*B. Lee Cooper, PhD*
*Wayne S. Haney, MDiv*

# Rock Music in American Popular Culture II: More Rock 'n' Roll Resources

*Pre-publication*
*REVIEWS,*
*COMMENTARIES,*
*EVALUATIONS . . .*

"**A** must for every musicologist! Dr. Cooper and Dr. Haney have done it again–painstaking research combined with incisive insights about the critical role popular music has played in mirroring and expressing the development of American culture over the past half-century. *Rock Music in American Popular Culture II* is an outstanding companion to its predecessor, *Rock Music in American Popular Culture I*. No serious music researcher or music library can do without either volume.

The milestone work that Cooper and Haney have done is to look beyond mere lists of records that fit various themes or recapitulation of various popular music sales charts. Instead, they have correlated the content of the songs to what was going on in the United States when these tunes were popular. They have shown how many of these themes are recurring from decade to decade. The continuing popularity of most of this music and the fact that mainstream America can still relate to it would indicate that despite all the cultural changes of the past 50 years, much has really stayed the same.

The only obvious question I am left with after reading *Rock Music in American Popular Culture II* is, when will the next volume of this series be available? I can't wait!"

**David A. Milberg, JD**
*Attorney at Law and Director*
*of Marketing, Keck, Mahin & Cate,*
*Chicago, IL*

"**C**ooper and Haney have done it again! Volume II of *Rock Music in American Popular Culture* continues the excellent work they initiated in Volume I. Researchers, teachers, students, and scholars will find a wealth of information in this volume to aid them in their explorations into rock music and its relationship to the culture as a whole.

The essays in this volume demonstrate rock's role as an affective and reflective force in American culture. Teachers will find it especially useful not only for the classroom strategies suggested but for the listing of resources they can draw on to enhance units in history and social studies courses. The essays are augmented by great lists of relevant songs within the subject areas (e.g., cars, disc jockeys, war, Halloween, legends, women, etc.) and, of course, by the usual comprehensive bibliographies of relevant sources.

*Rock Music in American Popular Culture II* is an invaluable resource for librarians, teachers, and scholars who are serious about the study of rock music and its place in American culture."

**Timothy E. Scheurer, PhD**
*Professor of Humanities,*
*Franklin University,*
*Columbus, OH*

"**C**ooper and Haney have written the second in what very well could be, and hopefully will be, a series of essay and review compilations that examine the influences of rock 'n' roll on society, and vice versa. Through recurring themes such as cars, marriage, and war; types of music such as soul, doo-wop, and regional music; individual 'legends,' from Frank Sinatra to Ahmet Ertegun to Paul McCartney; and such related phenomena as record collecting, rock journalism, and rock in motion pictures, Cooper and Haney exert their established brand of intellectual democracy to illustrate the inextricable links between popular music and everyday life in America. Scholarly yet accessible, this work is invaluable for jump-starting anesthetized students who cannot make the connection between scholarship and real life, and complacent librarians and other educators who cannot make the connection between popular culture and scholarship. Indeed, this book is not only highly recommended for libraries, but also to librarians, to whom Cooper and Haney have much to say and offer many challenges. This is a significant accomplishment of analysis and bibliography; let us stomp and cheer for another encore."

**Allen Ellis, MLS**
*Acting Head of Reference/*
*Associate Professor of Library Services,*
*Steely Library,*
*Northern Kentucky University*

*More pre-publication*
## REVIEWS, COMMENTARIES, EVALUATIONS . . .

"This lively study is a handbook of rock 'n' roll resources for all people who have ever heard or sung an American popular song. The authors look upon each chapter as a 'cultural snapshot,' with the whole work making 'a collage of life in the U.S.A.' It would be hard to find a subject not covered by the authors, including cigarettes, city life, radio programming, fads and nostalgia, horror films, legends, and many others. Each chapter is headed by a neat discussion of the phenomenon, followed by a listing of songs covering or discussing the subject.

But this book is more than the sum of its parts. As the authors say, rock music and American popular culture are inevitably linked. Rock music is now linked to classical music by such orchestras as the Boston Pops, Cincinnati Pops, Pittsburgh Symphony, and most others, as the directors and audiences realize the importance of rock music in American society. It goes everywhere.

This book goes with it. Nobody beats the authors in their sane, clear presentation of titles and social contexts. They put a song in your heart and a title in your head. The volume is a beehive of activity in popular music, all sugar and proteins with no stings. It belongs in everybody's pocket or purse."

**Ray B. Browne, PhD**
*Secretary/Treasurer,*
*Popular Culture Association*

"It is wonderful to see Lee Cooper and Wayne Haney write another very important and needed resource book about rock music. *Rock Music in American Popular Culture II* demonstrates that Cooper and Haney are on the top of their game. Even though this book will prove to be very valuable to popular culturalists, scholars, rock fans, and reference librarians, this again is a very important book for school teachers and their students. In a single record or in a series of records on a given topic, rock music provides teachers with a source of valuable information, editorial comments, and a 'feel' for a historical or contemporary event or topic. And the beauty of *Rock Music in American Popular Culture II* is that Cooper and Haney have provided all of these recorded sources, the themes, and the background information. The musical topics are endless, providing excellent teaching resources to develop motivating and exciting lessons for students. And don't forget the students. Rock 'n' roll is their music. Information in this wonderful book will give students many enjoyable opportunities to create their own meaningful lessons. As the Doobie Brothers used to exhort, 'Listen to the music,' people, especially you teachers, listen to *Rock Music in American Popular Culture II*."

**George W. Chilcoat**
*Associate Professor of Education,*
*Brigham Young University,*
*Provo, UT*

Harrington Park Press
An Imprint of The Haworth Press, Inc.

# Rock Music in American Popular Culture II
## *More Rock 'n' Roll Resources*

*HAWORTH* Popular Culture
Frank W. Hoffmann, PhD and William G. Bailey, MA
Senior Editors

New, Recent, and Forthcoming Titles:

*Arts & Entertainment Fads* by Frank W. Hoffmann
and William G. Bailey

*Sports & Recreation Fads* by Frank W. Hoffmann
and William G. Bailey

*Mind & Society Fads* by Frank W. Hoffmann
and William G. Bailey

*Fashion & Merchandising Fads* by Frank W. Hoffmann
and William G. Bailey

*Chocolate Fads, Folklore, and Fantasies: 1000+ Chunks of Chocolate
Information* by Linda K. Fuller

*The Popular Song Reader: A Sampler of Well-Known Twentieth Century
Songs* by William Studwell

*Great Awakenings: Popular Religion and Popular Culture*
by Marshall W. Fishwick

*The Christmas Carol Reader* by William Studwell

*Media-Mediated Relationships: Straight and Gay, Mainstream,
and Alternative Perspectives* by Linda K. Fuller

*The National and Religious Song Reader: Patriotic, Traditional,
and Sacred Songs from Around the World* by William E. Studwell

*Rock Music in American Popular Culture: Rock 'n' Roll Resources*
by B. Lee Cooper and Wayne S. Haney

*Rock Music in American Popular Culture II: More Rock 'n' Roll
Resources* by B. Lee Cooper and Wayne S. Haney

*The Americana Song Reader* by William E. Studwell

*Images of Elvis Presley in American Culture, 1977-1997: The Mystery
Terrain* by George Plasketes

# Rock Music in American Popular Culture II
## *More Rock 'n' Roll Resources*

B. Lee Cooper, PhD
Wayne S. Haney, MDiv

Harrington Park Press
An Imprint of The Haworth Press, Inc.
New York • London

Published by

Harrington Park Press, an imprint of The Haworth Press, Inc., 10 Alice Street, Binghamton, NY
13904-1580

Cover designed by Donna M. Brooks.

**Library of Congress Cataloging-in-Publication Data**

Cooper, B. Lee.
    Rock music in American popular culture II : more rock 'n' roll resources / B. Lee Cooper,
Wayne S. Haney.
        p.   cm.
    Includes bibliographical references, discographies, and index.
    ISBN 1-56023-877-1 (alk. paper).
    1. Rock music–United States–History and criticism. 2. Popular culture–United States–His-
tory–20th century. 3. Music and society. I. Haney, Wayne S. II. Title.
ML3534.C664 1996
781.66'0973–dc20
                                                                                        96-7919
                                                                                        CIP
                                                                                        MN

To the performing royalty of Rock 'n' Roll:

The Beatles
Chuck Berry
James Brown
Ray Charles
Eric Clapton
The Coasters
Sam Cooke
Creedence Clearwater Revival
Dion DiMucci
Fats Domino
The Drifters
Aretha Franklin
Jerry Lee Lewis
Little Richard
Delbert McClinton
Wilson Pickett
The Platters
Elvis Presley
Bonnie Raitt
Otis Redding
The Rolling Stones
Linda Ronstadt
Paul Simon
Jackie Wilson

# ABOUT THE AUTHORS

**B. Lee Cooper, PhD,** is Provost and Vice President for Academic Affairs at the University of Great Falls in Montana. He is an internationally published expert in the area of lyric analysis, popular culture bibliography, discography, and teaching methods in social studies. His previous publications include *Rock Music in American Popular Culture: Rock 'n' Roll Resources; Images of American Society in Popular Music; The Popular Music Handbook; The Literature of Rock II* with Frank W. Hoffmann; and *Popular Music Perspectives: Ideas, Themes, and Patterns in Contemporary Lyrics*. He is a member of the American Association of Higher Education, the American Culture Association, and the American Historical Association.

**Rev. Wayne S. Haney, BME, MDiv,** is Rector of Grace Episcopal Church in Lapeer, Michigan. Formerly Associate Director of the Academic Resource Center at Olivet College, Father Haney is an organist and computer specialist who has co-authored *Rock Music in American Popular Culture: Rock 'n' Roll Resources; Response Recordings: An Answer Song Discography, 1950-1990;* and *Rockabilly: A Bibliographic Resource Guide*.

# CONTENTS

# Acknowledgements

This anthology and its 1995 predecessor provide directions, discographies, and bibliographies designed to assist not only reference librarians but also rock music fans, popular culture enthusiasts, American Studies scholars, and public school teachers to probe the complexity of American society. Each chapter in this volume is a cultural snapshot. The entire work constitutes a collage of life in the United States. For rock 'n' roll troubadour Chuck Berry, being "Back in the U.S.A." meant grilled hamburgers, crowded freeways, and bustling urban life. Today McDonald's, multiscreen theaters, and mini-malls provide the social scenery for St. Louis natives. Joni Mitchell predicted it. Chrissie Hynde lamented it. And many current artists ranging from Ice-T and Public Enemy to Don Henley and Huey Lewis try to interpret it. Rock music and American popular culture are inevitably linked. The existence of the one is an audio manifestation of the other.

Frank W. Hoffmann and William L. Schurk have been staunch personal friends and invaluable inspirations for several decades. Their energy and enthusiasm for popular culture study is boundless. Professor Hoffmann, a teacher and librarian at Sam Houston State University in Huntsville, Texas, has a massive publication resume. He has authored a series of volumes exploring country, rhythm 'n' blues, and pop chart song listings for the trade journal *Cash Box*; he has co-authored *The Literature of Rock*, a multivolume bibliography identifying the most prominent books and articles available on popular music performers; he has written *Popular Culture and Libraries*, a volume designed to introduce librarians to the breadth of popular culture resources; and he has co-authored a series of studies on fads in American society. In 1993 he launched the scholarly journal *Popular Culture in Libraries*. This quarterly publication, assembled under Professor Hoffmann's energetic editorship, explores the interactions of mass media and information services, synthesized sound and automated bibliographies, popular culture and public services, and various issues of censorship, creativity, intellectual freedom, resource acquisition, and criticism of contemporary scholarship.

William L. Schurk is a galaxy apart from Hoffmann in style, personality, and the nature of his contributions to popular culture study. As Professor of Library Science and Sound Recording Archivist at the William T. Jerome Library on the campus of Bowling Green State University in Ohio, Schurk is frenetic yet focused, funny yet philosophical, and absolutely dedicated to the ongoing task of assembling the foremost collection of sound recordings in the world. The genius of Schurk, though, is his facile knowledge of recorded music. He is a human research encyclopedia. Rather than writing or publishing, though, he is constantly talking, telephoning, faxing, searching, bargaining, gathering, explaining, informing, illustrating, and assisting fans, students, teachers, scholars, and recording companies. He is a walking rock reference resource. Just as Hoffmann, his popular culture knowledge stretches across realms of comics, television shows, radio programs, games, animation, and so on. His conference presentations are legendary. His zeal for accumulating recordings to assist scholars in the academic investigation of popular music is crucial.

This collection of essays and reviews has its origin in the popular culture thoughts of Ray B. Browne and Russel B. Nye. Earlier writers championed vernacular investigation; later scholars have lauded the pursuit of the popular. But Browne and Nye are undeniably prime movers. They translated their ideas into programs, organizations, and movements. Browne, in particular, remains preeminent as a planner, dreamer, and academic schemer. The radical ideas about popular culture that he launched from his Bowling Green State University pulpit in the late 1960s are currently so dominant in academia that they have become "givens" in the geometry of contemporary culture research. Interdisciplinary exploration of cartoons, Christmas songs, Halloween, horror films, and science fiction is today the hallmark of popular culture study. Yet an anthology examining this variety of topics would have been unthinkable before Ray B. Browne and Russel B. Nye.

This volume pictures popular culture through an audio lens. Modern music provides lyric analysts, biographers, subject classification experts, and discographers with ample illustrations of commentaries on marriage, motion pictures, sex, war, and women. The essays compiled here differ markedly in style, structure, and length. Book reviews and science fiction stories are presented alongside footnoted historical investigations and biographical sketches. Both critical and laudatory conclusions are mixed throughout the text. The alphabetical topic format permits readers to select and concentrate on particular items of interest. Extensive literary resource and song title lists within the chapters, plus a lengthy bibliography at the end of the volume, offer additional sources for future inquiries.

Writers rely upon friends and professional colleagues for ideas, assistance, stimulation, criticism, and companionship while pursuing scholarly production. We gratefully acknowledge the superb books, articles, and conference papers produced by the following exceptional thinkers: Mark Booth, Ray B. Browne, Gary Burns, George O. Carney, George Chilcoat, Norm Cohen, R. Serge Denisoff, Howard A. DeWitt, Philip H. Ennis, Colin Escott, Reebee Garofalo, Archie Green, Charles Gritzner, Peter Hesbacher, Frank W. Hoffmann, David Horn, Hugo Keesing, Stephen Kneeshaw, John Litevich, J. Fred MacDonald, Jon McAuliffe, Hugh Mooney, Russel B. Nye, David Pichaske, Lawrence Redd, Jerome Rodnitzky, Roger B. Rollin, Fred E. H. Schroeder, Tom Schultheiss, Larry Stidom, Warren Swindell, and Joel Whitburn. Through record collecting and correspondence concerning audiotapes have come beneficial contacts with several shrewd, helpful persons: James A. Creeth, David A. Milberg, Frank Scott, and Chas "Dr. Rock" White.

Finally, our activities have enabled us to develop a cadre of professional friends who were sustaining and supportive during the inevitable research doldrums: Sue Ayotte, Stuart and Teresa Blacklaw, David and Maureen Boyd, Donna and Terry Brummett, Roger C. Buese, Dolores Chapman, Neil and Karen Clark, Marian Collins, Colby Currier, Norma Curtis, Cindy Eller, Charles and Jane Erickson, Shirley Erickson, Vicki Gallas, Frederick Gilliard, Susan Gray, Eric and Priscilla Hagen, Elna Hensley, Damon Lee, Don and Zella Morris, David Osmycki, Jack and Anne Patterson, Stuart Parsell, Kevin Rabineau, Todd and Connie Reynolds, Kenn Robbins, Donald and Sue Rowe (and Jessie, too), Shirley Ryan, Mary Schroth, Linda Jo Scott, Audrey Thompson, Stewart Tubbs, Donald Walker, Gary Wertheimer, James Wilson, Dirk G. Wood, and especially library historian/popular culture scholar Wayne A. Wiegand.

Authors also benefit from the loving, uncritical support of spouses, children, parents, and other relatives. This indispensable sustenance was provided by Jill E. Cooper, Michael L. Cooper, Laura E. Cooper, Julie A. Cooper, Nicholas A. Cooper, Kathleen M. Cooper, Charles A. Cooper, Patty Jo Cooper, Larry W. Cooper, Dustin Cooper, Leon Haney, Marian Haney, Mary Haney, Herbert Jones, Judy Jones, Carol Moore, and Harry Moore.

Yet another indispensable support to this project was in the area of computer technology support. A click of our computer keys and a squeak of our mouse go to Ellen Elder, Anita Kirk, and Laura Starr-Houghton for their invaluable assistance in the production of this work.

The final type of support that made this study possible was financial. Two agencies provided direct economic assistance. We wish to thank the Division of Fellowships and Seminars of the National Endowment for the Humanities (NEH) for awarding Lee Cooper a "Travel to Collections"

grant during 1985. We also acknowledge similar research funding provided by the Grants Committee and Board of Directors of the Association
for Recorded Sound Collections (ARSC) in 1990 and again in 1992. This
special financial support permitted lengthy periods of research access to
both literary and audio materials housed in the Sound Recordings Archive
in the William T. Jerome Library at Bowling Green State University.

*B. Lee Cooper and Wayne S. Haney*

# Preface

In 1995 The Haworth Press published *Rock Music in American Popular Culture*. This anthology examined 22 specific items from current life–baseball cards, Christmas carols, commercial catalogs, food, games, journalists and critics, memorabilia, nursery rhymes, and sports heroes–through the prism of contemporary song lyrics. The response to this integrated examination of popular culture was fascinating. Music fans noted the many facets of modern society that are influenced by rock performers' commentaries. Clearly Bruce Springsteen, Paul Simon, Madonna, the artist formerly known as Prince, and John Mellencamp do not sing in a vacuum. General readers expressed amazement at the infusion of rock rhythms, imagery, personalities, and lyrics into so many areas of everyday existence. If Elvis Presley and his postage stamp visage seem to be everywhere, the impact of rock music on American life is just as ubiquitous. Finally, popular culture scholars and researchers noted the pervasive manner in which the rock ethic–complete with antiauthoritarian dress, generation-gap principles, and sensual, suggestive (some might say "objectionable") lyrics–has captured the formats of corporate advertising and mass media broadcasting. Could a 1950s teenager ever have dreamed that the elected leader of the United States during the 1990s would be labelled "The Rock 'n' Roll President"?

Such positive perceptions have prompted a reprise of the music as a mirror of society theme. *Rock Music in American Popular Culture II* expands the net of social analysis. Transportation (cars and railroads), multiculturalism (ethnic diversity), communication (disc jockeys), gender issues (sex and women), and fear (Halloween and horror films) are examined in detail. Twenty-two new topics are included, with particular emphasis on such key twentieth-century concerns as war (lyrics from the First World War through the Persian Gulf conflict), city life, and marriage. The musical context touches each topic. It also elaborates the distinctive American pattern of isolating or compartmentalizing key issues. When Billy Joel disclaims social responsibility in "We Didn't Start the Fire" (1989), he is echoing the sentiments of disengagement voiced by civil rights pacifists, environmental ostriches, political neutrals, and fiscal conservatives. In contrast, Midnight Oil's "Beds Are Burning" (1988) cries for activism in realms of social justice, political morality, and personal ethics. Patterns of change in American society are clearly depicted throughout most of the chapters. Unfortunately, morality does not always triumph over materialism, and virtue does not eternally vanquish vice. Nevertheless, lyrics remain playful, creative, spontaneous, uplifting, and descriptive.

# Introduction

Information services are marvelously streamlined today. Computerized reference systems abound. Interlibrary loans enable small college faculty members to utilize materials previously available only to university professors. The past decade has seen the triumph of reference speed and resource outreach in library service. For popular culture researchers, however, the world of library information exchange remains selective, specialized, and isolated. This situation is not the result of insufficient computer power. Nor is it part of an organized plot to thwart popular culture studies. The difficulty stems from three interrelated factors. First, few reference librarians receive sufficient training in exploring popular culture resource options. Second, few libraries invest funds in materials that would assist popular culture scholars. Finally, the availability of guides, directories, handbooks, bibliographies, discographies, and other sourceworks for popular culture studies is far from universal among libraries and library schools.

My observations are grounded in experience rather than in formal information service training. I am a patron, not a librarian. Since 1968 I have taught courses in popular music, with particular emphasis on lyric analysis and thematic classification. Over the past 20 years I have written hundreds of articles, essays, and reviews on topics including television soundtracks, baseball cards, science fiction essays, radio disc jockeys, fairy tales, and bootleg records. I have benefitted from advice, guidance, counsel, proofreading, co-authoring, resource supplementing, and even housing provided by a variety of attentive, creative, diligent professional librarians. Similar assistance has been available to me during the completion of ten books. It would be a gross understatement to assert: "Some of my best friends are librarians!"

During the spring of 1990 I had the opportunity to participate on an American Culture Association panel exploring the topic "Popular Culture Research and Libraries." My remarks were divided into two segments. My initial concern was to outline those specific actions that might enable reference librarians to better serve popular culture scholars during the 1990s. The second part of my presentation consisted of the distribution of a bibliographic guide that identified numerous books and articles that

*1*

thoughtfully and perceptively explore the diverse realm of popular culture teaching and resources.

## CHALLENGES FOR LIBRARIANS

Popular culture researchers seldom seek theoretical analyses when they approach reference librarians. Similarly, such scholars are not pursuing random trivia. The nature of popular culture study requires the examination of materials that are often atypical, ephemeral, oversized (motion picture posters), undersized (postage stamps), technologically oriented (compact discs), and seldom catalogued in standard formats. From fads to folktales, from antique radio programs to contemporary television commercials, from baseball broadcasts to taped interviews with children's text writers—the requests are invariably mixed and seemingly unmanageable. In order to develop a systematic approach to meeting the information needs of popular culture researchers, the American Library Association (ALA) and those universities that educate future librarians must actively initiate and pursue the following policies and practices:

1. Assemble a national panel of library directors assigned to explore the current status and future needs of popular culture research.
2. Destroy all remnants of the "academic ghetto" mentality within the library profession that has either permitted omission or assigned low priority to the acquisition of popular culture materials.
3. Initiate a formal "Popular Culture Research Consulting Service" through American College and Research Libraries membership designed to evaluate information delivery options in small colleges as well as at major universities.
4. Extend the definition of the library community to include specialists in popular culture hobby fields (picture discs, Coca-Cola memorabilia, and baseball cards), collectors of fan-related materials (KISS Army activists [fans of this group were "officially" invited to join the KISS Army Fan Club], Beatles games, and Michael Jackson trading cards), editors of privately produced periodicals (*Fireball Mail, Reminiscing,* and *Elvis World*), and private record collectors.
5. Invite popular culture researchers to compile and submit annual information needs and service request reports to a designated ALA roundtable group.
6. Support the new national journal *Popular Culture in Libraries*.

7. Establish special researcher-in-residence grants at all universities with popular culture resource collections in order to enable scholars to spend extended time in information-rich environments.
8. Accumulate ephemeral materials with greater foresight (rather than just hindsight) in selected popular culture areas (political cartoons, comic books, cookbooks, and *Playboy* magazines).
9. Allocate funds to secure and catalog out-of-print books, magazines, and vinyl resources, particularly short-run specialty periodicals (*New Kommotion, Record Profile Monthly,* and *Record Digest*) and limited edition sound recordings.
10. Foster displays, circulate brochures, and publish reviews of recent works that are specifically designed to stimulate popular culture scholarship.
11. Commission and print an annual volume of essays to illustrate the variety of academic pursuits and scholarly contributions in the realm of popular culture research.
12. Develop a computerized reference system of popular culture research topics and resources.
13. Create an ALA-approved "Basic Library Collection of Popular Culture Research Materials Guide" to suggest recommended holdings for all college and university library directors.

## *SUGGESTED READING FOR LIBRARIANS*

The concluding section of this essay consists of a selected bibliography. This list of articles and books features the works and ideas of both librarians and popular culture scholars. This is not the "Basic Library . . . " guideline requested above, though. It is a combination of popular culture research perspectives, library service experiences and expectations, and a few model resource compilations. This bibliography is designed to spark debate and to stimulate further investigation of this topic. Hopefully, the ideas featured in the works of Frank Hoffmann, Barbara Moran, Gordon Stevenson, Wayne Wiegand, and others will foster constructive steps toward meeting the 1990s research needs of popular culture scholars.

### *Articles*

- Bell, Michael J. "The Study of Popular Culture," in *Handbook of American Culture–Volume Three* (Second Edition, Revised and Enlarged), edited by M. Thomas Inge (Westport, Connecticut: Greenwood Press, 1989), pp. 1459-1484.

- Blosser, Betsy J. and Gretchen Lagana. "Popular Culture in the Rare Book Room and Special Collections Department," *Journal of Popular Culture*, XXIII (Fall 1989), pp. 125-137.

- Bold, Rudolph. "Trash in the Library," *Library Journal*, CV (May 15, 1980), pp. 1138-1189.

- Browne, Ray B. "Libraries at the Crossroads: A Perspective on Libraries and Culture," *Drexel Library Quarterly*, XVI (July 1980), pp. 12-23.

- Browne, Ray B. "Popular Culture as the New Humanities," *Journal of Popular Culture*, XVII (Spring 1984), pp. 1-8.

- Browne, Ray B. "Popular Culture: Medicine for Illiteracy and Associated Education Ills," *Journal of Popular Culture*, XXI (Winter 1987), pp. 1-15.

- Browne, Ray B. "Redefining Literature," *Journal of Popular Culture*, XXIII (Winter 1989), pp. 11-21.

- Clarke, Jack A. "Popular Culture in Libraries," *College and Research Libraries*, XXXIV (May 1973), pp. 216-217.

- Cooper, B. Lee. "Information Services, Popular Culture, and the Librarian: Promoting a Contemporary Learning Perspective," *Drexel Library Quarterly*, XVI (July 1980), pp. 24-42.

- Cooper, B. Lee. "An Interview With Audio Center Director William L. Schurk," in *Images of American Society in Popular Music: A Guide to Reflective Teaching*, (Chicago: Nelson-Hall, Inc., 1982), pp. 127-144.

- Cooper, B. Lee. "An Opening Day Collection of Popular Music Resources: Searching for Discographic Standards," in *Twentieth-Century Popular Culture in Museums and Libraries*, edited by Fred E. H. Schroeder (Bowling Green, Ohio: Bowling Green State University Popular Press, 1981), pp. 226-255.

- Cooper, B. Lee. "Popular Culture: Teaching Problems and Challenges," in *Popular Culture and the Library: Current Issues Symposium II*, edited by Wayne A. Wiegand (Lexington: University of Kentucky Press, 1978), pp. 10-26.

- Cooper, B. Lee. "Rhythm 'n' Rhymes: Character and Theme Images from Children's Literature in Contemporary Recordings, 1950-1985," *Popular Music and Society*, XIII (Spring 1989), pp. 53-71.

- Denisoff, R. Serge. "A Short Note on Studying Popular Culture," *Popular Culture Methods,* I (August 1972), pp. 2-5.

- Fluck, Winfried. "Popular Culture as a Mode of Socialization: A Theory About the Social Functions of Popular Cultural Forms," *Journal of Popular Culture,* XXI (Winter 1987), pp. 31-46.

- Greeley, Andrew. "Agon and Empathos: A Challenge to Popular Culture," *Popular Culture Association Newsletter,* XV (April 1988), pp. 2-5.

- Gritzner, Charles F. "Country Music: A Reflection of Popular Culture," *Journal of Popular Culture,* XI (Fall 1978), pp. 857-864.

- Hilsabeck, Steven A. "The Blackboard Bumble: Popular Culture and the Recent Challenges to the American High School," *Journal of Popular Culture,* XVIII (Winter 1984), pp. 25-30.

- Kelm, Rebecca Sturm. "The Lack of Access to Back Issues of the Weekly Tabloids: Does It Matter?" *Journal of Popular Culture,* XXIII (Spring 1990), pp. 45-50.

- Lawrence, John Shelton. "A Critical Analysis of Roger B. Rollin's 'Against Evaluation'," *Journal of Popular Culture,* XII Summer 1978), pp. 99-112.

- Lewis, George H. "Between Consciousness and Existence: Popular Culture and the Sociological Imagination," *Journal of Popular Culture,* XV (Spring 1982), pp. 81-92.

- Lewis, George H. "Commercial and Colonial Stimuli: Cross Cultural Creation of Popular Culture," *Journal of Popular Culture,* XV (Fall 1981), pp. 142-156.

- Lewis, George H. "Uncertain Truths: The Promotion of Popular Culture," *Journal of Popular Culture,* pp. 31-44.

- Lewis, James R. "Adam and Eve on Madison Avenue: Symbolic Inversion in Popular Culture," *Studies in Popular Culture,* X (1987), pp. 74-82.

- McMullen, Haynes and Jay E. Daily. "Teaching the Use of Popular Materials in a Library School," in *Popular Culture and Libraries,* compiled by Frank W. Hoffmann (Hamden, Connecticut: Library Profession Publications/Shoe StringPress, Inc., 1987), pp. 41-52.

- Monaghan, Peter. "Icons of Popular Culture Are Grist for Historian's Research," *Chronicle of Higher Education,* XXXVI (September 13, 1989), p. 3A.

- Moran, Barbara B. "Popular Culture and Its Challenge to the Academic Library," in *Twentieth-Century Popular Culture in Museums and Libraries*, edited by Fred E. H. Schroeder (Bowling Green, Ohio: Bowling Green State University Popular Press, 1981), pp. 179-186.

- Moran, Barbara B. "The Popular Culture Collection Quandary: A Survey of Faculty Needs," *Collection Building*, (Spring 1983), pp. 13-17.

- Peterson, Richard A. "Where the Two Cultures Meet: Popular Culture," *Journal of Popular Culture*, XI (Fall 1977), pp. 385-400.

- Prechter, Robert R. "Elvis, Frankenstein, and Andy Warhol: Using Pop Culture to Forecast the Stock Market," *Barron's*, LXV (September 9, 1985), pp. 6-7, 26, 28ff.

- Rollin, Roger B. "Against Evaluation: The Role of the Critic of Popular Culture," *Journal of Popular Culture*, IX (Fall 1975), pp. 355-365.

- Rollin, Roger B. "Popular Culture: The Essential Humanity," *The Comparatist*, XIII (May 1989), pp. 98-108.

- Rollin, Roger B. "Son of 'Against Evaluation': Reply to John Shelton Lawrence," *Journal of Popular Culture*, XII (Summer 1978), pp. 113-117, pp. 355-365.

- Rollin, Roger B. "Trash Gratia Artis: Popular Culture As Literature," *Intellect*, (December 1976), pp. 191-194.

- Rollin, Roger B. " 'Words, Words, Words . . . ': On Redefining Literature," *Journal of Popular Culture*, XXIII (Winter 1989), pp. 1-10.

- Ryant, Carl "Oral History As Popular Culture," *Journal of Popular Culture*, XV (Spring 1982), pp. 60-66.

- Schroeder, Fred E. H. "The Discovery of Popular Culture Before Printing," *Journal of Popular Culture*, XI (Winter 1977), pp. 629-640.

- Schroeder, Fred E. H. "Extra-Academic Agents for Cultural Literacy in America," *Journal of American Culture*, XII (Spring 1989), pp. 17-23.

- Schroeder, Fred E. H. "How to Acquire, Access, Catalog, and Research a Popular Culture Collection for Your Museum of History, Technology, or Art for $97 Per Year," in *Twentieth-Century Popular Culture in Museums and Libraries*, (Bowling Green, Ohio: Bowling Green State University Popular Press, 1981), pp. 77-83.

- Schroeder, Janet K. "Studying Popular Culture in the Public Library: Suggestions for Cooperative Programs," *Drexel Library Quarterly*, XVI (July 1980), pp. 615-672.

- Schurk, William L. "Popular Culture and Libraries: A Practical Perspective," *Drexel Library Quarterly*, XVI (July 1980), pp. 43-52.

- Sewell, Robert G. "Trash or Treasure? Pop Fiction in Academic and Research Libraries," *College and Research Libraries*, XLV (November 1984), pp. 450-461.

- Stevenson, Gordon. "Popular Culture and the Academic Librarian," in *Popular Culture and the Library: Current Issues Symposium II*, edited by Wayne A. Wiegand (Lexington: University of Kentucky Press, 1978), pp. 28-51.

- Stevenson, Gordon. "Popular Culture and the Public Library," in *Advances in Librarianship—Volume Seven*, edited by Melvin J. Voight and Michael H. Harris (New York: Academic Press, 1977), pp. 177-229.

- Stevenson, Gordon. "Popular Culture Studies and Library Education," *Journal of Education for Librarianship*, XV (April 1977), pp. 235-250.

- Stevenson, Gordon. "The Wayward Scholar: Resources and Research in Popular Culture," *Library Trends*, XXV (April 1977), pp. 779-818.

- Tamke, Susan S. "Oral History and Popular Culture: A Method for the Study of the Experience of Culture," *Journal of Popular Culture*, XI (Summer 1977), pp. 267-279.

- Turner, Thomas N. "Using Popular Culture in the Social Studies" (No. 9 in Series Two of the How To Do It Series). Washington, DC: National Council for the Social Studies, 1979.

- Wiegand, Wayne A. "The Academic Library's Responsibility to the Resource Needs of the Popular Culture Community," in *Twentieth-Century Popular Culture in Museums and Libraries*, edited by Fred E. H. Schroeder (Bowling Green, Ohio: Bowling Green State University Popular Press, 1981), pp. 189-198.

- Wiegand, Wayne A. "Popular Culture: A New Frontier for Academic Libraries," *Journal of Academic Librarianship*, V (September 1979), pp. 200-204.

- Wiegand, Wayne A. "Taste Cultures and Librarians: A Position Paper," *Drexel Library Quarterly*, XVI (July 1980), pp. 1-11.

- Woodward, William. "America as a Culture (I): Some Emerging Lines of Analysis," *Journal of American Culture*, XI (Spring 1988), pp. 1-16.

- Woodward, William. "America as a Culture (II): A Fourfold Heritage," *Journal of American Culture*, XI (Spring 1988), pp. 17-32.

## Books

- Bigsby, C.W.E. (ed.). *Approaches to Popular Culture.* Bowling Green, Ohio: Bowling Green State University Popular Press, 1976.

- Bigsby, C.W.E. (ed.). *Superculture: American Popular Culture and Europe.* Bowling Green, Ohio: Bowling Green State University Popular Press, 1975.

- Brake, Robert J. (ed.). *Communication in Popular Culture.* Bowling Green, Ohio: Bowling Green State University Popular Press, 1975.

- Browne, Ray B. *Against Academia: The History of the Popular Culture Association/American Culture Association and the Popular Culture Movement, 1967-1988.* Bowling Green, Ohio: Bowling Green State University Popular Press, 1989.

- Browne, Ray B. (ed.). *Popular Culture and the Expanding Consciousness.* New York: John Wiley and Sons, Inc., 1973.

- Browne, Ray B. and Ronald J. Ambrosetti (eds.). *Popular Culture and Curricula* (revised edition). Bowling Green, Ohio: Bowling Green State University Popular Press, 1972.

- Browne, Ray B. and Marshall Fishwick (eds.). *Icons of America.* Bowling Green, Ohio: Bowling Green State University Popular Press, 1978.

- Browne, Ray B. and David Madden. *The Popular Culture Explosion: Experiencing Mass Media.* Dubuque, Iowa: William C. Brown Company, 1972.

- Bruner, David et al. *America Through the Looking Glass: A Historical Reader in Popular Culture.* Englewood Cliffs, New Jersey: Prentice-Hall, Inc., 1974.

- Buhle, Paul (ed.). *Popular Culture in America.* Minneapolis: University of Minnesota Press, 1987.

- Cawelti, John. *Adventure, Mystery, and Romance: Formula Stories as Art and Popular Culture.* Chicago: University of Chicago Press, 1976.

- Cooper, B. Lee. *Images of American Society in Popular Music: A Guide to Reflective Teaching.* Chicago: Nelson-Hall, Inc., 1982.

- Cooper, B. Lee. *The Popular Music Handbook: A Resource Guide for Teachers, Librarians, and Media Specialists.* Littleton, Colorado: Libraries Unlimited, Inc., 1984.

- Cooper, B. Lee. *Popular Music Perspectives: Ideas, Themes, and Patterns in Contemporary Lyrics.* Bowling Green, Ohio: Bowling Green State University Popular Press, 1990.

- Cooper, B. Lee. *A Resource Guide to Themes in Contemporary American Song Lyrics, 1950-1985.* Westport, Connecticut: Greenwood Press, 1986.

- Denisoff, R. Serge and Richard A. Peterson (eds.). *The Sounds of Social Change: Studies in Popular Culture.* Chicago: Rand McNally and Company, 1972.

- Fiske, John. *Reading the Popular.* Winchester, Massachusetts: Unwin Hyman, 1989.

- Fiske, John. *Understanding Popular Culture.* Winchester, Massachusetts: Unwin Hyman, 1989.

- Frith, Simon. *Sound Effects: Youth, Leisure, and the Politics of Rock 'n' Roll.* New York: Pantheon Books, 1981.

- Frith, Simon and Andrew Goodwon (eds.). *On Record: Rock, Pop, and the Written Word.* New York: Pantheon Books, 1990.

- Gans, Herbert J. *Popular Culture and High Culture: An Analysis and Evaluation of Taste.* New York: Basic Books, 1974.

- Geist, Christopher D., Ray B. Browne, Michael T. Marsden, and Carole Palmer (comps.). *Directory of Popular Culture Collections.* Phoenix: Oryx Press, 1989.

- Girgus, Sam. *The American Self: Myth, Popular Culture, and the American Ideology.* Albuquerque, New Mexico: University of New Mexico Press, 1980.

- Giroux, Henry A. and Roger I. Simon. *Popular Culture: Schooling and Everyday Life.* Westport, Connecticut: Bergin and Garvey, 1989.

- Gordon, Mark and Jack Nachbar (comps.). *Currents of Warm Life: Popular Culture in American Higher Education.* Bowling Green, Ohio: Bowling Green State University Popular Press, 1980.

- Gowans, Alan. *Learning to See: Historical Perspectives on Modern Popular/Commercial Arts.* Bowling Green, Ohio: Bowling Green State University Popular Press, 1981.

- Hoffmann, Frank W. and William G. Bailey. *Arts and Entertainment Fads*. Binghamton, New York: The Haworth Press, 1990.

- Hoffmann, Frank W. (comp.). *Popular Culture and Libraries*. Hamden, Connecticut: Library Professional Publications/Shoe String Press, Inc., 1984.

- Huebel, Harry Russell (ed.). *Things in the Driver's Seat: Readings in Popular Culture*. Chicago: Rand McNally and Company, 1972.

- Inge, M. Thomas (ed.). *Handbook of American Culture*, second edition, revised and enlarged (three volumes). Westport, Connecticut: Greenwood Press, 1989.

- Inge, M. Thomas (ed.). *Handbook of American Popular Literature*. Westport, Connecticut: Greenwood Press, 1988.

- LaForse, Martin W. and James A. Drake. *Popular Culture and American Life: Selected Topics in the Study of American Popular Culture*. Chicago: Nelson-Hall, Inc., 1981.

- Lance, David (ed.). *Sound Archives: A Guide to Their Establishment and Development*. London: International Association of Sound Archives, 1983.

- Landrum, Larry N. *American Popular Culture: A Guide to Information Sources*. Detroit, Michigan: Gale Research, 1982.

- Lax, Roger and Frederick Smith (comps.). *The Great Song Thesaurus* (updated edition). New York: Oxford University Press, 1988.

- Levine, Lawrence W. *Black Culture and Black Consciousness: Afro-American Folk Thought from Slavery to Freedom*. New York: Oxford University Press, 1977.

- Lewis, George H. (ed.). *Side-Saddle on the Golden Calf: Social Structure and Popular Culture in America*. Pacific Palisades, California: Goodyear Publishing Company, Inc., 1972.

- Lipsitz, George. *Time Passages: Collective Memory and American Popular Culture*. Minneapolis: University of Minnesota Press, 1990.

- Lohof, Bruce A. *American Commonplace: Essays on the Popular Culture of the United States*. Bowling Green, Ohio: Bowling Green State University Popular Press, 1982.

- Maltby, Richard (ed.). *Dreams for Sale: Popular Culture in the Twentieth Century*. London: Harrap Press, 1989.

- Marsden, Michael T., John G. Nachbar, and Sam L. Grogg, Jr. (eds.). *Movies As Artifacts: Cultural Criticism of Popular Film*. Chicago: Nelson-Hall, Inc., 1982.

- Mayo, Edith (ed.). *American Material Culture: The Shape of Things Around Us*. Bowling Green, Ohio: Bowling Green State University Popular Press, 1984.

- Middleton, Richard. *Studying Popular Music*. Milton Keynes, England: Open University Press, 1989.

- Nachbar, Jack, Deborah Weiser, and John L. Wright (comps.). *The Popular Culture Reader*. Bowling Green, Ohio: Bowling Green State University Popular Press, 1978.

- Nye, Russel B. (ed.). *New Dimensions in Popular Culture*. Bowling Green, Ohio: Bowling Green State University Popular Press, 1972.

- Nye, Russel B. *The Unembarrassed Muse: The Popular Arts in America*. New York: Dial Press, 1970.

- Rollin, Roger B. (ed.). *The Americanization of the Global Village: Essays in Comparative Popular Culture*. Bowling Green, Ohio: Bowling Green State University Popular Press, 1989.

- Root, Robert L., Jr. *The Rhetorics of Popular Culture: Advertising, Advocacy, and Entertainment*. Westport, Connecticut: Greenwood Press, 1987.

- Scheurer, Timothy E. (ed.). *American Popular Music—Volume One: The 19th Century and Tin Pan Alley*. Bowling Green, Ohio: Bowling Green State University Popular Press, 1989.

- Scheurer, Timothy E. (ed.). *American Popular Music—Volume Two: The Age of Rock*. Bowling Green, Ohio: Bowling Green State University Popular Press, 1989.

- Schroeder, Fred E. H. (ed.). *5000 Years of Popular Culture*. Bowling Green, Ohio: Bowling Green State University Popular Press, 1980.

- Schroeder, Fred E. H. (ed.). *Twentieth-Century Popular Culture in Museums and Libraries*. Bowling Green, Ohio: Bowling Green State University Popular Press, 1981.

- Ward, Alan. *A Manual of Sound Archive Administration*. Aldershot, Hants, England: Gower Publishing Company, Ltd., 1990.

- White, David Manning and John Pendleton (eds.). *Popular Culture: Mirror of American Life*. Del Mar, California: Publisher's, Inc., 1977.

- Wiegand, Wayne A. (ed.). *Popular Culture and the Library: Current Issues Symposium II*. Lexington: University of Kentucky Press, 1978.

- Wilson, Charles R. and William Ferris (ed.). *Encyclopedia of Southern Culture*. Chapel Hill: University of North Carolina Press, 1989.

# Chapter 1

# Answer Songs

Answer songs are tunes that respond to direct questions or continue to develop specific themes, ideas, or melody patterns from earlier songs. As a lyrical genre they are as old as the multiple verse ballads performed by medieval troubadours. In American tradition they are rooted in the verbal one-upmanship practiced by storytellers in barbershops, brothels, and bars along the Mississippi River. They are also linked to the joy of performers and audiences alike in perpetuating good melodies and in elaborating humorous tales. During the first half of the twentieth century, for example, many songs were recorded about the legendary exploits of John Henry, Frankie and Johnny, and Stagger Lee. This study is not concerned with either European balladry or pre-Cold War American tall tales, though. The purpose of this investigation is to examine various themes and styles in American answer song recordings from the 1950-1985 period. Although the majority of songs that trigger recorded responses are themselves highly popular, the same cannot be said of offshoot tunes. For this reason, answer discs are highly prized by most record collectors. Small pressings and limited sales of answer songs make them immediate rarities in the vinyl trade market. Beyond collecting though, these recordings are valuable cultural illustrations of several American traits. They are usually humorous, poking fun at a particular statement or a series of less-than-honorable activities; they invariably provide contrasting positions–personal and political–to previously stated viewpoints; they offer interesting, sometimes unexpected story-continuing options; and they often translate common phrases, domestic problems, or personal concerns into a popular cultural contest.

---

This essay by B. Lee Cooper was originally published as "Sequel Songs and Response Recordings: The Answer Record in Modern American Music, 1950-1985," *International Journal of Instructional Media*, XIII, No. 3 (1986), pp. 227-239. Reprint permission granted by the author, Editor Phillip J. Sleeman, and the Baywood Publishing Company.

Can the total field of answer songs be segmented into logical patterns for purposes of analysis? Not very easily. Yet close scrutiny shows that although the forms of response recordings remain relatively constant, the functions of answer songs vary dramatically. This leads to the differentiation of specific answer songs according to four categories: (1) answer to a direct question, (2) response to a statement or a command, (3) challenge to a position or ideology, and (4) continuation of a distinct storyline or theme.

The remainder of this essay examines answer songs within these categories. Selected illustrations of original hit recordings and the answer songs they generated are provided in tables within the text.

## ANSWER TO A DIRECT QUESTION

In 1961, a *Time* staff writer commented,

> So far, there are only half a dozen versions of "Are You Lonesome Tonight?," including the original by Elvis Presley which is now the nation's No. 1 hit. But if Elvis stays up there, there may well be a dozen variations of the theme. The "Lonesome" craze is the most blatant example of a pop music's latest fad: the answer record, which provides an answer to a question raised in an established hit.

The most easily explained justification for concocting a recording of an answer song is to respond to a direct question from a previous tune. The reactions to Elvis Presley's multiple pleas—"Are you lonesome tonight? Do you miss me tonight? Are you sorry we drifted apart?"—were consistent. Answer songs titled "Yes, I'm Lonesome Tonight" were launched by Thelma Carpenter, Linda Lee, Jo Anne Perry and Dodie Stevens. In addition, Jeanne Black sang "Oh, How I Miss You Tonight." The same kind of reassuring answers had greeted The Shirelles a year earlier when their song "Will You Love Me Tomorrow?" was answered by three different artists—"Yes, I Will Love You Tomorrow," "You Know I'll Love You Tomorrow," and "Not Just Tomorrow, But Always."

In 1956 Frankie Lymon and the Teenagers produced the hit "Why Do Fools Fall in Love?" The song's title appears at the end of a chain of questions ranging from "Why do birds sing so gay?" to "Why does my heart skip a crazy beat?" Humorously, the answer songs to this record remained in the family. Frankie's brother Lewis Lymon issued a tune that asserted "I Found Out Why." Not to be outdone, Frankie countered with his own answer record couched in the form of another question—"Who

Can Explain?" It is interesting to note that Frankie Lymon also released another answer–"I Put the Bomp"–in response to Barry Mann's 1961 hit "Who Put the Bomp (in the Bomp, Bomp, Bomp)?" Perhaps the most negative response to a recorded query was delivered by Hook McCoy. His reaction to Gary Burbank's soap opera-inspired question "Who Shot J.R.?" was "I Don't Give a Diddly Damn Who Shot J.R." Other answer tunes are listed below.

| Original Title, Record Number, and Artist | Release Date | Response Title, Record Number, and Artist |
|---|---|---|
| 1. "Are You Lonesome Tonight?" (RCA 57-7810) by Elvis Presley | 1960 | "Oh, How I Miss You Tonight" (Capitol 4492) by Jeanne Black |
| | | "Yes, I'm Lonesome Tonight" (Coral 6224) by Thelma Carpenter |
| | | "Yes, I'm Lonesome Tonight" (SHASTA 146) by Linda Lee |
| | | "Yes, I'm Lonesome Tonight" (Glad 1006) by Jo Anne Perry |
| | | "Yes, I'm Lonesome Tonight" (Dot 161667) by Dodie Stevens |
| 2. "Who Put the Bomp (in the Bomp, Bomp, Bomp)?" (ABC-Paramount 10237) by Barry Mann | 1961 | "We're the Guys" (Columbia 42162) by Bob and Jerry |
| | | "I Put the Bomp" (Roulette 4391) by Frankie Lymon |
| 3. "Who Shot J.R.?" (Ovatoin 1150) by Gary Burbank Band McNally | 1980 | "I Don't Give a Diddly Damn Who Shot J.R." (J-Ken 1015) by Hook McCoy |
| 4. "Why Do Fools Fall in Love" (Gee 1002) by Frankie Lymon and the Teenagers | 1956 | "I Found Out Why" (End 1000) by Lewis Lymon and the Teenchords |
| | | "Who Can Explain?" (Gee 1018) by Frankie Lymon and the Teenagers |

5. "Will You Love Me Tomorrow"      1960      "Not Just Tomorrow,
   (Scepter 1211)                                        But Always"
   by the Shirelles                                    (United Artists 290)
                                                             by Bertell Dache

                                                          "Yes, I Will Love You
                                                             Tomorrow"
                                                          (Atlantic 2091)
                                                          by Jon E. Holiday

                                                          "You Know I'll Love You
                                                             Tomorrow"
                                                          (Ry-An 501)
                                                          by Colly Williams

## *RESPONSE TO A STATEMENT OR COMMAND*

Among the most popular and frequently mentioned answer songs is Damita Jo's "I'll Save the Last Dance for You." This tune, released in response to The Drifters' 1960 statement "Save the Last Dance for Me," rose to Number 22 on the *Billboard* chart and remained a charted hit for 12 weeks. "You're Having the Last Dance with Me!" by The Townsmen was another reaction to The Drifters, but one that failed to achieve popular support. These tunes illustrate that no question is necessary in a song title to spark a creative answer. A direct statement or observation is enough to provoke a lyrical comment. Thus, Jim Reeves' 1959 telephone call plea "He'll Have to Go" was countered by the statement "He'll Have to Stay"; The Silhouettes' occupational dilemma in "Get a Job" was answered positively by The Heartbeats' "I Found a Job" and by The Miracles' "Got a Job"; and in 1962 Sam Cooke's "Bring It On Home to Me" admonition was heeded by Carla Thomas' "I'll Bring It Home to You."

One of the most broadly answered recordings was Ruth Brown's 1953 release "Mama (He Treats Your Daughter Mean)." The answers to this song were varied. First, appeals were made to the man of the house by two artists–Benny Brown and Scat Man Crothers–in "Papa." The Five Keys claimed "Mama, Your Daughter Told a Lie on Me." Sax Kari echoed this answer with "Hush Your Lyin' Mouth." Finally, Gloria Irving and Sax Kari took the hard line with the allegedly mistreated young woman by coldly observing "Daughter, That's Your Red Wagon." The following are additional examples of these types of answer songs:

| Original Title, Record Number, and Artist | Release Date | Response Title, Record Number, and Artist |
|---|---|---|
| 1. "Bring It on Home to Me" (RCA 8035) by Sam Cooke | 1962 | "I'll Bring It Home to You" (Atlantic 2163) by Carla Thomas |
| 2. "Get a Job" (Ember 1029) by The Silhouettes | 1957 | "I Found a Job" (Roulette 4054) by The Heartbeats |
| | | "Got a Job" (End 1016) by The Miracles |
| 3. "He'll Have to Go" (RCA 7643) by Jim Reeves | 1959 | "He'll Have to Stay" (Capitol 4368) by Jeanne Black |
| | | "He'll Have to Stay" (ABC 10097) by Corina Minette |
| 4. "Mama (He Treats Your Daughter Mean)" (Atlantic 986) by Ruth Brown | 1953 | "Papa" (Gotham 293) by Benny Brown |
| | | "Papa" (Recorded in Hollywood 142) by Scat Man Crothers |
| | | "Mama, Your Daughter Told a Lie on Me" (Aladdin 3175) by The Five Keys |
| | | "Daughter, That's Your Red Wagon" (States 115) by Gloria Irving and Sax Kari |
| | | "Hush Your Lyin' Mouth" (Great Lakes 1204) by Sax Kari and His Band |
| 5. "Save the Last Dance for Me" (Atlantic 2071) by The Drifters | 1960 | "I'll Save the Last Dance for You" (Mercury 71690) by Damita Jo |
| | | "You're Having the Last Dance with Me!" (Event 503) by The Townsmen |

| | | |
|---|---|---|
| 6. "Shop Around"<br>(Tamla 54034)<br>by The Miracles | 1960 | "Don'cha Shop Around"<br>(Guaranteed 219)<br>by Laurie Davis |
| | | "Don't Let Him Shop Around"<br>(Motown 1007)<br>by Debbie Dean |
| | | "Don't Have to Shop Around"<br>(Volt 127)<br>by The Mad Lads |

## CHALLENGE TO A POSITION OR IDEOLOGY

Lyrics often contain strong personal sentiments or partisan political perspectives that performers wish to communicate to others. It is understandable that such recordings prompt answer songs which either support the original ideas or offer contrasting opinions. The latter is the norm. Victor Lundberg's 1967 parental preaching in "An Open Letter to My Teenage Son" generated no fewer than six recorded responses. Although the 1960s were undoubtedly the golden era of politically motivated recordings and answers—led by the "Eve of Destruction" vs. "Dawn of Correction" verbal battle between Barry McGuire and The Spokesmen—it would be an error to think that conflicting sociological commentaries were limited to that decade. The naturalist educational philosophy of Supertramp in the 1979 tune "The Logical Song" was challenged by The Barron Knights' "The Topical Song." On a more personalized level, "Big Mama" Thornton's condemnation of her lover as a lazy "Hound Dog" was refuted by Rufus Thomas in 1953. The tag "Bear Cat" was created to capsule numerous female shortcomings. The table below provides a profile of personally biased, politically motivated answer songs.

| Original<br>Title, Record Number, and Artist | Release<br>Date | Response<br>Title, Record Number, and Artist |
|---|---|---|
| 1. "Eve of Destruction"<br>(Dunhill 4009)<br>by Barry McGuire | 1965 | "Dawn of Correction"<br>(Decca 31844)<br>by The Spokesmen |
| 2. "Hound Dog"<br>(Peacock 1612)<br>by Willie Mae ("Big Mama")<br>    Thornton | 1953 | "Bear Cat"<br>(Sun 181)<br>by Rufus Thomas |
| 3. "The Logical Song"<br>(A&M 2128)<br>by Supertramp | 1979 | "The Topical Song"<br>(Epic 50755)<br>by The Barron Knights |

4. "An Open Letter to My
      Teenage Son"
   (Liberty 55996)
   by Victor Lundberg

1967

"Hi Dad (An Open Letter)"
(Imperial 66272)
by Dick Clair

"Letter to Dad"
(Buddah 250)
by Every Father's Teenage
   Son

"A Teenager's Answer"
(Tower 383)
by Keith Gordon

"An Open Letter to My Father"
(Dragonet 009)
by Bob Random

"A Teenage Son's Open Letter
   to His Father"
(Date 1610)
by Robert Tamkim

"Letter from a Teenage Son"
(Philips 40503)
by Brand Wade

## CONTINUATION
## OF A DISTINCT STORYLINE OR THEME

Some answer songs are quite different from responses to a direct question or reactions to a statement or command. These tunes are actually extensions of previous hit recordings. They vary greatly. Sometimes they feature a new title with different lyrics, or the original title with supplementary lyrics; they may be produced by a new artist or by the performer of the original song; or they may employ a totally new melody, a slight variation of the original tune, or the same melody as the original recording. The key element to identifying these answer songs, though, is the fact that they continue to lyrically elaborate and expand upon a distinct storyline or theme which was launched in a previous recording.

Folklore is rich in extended storytelling. Popular recordings, which several scholars have identified as oral history resources, also present numerous examples of character and plot development through lyrical expansion. In the first half of the twentieth century, the primary subjects of such vinyl "soap operas" were steel drivin' man John Henry, notorious badman and murderer Stagger Lee, and the ill-fated couple Frankie and Johnny. It was not unexpected that tales of these characters would continue to be heralded after 1950 as well. But the best illustration of a highly popular song that generated not only a series of cover versions but also a number of answer recordings is the 1947 hit "Open the Door, Richard!" In addition to the major releases of this song in 1947 by composer Jack McVea (Black and White 792), by stage performer Dusty Fletcher (National 4012), and by recording giant Louis Jordan (Decca 23841), fourteen other versions were issued. In the same year, six answer songs also appeared. Thus, "Open the Door, Richard!" is an exemplary illustration of one of the most prolific answer-song generators in record history.

Although answer songs are created for all kinds of lyrical situations, the storytelling mode seems to generate responses in three distinct categories: comic reactions to comic situations; varying observations on family relations; and multiple viewpoints about sexual prowess. The best humor-oriented responses to novelty recordings include the answers to Larry Verne's 1960 "Mr. Custer," to The Royal Guardsmen's 1966 "Snoopy vs. The Red Baron," to Joe Tex's 1967 "Skinny Legs and All," and to Randy Newman's 1977 "Short People."

The domestic relations theme, which includes loved ones who are not yet married, is another rich source for answer songs. Classic illustrations include James Shepherd's traveling odyssey in "A Thousand Miles Away" and "Daddy's Home"; Ernie K-Doe's harangue against his "Mother-in-Law"; Johnny Cash's embarrassment at being "A Boy Named Sue"; Kenny Rogers' barroom interlude with the fickle "Lucille" and her hardworking husband; and the melancholy tale of Herman's Hermits about Mrs. Brown's lovely daughter. Although most of the answers to these tunes are comic, they generally expand upon the original situation and reach different conclusions than the original artist did.

The final examples within the continuation of distinct storyline areas are thematically oriented toward sexual prowess. The mildest incarnations of these lyrical brag-and-response activities are Gene Chandler's 1962 "Duke of Earl" and Etta James' 1955 "Wallflower" (which emerged later that same year as "Dance with Me Henry" by Georgia Gibbs). But while these songs utilized vague hints of romantic intent, two other tunes launched extended, outrageous, and unabashedly sexual tales of male and female indiscretions. In 1951 The Dominoes introduced the notorious Lovin' Dan. This "Sixty-Minute Man" promised every young woman an hour-long scene of kissin', huggin', squeezin', and blowin' his top. Tales of Dan's antics multiplied. In 1954 Hank Ballard and the Midnighters chanted "Work with Me Annie" to an amused and titillated radio and record-buying audience. The so-called Annie Series of answer recordings exploded when The Midnighters reported that "Annie Had a Baby" and could not work anymore. This group of songs, which are directly related to the more sanitized "Wallflower"/"Dance with Me Henry" set of records, constitute the best illustration of rampant answer tunes in the post-1950 period.

| Original<br>Title, Record Number, and Artist | Release<br>Date | Response<br>Title, Record Number, and Artist |
|---|---|---|
| 1. "A Boy Named Sue"<br>(Columbia 44944)<br>by Johnny Cash | 1969 | "A Girl Named Harry"<br>(Happy Tiger Era 102)<br>by Joni Credit |
| | | "My Name Is Sue (But I'm<br>a Girl)"<br>(Contrast 604)<br>by Johnny and Phil |
| | | "A Girl Named Johnny Cash"<br>(RCA 9839)<br>by Jane Morgan |
| | | "A Girl Named Sam"<br>(Starday 877)<br>by Louis Williams |
| 2. "Lucille"<br>(United Artists 929)<br>by Kenny Rogers | 1977 | "A Woman's Reply"<br>(Compass 003)<br>by Charlotte Hurt |
| | | "Thanks for Leaving, Lucille"<br>(Gusto/Starday 164)<br>by Sherri Jerrico |
| | | "Lucille's Answer"<br>(Epic 50444)<br>by Julie Jones |
| 3. "Mother-in-Law"<br>(Minit 623)<br>by Ernie K-Doe | 1961 | "Son-in-Law"<br>(Challenge 9109)<br>by The Blossoms |
| | | "Son-in-Law"<br>(Witch 101)<br>by Louise Brown |
| | | "My Mother-in-Law Is in My<br>Hair Again"<br>(Duke 378)<br>by Ernie K-Doe |

4. "Mr. Custer"
   (Era 3024)
   by Larry Verne

1960

"We're Depending on You
   Mr. Custer"
(Pip 100)
by The Characters

"Custer's Last Man"
(Motown 1002)
by Pop Corn and the
   Mohawks

"Ho Ho Mr. Custer"
(Personality 3501)
by Moe Nudenick

"Return of Mr. Custer"
(Era 3139)
by Larry Verne

5. "Mrs. Brown You've Got a
   Lovely Daughter"
   (MGM 13331)
   by Herman's Hermits

1965

"Mother Dear You've Got a
   Silly Daughter"
(Philips 40290)
by Sharon Black

"Mrs. James, I'm Mrs. Brown's
   Lovely Daughter"
(Capitol 5447)
by Connie Holiday

"Mrs. Schwartz You've Got
   an Ugly Daughter"
(Associated Artists 3065)
by Marty

"A Frightful Situation"
(Challenge 59292)
by Mrs. Brown's Lovely
   Daughter Carol

"Mrs. Green's Ugly Daughter"
(Diamond 183)
by Kenneth Young and the
   English Muffins

6. "Short People"
   (Warner Brothers 8492)
   by Randy Newman

1977

"Mr. Small"
(Vanguard 35200)
by The Mr. Men

"Tall People"
(Gusto 179)
by The Short People

"Tall People"
(Co-Star 101)
by Wee Willie Small

7. "Sixty-Minute Man"    1951
   (Federal 12022)
   by The Dominoes

"Petal Pushin' Papa"
(Federal 12114)
by The Dominoes

"Can't Do Sixty No More"
(Red Robin 108)
by The Du-Droppers (1952)

"Don't Stop Dan"
(King 4710)
by the Checkers (1954)

"Life of Ease"
(Great Lakes 1201)
by The Imperials (1954)

"Can't Do Sixty No More"
(Federal 12209)
by Billy Ward and the
    Dominoes (1955)

"The Hatchett Man"
(Spark 116)
by The Robins (1955)

"Dancin' Dan"
(Modern 1000)
by The Cadets (1956)

8. "Skinny Legs and All"    1967
   (Dial 4063)
   by Joe Tex

"I'll Take Those Skinny Legs"
(Twinight 106)
by Syl Johnson

"I'm Leroy—I'll Take Her"
(Jetstar 110)
by Bobby Patterson and the
    Mustangs

9. "Snoopy vs. The Red Baron"    1966
   (Laurie 3366)
   by The Royal Guardsmen

"Red Baron's Revenge"
(GNP 385)
by The Delicatessen

"The Return of the Red Baron"
(Laurie 3379)
by The Royal Guardsmen

10. "Stagger Lee" 1958 "Trail of Stagger Lee"
(ABC-Paramount 9972)  (Cornerstone 250)
by Lloyd Price  by Stella Johnson
and

"Stag-O-Lee" 1967 "The Return of Stagger Lee"
(Atlantic 2448)  (United Artists 277)
by Wilson Pickett  by Don Revels

  "The Ballad of Stagger Lee"
  (Kent 320)
  by The Senders

  "Return of Stagolee"
  (King 5186)
  by Titus Turner

11. "Taxi" 1972 "Sequel"
(Elektra 45770)  (Boardwalk 5700)
by Harry Chapin  by Harry Chapin

12. "A Thousand Miles Away" 1956 "500 Miles to Go"
(Rama 216)  (Gee 1047)
by The Heartbeats  by The Heartbeats

  "Daddy's Home"
  (Hull 740)
  by Shep and the Limelites
  (1961)

  "What Did Daddy Do"
  (Hull 751)
  by Shep and the Limelites

13. "The Wallflower" 1955 "Annie Met Henry"
(Modern 947)  (Modern 969)
by Etta James  by The Cadets
and

"Dance with Me Henry"  "Annie Met Henry"
(Mercury 70572)  (Chart 602)
by Georgia Gibbs  by The Champions

  "Hey, Henry!"
  (Modern 957)
  by Etta James

  "Henry's Got Flat Feet"
  (Federal 12224)
  by The Midnighters

  "Here Comes Henry"
  (Modern 1010)
  by Young Jesse

14. "Work with Me Annie"
(Federal 12169)
by The Midnighters

1954

"My Name Ain't Annie"
(King 4752)
by Linda Hayes and the
Platters

"Annie Don't Love Me No
More"
(Symbol 215)
by The Hollywood Flames

"Eat Your Heart Out Annie"
(Capitol 3512)
by The Jordimars

"Annie Get Your Yo-Yo"
(Duke 345)
by Little Junior Parker (1962)

"Annie's Back"
(Specialty 692)
by Little Richard (1964)

"Annie's Answer"
(Vee Jay 118)
by The El Doradoes

"Annie Had a Baby"
(Federal 12195)
by The Midnighters (1954)

"Annie's Aunt Fannie"
(Federal 12200)
by The Midnighters (1954)

"Annie Pulled a Humbug"
(Music City 746)
by The Midnights

"Annie Kicked the Bucket"
(Hollywood Star 789)
by The Nu-Tones

"Annie's Not an Orphan
Anymore"
(Challenge 919)
by Rochell and the Candles

"I'm the Father of Annie's
Baby"
(Bruce 118)
by Danny Taylor

This study constitutes only a preliminary investigation of the answer song phenomenon. The world of record collectors and sound recordings archives in libraries must be merged to provide vinyl resources necessary for further scholarship. The answer song, in all of its functional permutations, is a worthy subject for teaching and popular culture research.

# REFERENCES

Adams, Roy. "I Put the Bomp," *Record Exchanger*, No. 13 (1973), pp. 24, 26.

Buckley, Bruce R. "Frankie and Her Men: A Study of the Interrelationship of Popular and Folk Traditions" (PhD dissertation: Indiana University, 1961).

Cooper, B. Lee. "Bear Cats, Chipmunks, and Slip-In Mules: The 'Answer Song' in Contemporary American Recordings, 1950-1985," *Popular Music and Society,* XII (Fall 1988), pp. 57-77.

Cooper, B. Lee. "Response Recordings As Creative Repetition: Answer Songs and Pop Parodies in Contemporary American Music," *OneTwoThreeFour: A Rock 'n' Roll Quarterly*, No. 4 (Winter 1987), pp. 79-87.

Cooper, B. Lee. "Yes, Bearcat, I'll Save the Last Dance for You: Answer Songs and Sequel Tunes in American Popular Music, 1950-1985" (mimeographed paper and audiotape presentation at the 8th National Convention of The American Culture Association in April 1985).

Coucet, Sharon Arms. "Cajun: Songs and Psyche," *Journal of Popular Culture*, XXIII (Summer 1989), pp. 89-99.

Grevatt, Ren. "Answer Songs Aren't New!" *Melody Maker*, XXXV (November 5, 1960), pp. 6-7.

Hoffmann, Frank W. and William G. Bailey. "Answer Songs," in *Arts and Entertainment Fads* (New York: The Haworth Press, 1990), pp. 11-17.

Kahn, Ashley. "Stagolee," *WaveLength*, No. 85 (November 1987), pp. 22-23.

Kimberly, Nick "Answer Records," *Collusion*, No. 3 (July-September 1982), pp. 41-42.

Koppel, Martin. "The Answer Songs," *Soul Survivor*, No. 10 (Spring 1989), pp. 28-29.

Moonoogian, George. "The Answer Record in R&B," *Record Exchanger*, No. 22 (1976), pp. 24-25, 28.

Moonoogian, George. "Oh, That Annie!" *Record Exchanger*, No. 23 (1977), pp. 20-21.

Moonoogian, George and Chris Beachley. "Lovin' Dan: A Look Thirty Years Later—Does He Have 59 to Go?," *It Will Stand*, No. 20 (1980), pp. 4-7.

Morgan, John P. and Thomas C. Tulloss. "The Jake Walk Blues: A Toxicologic Tragedy Mirrored in American Popular Music," *Annals of Internal Medicine*, LXXXV (December 1976), pp. 804-808.

Noblett, Richard A. "Stavin' Chain: A Study of a Folk Hero—Part One," *Blues Unlimited*, No. 130 (May-August 1978), pp. 31-33.

Noblett, Richard A. "Stavin' Chain: A Study of a Folk Hero—Part Two," *Blues Unlimited*, No. 134 (March-June 1979), pp. 14-17.

Noblett, Richard A. "Stavin' Chain: A Study of a Folk Hero—Part Three," *Blues Unlimited*, No. 139 (Autumn 1980), pp. 31-33.

Noblett, Richard A. "Stavin' Chain: A Study of a Folk Hero—Part Four," *Blues Unlimited*, No. 142 (Summer 1982), pp. 24-26.

Oermann, Robert K. "Answer Songs: A Primer," in *Country: The Music and the Musicians*, edited by Paul Kingsbury and Alan Axelrod (New York: Abbeville Press, 1988), pp. 326-327.

Ralston, Richard D. "Bad Dude or Common Criminal: The Interrelationship of Contemporary and Folk Values in the Ballad of Stagolee" (mimeographed paper presented at the 14th National Convention of The Popular Culture Association in March 1984).

"Shame to You, Mac," *Time*, LXXXVII (January 6, 1961), p. 52.

Sandmel, Ben. "Whose Toot-Toot?" *Wavelength*, No. 56 (June 1985), pp. 24-28.

Seroff, Doug. "Open the Door Richard?" *Record Exchanger*, No. 20 (1975), pp. 10-11.

Stevenson, Gordon. "Race Records: Victims of Benign Neglect in Libraries," *Wilson Library Bulletin*, (November 1975), pp. 224-232.

Stidom, Larry. "Big Bad John (and Friends)," in *Izatso?! Larry Stidom's Rock 'n' Roll Trivia and Fact Book* (Indianapolis, Indiana: L. Stidom, 1986), p. 58.

Stidom, Larry. "Larry's Corner," *Record Digest*, No. 19 (June 15, 1978), p. 38.

Stidom, Larry. "Larry's Corner," *Record Digest*, Nos. 22/23 (August 1, 1978), pp. 24-28ff.

Stidom, Larry. "Larry's Corner," *Music World and Record Digest*, No. 40 (May 9, 1979), p. 10.

Stidom, Larry. "Sheb Wooley, a.k.a. Ben Colder: The Purple People Eater Revisited," *Goldmine*, No. 65 (October 1981), pp. 178-179.

Williams, Brett. *John Henry: A Bio-Bibliography.* Westport, Connecticut: Greenwood Press, 1983.

Woodford, Chris. "Don't Mess with My Toot-Toot!" *Now Dig This*, No. 31 (October 1985), p. 25.

Zucker, Mark J. "The Saga of Lovin' Dan: A Study in the Iconography of Rhythm and Blues Music of the 1950s," *Journal of Popular Culture*, XVI (Fall 1982), pp. 43-51.

# Chapter 2

# Cars

Chuck Berry epitomizes the folk artist of the Rock idiom. His style did not change because it did not have to; from the beginning it unconsciously expressed the responses of the artist and his audience to the ordinary realities of their world: to cars, girls, growing up, school, or music.

—Carl Belz

The motorcar is omnipresent in contemporary American society. David J. Neuman reported in 1974, "No mechanical convenience has so enthralled a jaded public as the automobile has the American masses. Certainly the television is used as often and for longer hours and the telephone is more plentiful, but the special relationship between an American and his/her car is based upon more than convenience . . . ." What is perhaps more unique than this elevated profile of the automobile is the ambivalent attitudes that characterize public opinion toward this enigmatic machine. As many observers have noted, an ironic love-hate relationship dominates the history of twentieth-century thought and writing about the motorcar. "The American automobile has traveled the whole circuit from hero to villain," notes Glen Jeansonne. "Once enshrined as a liberating and democratizing agent, it is now condemned as a major cause of pollution and congestion." Since its initial appearance, the automobile has been a subject of popular songs. From Billy Murray's "He'd Have to Get Under, Get Out and Get Under, to Fix Up His Automobile" to the hot

These essays by B. Lee Cooper were originally published as "Cruisin' and Playin' the Radio: Exploring Images of The American Automobile Through Popular Music," *International Journal of Instructional Media*, VII, No. 4 (1979-1980), pp. 327-334 and "Review of *The Illustrated Discography of Hot Rod Music, 1961-1965* by John Blair and Stephen J. McParland," *Popular Music and Society*, XV (Spring 1991), pp. 114-115. Reprint permissions granted by the author, Editor Phillip J. Sleeman, and the Baywood Publishing Company, and Editor R. Serge Denisoff and the Bowling Green State University Popular Press.

rod/surf scene tunes of the Beach Boys ("409," "Shut Down," "Little Deuce Coupe," and "Fun, Fun, Fun"), Jan and Dean ("Drag City," "Dead Man's Curve," and "The Little Old Lady from Pasadena"), and Ronny and the Daytonas ("G.T.O."), car-related songs have attracted record buyers. It is not peculiar, then, that the poet laureate of rock 'n' roll music–Chuck Berry–should also be one of the foremost spokesman among contemporary composers on the nature and impact of the motorcar on his fellow Americans. No other songwriter has demonstrated more lyrical ingenuity in introducing four-wheeled imagery to depict issues of freedom, mobility, sexual relationships, prosperity, and authority.

## *CHUCK BERRY*

Chuck Berry emerged as a popular recording star for Chess Records of Chicago in the summer of 1955. His first hit release–"Maybellene"– ranked as high as Number 5 on the *Billboard* "Top 100" charts. Despite the racist stigma that was often attached to rhythm-and-blues songs performed by black artists in the mid-1950s, Chuck Berry produced hit after hit. "Roll Over Beethoven" rose to Number 29; "School Day" peaked at Number 5 after 26 weeks on the *Billboard* list; "Rock and Roll Music" and "Johnny B. Goode" both climbed to the Number 8 position in 1957 and 1958, respectively; and "Sweet Little Sixteen" closed at Number 2 during a 16-week period of popularity. The Chuck Berry hit song phenomenon stretches from 1955 to the present. During the 1960s his recording productivity slowed considerably, but no less than eight of his 45 rpm releases reached the *Billboard* "Top 100." And in early 1970, on the strength of praise by The Beatles and the Rolling Stones and during a surge of rock 'n' roll nostalgia, Chuck Berry reasserted himself with a revised version of his classic "Reelin' and Rockin'" and a novelty song entitled "My Ding-a-Ling."

Chuck Berry has always been a youth-oriented performer. His consistent popularity among record buyers and concert audiences, the fact that he has always been a total performer (singer, writer, dancer, and musician), and the dramatic effect of so many of his songs on the entire field of popular music make him a seminal figure in contemporary audio production. The themes of his songs are manifestly personal. They demonstrate a minstrel's approach to modern life. Chuck Berry's song-poems are pointed observations and commentaries about the lifestyles of young people in urban-industrial America. He notes the lack of relevance in public school experiences ("School Day," "Too Much Monkey Business," and "Anthony Boy"); he depicts the universal reliance of young people on popular music as a means of emotional communication and celebration ("Rock and Roll Music," "Round and Round," and "Go, Go, Go"); he capsules the invigorating but confusing process of social maturation ("Almost Grown," "Sweet Little Sixteen," and "Sweet Little Rock and Roller"); he fabricates and breathes life into a series of twentieth-century Horatio Algers ("Johnny B. Goode," "Bye Bye Johnny," and "You Never Can Tell"); he condemns the fickleness of the female heart ("Nadine" and "Little Queenie"); and he describes the simplistic image of America to teenagers everywhere ("Back in the U.S.A.").

The thematic consistency of Chuck Berry's lyrics constitutes only one aspect of his uniqueness, though. He is also a creative force in language usage (a quality which H. L. Mencken would have applauded). In addition to employing standard slang terminology in his songs—"Machine" for automobile and "cruisin'" for driving—Chuck Berry initiates fascinating verbal images that come to symbolize the characters or scenes which he is describing. For instance, Johnny B. Goode does not just sit beside the railroad track and play his guitar. Instead he "strums to the rhythm that the (train's) drivers make . . . ." And the young man chasing the fickle Nadine does not just call out her name; he is described to be "campaign shoutin' like a Southern diplomat . . . ." Students at a dance do not just enjoy rock 'n' roll songs; they are "feelin' the music from head to toe . . . ." And finally, the young women of Chuck Berry's lyrical world inevitably face the transition period called "the grown-up blues" when they begin to wear "tight dresses and lipstick" and start "sportin' high heel shoes. . . ."

Recognizing Chuck Berry's orientation toward youth, his fascination with urban life and culture, and his folk-poet style of combining personal concerns with the confusion of complex community life and technological advances, it is hardly surprising that the automobile has emerged as a focal object in his lyrics. The following pages explore motorcar imagery in numerous songs written and performed by Chuck Berry.

## *"Maybellene"*

Fast cars and fickle females have sustained Chuck Berry's lyrics. "Maybellene" was the first. This 1955 tale illustrated two consistent themes in Chuck Berry's songs. First, the dude with the biggest most elegant car will invariably capture the attention of any girl ("Maybellene, why can't you be true?"); and second, the pursuit of a wayward woman is never final ("You've started back doin' the things you used to do."). The driver of the Cadillac Coupe de Ville remains unidentified, although one suspects that his financial resources far exceed those of the singing hero driving the V-8 Ford. Fate, in the form of a sudden cloudburst, enables the overheated Ford to catch the 110-mile-per-hour speeding Cadillac at the top of the hill. Then what happens? Chuck Berry does not depict a battle between the two drivers over the fair damsel. Instead, he returns to the original refrain—"Maybellene, why can't you be true?" Somehow, one senses that the man in the V-8 will be chasing again in the near future.

### *"Come On"*

This tune, both comic and tragic, finds a disabled automobile to be only one of a growing list of problems for a young man. "Everything is wrong," he declares, "since me and my baby parted." It may be difficult to establish a causal relationship between lost love and failing technology, but Chuck Berry does it. The hero's car will not start, and to further complicate matters, he loses his job and cannot afford to hire a mechanic. Dolefully observing his immobilized vehicle, the hero expresses the frustrated wish that ". . . somebody'd come along and run into it and wreck it." Perhaps a token amount of insurance money might be gained from such an accident, although certainly not enough to resolve all of the problems detailed in this down-and-out song.

### *"Nadine (Is That You?)"*

If dating a girl like Maybellene was a problem, having a fiancée like Nadine would be unbearable. Chuck Berry utilizes traffic congestion—crowded buses, loaded taxis, and endless lines of honking cars—to set the scene for this romantic chase. Nadine, who is reportedly always ". . . up to something new," is spotted doubling back from a corner and moving toward a coffee-colored Cadillac. As the hero calls out to gain her attention, she abandons the Caddie and gets into ". . . a yellow cab headin' up-town." The song provides no resolution since the pursuer is left at the mercy of his cab driver and must be content to be "leanin' out the taxi window tryin' to make her hear." Obviously private transportation is superior to public vehicles—and courtship via buses, on foot, or in cabs is depicted by Chuck Berry as a losing battle.

### *"No Money Down"*

A new Cadillac symbolizes power, sex, social mobility, notoriety, freedom, and . . . the end of the rainbow for the owner of a "broken down ragged Ford." The salesman in this tune is initially silent, but stands beneath a tempting "No Money Down" sign. When the prospective car buyer rolls into the lot, however, the dealer offers to put him in a car "that'll eat up the road." The salesman soon learns that he is facing a young man who knows exactly what he wants. And the list of accessories requested for the yellow, four-door Cadillac Coupe de Ville staggers the mind: wire-chromed wheels and a Continental spare, power steering and power brakes, air conditioning and automatic heat, "a full Murphy bed in my back seat" (Maybellene and Nadine beware!), short-wave radio, television, telephone ("You know I gotta talk to my baby when I'm ridin' alone."), four carburetors and two straight exhaust pipes, railroad air-horns, and a military spotlight. It seems doubtful that the proposed car deal is ever consummated. Nevertheless, the values of the would-be buyer are clearly articulated. A peppy, ostentatious buggy to replace a tired, drab Ford, and the whole world will be fine.

### *"Too Much Monkey Business"*

This song might bring to mind Jim Croce's "Workin' in the Car Wash Blues." The hero is really down on his luck. Too many bills and too much hard work. If it is not the antics of a woman trying to steal his freedom by forcing him to settle down, it is the mechanical thievery of a telephone operator stealing his dime, or the exile of Uncle Sam robbing him of physical autonomy and years of freedom through military service in Yokohama. The two automobile-related references in this song are brief. The first is a derogatory reference to the inferiority and sterility of military vehicles: "Army car! Arrgh...." The second is a negative attitude expressed about post-military employment at a local filling station: "Too many tasks, wipe the windows, check the tires, check the oil, dollar gas?!!!" There is no joyous speculation about owning the gas station or driving a Coupe de Ville, only frustration by being forced to endure . . . too much monkey business.

### *"No Particular Place to Go"*

This tune is Chuck Berry at his comic best. Initially, it appears to be a typical tale of automotive seduction. The boy is "cruising and playing the radio" with a sweet young thing seated close beside him. He steals a kiss, she whispers softly in his ear, and they continue ". . . cuddling more and driving slow, with no particular place to go." The romantic mood is shaken, however, when the car is unexpectedly transformed from a lovers' chariot into a four-wheeled chastity belt. Just as the couple is ready to take a stroll in the moonlight, the young woman discovers that her safety harness will not release. The final verse is classic Berry: "Riding along in my calaboose, still trying to get her belt unloose. All the way home I held a grudge, for the safety belt that wouldn't budge." Here is the motorcar as entrapment, a classic example of technologically enforced morality in contemporary song.

## "Move It"

This upbeat tune contains two illustrations of Chuck Berry's creative automobile imagery. The cars mentioned here are utilized as symbols of sexual liberation and senseless authority. In the first case, the singer yearns to possess a shapely disco queen who ". . . drives a mustang" and "let's her hair hang."

The second case is more complex. The driver of a 1955 Ford finds that his engine has mysteriously died on the freeway. Traffic begins to pile up behind him despite the fact that he has rolled the disabled car toward the curb and raised the hood to indicate mechanical distress. When Officer Lamar arrives, his only recommendation to resolve the automotive problem is a terse, "Move it!" The omission of a statement of sympathy, an offer of direct aid, or even a call for assistance is indicative of police mentality in high traffic areas. "You cannot stop it here! Get it out of here!" is the authoritarian patrolman's heartless refrain. The stalled automobile symbolizes unexpected trouble (a personal difficulty) as well as an opportunity for someone to offer assistance. But everyone else on the highway avoids the opportunity to be a good samaritan by simply ". . . tryin' to drive around." Only the policeman responds, unsatisfactorily.

## "Almost Grown"

Coming-of-age, that anthropological combination of physical maturation and economic independence, is a common theme in Chuck Berry's songs. The automobile is frequently a focal point for youthful expenditures: the addition of personalizing accessories (as in "No Money Down"), the never-ending quest for gasoline ("I'm burnin' aviation fuel—no matter what the costs."), and joy-riding in the countryside. From the perspective of the young man in this tune, the acquisition of a car is a symbol of social stability. He is a reformed soul who is ". . . doing all right in school," "hasn't broken any rules," "ain't never been in dutch" (with the police?), doesn't ". . . browse around too much," and doesn't "run around with no mob." In short, he is fairly respectable. But the undisguised sense of youthful uncertainty permeates the lyric. The "little car" he plans to buy will reportedly halt all his browsing and provide entry into the adult world.

### *"Wuden't Me"*

This song features Chuck Berry's sardonic use of the automobile and a minor traffic violation to underscore the social inequality that still exists in America. Instead of employing the make, model, and year of the car to identify the driver's personal background, the vehicle is introduced only to create the confrontation: "Oh boy, he ran a little stop sign in the South." The rest of the tale describes a quasi-legal incarceration in a Delta County jail, a fortunate escape, and the hot pursuit of the traffic offender by a Grand Dragon posse and seven Alabama bloodhounds. In mock humor, the singer of the tune continues to insist, "Wuden't Me."

### *"Carol"*

"Come into my machine so we can cruise on out," says Carol's would-be date. He wants to take her to a "swingin' little joint" that is located "Not too far back off the highway, not so long a ride." The romantic approach is straightforward. No frills. The automobile is simply a source of horizontal mobility. But the slang term "my machine," utilized to describe the young man's vehicle, hints that the engine may not be a stock variety and that the car's body may have been artistically personalized. Nonetheless, Carol is an object of pursuit—not unlike the fickle Maybellene and the fleeing Nadine—and both the automobile and the dancehall figure prominently in the lover's chase.

### *"If I Were"*

This highly speculative love song offers an automobile metaphor in which the desirable female is cast as a Mercedes Benz and the day-dreaming boy is a (Cadillac) Fleetwood Brougham. The idealized relationship is simple and straightforward: ". . . everytime I see you rollin' on the highway, I think I'd have to follow you home." There the Fleetwood longs to lodge in the Benz' double garage, bumper to bumper. Instead of just settling down and living happily ever after, the would-be Cadillac yearns for a fast-paced life where there is "nobody home but the Benz and the Brougham, ready, rarin' to roll out together." This is truly a four-wheeled fairy tale.

### *"You Never Can Tell"*

The message of this song—directed toward skeptical parents—is clear. Do not make snap judgments about the failure of teenage marriages. The automobile once again functions in several sociological ways. First, it illustrates economic stability and independence from the older generation; second, it establishes the individualistic style of the young couple under observation ("They bought a souped-up jitney, 'twas a cherry red fifty-three"); and finally, it becomes a source of personal pleasure and geographic mobility ("They drove it down to New Orleans to celebrate their anniversary"). The skepticism of the "old folks" apparently is not totally overcome by this single instance of marital bliss, though, as the refrain—"It goes to show you never can tell"—indicates.

### *"Back in the U.S.A."*

This paean to America, or more precisely to the urban centers of the United States ("New York, Los Angeles, oh, how I yearned for you. Detroit, Chicago, Chattanooga, Baton Rouge. Let alone just to be at my home back in ol' St. Lou."), is punctuated by two automobile-related yearnings. The returning world traveler, who exudes love for his home-land, indicates that high on his list of things "missed" are freeways and drive-ins. It should be obvious that traffic congestion and greasy hamburgers are not considered to be social problems to this urban patriot; instead, lines of cars zooming along multilane highways and dozens of automobiles sandwiched together beneath the watchful eyes of drive-in restaurant operators and their carhop employees are signs of social progress, economic stability, and personal joy.

Despite his numerous references to the automobile as a source of social mobility, Chuck Berry deviates from this prominent private transportation symbol in two of his most noted rags-to-riches tunes. For Johnny B. Goode ("Bye, Bye Johnny") it is the Greyhound bus which, funded by his mother's Southern Trust savings, whisks him from guitar playing beside a Louisiana railroad track to the gates of Hollywood. Similarly, the poor boy from Norfolk, Virginia ("The Promised Land") is transported by Greyhound bus from his hometown to Birmingham, Alabama, from there by train to New Orleans, Louisiana, and finally by plane from Houston, Texas to Los Angeles, California. The only possibility of auto transportation in this quest for life in "The Promised Land" occurs between New Orleans and Houston, but is depicted in lyrics that vaguely declare, "Somebody helped me get out of Louisiana, just to help me get to Houston Town." It might be that Chuck Berry is avoiding use of the automobile in these cases since his heroes are still unemployed and too young to have acquired even a used, battered Ford.

During the past 45 years Chuck Berry has chronicled the sociological impact of a particular segment of American technology faithfully and accurately. Undeniably he is the oral historian, the balladeer of teenage life. In 1970 journalist Michael Lydon accurately described him in one sentence: "Serious and comic as only a genius can be; arrogant, beautiful, and demonically energetic, Chuck has indelibly marked our times." What is seldom recognized, though, is the cogent, efficient manner in which this master lyricist has adapted the most common physical element of the youth culture—the automobile—to his own poetic ends. Hopefully, this study will generate further investigation of Chuck Berry's expansive portfolio of tunes.

In the meantime one cannot ignore the fact that the automobile will apparently remain a topic of sharply divided opinion and national attention during the coming decade. Just as Chuck Berry has explored the sociology and psychology of the motorcar for the younger generation, other poets (probably with less rhythm—but not with less blues) will attempt to come to grips with the complex issues of traffic congestion, the energy crisis, environmental pollution, and the dozens of other concerns related to America's love-hate relationship with the automobile. As one student of popular culture sagely noted,

> Whatever the future holds for the automobile, it seems that for Americans the car is here to stay, in large part because it is a powerful iconic focus for the national ideals of individualism, freedom, and personal power. And the songs that celebrate this great American icon will continue to strike a responsive chord in the American psyche.

This should mean Chuck Berry's tunes—old and new—will continue to be vital, valuable commentaries on humans and their favorite machine.

## *HOT RODS*

*The Illustrated Discography of Hot Rod Music, 1961-1965.* Compiled by John Blair and Stephen J. McParland. Ann Arbor, Michigan: Popular Culture, Ink., 1990. Illustrated pp. 167.

John Blair and Stephen J. McParland have isolated a moment in American cultural history. Between 1961 and 1965 youthful interest in automobiles and rock music crescendoed. Blair and McParland contend that the early 1960s focus on teen rituals–dating, authority challenging, peer pleasing, money earning, job hunting, and even surfing–is clearly depicted in hot rod music. Led by The Beach Boys, Jan and Dean, The Hondells, The Ripchords, Ronny and the Daytonas, and The Routers, an onslaught of car songs dominated popular music charts and lionized the automobile as America's prime icon. The triumph of The Beatles and the subsequent British invasion ended, or at least redirected, youthful attention from this four-wheeled mania toward hairstyles, hip garb, and the hoary spectre of a southeast Asian war.

*The Illustrated Discography of Hot Rod Music, 1961-1965* is a treasurehouse of records, album art, and commercial advertisement. Blair and McParland feature alphabetized lists of single recordings and 33 1/3 rpm albums. Numerous picture sleeves, album covers, photographs of popular music groups, and magazine advertisements for both cars and discs are interspersed throughout the lengthy, detailed discography. The authors also provide brief appendixes that feature "Compilation Albums by Label," "Glossary of Hot Rod and Racing Terms," "U.S. Releases of Foreign Hot Rod Recordings," "Hot Rod Music and Hollywood–The Sixties," and "Hot Rod Recordings on the Top 100." The text concludes with a short bibliography and three very helpful indexes.

The genius of this work, not unlike John Blair's earlier *The Illustrated History of Surf Music, 1961-1965*, is its clear focus on a distinctive instance of musical/cultural linkage. However, one might have hoped for a broader perspective from Blair and McParland when examining auto/audio interaction in twentieth-century US history. Even if the numerous pre-1950 tunes are ignored, it is difficult to discuss rock groups and car tunes without focusing on the contributions of Chuck Berry, Bruce Springsteen, Aretha Franklin, Billy Ocean, Billy Emerson, Eddie Cochran, Natalie Cole, and even DJ Jazzy Jeff and the Fresh Prince. Hopefully, Blair and McParland will consider expanding their narrow hot rod music view (1961-1965) to encompass the 40-year image of automobiles in all rock era lyrics (1950-1990).

Blair and McParland's beautifully illustrated volume is valuable to popular culture scholars, music fans, record collectors, and classic car enthusiasts. It captures the post-Elvis pre-Beatles era of rock and defines the cruisin' mania even more clearly than the film *American Grafitti*. The thorough introductory comments by the authors make this fact-filled compendium of car songs even more interesting and helpful for record researchers. This volume ought to be dedicated to . . . "Mustang Sally," "The Little Old Lady from Pasadena," and any reckless teenager who ever felt the challenge of "Dead Man's Curve."

# REFERENCES

Alexander, Shana. "Love Songs to the Carburetor," *Life*, LVII (November 6, 1964), p. 33.

Ames, Roy Clifton. "Cars in Song," *Special-Interest Autos*, (January/February, 1977), pp. 40-45.

Belasco, Warren. "Motivatin' with Chuck Berry and Frederick Jackson Turner," in *The Automobile and American Culture,* edited by David L. Lewis and Laurence Goldstein (Ann Arbor: University of Michigan Press, 1983), pp. 262-279.

Belz, Carl. "Chuck Berry: Folk Poet of the Fifties," in *The Story of Rock* (second edition) (New York: Harper and Row, 1972), pp. 61-66.

Berry, Chuck. *Chuck Berry–The Autobiography.* New York: Harmony Books, 1987.

Cooper, B. Lee. "Chuck Berry and the American Motor Car," *Music World*, No. 86 (June 1981), pp. 18-23.

Cooper, B. Lee. "Nothin' Outrun My V-8 Ford: Chuck Berry and the American Motorcar, 1955-1979," *JEMF Quarterly*, XVI (Spring 1980), pp. 18-23.

Cooper, B. Lee. "Transportation Systems," in *A Resource Guide to Themes in Contemporary American Song Lyrics, 1950-1985,* edited by B. Lee Cooper (Westport, Connecticut: Greenwood Press, 1986), pp. 235-252.

"Country Cads," *Newsweek*, LXXV (April 13, 1970), pp. 84-86.

Danker, Frederick E. "Trucking Songs: A Comparison with Traditional Occupational Song," *Journal of Country Music*, VII (January 1978), pp. 78-86.

Demento, Dr. " 'Check Out My Custom Machine': Vehicular Traffic Through the Ages," *Wax Paper*, II (April 29, 1977), pp. 16-19.

Denfeld, D. "Woody and Rag Are Dead: A Consideration of the Three Stages of American Automobile Consciousness," *Journal of Popular Culture*, VIII (Sparing 1974), pp. 148-153.

Dettelbach, Cynthia Golomb. *In the Driver's Seat: The Automobile in American Literature and Popular Culture.* Westport, Connecticut: Greenwood Press, 1976.

DeWitt, Howard A. *Chuck Berry: Rock 'n' Roll Music* (second edition). Ann Arbor, Michigan: Pierian Press, 1985.

Duke, Maurice. "The Automobile," in *The Handbook of American Popular Culture–Volume One,* edited by M. Thomas Inge (Westport, Connecticut: Greenwood Press, 1978), pp. 27-48.

Duke, Maurice. "Motor Vehicle Museums," in *Twentieth-Century Popular Culture in Museums and Libraries,* edited by Fred E. H. Schroeder (Bowling Green, Ohio: Bowling Green State University Popular Press, 1981), pp. 158-176.

Flink, James J. *The Car Culture.* Cambridge, Massachusetts: MIT Press, 1975.

Flink, James J. "Three Stages of American Automobile Consciousness," *American Quarterly*, XXIV (October 1972), pp. 451-473.

Gammage, Grady, Jr. and Stephen L. Jones. "Orgasm in Chrome: The Rise and Fall of the Automobile Tailfin," *Journal of Popular Culture*, VIII (Spring 1974), pp. 132-147.

Hawkins, Richard. "The Automobile As a Vehicle of Engagement" (mimeographed paper presented at the 10th National Convention of the Popular Culture Association in April 1980).

Higgins, James V. "Rock 'n' Cars Make Beautiful (?) Music Together," *Detroit News*, (October 15, 1986), pp. F-1,2.

Hoffmann, Frank W. and William G. Bailey. "Car Songs," in *Arts and Entertainment Fads* (New York: The Haworth Press, 1990), pp. 61-62.

Hossain, Tony. "A Rich Slice of the American Pie," *Friends*, XXXVII (August 1980), pp. 26-28.

Jeanes, William. "Doo-Wopping the American Dream," *Car and Driver*, (March 1985), pp. 85-89.

Jeansonne, Glen. "The Automobile and American Morality," *Journal of Popular Culture*, VIII (January 1974), pp. 125-131.

Kornheiser, Tony. "Radio Daze," *Life*, XIII (June 1990), pp. 89-95.

Lewis, David L. "Sex and the Automobile: From Rumble Seats to Rockin' Vans," *Michigan Quarterly Review*, XX (Winter 1981), pp. 518-528.

Lewis, David L. and Lawrence Goldstein (eds.). *The Automobile and American Culture*. Ann Arbor: University of Michigan Press, 1983.

Lipsitz, George. "'Living in the U.S.A!': Chuck Berry and St. Louis Rock and Roll, 1945-1960." (Mimeographed paper presented at the 12th National Convention of the Popular Culture Association in April 1982.)

Lydon, Michael. "Chuck Berry Lives!" *Ramparts*, VIII (December 1969), pp. 47-56.

Moorhouse, H. F. "Racing for a Sign: Defining the 'Hot Rod', 1945-1960," *Journal of Popular Culture*, XX (Fall 1986), pp. 83-96.

Morrow, Lance. "Cars: The American Passion," *Life*, XIII (June 1990), pp. 48-52.

Neuman, David J. "From Bumper . . .," *Journal of Popular Culture*, VIII (Spring 1974), pp. 123-124.

Newman, Ralph M. "The Chuck Berry Story: Long Lives Rock and Roll," *Time Barrier Express*, No. 27 (April/May 1980), pp. 34-36.

Perrin, Mark. "Crazy 'Bout Automobiles," *Now Dig This*, No. 83 (February 1990), pp. 8-9.

Rae, John B. *The American Automobile: A Brief History*. Chicago: University of Chicago Press, 1965.

Rae, John B. *The Road and the Car in American Life*. Cambridge, Massachusetts: MIT Press, 1971.

Rollin, Roger B. "*Deus in Machina:* Popular Culture's Myth of the Machine," *Journal of American Culture*, II (Summer 1979), pp. 287-308.

Schurk, William L. "Unhurried Views of Auto-Erotica: A Singalong." (Mimeographed paper presented at the 11th National Convention of the Popular Culture Association in March 1981.)

"Transportation in American Popular Songs: A Bibliography of Items in the Grosvenor Library," *The Grosvenor Library Bulletin*, XXVII (June 1945), pp. 61-106.

White, Lawrence J. *The Automobile Industry Since 1945*. Cambridge, Massachusetts: Harvard University Press, 1971.

Wright, John. "Car Tunes: Lyrics on the Automobile." (Mimeographed paper and audio presentation at the 7th Annual Meeting of the Midwest Popular Culture Association in October 1979.)

Wright, John L. "Croonin' About Cruisin'," in *The Popular Culture Reader*, edited by Jack Nachbar, Deborah Weiser, and John L. Wright (Bowling Green, Ohio: Bowling Green State University Popular Press, 1978), pp. 109-117.

# Chapter 3

# Cigarettes

Since 1945 the American public has witnessed a dramatic change in the image of cigarette use. Teachers should employ the cultural themes that have evolved during this five-decade period to illustrate the complexity of smoking, personal behavior, and social life. This study provides a discography of more than 100 recordings that illustrate diverse tobacco-related images, including contemplation and reflection, reverie and romance, rebellion and experimentation, frustration and self-ridicule, and condemnation and mockery. By combining several years of negative public health data, political pressuring and legal mandates, and mixed journalistic commentaries with 50 years of lyrical observations, social studies instructors can creatively demonstrate the shifting climate of attitudes toward cigarette smoking in the United States.

Nothing better illustrates the shift in America's image of cigarette smoking over the past 50 years than popular song lyrics. Although Hollywood films and television programs offer ample visual evidence of tobacco use, post-World War II recordings contain a remarkably informative verbal network of tobacco-related terms, stock cigarette-use situations, and stereotypic smoker personalities. By listening to lyrics, students can readily identify such diverse attitudes, feelings, and behaviors as:

- The uninhibited joy of smokers ("A Cigarette, Sweet Music and You"–1957)
- The isolation and loneliness of a singular figure at a cloudy cabaret setting ("Smoky Places"–1961)
- The annoyance felt by friends or family members over an individual's excessive tobacco use ("Smoke! Smoke! Smoke! (That Cigarette)"–1947)

This essay by B. Lee Cooper and William L. Schurk was originally published as "Smokin' Songs: Examining Tobacco Use as an American Cultural Phenomenon Through Contemporary Lyrics," *International Journal of Instructional Media*, XXI, No. 3 (1994), pp. 261-268. Reprint permission granted by the authors, Editor Phillip J. Sleeman, and the Baywood Publishing Company.

- The personal depression and helplessness caused by addiction to nicotine ("I Can't Quit Cigarettes"–1966)
- The youthful rebellion found in snatching secret cigarette breaks ("Smokin' in the Boys' Room"–1985)
- The reveries of past lovers and former friends conjured by matchsticks, cigarettes, smoke rings, and ashtrays ("Lipstick Traces (on a Cigarette)"–1962)
- The inability to comprehend the reasons for continued tobacco use ("Another Puff"–1972)

The chronological record list provided below features more than 100 songs. These tunes can be rearranged for instructional purposes to create various personal and social perspectives on tobacco-related issues and themes in recent US history.

- "Cigarettes, Whiskey, and Wild, Wild Women"
  (Victor 20-2199)
  Sons of the Pioneers (1947)

- "Smoke! Smoke! Smoke! (That Cigarette)
  (Capitol Americana 40001)
  Tex Williams (1947)

- "Cigarette Song (Always Grabbing Someone's Butt)"
  (Pearl 74)
  Larry Vincent (1948)

- "Don't Smoke in Bed"
  (Capitol 10120)
  Peggy Lee (1948)

- "Coffee, Cigarettes, and Tears"
  (Apollo 1177)
  Larks (1950)

- "Coffee and Cigarettes"
  (Columbia CL 6199)
  Johnnie Ray (1952)

- "Smoke Rings"
  (Capitol 2123)
  Les Paul and Mary Ford (1952)

- "Smoking My Sad Cigarette"
  (Columbia 39951)
  Jo Stafford (1953)

- "Smoke from Your Cigarette"
  (Coral 61363)
  Billy Williams Quartet (1955)

- "Smoke Another Cigarette"
  (Mercury MG 20179)
  Harry Revel (1956)

- "While a Cigarette Was Burning"
  (Mercury MD 20098)
  Patti Page (1956)

- "Ashtrays for Two"
  (Coral CRL 57060)
  Bob Crosby (1957)

- "Share with Me a Lonely Cigarette"
  (Decca DL 8452)
  Daniel DeCarlo (1957)

- "Three Cigarettes in an Ashtray"
  (Decca 30406)
  Patsy Cline (1957)

- "A Cigarette, Sweet Music, and You"
  (Capitol SW 845)
  Fred Waring and the Pennsylvanians (1957)

- "Cigarettes and Coffee Blues"
  (Columbia 41268)
  Lefty Frizzell (1958)

- "Got a Match?"
  (ABC Paramount 9931)
  Frank Gallop (1958)

- "Let's Have a Cigarette Together"
  (RCA Victor LSP 1799)
  Vaughn Monroe (1958)

- "Charlie Brown"
  (ATCO 6132)
  Coasters (1959)

- "Don't Smoke in Bed"
  (Bethlehem 11055)
  Nine Simone (1960)

- "Cigarettes"
  (Columbia CS 8480)
  Yaffa Yarkoni (1961)

- "Jet Song" from *West Side Story*
  (Columbia 2070)
  Russ Tamblyn (1961)

- "Saved"
  (Atlantic 2099)
  LaVern Baker (1961)

- "Smoke! Smoke! Smoke! (That Cigarette)"
  (Columbia 8535)
  Jimmy Dean (1961)

- "Smoky Places"
  (Tuff 1808)
  Corsairs (1961)

- "Cigarette Girl"
  (Jubilee JGM 1035)
  Bob Peck (1962)

- "Lipstick Traces (on a Cigarette)"
  (Minit 644)
  Benny Spellman (1962)

- "Twenty Cigarettes"
  (Columbia CS 8687)
  Little Jimmy Dickens (1962)

- "When You Smoke Tobacco"
  (Mercury MG 20781)
  Ernie Sheldon (1962)

- "Cigarette"
  (Original Sound 32)
  Visions (1963)

- "Cigarettes and Coffee Blues"
  (Columbia 42701)
  Mary Robbins (1963)

- "Cigarettes, Whisky, and Wild, Wild Women"
  (Warner Brothers 5336)
  Johnny Nash (1963)

- "Smoke Rings"
  (RCA Victor LSP 2673)
  Sam Cooke (1963)

- "Down to My Last Cigarette"
  (Columbia 43120)
  Billy Walker (1964)

- "My Cigarette and I"
  (Columbia CL 2149)
  J's With Jamie (1964)

- "Smoke from Your Cigarette"
  (Chattahoochie 649)
  Drake Sisters (1964)

- "Cigarettes and Whiskey"
  (Arvee A-434)
  Sammy Jackson (1965)

- "Get off of My Cloud"
  (London 9792)
  The Rolling Stones (1965)

- "King of the Road"
  (Smash 1965)
  Roger Miller (1965)

- "Lipstick Traces (on a Cigarette)"
  (Imperial 66102)
  O'Jays (1965)

- "Smoke, Drink, Play 21"
  (Dot 16806)
  Tony Williams (1965)

- "Cigarettes and Coffee"
  (Volt 413)
  Otis Redding (1966)

- "I Can't Quit Cigarettes"
  (Decca 31931)
  Jimmy Martin (1966)

- "Tobacco"
  (RCA Victor LSP 3601)
  George Hamilton IV (1966)

- "Cigarette Ashes"
  (Epic LN 24249)
  Ed Henry (1967)

- "One Little Packet of Cigarettes"
  (MGM SE 4478)
  Herman's Hermits (1967)

- "Cigarette"
  (Adelphi AD 1001)
  Mike Stewart (1968)

- "May I Light Your Cigarette?"
  (MGM SE 4568)
  Beacon Street Union (1968)

- "Smoke, Smoke, Smoke–'68"
  (Boone 1069)
  Tex Williams (1968)

- "Cigarette Smoking"
  (Liberty 56128)
  Brother Sammy Shore (1969)

- "The Cigarette Song" from *Promenade*
  (RCA Victor LSO 1161)
  Sana Schaeffer, Ty Connel, and Gilbert Price (1969)

- "Smoke Smoke Smoke (but Not Around Me)"
  (Monument 1108)
  Grandpa Jones (1969)

- "Cigarette Grubber"
  (GRT 22)
  Sam Taylor Jr. (1970)

- "Blue Money"
  (Warner Brothers 7462)
  Van Morrison (1971)

- "Cigarette Blues"
  (Blue Goose BG 2005)
  Roger Hubbard (1971)

- "I Love Them Nasty Cigarettes"
  (Chart 5112)
  Jim Nesbitt (1971)

- "Another Puff"
(RCA 0613)
Jerry Reed (1972)

- "Tobacco, White Lightning, and Women Blues No. 2"
(Capitol SW 874)
Buck Owens (1972)

- "Smoke"
(Kama Sutra KSBS 2069)
Roger Cook (1973)

- "Smoke! Smoke! Smoke! (That Cigarette)"
(Paramount 0216)
Commander Cody And His Lost Planet Airmen (1973)

- "Smokin' in the Boys' Room"
(Big Tree 16011)
Brownsville Station (1973)

- "Cigarettes and Muscatel Wine"
(Prince 1008)
Little Joe Cale (1974)

- "Fool for a Cigarette"
(Reprise MS 2179)
Ry Cooder (1974)

- "Should I Smoke"
(Warner Brothers BS 2827)
Badfinger (1974)

- "Smokin' Room"
(ABC 11427)
Rufus (1974)

- "Smoking Cigarettes"
(Capitol ST 2823)
Golden Earring (1974)

- "Workin' at the Car Wash Blues"
(ABC 11447)
Jim Croce (1974)

- "Candy, Brandy and a Carton of Cigarettes"
(Golden Crest CR 3044)
Lou Carter (1975)

- "Smoking"
  (Virgin V 2056)
  Keith Hudson (1976)

- "Flick the Bic"
  (RSO RS 13017)
  Rick Dees (1977)

- "Lipstick Traces"
  (Mercury 55005)
  Jimmie Peters (1977)

- "A Beer and a Cigarette"
  (Stiff 940573)
  Terraplane (1978)

- "Cigarettes"
  (Mercury 55005)
  City Boy (1978)

- "The Gambler"
  (United Artists 1250)
  Kenny Rogers (1978)

- "Smoke Rings and Wine"
  (Marlin 2210)
  Ralph MacDonald (1978)

- "You Burn Me Up–I'm a Cigarette"
  (EG LP 101)
  Robert Fripp (1979)

- "Caffeine, Nicotine, Benzedrine (and Wish Me Luck)"
  (RCA 12157)
  Jerry Reed (1981)

- "Smokin' and Drinkin'"
  (TK 1042)
  James Brown (1981)

- "Tryin' to Live My Life Without You"
  (Capitol 5092)
  Bob Seger (1981)

- "A Beer and a Cigarette"
  (Johanna JHN 3008)
  Hanoi Rocks (1983)

- "Reasons to Quit"
  (Epic 03494)
  Merle Haggard and Willie Nelson (1983)

- "Cigarette Head"
  (Reuben Kincade RKP 001)
  Hype (1984)

- "Cigarettes"
  (Flat Black Music FN 1002)
  Full Nelson (1985)

- "Smokin' in the Boys' Room"
  (Elektra 69625)
  Motley Crue (1985)

- "Cigarette"
  (Enigma 73208)
  Smithereens (1986)

- "Smoke Rings"
  (Warner Brothers 25400)
  Laurie Anderson (1986)

- "Cigarettes of a Single Man"
  (A & M SP 5161)
  Squeeze (1986)

- "No Smoking"
  (Enigma SV 73276)
  Todd Rundgren (1987)

- "I'm Down to My Last Cigarette"
  (Sire 27919)
  k.d.lang (1988)

- "Love Is Like a Cigarette"
  (Panagaea Pan 42137)
  Kip Hanrahan (1988)

- "Smoke Another Cigarette"
  (Geffen GHS 24201)
  Toll (1988)

- "Cigarette"
  (Mammoth 9663)
  Sidewinders (1989)

- "Cigarette in the Rain"
  (Warner Brothers 26002)
  Randy Crawford (1989)

- "Opposites Attract"
  (Virgin 99158)
  Paula Abdul (1989)

- "Pack 'O Smokes"
  (Scot 2)
  Prisonshake (1989)

- "Cigarette"
  (More 224-K05-5)
  Nude Swirl (1990)

- "Cigarette Breath"
  (Elektra 60890)
  Shinehead (1990)

- "Smoking Lounge"
  (Horton/Reflex HR 008)
  Helltrout (1990)

- "Ashtray"
  (Lookout 62)
  Screeching Weasel (1992)

- "Cigarette Ashes on the Floor"
  (Giant 24452)
  Miki Howard (1992)

- "Smokers"
  (Munstor MR 0230)
  Cancer Moon (1992)

- "Three on a Match"
  (Big Money Inc. BMI 039)
  Mickey Finn (1993)

## REFERENCES

Breed, Warren and James R. DeFoe. "Drinking and Smoking on Television, 1950-1982," *Journal of Public Health Policy*, 5 (June 1984), pp. 257-270.
Cooper, B. Lee. "Examining the Medical Profession Through Musical Metaphors," *International Journal of Instructional Media*, XXI, No. 2 (1994), pp. 155-163.

Cooper, B. Lee and William L. Schurk. "Doctor, Doctor Give Me the News: Medical Images and Metaphors in Modern Music, 1950-1990," *Popular Culture in Libraries*, in press.

Cooper, B. Lee and William L. Schurk. "Processing Health Care Images from Popular Culture Resources: Physicians, Cigarettes, and Medical Metaphors in Contemporary Recordings," *Popular Music and Society,* XVII (Winter 1993), pp. 105-124.

Dillow, Gordon L. "Thank You for Not Smoking: The Hundred-Year War Against the Cigarette," *American Heritage*, (February/March 1981), pp. 94-107.

Goodman, Jordon. *Tobacco in History: The Cultures of Dependence.* New York: Routledge, 1993.

Headman, David G., Michael D. Later, Cheryl L. Upright, and Nathan Maccoby. "How an Unhealthy Product Is Sold: Cigarette Advertising in Magazines, 1960-1985," *Journal of Communication*, 37 (Autumn 1987), pp. 95-106.

Mintz, Morton. "The Artful Dodgers," in *Crisis in American Institutions* (ninth edition), edited by Jerome H. Skolnick and Elloit Currie (New York: Harper Collins College Publishing, 1994), pp. 39-49.

National Commission on Smoking and Public Policy. *A National Dilemma: Cigarette Smoking, or the Health of Americans.* New York: American Cancer Society, 1978.

Troyer, Ronald J. and Gerald E. Markle. *Cigarettes: The Battle Over Smoking.* New Brunswick, New Jersey: Rutgers University Press, 1983.

Wagner, Susan. *Cigarette Country: Tobacco in American History and Politics.* New York: Praeger Books, 1971.

White, Larry C. *Merchants of Death: The American Tobacco Industry.* New York: Beech Tree Books/William Morrow and Company, 1988.

Yankauer, Alfred. "Smoking and Health: A 25-Year Perspective," *American Journal of Public Health*, 79 (February 1989), pp. 141-143.

# Chapter 4

# City Life

The relationship between modern music and the metropolis has been a subject of scholarly investigation for many years. Even in fields of American music where rural themes have traditionally been dominant, a shift of lyrical emphasis has occurred since World War II. One writer described this phenomenon by stating, "The first observation that needs to be made about Country and Western music is that it is neither 'Country' nor 'Western.' It draws most of its imagery from the town or city (or the highways leading into the city), and its geographical center of gravity is not western but southeastern." This assertion can be expanded into a human perspective through the following observation: "It is no longer interested in the open range, the cattle-drive, or the cowboy at the campfire. Today's C&W hero is frequently a city-dwelling working man struggling with the complexities of modern urban—or suburban life." The author of these observations, Peter Thorpe, illustrates this view of the new "country" hero by referring to Merle Haggard's lyrical saga of the bewildered, ambivalent fellow in "Workin' Man Blues."

For history teachers, the shifting images of urban life in American society offer excellent opportunities for instructional innovation. It is significant to note that British sociologist Charlie Gillett contends that contemporary music became the dictionary, barometer, microscope, gyroscope, and source of social etiquette for American youth during the 1950s. Gillett notes that:

> . . . during the mid-fifties, in virtually every urban civilization in the world, adolescents staked out their freedom in the cities, inspired and reassured by the Rock and Roll beat. Rock and Roll was perhaps the

---

This study by B. Lee Cooper was originally published as "Music and the Metropolis: Lyrical Images of Life in American Cities. 1950-1980," *Teaching History*, VI (Fall 1981), pp. 72-84. Reprint permission granted by the author and editor of *Teaching History*, Stephen Kneeshaw.

first form of popular culture to celebrate without reservation characteristics of city life that had been among the most criticized. In Rock
and Roll, the strident, repetitive sound of the city life were, in effect,
reproduced as melody and rhythm. (p. viii)

If the city was a confusing mechanized jungle, the rhythmic translation
of survival and success was often found in the lyrics provided on record
albums, over radios, and on jukeboxes. The following pages will expand
upon and update Gillett's observations. The personalized perspectives provided in song lyrics demonstrate how contemporary singers and songwriters
assemble attitudes, ideas, events, and values that may help history teachers
and their students to formulate and define the concept of "urban existence."

> When I look back,
> Boy, I must have been green.
> Boppin' in the country,
> Fishin' in a stream.
> Lookin' for an answer,
> Tryin' to find a sign,
> Until I saw your city lights,
> Honey, I was blind.
>
> —"Honky Cat"
> by Elton John

> They're dancing in Chicago
> Down in New Orleans,
> In New York City,
> All we need is music, sweet music.
>
> —"Dancing in the Street"
> by Martha and the Vandellas

Media analytists often use television as a barometer of public opinion.
Karl E. Meyer focused on prime-time programming between 1958 and
1975 to demonstrate the growth of "urbanized thinking" among contem-
porary Americans. While frontier sagas such as *Gunsmoke*, *Wagon Train*,
*Have Gun-Will Travel*, *Rifleman*, *Maverick*, *Wells Fargo*, *Wyatt Earp*, and
*Cheyenne* dominated evening television programming during the late
1950s, urban situation comedies reigned in the nighttime spotlight two
decades later. The top-rated shows of 1975 included *All in the Family*,
*Laverne and Shirley*, *Sanford and Son*, *Rhoda*, *Welcome Back Kotter*,
*Kojak*, and *The Mary Tyler Moore Show*. Meyer observed:

Sooner or later, Americans had to come to terms with a reality we sought to deny or ignore–that we are in essence a nation of city slickers, that the urban way of life is the norm, that far more of us live in apartment houses than in clapboards in Stockbridge or on peanut farms in Plains. . . . No longer invisible on prime time, the big city is ubiquitous. Not only do the most popular sitcoms have a clearly defined urban setting, but their themes reflect urban concerns: racial friction, single living, changing sex roles, office politics, generational conflict, and so forth. For the first time since its inception, television is presenting a recognizable cross-section of big-city denizens: blue collar and white collar, ethnic and unwhite, doctor, lawyer, beggarman, and shrink. (p. 16)

Although Meyer may be correct, the signs of this social change had been reflected in another medium much earlier. In fact, popular music anticipated television's urban theme commitment by two decades. As a mirror of city life in the 1950s, 1960s, and 1970s, song lyrics were more attentive to urban issues than television because of their city-based artistic originators and their youthful audience. One clear illustration of the urban perspective that undergirds popular music may be noted in the following titles of recently published books which examine the singers, songs, composers, rhythmic styles, and record companies in contemporary music: *Chicago Breakdown* (1975) by Mike Rowe; *Jazz City: The Impact of Our Cities on the Development of Jazz* (1978) by Leroy Ostransky; *Jazz Style in Kansas City and the Southwest* (1971) by Ross Russell; *The Jefferson Airplane and the San Francisco Sound* (1969) by Ralph J. Gleason; *Motown and the Arrival of Black Music* (1971) by David Morse; *The Nashville Sound: Bright Lights and Country Music* (1970) by Paul Hemphill; *The New Haven Sound, 1946-1976* (1977) by Paul Lepri; *The Sound of the City: The Rise of Rock and Roll* (1971) by Charlie Gillett; *The Sound of Philadelphia* (1975) by Tony Cummings; *They All Sang on the Corner: New York City's Rhythm and Blues Vocal Groups of the 1950's* (1973) by Philip Groia; *Uptown–The Story of Harlem's Apollo Theatre* (1971) by Jack Schiffman; *Urban Blues* (1966) by Charles Keil; *Walking to New Orleans: The Story of New Orleans Rhythm and Blues* (1964) by John Broven.

Beyond scholarly titles, though, the relationship between American popular music and metropolitan population centers can be documented through the familiar linkages of city names with distinctive singing styles. One commonly associates New Orleans and Kansas City with jazz, St. Louis and Chicago with the blues, Nashville with country music, New York with rhythm and blues, Detroit with the "Motown Sound," and

Memphis with soul sounds. The all-pervasive disco tempo, according to Stephen Holden, "suggests the heartbeat of modern urban life."

What has not been widely acknowledged is the fact that contemporary tunes can be utilized as a rich source of social commentary as well as a bundle of danceable rhythmic patterns. The realm of popular music is much more complex than the relatively narrow television programming schedule. Although courtship themes continue to dominate contemporary lyrics quantitatively, examples abound of urban-related social and political commentaries in the music of the past thirty years. These metropolitan lifestyle observations can be found in all major forms of modern music— pop, soul, and country. Although certain singers have become associated with both pro-urban and antiurban tunes, this ideological connotation is neither consistent nor necessarily intentional. It would be as unfair to attribute universal anticity feelings to John Denver ("Thank God I'm a Country Boy") and Glen Campbell ("Country Boy (You Got Your Feet in L.A.)") as it would be to ascribe totally pro-urban attitudes to Chuck Berry ("Back in the U.S.A."). In order to be instructive rather than propagandistic, teachers must use a variety of songs and artists to illustrate the multiplicity of images of urban life in American popular music between 1950 and 1980.

> You grew up riding the subways,
> Runnin' with people up in Harlem,
> Down on Broadway.
> You're no tramp,
> But you're no lady—
> Talkin' that street talk.
> You're the heart and soul of
> New York City.
>
> —"Native New Yorker"
> by Odyssey

> Thousands of lives wasting away,
> People living from day to day.
> It's a challenge just stayin' alive,
> 'Cause in the ghetto—only the strong survive.
>
> —"Masterpiece"
> by The Temptations

Is Chicago the happy-go-lucky, "toddlin' town" described by Frank Sinatra? Or is it really a center of political repression as Graham Nash asserts? And if State Street is really such a great street, what does Jim

Croce mean when he calls the South Side of Chicago "the baddest part of town"? Did the death of Mayor Richard Daley and the election of Jane Byrne meet the Chi-Lites' request for a redistribution of political power in the Windy City? Do young blacks in Chicago still believe, as Lou Rawls obviously does, that it is possible to escape from the ghetto? Even though there are no correct answers to these questions, any teacher should recognize the value of asking his or her students to examine them.

Translating lyric-based social or political themes into active classroom discussions does not limit an instructor to one particular pedagogical approach. However, certain fundamental understandings must be established between the teacher and the students before lyrical analysis can be utilized. First, the songs should not be randomly chosen; they must be carefully selected to illustrate specific urban-related ideas. Second, the values and ideas expressed in a single song must be open for critical examination by the class. Neither the singer nor the songwriter should be biographically "interpreted"—only the context of the lyric should be reviewed and discussed. Third, an open classroom atmosphere must prevail during the discussion stage or the technique of utilizing popular culture resources will become as deadening as using a traditional textbook. Students must be encouraged to challenge each other's ideas and be permitted to introduce additional songs to enhance, contradict, or broaden a particular theme.

To demonstrate the expansive characteristics of this instructional approach, let me report on the unanticipated responses from one of my own history classes. My instructional goal was to illustrate to a group of college freshmen the following hypothesis: "The city has replaced the frontier in the minds of many twentieth-century Americans as the place where freedom, fame, and fortune can be readily attained. The inhibiting factors of rural life can be overcome by moving to the big city." The songs I selected to depict the argument for increased opportunities for social mobility through metropolitan relocation were: Dave Loggin's "Please Come to Boston," Chuck Berry's "Johnny B. Goode," and Elvis Presley's "Promised Land."

No sooner had I played these songs and launched into the "small town narrowness vs. big city opportunity" theme than my students confronted me with three different perceptions of urban existence. One group claimed that I was ignoring such vital small town virtues as love, individual concern, time for experimentation, human understanding, and the general simplicity of life. Among the recordings offered to illustrate these characteristics were John Denver's "Thank God I'm a Country Boy" and Merle Haggard's "Okie from Muskogee." Other students asserted that urban life may crush the spirit of a talented individual because it lacks sensitivity, tends to foster loneliness and isolation, and creates a morbid fear of failure. Several songs were suggested to illustrate this position: Bobby Bare's "Detroit City," Jim Croce's "Workin' in the Car Wash Blues," Gladys Knight and the Pips' "Midnight Train to Georgia," and The Spinners' "I'm Comin' Home." A third group of students built their case against my original hypothesis on the suggestions of the second. These students argued that more people are currently leaving urban situations to find personal gratification (Canned Heat's "Goin' Up the Country" and Crosby, Stills, Nash, and Young's "Woodstock"), to escape the materialistic pressures of urban existence (Mac Davis's "Stop and Smell the Roses" and Ray Steven's "Mr. Businessman"), or just to return to more friendly, more familiar surroundings (Don Williams' "Tulsa Time" and Roger Miller's "Kansas City Star").

Even though I attempted to counter this barrage of arguments and recordings with illustrations of urban enjoyment, including Petula Clark's "Downtown," Scott MacKenzie's "San Francisco," and Frank Sinatra's "Chicago," I continued to encounter a movement by half of my students that categorically denied my initial "streets paved with gold" stereotype of urban life. Finally, a fourth group of students even suggested that migration from a rural setting into the city might occur for totally nonselfish, nonmaterialistic reasons. This small contingent argued, using John Sebastian's "Welcome Back," Timmy Thomas's "Why Can't We Live Together," and Rare Earth's "Hey Big Brother," that idealistic social reforms could be initiated by persons who were coming into a city seeking to improve the quality of urban politics, education, and race relations. Sensing an unrealistic overemphasis on humanitarianism and a failure to acknowledge the more materialistic elements of working life in the city, yet another student noted that employment opportunities in the city were often repetitive, boring, and dehumanizing. He made his case with lyrics from BTO's "Takin' Care of Business," The Easybeats's "Friday on My Mind," The Vogues's "Five O'Clock World," and The O'Jays' "For Love of Money."

By the time this three-day classroom exchange on the nature of rural existence, social mobility, and urban life had run its course, my students clearly perceived that people in the United States could be simultaneously attracted to and repelled by the city. They saw both advantages and disadvantages to living, working, and seeking to change the nature of American metropolitan areas. From this broadened mindset, I then assigned portions of three books to be read and reviewed by the entire class. These literary resources were: Sinclair Lewis's *Main Street*, Jacob Riis's *How the Other Half Lives*, and Ulf Hannerz's *Soulside: Inquires into Ghetto Culture and Community*.

This tired city was somebody's dream,
Billboard horizons as black as they seem.
Four level highways across the land,
We're building a home for the family of man.

—"The Family of Man"
by Three Dog Night

Well south side of Chicago,
Is the baddest part of town.
And if you go down there,
You better just beware,
Of a man named Leroy Brown.

—"Bad, Bad, Leroy Brown"
by Jim Croce

Welcome to the beat of a city street,
Walk on now and don't be shy,
Take a closer look at the people you meet,
And notice the fear in their eye,
Yeah, watching the time passing by.

—"Hey Big Brother"
by Rare Earth

Uptown got its hustlers,
The Bowery got its bums,
Forty-Second Street got big Jim Walker,
He's a pool shootin' son-of-a-gun.

—"You Don't Mess Around with Jim"
by Jim Croce

Suggesting that contemporary lyrics be utilized in high school and college classrooms is hardly original. However, few history teachers have employed the rich potential in pop records for studying urban life in America. The use of song lyrics combines varying descriptive elements of biography, fantasy, memory, illusion, fact, and folklore. Such a strange mixture of resources may not please traditionally trained historians, statistically oriented sociologists, or other scholars who currently instruct classes in urban society. Initial hostility may be overcome, however, if these critics will accept the fundamental pedagogical principle that student motivation ("recognition of personal problems or social conflict situations") is an absolute prerequisite for generating serious reflective thought on any subject.

Several lesson plans outlining the specific teaching approach which I am advocating are provided below. They are designed to create questions, uncertainty, cognitive dissonance, conflicts and controversy within students' minds by representing at least two different lyrical orientations on a single issue relating to metropolitan existence. The imagery provided in popular songs is highly familiar to, but generally uncritically received by, the majority of young listeners. From the most simple to the most complex lyric structures, certain basic themes can be constructed from selected groups of contemporary tunes.

### Sample Lesson Plans

#### The Changing Image of the Metropolis

For Reflection:

How has the image of American city life changed during the past three decades?

Major Concepts to be Investigated:

| | | |
|---|---|---|
| population density | ghetto | ethnic groups |
| cultural opportunities | suburbia | urban renewal |
| labor unions | ecology | industrial growth |

Songs and Performers to be Referenced:

1950-1959 tunes

"Chicago" (Capitol 3793) by Frank Sinatra
"New York's My Home" (Decca 30111) by Sammy Davis Jr.
"Mack the Knife" (Atco 6147) by Bobby Darin
"Back in the U.S.A." (Chess 1729) by Chuck Berry
"Kansas City" (Fury 1023) by Wilbert Harrison

1959-1969 Tunes

"Detroit City" (RCA Victor 47-8183) by Bobby Bare
"Twelve Thirty" (Dunhill 4099) by The Mamas and the Papas
"San Franciscan Nights" (MGM 13769) by The Animals
"Subterranean Homesick Blues" (Columbia 43242) by Bob Dylan
"Summer in the City" (Kama Sutra 250) by The Lovin' Spoonful

1970-1979 Tunes

"Bright Lights, Big City" (Capitol 3114) by Sonny James
"Stayin' Alive" (RSO 885) by the Bee Gees
"Hot Child in the City" (Chrysalis 2226) by Nick Gilder
"On Broadway" (Warner Brothers 8542) by George Benson
"In the Ghetto" (Fame 91000) by Candi Staton

### Urban Decadence and Social Decline

For Reflection:

> Why do many people claim that the increasing urban population has produced a general decline in the quality of American life?

Major Concepts to be Investigated:

| | | |
|---|---|---|
| pollution | racism | political repression |
| alienation | materialism | moral decay |
| poverty | violence | artificiality |
| bigotry | unemployment | prostitution |

Songs and Performers to be Referenced:

> "For Love or Money" (Philadelphia International 3544) by The O'Jays
> "Freddie's Dead" (Curtom 1975) by Curtis Mayfield
> "Masterpiece" (Gordy 7126) by The Temptations
> "I'm Gonna Move to the Outskirts of Town" (Impulse 202) by Ray Charles
> "Runaway Child, Running Wild" (Gordy 7084) by The Temptations
> "Takin' It to the Street" (Warner Brothers 8196) by The Doobie Brothers
> "Lido Shuffle" (Columbia 10491) by Boz Scaggs
> "Life in the Fast Lane" (Asylum 45403) by The Eagles
> "Hey Big Brother" (Rare Earth 5038) by Rare Earth
> "Baker Street" (United Artists 1192) by Gerry Rafferty
> "Mr. Businessman" (Monument 1083) by Ray Stevens
> "Movin' Out (Anthony's Song)" (Columbia 10708) by Billy Joel
> "Ball of Confusion" (Gordy 7099) by The Temptations
> "In the Ghetto" (Fame 91000) by Candi Staton
> "People Are Strange" (Elektra 45621) by The Doors
> "American Woman" (RCA 74-0325) by The Guess Who
> "Mrs. Robinson" (Columbia 44511) by Simon and Garfunkel
> "Monster" (Dunhill 4221) by Steppenwolf

### City Life and Black Americans

For Reflection:

> How has the urban environment affected the social, political, and economic development of black men and women in modern America?

Major Concepts to be Investigated:

| | | |
|---|---|---|
| racism | social mobility | equal opportunity |
| ghetto | political involvement | affirmative action |
| education | economic incentive | |

Songs and Performers to be Referenced:

> "On Broadway" (Atlantic 2182) by The Drifters
> "Johnny B. Goode" (Chess 1691) by Chuck Berry
> "Uptown" (Philles 102) by The Crystals

"Bright Lights, Big City" (Vee-Jay 398) by Jimmy Reed
"You Haven't Done Nothin'" (Tamla 54252) by Stevie Wonder
"Promised Land" (Chess 1916) by Chuck Berry
"Superfly" (Curtom 1978) by Curtis Mayfield
"For the Love of Money" (Philadelphia International 3544) by The O'Jays
"Down and Out in New York City" (Polydor 14168) by James Brown
"Masterpiece" (Gordy 7126) by The Temptations
"Natural Man" (MGM 14262) by Lou Rawls
"Freddie's Dead" (Curtom 1975) by Curtis Mayfield
"Inner City Blues (Make Me Wanna Holler)" (Tamia 54209) by Marvin
     Gaye
"Almost Grown" (Chess 1722) by Chuck Berry
"Money Honey" (Atlantic 1006) by The Drifters
"Dead End Street" (Capitol 5869) by Lou Rawls
"The Ghetto" (Atco 6719) by Donny Hathaway

### The Urban Male

For Reflection:

Is the popular image of the urban male positive or negative?

Major Concepts to be Investigated:

| | | |
|---|---|---|
| self-motivation | individual character | intimidation |
| authority | violence | materialism |
| dignity | honesty | perseverance |
| chauvinism | power | |

Songs and Performers to be Referenced:

"Movin' Out (Anthony's Song)" (Columbia 10708) by Billy Joel
"You Don't Mess Around with Jim" (ABC 11328) by Jim Croce
"Mack the Knife" (Atco 6147) by Bobby Darin
"Take a Letter Maria" (Atco 6714) by R. B. Greaves
"Boy from New York City" (Blue Cat 102) by The Ad Libs
"Mr. Businessman" (Monument 1083) by Ray Stevens
"Bad, Bad Leroy Brown" (ABC 11359) by Jim Croce
"Taxi" (Elektra 45770) by Harry Chapin
"Big Boy Pete" (Arvee 595) by The Olympics
"Workin' in the Car Wash Blues" (ABC 11447) by Jim Croce
"Trouble Man" (Tamla 54228) by Marvin Gaye
"Theme from Shaft" (Enterprise 9038) by Isaac Hayes
"Kansas City Star" (Smash 1965) by Roger Miller
"My Life" (Columbia 10853) by Billy Joel
"Rhinestone Cowboy" (Capitol 4095) by Glen Campbell

### The Urban Troubadour

For Reflection:

> Why do some contemporary singers and songwriters focus their lyrical attention on the nature and meaning of urban life?

Major Concepts to be Investigated:

| | | |
|---|---|---|
| autobiography | experience | biography |
| nostalgia | folk song | reflection |
| troubadour | individualism | balladeer |

Songs and Performers to be Referenced:

Jim Croce Tunes

"You Don't Mess Around with Jim" (ABC 11328)
"Operator (That's Not the Way It Feels)" (ABC 11335)
"Bad, Bad Leroy Brown" (ABC 11359)
"I Got a Name" (ABC 11389)
"Workin' at The Car Wash Blues" (ABC 11447)

Chuck Berry Tunes

"School Day" (Chess 1653)
"Sweet Little Sixteen" (Chess 1683)
"Johnny B. Goode" (Chess 1691)
"Back in the U.S.A." (Chess 1729)
"You Never Can Tell" (Chess 1906)
"Promised Land" (Chess 1916)

Curtis Mayfield Tunes

"Future Shock" (Curtom 1987)
"Superfly" (Curtom 1978)
"Freddie's Dead" (Curtom 1975)
"Choice of Colors" (Curtom 1943)
"We're a Winner" (ABC 11022)

Stevie Wonder Tunes

"You Haven't Done Nothin'" (Tamla 4252)
"Living for the City" (Tamla 54242)
"Superstition" (Tamla 54226)
"Heaven Help Us All" (Tamla 54200)

## REFERENCES

Burt, Rob. *Surf City/Drag City.* New York: Sterling Publishing Company, 1986.
Cantor, Louis. *Wheelin' on Beale: How WDIA-Memphis Became the Nation's First All-Black Radio Station and Created the Sound That Changed America.* New York: Pharos Books, 1992.

Carney, George O. "Geography of Music: Inventory and Prospect," *Journal of Cultural Geography*, X (Spring-Summer 1990), pp. 35-48.

Carney, George O. (ed.). *The Sounds of People and Places: A Geography of American Folk and Popular Music* (third edition). Lanham, Maryland: Rowman and Littlefield, Inc., 1994.

Chambers, Ian. *Urban Rhythms*. London: Macmillan Publishers, Ltd., 1985.

Cooper, B. Lee. "Audio Images of the City," *Social Studies*, LXXII (May-June 1981), pp. 130-136.

Cooper, B. Lee. "Urban Life in Popular Music," in *Images of American Society in Popular Music: A Guide to Reflective Teaching* (Chicago: Nelson-Hall, Inc., 1982), pp. 97-110.

Cummings, Tony. *The Sound of Philadelphia*. London: Methuen Press, 1975.

Demento, Dr. "Big Apple Dreamin': New York in Song From 'Coney Island Baby' to 'Nights on Broadway,'" *Waxpaper*, II, No. 9 (August 26, 1979), pp. 23-25.

Endres, Clifford. *Austin City Limits: The Story Behind Television's Most Popular Country Music Program*. Austin: University of Texas Press, 1987.

Escott, Colin, with Martin Hawkins. *Good Rockin' Tonight: Sun Records and the Birth of Rock 'n' Roll*. New York: St. Martin's Press, 1991.

Fein, Art. *The L.A. Musical History Tour: A Guide to the Rock and Roll Landmarks of Los Angeles*. Winchester, Massachusetts: Faber and Faber, 1990.

Friedlander, Lee. *The Jazz People of New Orleans*. London: Jonathan Cape, 1992.

Gillett, Charlie. *The Sound of the City: The Rise of Rock and Roll* (revised and expanded edition). New York: Pantheon Books, 1983.

Gleason, Ralph J. *The Jefferson Airplane and the San Francisco Sound*. New York: Ballantine Books, 1969.

Goyenar, Alan. *Meeting the Blues: The Rise of the Texas Sound*. Dallas: Taylor Publishing Company, 1988.

Guralnick, Peter. *Sweet Soul Music: Rhythm and Blues and the Southern Dream of Freedom*. New York: Harper and Row, 1986.

Hannusch, Jeff. (a.k.a. almost slim). *I Hear You Knockin': The Sound of New Orleans Rhythm and Blues*. Ville Platte, Louisiana: Swallow Press, 1985.

Henderson, Floyd M. "The Image of New York City in American Popular Music of 1890-1970," *New York Folklore Quarterly*, XXX (December 1974), pp. 267-278.

Holden, Stephen. "Disco: The Medium Is the Message," *High Fidelity*, XXIX (August 1979), p. 105.

Keil, Charles. *Urban Blues*. Chicago: University of Chicago Press, 1966.

Kenney, William Howland. *Chicago Jazz: A Cultural History, 1904-1930*. New York: Oxford University Press, 1993.

Lepri, Paul. *The New Haven Sound, 1946-1976*. New Haven, Connecticut: United Printing Services, Inc., 1977.

Lichtenstein, Grace and Laura Dankner. *Musical Gumbo: The Music of New Orleans*. New York: W. W. Norton and Company, 1993.

Loza, Steven. *Barrio Rhythm: Mexican American Music in Los Angeles*. Urbana: University of Illinois Press, 1993.

MacLean, Hugh and Vernon Joynson (comps.). *An American Rock History–Part Three: Chicago and Illinois*. Telford, Shropshire, England: Borderline Productions, 1992.

MacLeod, Bruce A. *Club Date Musicians: Playing the New York Party Circuit*. Urbana: University of Illinois Press, 1993.

McDonough, Jack. *San Francisco Rock: The Illustrated History of San Francisco Rock Music*. San Francisco: Chronicle Books, 1985.

McKee, Margaret and Fred Chisenhall. *Beale Black and Blue: Life and Music on Black America's Main Street*. Baton Rouge: Louisiana State University Press, 1981.

Meyer, Karl E. "Love Thy City: Marketing the American Metropolis," *Saturday Review*, VI (April 29, 1979), p. 16.

Moore, MacDonald Smith. *Yankee Blues: Musical Culture and American Identity*. Bloomington: Indiana University Press, 1985.

Ostransky, Leroy. *Jazz City: The Impact of Our Cities on the Development of Jazz*. Englewood Cliffs, New Jersey: Prentice-Hall, Inc., 1978.

Pearson, Nathan W., Jr. *Goin' to Kansas City*. Urbana: University of Illinois Press, 1987.

Peretti, Burton W. *The Creation of Jazz: Music, Race, and Culture in Urban America*. Urbana: University of Illinois Press, 1992.

Pettigrew, Jim. "From Rhythm 'n' Blues to Disco: A Broad Overview of Atlanta Music Since 1945," *Atlanta Historical Bulletin*, XXI (Summer 1977), pp. 114-138.

Pruter, Robert. *Chicago Soul*. Champaign-Urbana: University of Illinois Press, 1991.

Rooney, John F., Jr., Wilbur Zelinsky, and Dean R. Louder. (gen. eds.). *This Remarkable Continent: An Atlas of United States and Canadian Society and Cultures*. College Station, Texas: For the Society for the North American Cultural Survey by Texas A&M University Press, 1982.

Rowe, Mike. *Chicago Breakdown*. New York: Drake Publishers, 1975.

Scott, Quinta and Susan Croce Kelly. *Route 66: The Highway and Its People*. Norman: University of Oklahoma Press, 1988.

Schlatti, Gene and David Seay. *San Francisco Nights: The Psychedelic Music Trip, 1965-1968*. New York: St. Martin's Press, 1985.

Shank, Barry. *Dissonant Identities: The Rock 'n' Roll Scene in Austin, Texas*. Hanover, New Hampshire: University Press of New England, 1994.

Smith, Michael P. *A Joyful Noise: A Celebration of New Orleans Music*. Dallas, Texas: Taylor Publishing Company, 1990.

Snyder, Tom. *The Route 66 Traveler's Guide and Roadside Companion*. New York: St. Martin's Press, 1990.

Thorpe, Peter. "I'm Movin' On: The Escape Theme in Country and Western Music," *Western Humanities Review*, XXIV (Autumn 1970), pp. 307-318.

Walker, Dave. *American Rock 'n' Roll Tour*. New York: Thunder's Mouth Press, 1992.

Wallis, Michael. *Route 66: The Mother Road*. New York: St. Martin's Press, 1990.

Willoughby, Larry. *Texas Rhythm/Texas Rhyme: A Pictorial History of Texas Music*. Austin: Texas Monthly Press, Inc., 1984.

Wootton, Richard. *Honky Tonkin': A Travel Guide to American Music*. Charlotte, North Carolina: East Woods Press, 1980.

Zonn, Leo (ed.). *Place Images in Media: Portrayal, Experience, and Meaning*. Savage, Maryland: Rowman and Littlefield, Inc., 1990.

Chapter 5

# Disc Jockeys

## *STATION WDIA IN MEMPHIS*

*Wheelin' on Beale: How WDIA-Memphis Became the Nation's First All-Black Radio Station and Created the Sound That Changed America*. By Louis Cantor. New York: Pharos Books, 1992. Illustrated. 264 pp.

In *Wheelin' on Beale*, radio technician and historian Louis Cantor weaves the colorful tapestry tale of the emergence and growth of WDIA, the 50,000 watt Goodwill Station of Memphis, Tennessee. This chronological garment expands from the creation of the broadcasting corporation in 1947 to the present day. The station grew like a huge quilt of many hues and colors between 1948 and 1957 when original owners Bert Ferguson and John Pepper sold out to Egmont Sonderling of Chicago. Cantor focuses on this early broadcasting period as the confluence of luck, skilled management, powerful and talented radio personalities, and deep community commitment. The success of WDIA in the 1950s was a triumph for integrated staffing and creative thinking. Ironically, the decline of WDIA occurred because of resegregation of personnel and acquiescence to herd mentality. Cantor displays the whole-cloth staffing journey from all-white, to integrated black-and-white, to predominantly black, with brilliant insight, rich illustration, and heartfelt compassion. There are many heroes in *Wheelin' on Beale*. Courageous founder and general manager Bert Ferguson is lauded as a Branch Rickey-type figure, who carefully bal-

The initial review by B. Lee Cooper is scheduled to be published in *Popular Culture in Libraries*. Reprint permission granted by the author, Editor Frank Hoffmann, and The Haworth Press. The second essay, titled "Redefining Those Oldies But Goodies Playlist: Radio Programming, Market Expansion, and America's Musical Heritage," is scheduled to be published in *Journal of Radio Studies*. Reprint permission granted by the author, Editor Frank Chorba, and the *Journal of Radio Studies*.

anced financial savvy with community responsibility. Nat D. Williams is WDIA's Jackie Robinson. He was the first black disc jockey in Memphis on a station that ultimately became the first in the nation to adopt an all-black programming format. Other WDIA team leaders, both white and black, included Program Director David James, Programming Continuity Director Chris Spindel, News Editor Marie Wathen, and the masterful, mirthful, magical deejays Maurice "Hot Rod" Hulbert, A.C. "Moolah" Williams, Theo "Bless My Bones" Wade, Rufus Thomas, Willa Monroe, B.B. King, Robert "Honeyboy" Thomas, and Martha Jean "The Queen" Steinberg. Cantor skillfully recreates the on-the-air bantering and distinctive patois of many WDIA disc jockeys. He also lovingly documents their devotion to 1950s R&B music, to the black community in Memphis, and to the reality of work as play.

*Wheelin' on Beale* is well-documented, carefully researched, and meticulously objective. Cantor not only lauds his heroes, but he also portrays their foibles and shortcomings. The author is generous in his acknowledgment of broadcasting competitors (Dewey Phillips' *Red, Hot, and Blue* show on WHBQ), thorough in his investigation of previous black announcers (Jack L. Cooper's *All-Negro Hour* in Chicago in 1929), critical of the white-dominated power structure at WDIA, and saddened that the city of Memphis still bears the stigma of Martin Luther King Jr.'s death on April 4, 1968. Although Cantor is conversant with the foremost scholars on Beale Street history (Margaret McKee and Fred Chisenhall) and black radio broadcasting (Mark Newman, J. Fred MacDonald, and Kip Lornell), this volume is unmistakably a groundbreaking oral investigation drawn from the notes and memories of WDIA participants and observers. Youthful readers may not appreciate–or might even be offended by–the antique-sounding programs featured on WDIA: *Tan Town Jamboree, Sepia Swing Club, Hoot 'n' Holler, Wheelin' On Beale*, and *Hallelujah Jubilee*. But no one should overlook the magnificent roots of volunteerism, community involvement, philanthropy, and racial pride that were established via WDIA's Goodwill Announcements, Goodwill Revue, Starlight Revue, and Goodwill Fund, Inc. contributions to local school busing, disabled children, Little League baseball, and homeless children. The early 1950s beneficence of Bert Ferguson and Nat D. Williams parallel the early 1990s concerns shown by Jimmy Carter and Jesse Jackson.

### GOLDEN OLDIES PROGRAMMING

Most people develop their tastes in music during the years when they first begin dating and having sex. Once established, these preferences often persist throughout the adult years. One generation may have always liked the big band sound of Glen Miller, another the exciting beat of Elvis Presley, another the driving guitar of Eric Clapton, and another the electrifying rhythms of Michael Jackson. . . . Of course, radio programmers have known about the cohort effect for years. And successful advertising experts usually key the pace, sound, and mood of their commercials to the particular cohort they're trying to reach. . . . Mature consumers are more interested in purchasing experiences than things. . . .

–from *Age Wave* (1990)
by Ken Dychtwald and Joe Flower

Listening to "Golden Oldies" radio stations can be immensely enjoyable. Significant numbers of Americans tune in daily to hear Buddy Holly, The Beatles, Connie Francis, Dusty Springfield, and The Monkees sing their 1950s and 1960s hit tunes. WIBM-FM of Lansing, Michigan is typical of most current oldies-but-goodies stations. It is my channel of choice. The music is dominant, with news announcers and disc jockeys limiting their banter. The pop and hiss and occasional scratch of vinyl 45s has been replaced by cassette tapes or compact discs, of course. Yet The Five Satins, The Drifters, The Shirelles, The Four Seasons, and the Rolling Stones continue to wail "In the Still of the Night," "This Magic Moment," "Soldier Boy," "Sherry," and "Get off of My Cloud" to listeners' delight.

It is undeniable that the concept of classic rock radio is functional. Programming music from 1955 to 1970 (or even through the late 1970s) attracts a sizable cohort of listeners, which in turn makes advertisers willing to purchase air spots. But being functional is not necessarily being creative. And being functional does not mean that some aspects of the present program format are not dysfunctional. That is, capturing a small portion of the popular market may be a reasonable goal. But building upon that market base, enlarging interest and broadening listener appeal, and achieving enhanced shares of various age/sex/income cohorts is the key to radio sales success. Although honing a distinctive niche within a regional audience is always a beneficial starting point, it is imperative that growth be projected and secured through strategic management. For Golden Oldies station directors and their classic rock disc jockeys, this means more than just appearances at high schools, public service announcements, cash prizes and free concert passes, or other forms of community involvement. These are worthy promotional gambits. But the major challenge to achieving program longevity is related to the aesthetic, artistic elements in the music. Without listener enthusiasm for the specific recordings being broadcast, even the most talented disc jockeys, the best sales directors, and the most gifted station managers are doomed. The Doobie Brothers provided excellent guidance in 1972 when they urged all of us to "Listen to the Music."

What can be done to improve programming on Golden Oldies stations? How can the current audience be retained, while new listeners are attracted? What strategies should be initiated to make a historically static playlist more dynamic, creative, and innovative?

## Deepening the Historical Playlist

A debate is currently raging among record collectors, popular music scholars, recording artists, and rock fans concerning the roots of rock 'n' roll music. Although concern about this subject can be traced back to Lawrence Redd, Arnold Shaw, and Nick Tosches, it is currently being fanned by Morgan Wright, Jim Dawson, and Steve Propes. The audio turn of this debate clearly belongs to Golden Oldies programmers. No longer content to claim "Heartbreak Hotel" (1956), "Gee" (1954), or even "Sixty-Minute Man" (1951) as the first rock tune, knowledgeable, articulate, persuasive writers and CD producers are extending the public's vision of rock's roots back into the 1940s. Astute directors at Golden Oldies stations should follow this lead and begin to program special segments that pay tribute to recordings by Big Joe Turner, Louis Jordan, The Mills Brothers, The Ink Spots, Roy Brown, Amos Milburn, Wynonie Harris, and Johnny Otis.

Beyond the benefits of promoting "new" old music, the Golden Oldies station can legitimately claim to be serving both an historical mission and a socially responsible experiment in cultural diversity. The segregation of most R&B performers (Hank Ballard and the Midnighters, Billy Ward and the Dominoes, and even Fats Domino) and many country artists (Moon Mullican, Hank Williams, and even Bill Haley) from early 1950s pop radio and pop music charts would amaze most younger listeners. Similarly, numerous current fans of British rockers or American heavy metal bands might be fascinated to hear song titles from the 1970s and 1980s performed by "unknown" artists such as Muddy Waters, Bo Diddley, Joe Liggins, or Arthur "Big Boy" Crudup. The roots-of-rock segments might also promote better understanding of African-American performers, country music rhythms and artists, regional sources of music, the humor that exists in lyrics, and the group harmony basis for both doo-wop groups and pop duos.

## *Acknowledging Artistic Longevity*

British journalists often chide American music fans for being both fickle and ahistorical. For the most part, these charges are valid. "Once a star, always a star" is the fandom norm in the United Kingdom. From Lonnie Donegan and Cliff Richard to The Sex Pistols and Boy George (of Culture Club), recognition for musical success is considered a lifetime claim to fame, if not necessarily to personal fortune. Bill Haley, Gene Vincent, Jerry Lee Lewis, The Everly Brothers, and hundreds of American recording artists of 1950s and 1960s vintage often sought refuge with the adoring British public late in their careers. Unfortunately, their own countrymen had developed a mysterious amnesia about the magic of their music.

Golden Oldies stations should be the aesthetic conscience of American popular music. Celebrity ought to be continually celebrated. For The Monotones this is quite simple: play "Book of Love." The same is true for numerous one-hit wonder singers and groups including The Edsels, The Paradons, Jewel Akens, The Five Du-Tones, Eddie Fontaine, and Harold Dorman. But what about artists that have extended recording careers? Is it legitimate to acknowledge their recorded contributions during the 1950s and 1960s–and then to behave as if they ceased performing after 1970? This dilemma exists with such prominent stars as Ray Charles, Aretha Franklin, Smokey Robinson, and Stevie Wonder. The artistry of these music industry giants may indeed be rooted in early audio triumphs–"What'd I Say" (1959), "Respect" (1967), "Shop Around" (1960), and "Fingertips" (1963). But unlike the sadly deceased Buddy Holly, Ritchie Valens, Bobby Darin, Jim Croce, and Otis Redding, these magnificent performers have continued to light up our lives with new releases. It is a gross error for Golden Oldies programmers to slavishly follow random date guidelines rather than actively tracking the dynamic careers of oldies heroes and heroines. The Doobie Brothers' release "The Doctor" (1989), for instance, is as good as any of their early 1970s hit recordings; the same can be said for any of the Rolling Stones' 1980s releases.

By tracing an artists' audio achievements from the 1950s and 1960s up to the present, a Golden Oldies station adds credence to its reason for being, provides additional historical information about American musical culture, and honors publicly acknowledged recording giants in one gesture. Electing to ignore the artist formerly known as Prince, Madonna, Milli Vanilli, and Run-D.M.C. is reasonable in regard to defining a stylistic and time-frame playlist. However, it is an error to become artificially trapped in a narrow time warp that fails to acknowledge the continuity and longevity of brilliant performers.

## Promoting Roots Recordings

The contribution of Golden Oldies stations to sustaining interest and awareness of black vocal harmony (The Flamingos, The Moonglows, The Five Satins, and The Orioles), rockabilly music (Carl Perkins, Eddie Cochran, Jerry Lee Lewis, and Elvis Presley), rock 'n' roll (Chuck Berry, Larry Williams, Frankie Ford, and Little Richard), and novelty tunes (Nervous Norvus, Big Bopper, Clarence "Frogman" Henry, and The Coasters) is immeasurable. The heritage of the 1950s and 1960s deserves to be broadcast daily and displayed as a fascinating, ornate tapestry of divergent musical styling. But roots must produce limbs and leaves, or they are judged to be dead. Occasionally, it is the obligation of Golden Oldies program directors to demonstrate the historic connections between classic rock tunes and current pop hits, between vintage artists' styles and contemporary performers' sounds. Such audio linkage gives meaning and amplified justification for continuing attention to oldies.

There are three relatively easy ways to establish connections between early rock music and modern recordings. First, echoes of persistent themes or rhythm patterns can be identified. By playing Marty Stuart's "Arlene" (1985) next to Carl Perkin's "Movie Magg" (1956) and "Honey Don't" (1956), for example, a disc jockey can readily demonstrate the consistency of rockin' guitar sounds and lyrical imagery in the rockabilly genre. Similar comparisons might be made between Hank Ballard's "Work with Me Annie" (1954) and Tone-Loc's "Wild Thing" (1988), or Jackie Wilson's "Doggin' Around" (1960) and Simply Red's "If You Don't Know Me By Now" (1989). Second, re-releases of classic rock songs provide special opportunities to illustrate that there are hundreds and hundreds of 1950s and 1960s recordings that have become popular "Standards" during the rock era. Lengthy salutes to the classic tunes of early rock artists may be found on several recent motion picture soundtrack releases. In 1991, for example, the compact disc titled *The Commitments* (MAD 10286) featured an Irish band performing "Mustang Sally" (Wilson Pickett), "Treat Her Right" (Roy Head), "Try a Little Tenderness" (Otis Redding), "I Can't Stand the Rain" (Ann Peebles), "The Dark End of the Street" (James Carr), and "Chain of Fools" (Aretha Franklin). Single releases that reprise the hits of early rock, R&B, and soul stars are even more common. Note The Manhattans' spectacular 1985 version of "You Send Me" (Sam Cooke), the Boyz II Men 1993 reprise of "In the Still of the Nite (I'll Remember)" (The Five Satins), and the Rolling Stones' 1986 hit "Harlem

Shuffle" (Bob and Earl). Finally, Golden Oldies stations ought to call their listeners' attention to contemporary performers who function as revivalists of early rock tunes. The exceptional reissues of Michael Bolton ("Georgia on My Mind" and "(Sittin' On) The Dock of the Bay"), Dave Edmunds ("I Hear You Knockin'"), Michael Henderson ("To Be Loved"), Joe Cocker ("Unchain My Heart"), New Edition ("Earth Angel"), and The Nylons ("Kiss Him Goodbye") deserve playing time on oldies stations along with the earlier recordings by the original artists–Ray Charles, Otis Redding, Fats Domino, Jackie Wilson, The Penguins, and Steam.

Playing new artists will not corrupt the playlist philosophy of honoring songs from the mid-twentieth century. It will also accomplish two positive ends. The present generation will realize that American music is far more than just a current affair. Obviously, "Georgia on My Mind" had a Hoagy Carmichael history long before Ray Charles stylized the tune. Similarly, Smiley Lewis recorded "I Hear You Knocking" before Fats Domino did. The extended life of songs ought to be an educational perspective shared by Golden Oldies broadcasters. The fact that current stars elect to record previously performed classic tunes heightens the inherent value of the recorded repertoire presented on Golden Oldies programs.

### Conclusion

The decline of vinyl sales during the 1980s signalled the death of the 45 rpm record. Neither cassettes singles nor CD singles have proven to be as popular in terms of commodity sales as the old black plastic discs. Nevertheless, it is still individual songs rather than albums that make up *Billboard*'s "Hot 100" chart. Not surprisingly, many Golden Oldies stations conduct their own polls–generally among their own listeners–to establish the "Top 50," "Top 100," or "Top 500" favorite recordings of all time. Selections invariably include "Yesterday," "In the Still of the Night," "Satisfaction," "In the Midnight Hour," "Runaround Sue," and "Don't Be Cruel."

If these tunes are to survive as more than one generation's favorites, though, they must receive greater cross-generational exposure. Resilient touring acts such as Ray Charles, the Rolling Stones, James Brown, Aretha Franklin, Stevie Wonder, Elton John, and The Everly Brothers have always succeeded in mixing their newest releases with their traditional tunes. To maintain vitality, to acknowledge continuing artistic creativity, and to market a distinctive playlist to an increasingly larger (not just increasingly older) listening population, Golden Oldies stations must revise their programming perspective. Bob Seger was only partially correct when he urged us to simply "get those old records off the shelf."

Chuck Berry, the Poet Laureate of the 1950s, was more on target for enlightening oldies station programmers when he sang, "Just let me hear some of that rock 'n' roll music, any old way you choose it. . . ."

# REFERENCES

Anderson, Bruce, Peter Hesbacher, K. Peter Etzkorn, and R. Serge Denisoff. "Hit Record Trends, 1940-1977," *Journal of Communication*, XXX (Spring 1980), pp. 31-43.
Aquila, Richard. *That Old Time Rock and Roll: A Chronicle of an Era, 1954-1963*. New York: Schirmer Books, 1989.
Baehr, Helen and Michele Ryan. *Shut Up and Listen! Women and Local Radio—A View From the Inside*. London: Comedia Press, Ltd., 1984.
Barnes, Ken. "Top 40 Radio: A Fragment of the Imagination," in *Facing the Music*, edited by Simon Frith (New York: Pantheon Books, 1988), pp. 8-50.
Berry, Peter E. . . . *And the Hits Just Keep on Comin'*. Syracuse, New York: Syracuse University Press, 1977.
Bronson, Fred. *The Billboard Book of Number One Hits* (revised and enlarged edition). New York: Billboard Publications, Inc., 1988.
Busnar, Gene. *It's Rock 'n' Roll: A Musical History of the Fabulous Fifties*. New York: Wanderer Books, 1979.
Cantor, Louis. *Wheelin' on Beale: How WDIA-Memphis Became the Nation's First All-Black Radio Station and Created the Sound That Changed America*. New York: Pharos Books, 1992.
Chapple, Steve and Reebee Garofalo. *Rock 'n' Roll Is Here to Pay: The History and Politics of the Music Industry*. Chicago: Nelson-Hall, Inc., 1977.
"Chronological Display of Radio Station Surveys, 1955-1990," *DISCoveries*, IV (July 1991), pp. 15-105.
Cooper, B. Lee. "From Anonymous Announcer to Radio Personality, From Pied Piper to Payola: The American Disc Jockey, 1950-1970," *Popular Music and Society*, XIV (Winter 1990), pp. 89-95.
Cooper, B. Lee. *Images of American Society in Popular Music: A Guide to Reflective Teaching*. Chicago: Nelson-Hall, Inc., 1982.
Cooper, B. Lee. *The Popular Music Handbook: A Resource Guide*. Littleton, Colorado: Libraries Unlimited, Inc., 1984.
Cooper, B. Lee. *Popular Music Perspectives: Ideas, Themes, and Patterns in Contemporary Lyrics*. Bowling Green, Ohio: Bowling Green State University Popular Press, 1991.
Cooper, B. Lee. "Promoting Social Change Through Audio Repetition: Black Musicians As Creators and Revivalists, 1953-1978," *Tracking: Popular Music Studies*, II (Winter 1989), pp. 26-46.
Cooper, B. Lee. "Repeating Hit Tunes, A Cappella Style: The Persuasions As Song Revivalists, 1967-1982," *Popular Music and Society*, XIII (Fall 1989), pp. 17-27.

Cooper, B. Lee. *A Resource Guide to Themes in Contemporary Song Lyrics, 1950-1985*. Westport, Connecticut: Greenwood Press, 1986.

Cooper, B. Lee. "Review of the CHUM Chart Book, 1957-1983: A Complete Listing of Every Charted Record by Ron Hall," *ARSC Journal*, XIX, Nos. 2-3 (1987), pp. 96-101.

Cooper, B. Lee. "Review of *Don Sherwood: The Life and Times of the World's Greatest Disc Jockey* by Laurie Harper," *Popular Culture in Libraries*, I, No. 1 (1993), pp. 157-158.

Cooper, B. Lee. "Review of *The Heart of Rock and Soul: The 1001 Greatest Singles Ever Made* by Dave Marsh," *Michigan Academician*, XXIII (Spring 1991), pp. 203-205.

Cooper, B. Lee. "Review of *Rock 'n' Roll on Compact Disc* by David Prakel, *Rock on CD* by David Sinclair, and *A Guide to Oldies on Compact Disc* by Mike Callahan," *Blue Suede News*, No. 21 (1992), pp. 20-21.

Cooper, B. Lee. "Review of *Rock on Almanac* by Norm N. Nite, *The Harmony Illustrated Encyclopedia of Rock* (sixth edition), and *That Old Time Rock and Roll* by Richard Aquila," *Journal of Popular Culture*, XXIV (Summer 1990), pp. 175-177.

Cooper, B. Lee. "Review of *The Rockin' 40's* (Hoy CD 40-S-01) by Morgan Wright and *What Was the First Rock 'n' Roll Record?* by Jim Dawson and Steve Propes," *Popular Music and Society*, XVII, (Summer, 1993), p. 134.

Cooper, B. Lee. "Review of *Rockin' the Classics and Classicizin' the Rock: A Selectively Annotated Discography* by Janell R. Duxbury," *ARSC Journal*, XIX Nos. 2-3 (1987), pp. 94-95.

Cooper, B. Lee. "Review of *Rockin' the Classics and Classicizin' the Rock: A Selectively Annotated Discography—First Supplement* by Janell R. Duxbury," *Popular Music and Society*, XVI (Summer 1992), pp. 116-117.

Cooper, B. Lee. "Review of *Television Theme Recordings: A Discography* by Steve Gelfand," *Popular Music*, VIII (January 1988), pp. 116-117.

Cooper, B. Lee. "Review of *TV Theme Soundtrack Directory and Discography with Cover Versions* by Craig W. Pattillo," *Popular Music and Society*, XIV (Winter 1990), pp. 115-116.

Cooper, B. Lee and Wayne S. Haney. *Response Recordings: An Answer Song Discography*. Metuchen, New Jersey: Scarecrow Press, Inc., 1990.

Cooper, B. Lee and Wayne S. Haney. *Rock Music in American Popular Culture: Rock 'n' Roll Resources*. Binghamton, New York: The Haworth Press, 1995.

Courtney, Ron. "Blues in the Night: The Story of WLAC Radio," *Goldmine*, No. 93 (February 1984), pp. 183-184.

Curtis, Jim. *Rock Eras: Interpretations of Music and Society, 1954-1984*. Bowling Green, Ohio: Bowling Green State University Popular Press, 1987.

Daniel, Sherry. "Dick Biondi's Legacy," *DISCoveries*, No. 61 (June 1993), pp. 36-41.

Daniel, Sherry. "Fares of the Airwaves," *DISCoveries*, No. 60 (May 1993), p. 20.

Daniel, Sherry. "Fares of the Airwaves," *DISCoveries*, No. 62 (July 1993), pp. 114-115.

Daniel, Sherry. "Fares of the Airwaves," *DISCoveries*, No. 66 (November 1993), p. 125.

Daniel, Sherry. "Fares of the Airwaves," *DISCoveries*, No. 67 (December 1993), p. 60.

Daniel, Sherry. "Fares of the Airwaves," *DISCoveries*, No. 68 (January 1994), p. 104.

Dawson, Jim and Steve Propes. *What Was the First Rock 'n' Roll Record?* Boston, Massachusetts: Faber and Faber, 1992.

Delfinger, Gary (comp.). *The Rock 'n' Roll Oldies Car Songbook*. Philadelphia: Running Press, 1987.

DeLuca, David. "The Mad, Mad Daddy of Cleveland Radio," *Cleveland Magazine*, (September 1984), pp. 82-85.

Denisoff, R. Serge. "The Evolution of Pop Music Broadcasting, 1920-1972," *Popular Music and Society*, II (Spring 1973), pp. 202-226.

Denisoff, R. Serge. "The Gatekeepers of Radio," in *Solid Gold: The Popular Record Industry* (New Brunswick, New Jersey: Transaction Books, 1975), pp. 216-282.

Dexter, Dave, Jr. "Disc Jockey: Origin of the Species, 1930-1945," *Billboard*, (December 27, 1969), pp. 56-58.

Downey, Pat. *The Golden Age of Top 40 Music (1955-1973) on Compact Disc*. Boulder, Colorado: Pat Downey Enterprises, 1992.

Erlewine, Michael and Scott Bultman (eds.). *All Music Guide*. San Francisco: Miller Freeman, Inc., 1992.

Gillett, Charlie. *The Sound of the City: The Rise of Rock and Roll* (revised and expanded edition). New York: Pantheon Books, 1983.

Goldstein, Stewart and Alan Jacobson. *Oldies But Goodies: The Rock 'n' Roll Years*. New York: Masong Charter, 1977.

Griggs, Bill. "Spotlight on Dick Jacobs," *Rockin' 50s*, No. 38 (October 1992), pp. 8-15.

Hadley, Daniel J. "'Ride the Rhythm': Two Approaches to D. J. Practice," *Journal of Popular Music Studies*, V (1993), pp. 58-67.

Harper, Laurie. *Don Sherwood: The Life and Times of "the World's Greatest Disc Jockey."* Rocklin, California; Prima Publishing and Communications, 1989.

Hesbacher, Peter. "Sound Exposure in Radio: The Misleading Nature of the Station Playlist," *Popular Music and Society*, III (Summer 1974), pp. 189-201.

Hesbacher, Peter. Robert Downing and David G. Berger, "Record Roulette: What Makes It Spin?" *Journal of Communication*, XXV (Summer 1975), pp. 74-85.

Hoffmann, Frank W. (comp.). *The Cash Box Singles Charts, 1950-1981*. Metuchen, New Jersey: Scarecrow Press, Inc. 1983.

Hoffmann, Frank W. (comp.). *The Literature of Rock, 1954-1978*. Metuchen, New Jersey: Scarecrow Press, Inc., 1981.

Hoffmann, Frank W. "Radio," in *Popular Culture and Libraries* (Hamden, Connecticut: Library Professional Publications/Shoe String Press, Inc., 1984), pp. 206-216.

Hoffmann, Frank W. and William G. Bailey. *Arts and Entertainment Fads*. Binghamton, New York: The Haworth Press, Inc., 1990.

Hoffmann, Frank W. and B. Lee Cooper (comps.). *The Literature of Rock II, 1979-1983* (two volumes). Metuchen, New Jersey: Scarecrow Press, Inc., 1986.

Hoffmann, Frank W. and B. Lee Cooper (comps.). *The Literature of Rock III, 1984-1990* (two volumes). Metuchen, New Jersey: Scarecrow Press, Inc., 1994.

Holiday, Jon. "It's More Than Just Nostalgia," *Billboard*, XCV (June 18, 1983), p. 10.

Hugunin, Marc. "ASCAP, BMI, and the Democratization of American Popular Music," *Popular Music and Society*, VII (Winter 1979), pp. 8-17.

Jackson, John A. *Big Beat Heat: Alan Freed and the Early Years of Rock and Roll*. New York: Schirmer Books 1991.

Jancik, Wayne. *The Billboard Book of One-Hit Wonders*. New York: Billboard Books/Watson-Guptill Publications, 1990.

Jones, Peter. "Wolfman Jack: Ah-Oooo!" *Goldmine*, No. 290 (September 6, 1991), pp. 64-68.

Kamin, Jonathan. "Taking the Roll Out of Rock 'n' Roll: Reverse Acculturation," *Popular Music and Society*, IV (Fall 1975), pp. 170-187.

Kinder, Bob. *The Best of the First: The Early Days of Rock and Roll*. Chicago: Adams Press, 1986.

King, Stephen. "Between Rock and a Soft Place," *Playboy*, XXIX (January 1982), pp. 120-122ff.

Lujack, Larry. *Super Jock: The Loud, Frantic, Nonstop World of Rock Radio DJ*. Chicago: Henry Regnery, 1975.

Lull, James, Lawrence Johnson, and Carol E. Sweeney. "Audiences for Contemporary Radio Formats," *Journal of Broadcasting*, XXII (Fall 1978), pp. 139-153.

MacDonald, J. Fred. *Don't Touch That Dial! Radio Programming in American Life, 1920-1960*. Chicago: Nelson-Hall, Inc., 1979.

MacFarland, David T. *The Development of the Top 40 Radio Format*. Salem, New Hampshire: Ayer Company, Publishers, 1979.

Marion, Jean-Charles. "The New York Disc Jockeys," *Record Exchanger*, No. 31 (1983), pp. 16-17, 24.

Marsh, Dave. *Fortunate Son*. New York: Random House, 1985.

Marsh, Dave. *The Heart of Rock and Soul: The 1001 Greatest Singles Ever Made*. New York: New American Library, 1989.

Marsh, Dave, Lee Ballinger, Sandra Choron, Wendy Smith, and Daniel Wolff. *The First Rock and Roll Confidential Report: Inside the Real World of Rock and Roll*. New York: Pantheon Books, 1985.

McFarlin, James. "Solid Gold: Detroit Radio Is Mining Yuppie Listeners in a Gold Rush," *Detroit News* (September 22,1988), pp. 1C, 5C.

Miller, Chuck. "Equal Time for New Music," *Billboard*, XCIV (December 25, 1982), p. 12.

Morrissey, Michael. "Promoting Beyond the Top 10," *Billboard*, XCVI (September 8, 1984), p. 10.

Morrow, Bruce and Laura Baudo. *Cousin Brucie! My Life in Rock 'n' Roll Radio*. New York: Beech Tree Books/William Morrow and Company, Inc., 1987.

Morthland, John. "The Rise of Top 40 AM," in *The Rolling Stone Illustrated History of Rock and Roll* (revised edition), edited by Jim Miller (New York: Random House/Rolling Stone Press Books, 1980), pp. 92-95.

Newman, Mark. *Entrepreneurs of Profit and Pride: From Black Appeal to Radio Soul*. New York: Praeger Books, 1988.

Osgood, Dick. *WYXIE Wonderland: Diary of a Radio Station*. Bowling Green, Ohio: Bowling Green State University Popular Press, 1981.

O'Shea, Shad. *Just for the Record*. Cincinnati, Ohio: Positive Feedback Books, 1987.

Passman, Arnold. *The Dee Jays*. New York: Macmillan Company, 1971.

Paytress, Mark. "Alan Freed," *Record Collector*, No. 165 (May 1993), pp. 110-112.

Peterson, Richard A. and Russell B. Davis, Jr. "The Contemporary American Radio Audience," Popular Music," *American Sociological Review*, XL (April 1975), pp. 158-173.

Pitts, Michael R. *Radio Soundtracks: A Reference Guide* (second edition). Metuchen, New Jersey: Scarecrow Press, 1986.

Pollock, Bruce. *When Rock Was Young: A Nostalgic Review of the Top 40 Era*. New York: Holt, Rinehart and Winston, 1981.

Pollock, Bruce. *When the Music Mattered: Rock in the 1960s*. New York: Holt, Rinehart and Winston, 1983.

Pruter, Robert. "The Emergence of Soul Radio," in *Chicago Soul* (Champaign-Urbana: University of Illinois Press, 1991), pp. 12-19.

Redd, Lawrence N. *Rock Is Rhythm and Blues: The Impact of Mass Media*. East Lansing: Michigan State University Press, 1974.

Rothenbuhler, Eric W. and Tom McCourt. "Commercial Radio and Popular Music: Processes of Selection and Factors of Influence," in *Popular Music and Communication* (second edition), edited by James Lull (Newbury Park, California: Sage Publications, Inc., 1992), pp. 101-115.

Ryan, John. *The Production of Culture in the Music Industry: The ASCAP-BMI Controversy*. Lanham, Maryland: University of America, Inc., 1985.

Scheurer, Timothy E. (ed.). *American Popular Music–Volume Two: The Age of Rock*. Bowling Green, Ohio: Bowling Green State University Popular Press, 1989.

Sheppard, Roy. *The DJ's Handbook: From Scratch to Stardom*. Poole, Dorset, England: Javelin Books, 1986.

Shields, Steven O. (comp.). "A Selected Bibliography of Scholarly Articles and Dissertations on Radio Studies," *Journal of Radio Studies*, I (1992), pp. 169-172.

Sklar, Rick. *Rocking America–An Insider's Story: How the All-Hit Radio Stations Took Over*. New York: St. Martin's Press, 1984.

Smith, Joe, edited by Mitchell Fink. *Off the Record: An Oral History of Popular Music.* New York: Warner Books, 1988.

Smith, Wes. *The Pied Pipers of Rock 'n' Roll: Radio Deejays of the '50s and '60s.* Marietta, Georgia: Longstreet Press, Inc., 1989.

Tamarkin, Jeff. "Don K. Reed: New York's Doo-Wop Disc Jockey," *Goldmine,* No. 64 (September 1981), pp. 10-11.

Trubia, Charlie. "Romancing the 25-to-54 Demographic: Advertisers Focus on New Heart of Buying Power," *Billboard,* XCVIII (February 8, 1986), p. 21.

Wade, Dorothy and Justine Picardie. *Music Man: Ahmet Ertegun, Atlantic Records, and the Triumph of Rock 'n' Roll.* New York: W.W. Norton and Company, Inc., 1990.

Wilkinson, Tony. "Jim Pewter–The Spirit of Alan Freed Lives On." *Now Dig This,* No. 73 (April 1989), p. 9.

Williams, Gilbert A. "The Black Disc Jockey as a Cultural Hero," *Popular Music and Society,* X (Summer 1986), pp. 79-90.

Chapter 6

# Doo-Wop Harmony

## *THE MAGNIFICENTS*

*Du-Wop*. By Johnny Keyes. Chicago: Vesti Press, 1991 (c. 1987). Illustrated. 94 pp. Paperback. (Available from publisher at Apartment 606, 1857 East 71st Street, Chicago, Illinois 60649).

This is the memoir of a black artist who adores vocalizing and feels obligated to share his professional experiences with friends, doo-wop fans, and would-be performers. Johnny Keyes still dreams about the 1950s, when music was more important than marketing, when streetcorner buddies differed dramatically from studio musicians, and when both performing and recording were "live" activities without the benefits of artificial electronic enhancement or "canned" multitrack taping support. The author writes plainly. But he is no Hemingway. Still, the text is compelling because it captures the essence of one man's struggle against the calamities of commercial music. The joy of singing, the electricity of public performance is sufficient reward to feed an artist's soul. Nevertheless, the artist's body demands food, shelter, and clothing, and adult well-being demands a modicum of financial security as the teenage years recede. Keyes' study is neither comedy nor tragedy. It is the sensitive biography of a talented vocalist in America's turbulent rock 'n' roll age.

Keyes was the lead singer for Tam and the Tam O'Shanters, a high school vocal group formed in 1953. They adopted the professional name

The initial review by B. Lee Cooper was originally published as "Review of *Du-Wop* by Johnny Keyes," *Popular Music and Society*, XVI (Spring 1992), pp. 98-99. Reprint permission granted by the author, Editor R. Serge Denisoff, and the Bowling Green State University Popular Press. The second review by B. Lee Cooper is scheduled to be published in *Popular Culture in Libraries*. Reprint permission granted by the author, Editor Frank Hoffmann, and The Haworth Press.

Magnificents at the request of Chicago's WAAF disc jockey "The Magnificent" Montague. Their initial recording for the local Vee-Jay label was "Up on the Mountain." The Magnificents attained Number 9 on the juke box chart, Number 14 on the R&B best-seller list, and Number 15 on the disc jockey parade of hits. Their journey to musical fame and fortune as record stars seemed assured. Keyes describes the group's numerous activities of 1956 and 1957 in loving detail, and provides reproductions of telegrams, backstage snapshots, Apollo Theatre posters, and American Guild of Variety Artists (AG-VA) engagement contracts to illustrate these endeavors. Keyes describes an impromptu backstage meeting with Elvis Presley in Memphis ("And we learned that Elvis was a very friendly and interesting person to talk with, but he wasn't the King of Rock 'n' Roll. Little Richard is."), the thrill of performing at the Paramount Theatre as part of Alan Freed's "Holiday of Stars," and the process of joining The Sharps to sing backup for the 1957 Thurston Harris hit "Little Bitty Pretty One."

*Du-Wop* is chock-full of anecdotal reflections. Keyes details financial rip-offs by unscrupulous club owners; condemns the "cover recordings" of white performers such as Pat Boone and The Diamonds; explains the need to "look sharp" via special makeup, hair processing, and stage costuming; and cites generational conflicts between older instrumental musicians and younger doo-wop vocal groups. Two messages dominate Keyes' preaching. Remain true to your own original, distinctive singing style and be persistent about public performing. In the author's words, "If you can resist the pitfall of logical and rational thinking and just hold on to your dream, you'll outlive most of the competition anyway and your time will arrive, even if it is a result of some sort of cosmic process of elimination" (p. 56). For Keyes, hit record recognition arrived on July 15, 1956—and never returned again. His description of the daily "I Only Have Eyes For You" doo-wop singing break that he and four other postal workers take at 5:30 each evening is genuinely heart-rending.

Although listed at only 94 pages, *Du-Wop* is actually twice that size. Keyes provides a spectacular array of stunning black-and-white doo-wop and R&B group publicity photos in unpaginated fashion throughout the text. From The King Cole Trio, The Cats and the Fiddle, and The Four Ink Spots to The Spaniels, The Moonglows, and The Clovers, the full-page pictures alone make this book a rare value at the low price tag. This study has merit as history, biography, and pictorial art. No music librarian, audio archivist, popular culture enthusiast, American studies researcher, African-American historian, or doo-wop record fan should miss this publication.

## RECORD COLLECTING

*Collecting Rare Records: A Guide to Take You Through the World of Rare Records.* By Lou Silvani. Bronx, New York: Times Square Records, 1992. Illustrated. 321 pp.

*Doo-Wop: The Forgotten Third of Rock 'n' Roll.* By Anthony J. Gribin and Matthew M. Schiff. Iola, Wisconsin: Krause Publications, 1992. Illustrated. 616 pp.

Louis Silvani has created a spectacular guide for collectors of rare vocal group recordings from the 1940s, 1950s, 1960s, and 1970s. This volume is arranged alphabetically by record label–from A, AJ, Aardell, Abbey, and ABC to Way Out, X Tra, YRS, and Zebra. Each entry features the reproduction of the record label, a sample citation for a specific vocal group, the A- and B-sides of a single release, and the year of the recording. Specific points of guidance concerning variations in label colors and other information about groups, songs, or companies is generously noted throughout the oversized volume. The text is also peppered with handsome black-and-white photographs of classic R&B and doo-wop groups. The study concludes with a helpful alphabetical "Index" organized by performing group names–from Academics, Accents, Nicky Addeo, Adelphis, and Admirals to Zephyrs, Ben Zeppa, Zeroes, George Zimmerman, and Zodiacs.

*Collecting Rare Records* is not a comprehensive discography. It is an instructional guide, intended to alert both amateurs and professionals to the verbal and marketing intricacies of record production, distribution, and bootlegging. Despite providing a brief introductory commentary on the "Development of Black Vocal Groups" (pp. xv-xx), the main thrust of the book is technical rather than historical. This is not a criticism, though. Silvani's designated audience is oriented toward analysis of vintage vinyl treasures. Likewise, most vocal group harmony collectors have lifetime memories (or nostalgic mythologies) of The Five Satins, The Harptones, The Crows, The Jesters, and The Flamingos. But Silvani does provide superb trivia material by identifying the names of obscure record company founders and seldom-mentioned vocal group participants within the label citation system. This study is a godsend to music lovers, greedy investors, and R&B record hunters.

Normally the publication of a book like *Collecting Rare Records* would be an unparalleled find during any year. This was not true in 1992. Anthony J. Gribin and Matthew M. Schiff produced a truly remarkable salute to 1950s and 1960s vocal groups in that same year. *Doo-Wop: The Forgotten Third of Rock 'n' Roll* is an ideal blend of historical perspective, discographic display, bibliographic compilation, and musical devotion. It provides the perfect introduction for youthful listeners who are unaware of the tremendous influence of doo-wop styling on contemporary American music. Even the most dedicated black music scholars and knowledgeable record collectors will be amazed at the amount of information accumulated in this single resource. Gribin and Schiff have really done their vinyl homework.

The heart of *Doo-Wop* is a huge "Songography" (pp. 151-606). This listing is arranged alphabetically by performing group names—from A-Tones, Accents, and Acorns to Zippers, Zircons, and Zodiacs—and features two-sided record titles, years of release, and record company names and numbers. This clear, authoritative disc data is invaluable. For doo-wop researchers, it exceeds even the superb discographic efforts of Fernando Gonzales and Jeff Kreiter. No group harmony afficiando or black music scholar will be able to explore the 1952-1963 era without consulting this magnificent guide.

Even more impressive is the rich introductory section that precedes the "Songography." In 150 fact-filled, perceptive pages the authors delineate their own thoughtful interpretation of doo-wop music. The central premise of this study is that rockabilly and rhythm 'n' blues have for too long received the lion's share of attention as rock's roots. Doo-wop deserves more recognition and greater documentation. Gribin and Schiff examine the frequency of doo-wop radio airplay, the combination of vocal styling, instrumentation, and lyrics in doo-wop recordings, the pop/gospel/R&B roots of the doo-wop sound, primary group exponents of the music (Five Satins, El Dorados, Flamingos, Frankie Lymon and the Teenagers, Coasters, The Platters, and The Chantels), urban teen subculture of the doo-wop era, the changing technology of disc size and transistor radios during the 1950s, the unique broadcasting styles of personality disc jockeys (Alan Freed, Jocko Henderson, Peter Tripp, and Tommy "Dr. Jive" Smalls), the rise of independent record labels, and various genre idiosyncracies including the creation of distinctive group names (for birds, precious gems, automobiles, and flowers), classic doo-wop tunes ("Somewhere Over the Rainbow," "A Sunday Kind of Love," and "Gloria"), and peculiar lyrical topics (jungle scenes, Mexican romances, Oriental dating fantasies, weddings, returning soldiers, nursery rhyme characters, and nonsense syllables). The illustrative detail is wonderful. The clarity of writing is beneficial. And the uninhibited zeal of the authors is undeniably infectious.

Doo-wop has finally been delivered from the bondage of literary obscurity. This study presents both a musical history and discography worthy of its contribution to American popular records. It is regrettable that so few young music listeners will ever encounter the rich, inspiring vocal harmonies of The Five Keys, The Drifters, or Nolan Strong and the Diablos–and must settle instead for a toneless Tone-Loc or the dynamic but nonmelodic Hammer. At least black film director Spike Lee recognized the soulful roots sound of doo-wop in his brilliant 1990 soundtrack Do it a Cappella (Elektra 60953). For Gribin and Schiff, the history of vocal harmony groups is a treasure, a pleasure, and an authentic measure of rock 'n' roll's softer, more simple magic.

While all doo-wop enthusiasts will enjoy both *Collecting Rare Records* and *Doo-Wop: The Forgotten Third of Rock 'n' Roll*, the Gribin and Schiff study is a book that shouts for special recognition and echoes with authority as an exploration of a key genre of America's popular music past.

## REFERENCES

Brown, Geoff. "Doo-Wop," *The History of Rock*, No. 4 (1982), pp. 69-73. Busnar, Gene. *It's Rock 'n' Roll: A Musical History of the Fabulous Fifties*. New York: Wanderer Books, 1979.

Clark, Alan (comp.). *Rock and Roll Memories–Number One*. West Covina, California: Alan C. Lungstrum/National Rock and Roll Archives, 1987.

Clark, Alan (comp.). *Rock and Roll Memories–Number Two*. West Covina, California: Alan C. Lungstrum/National Rock and Roll Archives, 1987.

Clark, Alan (comp.). *Rock and Roll Memories–Number Three*. West Covina, California: Alan C. Lungstrum/National Rock and Roll Archives, 1988.

Clark, Alan (comp.). *Rock and Roll Memories–Number Four*. West Covina, California: Alan C. Lungstrum/National Rock and Roll Archives, 1989.

Clark, Alan (comp.). *Rock and Roll Memories–Number Five*. West Covina, California: Alan C. Lungstrum/National Rock and Roll Archives, 1990.

Clark, Alan (comp.). *Rock and Roll Memories–Number Six*. West Covina, California: Alan C. Lungstrum/National Rock and Roll Archives, 1991.

Clark, Alan (comp.). *Rock and Roll Memories–Number Seven*. West Covina, California: Alan C. Lungstrum/National Rock and Roll Archives, 1992.

Clark, Alan (comp.). *Rock and Roll Memories–Number Eight*. West Covina, California: Alan C. Lungstrum/National Rock and Roll Archives, 1993.

Cooper, B. Lee. "Repeating Hit Tunes, A Cappella Style: The Persuasions As Song Revivalists, 1967-1982," *Popular Music and Society*, XIII (Fall 1989), pp. 17-27.

Cooper, B. Lee. "Review of *Clyde McPhatter: A Biographical Essay* by Colin Escott," *Popular Music and Society*, XIII (Summer 1989), pp. 113-115.

Cooper, B. Lee. "Review of *Group Collector's Record Guide* by Jeff Kreiter," *Popular Music and Society*, XIV (Winter 1990), pp. 116-117.

Cooper, B. Lee. "Review of *Shake, Rattle, and Roll–The Golden Age of American Rock 'n' Roll: Volume One–1952-1955* by Lee Cotten," *Sonneck Society Bulletin*, XV (Summer 1989), p. 91.

Cummings, Tony. "Doo-Wop: The Streetcorner Harmonisers," in *The Sound of Philadelphia* (London: Methoven Books, 1975), pp. 24-33.

Dawson, Jim and Steve Propes. *What Was the First Rock 'n' Roll Record?* Boston: Faber and Faber, 1992.

Engel, Edward R. *White and Still All Right: White Group Histories of the '50s and Early '60s—Volume One.* New York: Crackerjack Press, 1977.

Ewalt, Bob. "Review of *Doo-Wop: The Forgotten Third of Rock 'n' Roll* by Anthony J. Gribin and Matthew M. Schiff," *Now Dig This,* No. 115 (October 1992), p. 15.

Ferlingere, Robert D. (comp.). *A Discography of Rhythm and Blues and Rock 'n' Roll Vocal Groups, 1945 to 1965.* Hayward, California: California Trade School, 1976.

Fry, Macon. "Doo-Wop Without Pop-Hiss," *Wavelength,* No. 125 (March 1991), p. 9.

Goldstein, Stewart and Alan Jacobson. *Oldies But Goodies: The Rock 'n' Roll Years.* New York: Mason Charter, 1977.

Gonzalez, Fernando (comp.). *Disco-File: The Discographical Catalog of American Rock and Roll and Rhythm and Blues Vocal Harmony Groups, 1902 to 1976* (second edition). Flushing, New York: F.L. Gonzalez, 1977.

Gray, Michael H. (comp.). *Bibliography of Discographies: Volume Three—Popular Music.* New York: Bowker Company, 1983.

Grendysa, Peter. "Fortune Records: In a Few Words . . . ," *Goldmine,* No. 142 (January 3, 1986), p. 18.

Gribin, Anthony J. and Matthew M. Schiff. *Doo-Wop: The Forgotten Third of Rock 'n' Roll.* Iola, Wisconsin: Krause Publications, 1992.

Groia, Phil. *They All Sang on the Corner; New York City's Rhythm and Blues Vocal Groups of the 1950s.* Setauket, New York: Edmond Publishing Company, 1974.

Hansen, Barry. "Doo-Wop," in *The Rolling Stone Illustrated History of Rock and Roll* (fully revised and updated), edited by Anthony DeCuretis and James Henke, with Holly George-Warren (New York: Random House, 1992), pp. 92-101.

Hirschberg, David. "The Doo-Wop Hall of Fame Awards: The People's Choice," *Now Dig This,* No. 112 (July 1992), pp. 8-10.

Javna, John. *The Doo-Wop Sing-Along Songbook.* New York: St. Martin's Press, 1986.

Kaye, Lenny. "The Best of Acappella," in *The Penguin Book of Rock and Roll Writing,* edited by Clinton Heylin (New York: Penguin Books, 1992), pp. 22-37.

Keyes, Johnny. *Du-Wop.* Chicago: Vesti Press, 1991.

Kocandrle, Mirek. "Doo-Wop," in *The History of Rock and Roll: A Selective Discography* (Boston: G.K. Hall and Company, 1988), pp. 45-54.

Kreiter, Jeff (comp.). *45 R.P.M. Group Collector's Record Guide: A Guide to Valuable Recordings of Group Harmony From 1950-1965* (third edition). Wheeling, West Virginia: Boyd Press, 1990.

Lepri, Paul. *The New Haven Sound, 1946-1976.* New Haven, Connecticut: Paul Lepri, 1977.

McGarvey, Seamus. "New York Rock 'n' Roll and Doo-Wop—Paul Winley and Winley Records Interviewed," *Now Dig This*, No. 75 (June 1989), pp. 27-31.

Nichols, Pete. "Doo-Wop," *Record Collector*, No. 87 (November 1986), pp. 24-27.

Nichols, Pete. "Doo-Wop," *Record Collector*, No. 88 (December 1986), pp. 45-49.

Nite, Norm N. (comp.). *Rock on—The Illustrated Encyclopedia of Rock 'n' Roll: Volume One—The Solid Gold Years* (updated edition). New York: Harper and Row, 1982.

Pavlow, Al. *Big Al Pavlow's the Rhythm 'n' Blues Book: A Disc-History of Rhythm 'n' Blues*. Providence, Rhode Island: Music House Publishing, 1983.

Paytress, Mark. "Review of *Doo-Wop: The Forgotten Third of Rock 'n' Roll* by Anthony J. Gribin and Matthew M. Schiff," *Record Collector*, No. 162 (February 1993), p. 159.

Propes, Steve. *Golden Goodies: A Guide to '50s and '60s Popular Rock and Roll Record Collecting.* Radnor, Pennsylvania: Chilton Book Company, 1975.

Raper, Jim. "Doo-Wop on 45 R.P.M.," *Now Dig This*, No. 109 (April 1992), pp. 10, 32.

Rhode, H. Kandy, with research assistance from Laing Ned Kandel. *The Gold of Rock and Roll, 1955-1967*. New York: Arbor House, 1970.

Settle, Kenneth. "Fortune Records," *Goldmine*, No. 88 (September 1983), pp. 59-61, 64.

Shaw, Arnold. *Honkers and Shouters: The Golden Years of Rhythm and Blues*. New York: Collier Books, 1978.

Shaw, Arnold. *The Rockin' 50s: The Decade That Transformed the Pop Music Scene*. New York: Hawthorn Books, Inc., 1974.

Silvani, Lou. *Collecting Rare Records: A Guide to Take You Through the World of Rare Records*. Bronx: Times Square Records, 1992.

Smith, Wes. *The Pied Pipers of Rock 'n' Roll: Radio Deejays of the '50s and '60s*. Marietta, Georgia: Longstreet Press, Inc., 1989.

Tamarkin, Jeff. "Acappella in the '80s: It's Not Just Doo-Wop Anymore," *Goldmine*, No. 210 (August 13, 1988), pp. 22, 79.

Tamarkin, Jeff. "Ambient Sound Records: Group Harmony in the '80s," *Goldmine*, No. 70 (March 1982), pp. 20, 22-23.

Tamarkin, Jeff. "Don K. Reed: New York's Doo-Wop Disc Jockey," *Goldmine*, No. 64 (September 1981), pp. 10-11.

Tosches, Nick. *Unsung Heroes of Rock 'n' Roll: The Birth of Rock 'n' Roll in the Dark and Wild Years Before Elvis*. New York: Charles Scribner's Sons, 1984.

Warner, Alan. *Who Sang What in Rock 'n' Roll: 500 Revered, Revived, and Much Recorded Songs From the Rock Era*. London: Blandford Press, 1990.

Whitburn, Joel (comp.). *Top Rhythm 'n' Blues Singles, 1942-1988*. Minomonee Fall, Wisconsin: Record Research, Inc., 1988.

# Chapter 7

# Fads and Nostalgia

## *TWO CENTURIES OF MUSIC*

*A Twentieth-Century Musical Chronicle: Events, 1900-1988.* Compiled by Charles J. Hall. Westport, Connecticut: Greenwood Press, 1989. 347 pp.

*A Nineteenth-Century Musical Chronicle: Event, 1800-1899.* Compiled by Charles J. Hall. Westport, Connecticut: Greenwood Press, 1989. 374 pp.

These two volumes contain a gold mine of factual information about classical or "art" music, plus occasional highlights related to jazz and other popular genres. Andrews University music historian Charles J. Hall has organized this reference guide in a clear, consistent chronological format. Each year constitutes a complete chapter. In turn, each chapter surveys the following annual subjects: world events; cultural highlights (Pulitzer Prizes, art, and literature); births and deaths of prominent musicians; professional debuts (Metropolitan Opera, elsewhere in the United States, and worldwide); new positions (conductors and educators); artistic prizes and honors; biographical highlights; institutional openings (performing groups and festivals); musical literature; and musical compositions. The appearance of name after name creates a biographical collage of international musicianship over two centuries.

Two of these four reviews by B. Lee Cooper were originally published in *Journal of Popular Culture* and *Michigan Academician*. Reprint permission granted by the author, Managing Editor Pat Browne, and Bowling Green State University Popular Press, and Editor Kathleen Duke and the Michigan Academy for Science, Arts, and Letters.

The concept of providing annual listings to depict the evolution of music, literature, and art is not new. International fact surveys include *Chronology of Culture* (Van Nostrand Reinhold, 1984) by John Paxton and Sheila Fairfield and *The Timetables of History* (Touchstone, 1982) by Bernard Gron; American experiences are featured in *American Chronicle, 1920-1980* (Atheneum, 1987) by Lois Gordon and Alan Gordon, and *The Timetables of American History* (Touchstone, 1981) by Laurence Urdang. Music is only a minor factor in these four volumes. The most recent music-focused American chronology is *Rock on Almanac* (Harper and Row, 1989) by Norm N. Nite. The two Hall volumes are clearly modeled after most standard historical chronologies, though with a distinct musical emphasis.

In 1983 the Greenwood Press issued a text titled *Year by Year in the Rock Era: Events and Conditions Shaping the Rock Generations That Reshaped America*. Compiled by Herb Hendler, this exceptional study utilized the annual survey format—but sought to link and associate popular culture content (fashion, fads, slang, and trivia), media and literature (films, television, books, and comics), social statistics (census figures and demographic reports), and specific historical events with the emerging contemporary music (performers, juke box plays, dances, and rock journalism). This hallmark study, stressing the integration of music and culture, is apparently unknown to Hall. Too bad. The Greenwood editorial staff should have challenged Hall to move away from the more traditional fact-upon-fact isolation toward Hendler's more informative, insightful, integrative approach. Of course, some might argue that classical compositions and professional artists are less influenced by annual historical circumstance than either pop songs or rock performers. However, this type of a historical assertion calls into question the basic rationale for printing the two volumes being reviewed here.

Music reference librarians will enjoy the clarity of Charles J. Hall's chronicles. But music historians should demand much, much more than a mere chronology—especially since Hendler has established such a superb music-oriented standard.

## ROCK ERA TRENDS

*Year by Year in the Rock Era: Events and Conditions Shaping the Rock Generations That Reshaped America.* By Herb Hendler. Westport, Connecticut: Greenwood Press, 1983. Illustrated, with Statistical Tables. 350 pp.

Herb Hendler, former American record company executive and founder of London's Franklin School of Contemporary Studies, has assembled a fact-filled compendium depicting three decades of life in the United States. *Year by Year in the Rock Era* is a statistical, nostalgic, reflective review of youth-oriented America from 1954-1981. The text is structured chronologically. Each chapter examines a single year by presenting several paragraphs or lists featuring the following items: (1) rock artists, (2) juke box hits, (3) popular dances, (4) news of the rock scene, (5) national and international events, (6) statistical information about life in America, (7) teen/college lifestyles, (8) fashions, (9) fads, (10) argot, jargon, and slang, and (11) factual trivia. Beyond these 250 year-by-year pages, the author also provides 100 pages of economic tables ("Cost of Living Prices," "Car Prices," and "College Tuition Fees"), lists of popular films, and compilations of hit television shows, comic strips, and books and magazines that catered to youthful interests. A superb, though unannotated, bibliography of scholarly books is also included.

Hendler's stated goal is to offer sociologists, popular culture scholars, and nostalgia buffs a synthesized resource guide to rock history/social mores/interesting trivia/economics. Of course a 28-year dose of business trends, demographics, historical events, celebrity names, and political activities can be overwhelming, but Hendler achieves readability, clarity, and credibility. In comparison to several other rock almanac-type books—Sean Brickell and Rich Rothschild's *The Pages of Rock History: A Day-by-Day Calendar of the Births, Deaths, and Major Events* (1983), Gene Busnar's *It's Rock 'n' Roll* (1979), and Dan Formento's *Rock Chronicle: A 365 Day-by-Day Journal of Significant Events in Rock History* (1982)—Hendler's work is superior in terms of statistical content, organizational consistency, and quality of editorial preparation. *Year by Year in the Rock Era* will undoubtedly become a key resource for all students of trends in contemporary fashion, language, film, sexual mores, and music.

The author's "Introduction" is both satisfying and mystifying. To Hendler's credit, he asserts that his book is designed to be utilized by the broadest possible audience to explore (for either personal fun or more serious scholarly purposes) this nation's cultural history. Unfortunately, Hendler then commences to interpret his own work by imposing an uncharacteristically restrictive perspective. First, he argues that the "Rock Era" begins in 1954 (even Hendler acknowledges that this assumption is still widely debated) and ends in 1981. The latter point is lamely based upon the 1982 format switch from "Top 40" rock programming to talk/interview presentations by New York radio station WABC-AM. It would have been much more reasonable for the author simply to admit the obvious. Both the beginning and ending dates in such an extended cultural resource work are largely arbitrary. A second problem with Hendler's furtive interpretation is the tendency to state judgments without providing adequate factual background to justify the assertions. Two classic rock era studies that skillfully combine sociological statistics and recording industry data with logical, cogent generalizations are Charlie Gillett's *The Sound of the City: The Rise of Rock and Roll* (1970) and Simon Frith's *Sound Effects: Youth, Leisure, and the Politics of Rock 'n' Roll* (1981). The third mystifying problem is Hendler's apparent myopia toward events of overarching significance to the 28 years that he is investigating. The post-World War II period in the United States is unified and influenced by more than just youth-oriented music and fads. Internationally, the Cold War and the growing threat of nuclear holocaust function as dreadful political and psychological constants; domestically, minority struggles for civil rights, social justice, and economic security are predominant issues. Finally, since Hendler depicts the Rock Era as cyclical in evolution—emergence, acceptance, dominance, and decline—he glosses over the fact that popular music has consistently been regarded as morally corrupting, aesthetically void, and atheistic (if not satanically inspired) by many Americans since 1954. Similarly, the triumphs of Australian rockers (AC/DC, The Little River Band, and Men At Work), the financial success of rock videos, compact discs, and MTV, and the musical impact of the newest British Invasion (Culture Club, The Eurythmics, and many, many others) hardly augur the demise of the Rock Era.

Despite these unexplainable interpretative glitches, *Year By Year in the Rock Era* is a work that deserves high praise and public attention. Hendler is preaching a cultural message that is certainly worth noting. Social change in America since 1954 is occurring at an ever-accelerating rate. It is the myriad facets of popular culture that most clearly illustrate this fact, and rock music/youthful society are unquestionably primary indicators of things as they are and things as they might be. As Johnny Otis sagely observed, "Listen to the Lambs." Hendler has selected a reasonable time frame and provided a wealth of qualitative and quantitative material for others to analyze. This is a valuable service. His book is clearly organized and interesting. It is a step ahead of the increasingly numerous Guinness books—and far more noteworthy than the numerous trivia and nostalgia texts that have flooded the publication marketplace since 1980. Few authors would have had the patience, humor, and insight to produce a book such as *Year by Year in the Rock Era*. It is fortunate that Hendler has accomplished this task.

## BIOGRAPHICAL SKETCHES

*Rock on Almanac: The First Four Decades of Rock 'n' Roll—A Chronology.* Compiled by Norm N. Nite. New York: Harper and Row, 1989. Illustrated. 532 pp.

*The Harmony Illustrated Encyclopedia of Rock* (sixth edition). By Pete Frame, John Tobler, Ed Hanel, Roger St. Pierre, Chris Trengove, John Beecher, Clive Richardson, Gary Cooper, Marshal Hanlon, and Linda Sandahl. New York: Harmony Books, 1989. Illustrated. 208 pp.

*The Old Time Rock and Roll: A Chronicle of an Era, 1954-1963.* By Richard Aquila. New York: Schirmer Books, 1989. Illustrated. 370 pp.

As rock 'n' roll moves into the 1990s, its history is being revised. Perhaps this was inevitable. All revolutions, especially successful ones, are eventually co-opted, tamed, civilized, and toned down to textbook proportions. Even the most radical change eventually is depicted as an irresistible, evolutionary pattern. The heroes of cultural rebellions either die or, in their twilight years, gain medals of recognition and Hall of Fame inductions. From Chuck Berry and Little Richard to Jerry Lee Lewis and Elvis Presley, the original "bad boys" are presently imaged as outrageous jokers or relatively harmless boy-next-door/rowdy schoolboy rebels. The random violence, sexuality, strong antiauthority elements of 1950s rock 'n' roll is thus translated into social pranksterism. The fact that black music became white music, obscure country bar bands became national celebrities, and the days of Eisenhower calm eventually erupted into civil strife during the 1960s slips from public memory. Amnesia triumphs.

Three books published within the past year illustrate this bowdlerizing trend. *That Old Time Rock and Roll: A Chronicle of an Era, 1954-1963* by Richard Aquila, *Rock on Almanac: The First Four Decades of Rock 'n' Roll* by Norm N. Nite, and the sixth edition of *The Harmony Illustrated Encyclopedia of Rock* contribute to the obliteration and assimilation of rock music into mainstream pop. Clearly such mellowing has occurred as the American youth music movement expanded to encompass 35 years and several generations of teenagers. But the historical perspective in each of these volumes is unitary rather than divergent. Chuck Berry equals Richard Marx equals Bob Marley equals Dolly Parton equals INXS equals Slim Harpo. Aquila, Nite, and the talented picture/text/discography team from Harmony's writing stable overwhelm readers with ornaments, bright lights, and tinsel—but they neglect to explain the birthright story behind their celebration.

Maybe such overview criticism is undeserved. Taken as individual studies, how do these books stand up to their literary competition in the realms of almanacs, encyclopedias, and song lists? Truthfully, they are inferior. Norm N. Nite's *Rock on Almanac* lists almost everything imaginable (news highlights, sports winners, music events, debut artists, monthly hit tunes, top annual singles and albums, Grammy winners, births and deaths, movies, Academy Award winners, and television shows). Unfortunately, this task has been more skillfully accomplished by Herb Hendler in *Year by Year in the Rock Era: Events and Conditions Shaping the Rock Generations That Reshaped America* (Greenwood Press, 1983) and more specifically chronicled in *The Rolling Stone Rock Almanac: The Chronicles of Rock and Roll* (Rolling Stone Press Book, 1983) and *Rock Day by Day* (Guinness Books, 1987). One suspects that the future appearance of more highly detailed studies, such as Lee Cotten's *Shake, Rattle, and Roll—The Golden Age of American Rock 'n' Roll: Volume One, 1952-1955* (Pierian Press, 1989) will render the overly general *Rock on Almanac* obsolete.

*The Harmony Illustrated Encyclopedia of Rock*, a longtime reference guide for teenagers—old and young—is fun. It has many, many photographs of performers and album covers, brief discographies of U.S.- and U.K.- charted singles and albums, and several elegant Pete Frame "Family Tree" charts of rock band formations, unifications, and destructions. But the volume lacks authority—specificity, detail and balance. For both casual readers and serious researchers, initial investigations of rock biographies ought to begin with Phil Hardy and Dave Laing's *Encyclopedia of Rock* (Aquarius Books, 1977), Irwin Stambler's *The Encyclopedia of Pop, Rock, and Soul*, revised edition (St. Martin's Press, 1989), and Barry Lazell's *Rock Movers and Shakers: An A to Z of the People Who Made Rock Happen* (Billboard Publications, 1989). None of these latter studies is perfect, but each is better than Harmony's sixth edition.

Richard Aquila is a talented essayist and a fine popular culture analyst. Neither of these traits is brought to bear on the material presented in *That Old Time Rock and Roll*. Although the black-and-white photographs in the book are priceless, the rest of the volume is inferior as an almanac (see Hendler above), ho-hum as a biographical encyclopedia (see Stambler above), and poorly documented as a subject classification resource. This latter activity has been more thoroughly researched and more thoughtfully presented in Bob Macken, Peter Fornatale, and Bill Ayres' *The Rock Music Source Book* (Doubleday, 1980), Jeff Green's *The 1987 Green Book: Songs Classified by Subject* (Professional Desk References, 1986), and B. Lee Cooper's *A Resource Guide to Themes in Contemporary American Song Lyrics, 1950-1985* (Greenwood Press, 1986).

Why are the three books reviewed here on the market when superior studies are already available? Because publishers know how to squeeze money from the popular music youth market. Norm N. Nite has been reaping royalties from superficial rock reference publications since he issued the initial volume of his three-volume opus *Rock On: The Illustrated Encyclopedia of Rock 'n' Roll–The Golden Years* (Thomas Crowell, 1974). The cumulative impact of such surface-riding studies is to diminish the historical significance of music in American society from 1950 to the present. That is too bad. It undermines the pioneering works of Simon Frith, R. Serge Denisoff, David Picaske, Peter Guralnick, Charles Hamm, George Carney, Howard DeWitt, and hundreds of other sociologists, historians, journalists, and popular music scholars. At best, these three books might spark the interest of a 12-year-old to listen to a Buddy Holly album, to read Chuck Berry's autobiography, or to roam through library stacks in search of Charlie Gillett's magnificent *Sound of the City*.


## FADS

*Panati's Parade of Fads, Follies, and Manias: The Origins of Our Most Cherished Obsessions.* By Charles Panati. New York: Harper Collins Publishers, 1991. Illustrated. 491 pp.

Without humility, popular culture researcher and master fad-finder Charles Panati describes himself as "the foremost specialist on everything." This is the ideal background for creating a decade-by-decade review of twentieth-century American fads, follies, and manias. Panati's clearly structured text features chapter-length commentaries on "Fads, Follies, and Trends," "Fairs and Expos," "Dance Crazes," "Popular Songs," and "Bestselling Books" from 1890 to 1990. "Radio Hits" are also examined for the 1930s and "Television Hits" are explored from the 1940s to the present. This is not just a book of lists, though. The author provides exceptionally detailed, thoughtful, readable descriptions for everything from "Jazz Age Jargon," "Goldfish Swallowing," "Zoot Suit with a Reet Pleat and a Peg Leg," and "Kilroy Was Here" to "Davey Crockett Hats," "I Love Lucy," "Macrame," and "Rubik's Cube."

The only recent volume that rivals Panati's work for detailed analysis of specific popular culture icons is *Arts and Entertainment Fads* (The Haworth Press, 1990) by Frank W. Hoffmann and William G. Bailey. This earlier study examines only 120 topics compared to more than 20 times that number of subjects in *Fads, Follies, and Manias*. However, Hoffmann and Bailey clearly outshine Panati by providing multiple bibliographic references for each entry, by cross-referencing all citations in an "Appendix," and by providing a thorough Index. It is unpardonable for the sagacious Panati to omit an alphabetized index for this otherwise magnificent resource guide.

An especially strong theoretical "Introduction" enables Panati to justify his interest in "A Century of Popular Culture" (pp. 1-8). The author notes that four themes repeatedly surface and commingle throughout his work: (1) The Pervasiveness of Popular Culture; (2) The Power of Nostalgia; (3) The Mass Appeal of Faddishness; and (4) Americans' Use of Leisure Time. Trends, crazes, manias, and luxuries became possible as the western frontier closed, as artistic individualism surfaced, as work days were standardized, as communication media improved and diversified, and as "the pursuit of happiness" became boundless. *Fads, Follies, and Manias* is a rollicking resource celebration for both research and casual reading. No one interested in American culture should miss this expansive study of facts and fun.

> *Handbook of American Popular Culture—Three Volumes* (second edition, revised and enlarged). Edited by M. Thomas Inge. Westport, Connecticut: Greenwood Press, 1989. 1,580 pp.

This exceptional bibliographic reference guide is a literary salute to Ray B. Browne and the academic popular culture movement that he initiated in 1967. It is ironic that M. Thomas Inge, a scholar of immense energy, creativity, and diversity, should produce an expanded version of his landmark 1978-1981 compilation in 1989. Earlier in the same year Browne issued *Against Academia: The History of the Popular Culture Association/American Culture Association and the Popular Culture Movement, 1967-1988*. The strange thing is that Inge's work, from the editor's brief but perceptive "Introduction" through the expansive, multitopic chapters, speaks more eloquently to Browne's far-reaching intellectual influence than does the Bowling Green professor's own organizational autobiography.

The *Handbook of American Popular Culture* is presented in 46 alphabetical chapters, beginning with "Advertising," "Almanacs," and "Animation" and ending with "Television," "Trains and Railroading," and "Women." There is also an appended essay on "The Study of Popular Culture." The contributors are decidedly academic in orientation. Their records of scholarly publication are awesome, and their geographical distribution throughout the United States demonstrates the national perspective that shapes this guide. While one might wish to suggest the addition of other dominant popular culture thinkers–J. Fred MacDonald (radio and television), Ron Denisoff (records and the record industry), Roger Rollin (popular culture theory), Gary Burns (film), Frank W. Hoffmann (music), and Norm Cohen (railroads)–it is difficult to challenge the quality of the essays produced by Inge's army of writers.

Each section of the *Handbook* is structured as a bibliographic essay. First, the writer succinctly defines the scope of his or her investigation; then a historical perspective is presented on the topic; next a popular culture image is established, with specific illustrations provided and events or leading personalities profiled; and finally, reference works are cited, research collections are identified, studies of history and criticism are surveyed, and a massive bibliography is provided. The thoroughness of each essay is truly remarkable.

Has Inge omitted anything from this revised edition of his original *Handbook*? Regrettably, he has. In the "Introduction" he explains that previously included topics such as comic books, detective and mystery novels, popular history and biography, science fiction, verse and popular poetry, westerns, and young adult fiction have been segregated into a separate volume titled *Handbook of American Popular Literature* (1988). This is a startling mistake. Inge should have continued to integrate these elements, even at the cost of producing a four-volume work. The impact of the revised 1989 *Handbook* is diminished by such segmentation. It is hard to imagine that inclusive popular culture thinkers such as Ray Browne, Russel B. Nye, or John Cawelti could look positively at such segmentation in a Handbook that initially championed cross-disciplinary thought. Browne's most fierce academic battles have been waged to break down the artificial departmental barriers between literature, history, science, and the arts. Hopefully, the 1999 edition of Inge's *Handbook* will be a five-volume triumph that includes not only pulp and dime novels, fantasy, children's literature, and Big Little Books, but also fads, stand-up comics, futurists, and even educational trends.

The $150 price tag for the *Handbook of American Popular Culture* may seem steep. Yet, no serious student of contemporary American civilization can afford to miss the bibliographic surveys provided in these three volumes. This is a sterling set of essays–a most fitting literary acknowledgment to the giant whose shoulders stills support the American popular culture movement: Ray B. Browne.

# REFERENCES

Aquila, Richard. *That Old Time Rock and Roll: A Chronicle of an Era, 1954-1963*. New York: Schirmer Books, 1989.

Betrock, Alan. *Hitsville:The 100 Greatest Rock 'n' Roll Magazines, 1954-1968*. Brooklyn, New York: Shake Books, 1991.

Bronson, Fred. *The Billboard Book of Number One Hits* (revised and enlarged edition). New York: Billboard Publications, Inc., 1988.

Clarke, Donald (ed.). *The Penguin Encyclopedia of Popular Music*. New York: Viking Penguin, Inc., 1989.

Cooper, B. Lee. "From Anonymous Announcer to Radio Personality, from Pied Piper to Payola: The American Disc Jockey, 1950-1970," *Popular Music and Society*, XIV (Winter 1990), pp. 89-95.

Cooper, B. Lee and Wayne S. Haney. *Response Recordings: An Answer Song Discography*. Metuchen, New Jersey: Scarecrow Press, Inc., 1990.

Curtis, Jim. *Rock Eras: Interpretations of Music and Society, 1954-1984*. Bowling Green, Ohio: Bowling Green State University Popular Press, 1987.

DeCurtis, Anthony and James Henke, with Holly George-Warren (eds.). *The Rolling Stone Illustrated History of Rock and Roll* (fully revised and updated). New York: Random House, 1992.

Hardy, Phil and Dave Laing. *The Faber Companion to 20th-Century Popular Music*. London: Faber and Faber, 1990.

Hoffmann, Frank W. and William G. Bailey. *Arts and Entertainment Fads*. Binghamton, New York: The Haworth Press, 1990.

Jancik, Wayne. *The Billboard Book of One-Hit Wonders*. New York: Billboard Books/Watson-Guptill Publications, 1990.

Larkin, Colin (ed.). *The Guinness Encyclopedia of Popular Music* (four volumes). Enfield, Middlesex, England: Guinness Superlatives, Ltd., 1993.

Lazell, Barry, with Dafydd Rees and Luke Crampton (eds.). *Rock Movers and Shakers: An A to Z of the People Who Made Rock Happen*. New York: Billboard Publications, Inc., 1989.

Nite, Norm N. (comp.). *Rock On Almanac: The First Four Decades of Rock 'n' Roll—A Chronology*. New York: Harper and Row, 1989.

Nite, Norm N. (comp.). *Rock On—The Illustrated Encyclopedia of Rock 'n' Roll: Volume One—The Solid Gold Years* (updated version). New York: Harper and Row, 1982.

Nite, Norm N., with Ralph M. Newman (comp.). *Rock On—The Illustrated Encyclopedia of Rock 'n' Roll: Volume Two—The Years of Change, 1964-1978* (updated edition). New York: Harper and Row, 1984.

Nite, Norm N., with Charles Crespo (comps.). *Rock On—The Illustrated Encyclopedia of Rock 'n' Roll: Volume Three—The Video Revolution, 1978 to the Present*. New York: Doubleday and Company, Inc., 1984.

Ochs, Michael. *Rock Archives: A Photographic Journey Through the First Two Decades of Rock and Roll*. New York: Doubleday and Company, Inc., 1984.

Pareles, Jon and Patricia Romanowski (eds.). *The Rolling Stone Encyclopedia of Rock and Roll*. New York: Rolling Stone Press/Summit Books, 1983.

Propes, Steve. *Golden Goodies: A Guide to 50's and 60's Popular Rock and Roll Record Collecting*. Radnor, Pennsylvania: Chilton Book Company, 1975.

Propes, Steve. *Golden Oldies But Goodies: A Guide to 50's Record Collecting*. New York: Colier Books, 1973.

Shannon, Bob and John Javna. *Behind the Hits: Inside Stories of Classic Pop and Rock and Roll*. New York: Warner Books, 1986.

Stambler, Irwin (comp.). *The Encyclopedia of Pop, Rock, and Soul* (revised edition). New York: St. Martin's Press, 1989.

Ward, Ed, Geoffrey Stokes, and Ken Tucker. *Rock of Ages: The Rolling Stone History of Rock and Roll*. New York: Rolling Stone Press/Summit Books, 1986.

Warner, Alan. *Who Sang What in Rock 'n' Roll: 500 Revered, Revived, and Much Recorded Songs From The Rock Era*. London: Blandford Press, 1990.

Whitburn, Joel (comp.). *Pop Memories, 1890-1954: The History of American Popular Music*. Menomonee Falls, Wisconsin: Record Research, Inc., 1986.

# Chapter 8

# Halloween

Sound recordings archivists cannot always predict patron requests. However, they should anticipate recurring audio needs. This is especially true in respect to annual requests related to religious celebrations, national holidays, or other special occasions. Numerous reports on recordings related to Christmastime are available. However, there are few systematic audio resource listings on events such as graduation day, birthday parties, anniversaries, Valentine's Day, April Fool's Day, or even Sweetest Day. Family members, disc jockeys, student council members, department store managers, husbands and wives, flower store owners, candy merchants, and other community members could benefit from knowing about such theme-related songs as "My Funny Valentine," "Happy, Happy Birthday Baby," "Sweets for My Sweet," and "What Are You Doing New Year's Eve?"

Halloween, the popular trick-or-treat festival that occurs every October 31st, is celebrated in numerous ways. The traditional creation of individually carved pumpkin faces has expanded and spawned a new industry of orange-faced leaf bags; the sharing of cookies with gaily dressed neighborhood children has become a ritual of candy distribution sanctioned by entire cities; and homemade prince, fireman, and clown costumes have been supplemented with Ninja Turtle, Batman, and Bart Simpson outfits purchased in city stores. Beyond orange vegetables, sweet treats, and costumes of workers and movie characters, Halloween is undeniably a world of sound. Squeals and whispers, shrieks and giggles, roars and screams—all of these vocalizations occur. Many families also play recordings of "scary" music, with occasional voice-over cries, to create the mood of fright on trick-or-treat night.

---

This essay by B. Lee Cooper was originally published as "A Haunting Question: Should Sound Recordings Archives Promote the Circulation of Horror Material?" *Popular Culture in Libraries*, I, No. 3 (1993), pp. 45-58. Reprint permission granted by the author, Editor Frank W. Hoffmann, and The Haworth Press.

Despite much Gothic imagery to the contrary, Halloween is an evening of comedy. The night of Count Dracula, Frankenstein's monster, the were-wolf, the mummy, and even Freddie Krueger is designed to provoke laughter rather than terror. The fun of the masquerade clearly supersedes feigned fright over masked ugliness. The thrill of the unexpected, the unanticipated is never designed to sustain uncomfortable feelings. "Boo!" elicits short fright, not danger. The torrent of laughter following a momentary scare is both a relief and a joy, as well as an anticipation of yet a better moment of startling surprise.

Haunting as humor is broadly illustrated throughout American commercial recordings. Archivists should recognize this fact. They should also join in the annual Halloween celebration by encouraging and contributing to the audio enjoyment beginning immediately after Labor Day. Archivists should circulate a detailed list of Halloween songs that are available for listening. Targets for this information can include television programmers, radio station managers, student activities directors, scout troop leaders, high school student council advisors, church youth group supervisors, and local theater managers. Each of these program planners might find the information and resources being suggested to be precisely the kind of audio Halloween fun they are seeking. Fun remains the central focus. But the sound recording archive can secure additional visibility, publicity, and even notoriety from sponsoring a special "Sounds of Halloween" program. The ultimate goal of this activity would be to raise the consciousness of community leaders about the location, audio resources, and the director of a year-round public service area. This entrepreneurial focus should make library work seem both responsive and flexible.

What specific kinds of Halloween-related sound recordings offer the laughter, the stories, and the music that will conjure the appropriate haunting feelings? The following discography features a variety of 45 rpm recordings. They are arranged in eight preselected themes that might suggest potential promotional ideas. Beyond the individual song titles listed below, a brief list of album-length compilations is also recommended.

### Casting Spells, Mixing Potions, and Practicing Voodoo

- "Black Magic Woman"
  (Columbia 45270)
  Santana (1970)

- "Castin' My Spell"
  (Capitol 4168)
  The Johnny Otis Show with Marci Lee (1959)

- "Got My Mojo Working"
(Chess 1962)
Muddy Waters (1956)

- "I Put a Spell on You"
(Okeh 7072)
Screamin' Jay Hawkins (1956)

- "I'm Your Hoochie Coochie Man"
(Chess 1560)
Muddy Waters (1954)

- "Ju Hand"
(MGM 13365)
Sam The Sham and the Pharaohs (1965)

- "Ju Woman"
(Columbia 45290)
Diane Kolby (1971)

- "Love Potion No. 9"
(United Artists 180)
The Clovers (1959)

- "Supernatural Voodoo Woman"
(Soul 35112)
The Originals (1974)

- "That Old Black Magic"
(Decca 29541)
Sammy Davis, Jr. (1955)

- "Under Your Spell Again"
(Imperial 66144)
Johnny Rivers (1965)

- "Voodoo"
(RCA 10127)
Screamin' Jay Hawkins (1975)

- "Voodoo Doll"
(A&M 1656)
Wild Cherry (1975)

- "Voodoo Magic"
(GRC 2033)
Wild Cherry (1975)

- "Voodoo Man"
  (Mercury 71266)
  The Del Vikings (1958)

- "Voodoo Woman"
  (Elektra 45670)
  Simon Stokes and the Nighthawks (1969)

- "Who Do You Love"
  (Swan 4162)
  The Sapphires (1964)

## Count Dracula and Other Vampires

- "Omar the Vampire"
  (Four Star 1016)
  The Hamburger Brothers (1975)

- "Screamin' Ball (at Dracula Hall)"
  (Roulette 1313)
  The Duponts (1958)

- "Vampire"
  (Triumph 54)
  The Bel-Aires (1963)

## Demons and Devils

- "The Devil"
  (Jeremiah 1011)
  Hoyt Axton (1981)

- "The Devil Went Down to Georgia"
  (Epic 507000)
  The Charlie Daniels Band (1979)

- "Devil's Son"
  (London 1047)
  The Rattles (1973)

- "Little Demon"
  (Okeh 7072)
  Screamin' Jay Hawkins (1956)

- "Lucifer"
  (Capitol 2748)
  Bob Seger System (1970)

### *Evil Behavior and Violence*

- "Bad, Bad Leroy Brown"
  (ABC 11359)
  Jim Croce (1973)

- "Bad to the Bone"
  (EMI-American 8140)
  George Thorogood and the Destroyers (1982)

- "Big Boy Pete"
  (Arvee 595)
  The Olympics (1960)

- "Crawlin' King Snake"
  (Modern 714)
  John Lee Hooker (1949)

- "Evil Ways"
  (Columbia 45069)
  Santana (1970)

- "I'm Bad"
  (Checker 842)
  Bo Diddley (1956)

- "I'm Ready"
  (Checker 1579)
  Muddy Waters (1954)

- "Lucretia MacEvil"
  (Columbia 45235)
  Blood, Sweat and Tears (1970)

- "Mack the Knife"
  (Atco 6147)
  Bobby Darin (1959)

- "Mean Woman Blues"
  (Monument 824)
  Roy Orbison (1963)

- "Polk Salad Annie"
  (Monument 1104)
  Tony Joe White (1969)

- "Ramblin' Gamblin' Man"
  (Capitol 2297)
  Bob Seger System (1968)

- "Smackwater Jack"
(Ode 66019)
Carole King (1971)

## *Fortune Tellers, Gypsies, and Tarot Cards*

- "Fortune Teller"
(World Pacific 77851)
The Hardtimes (1967)

- "Fortune Teller"
(Mini 644)
Benny Spellman (1962)

- "Fortuneteller"
(Del-Fi 4177)
Bobby Curtola (1962)

- "Fortune Telling Cards"
(MGM 11587)
Billy Eckstine (1953)

- "Gypsy Woman"
(ABC-Paramount 10241)
The Impressions (1961)

## *Ghosts, Goblins, and Haunted Houses*

- "Ghostbusters"
(Arista 9212)
Ray Parker, Jr. (1984)

- "Haunted House"
(Hi 2076)
Jumpin' Gene Simmons (1964)

- "The Haunted House of Rock"
(Jive 9031)
Whodini (1983)

- "Riders in the Sky (A Cowboy Legend)"
(RCA Victor 3411)
Vaughn Monroe and His Orchestra (1949)

## *Halloween*

- "Halloween"
  (Bellaire 113)
  The Friendly Ghosts

## *Monsters from Outer Space*

- "Martian Hop"
  (Chairman 4403)
  The Ran-Dells (1963)

- "The Purple People Eater"
  (MGM 12651)
  Sheb Wooley (1958)

- "The Purple People Eater Meets the Witch Doctor"
  (Mercury 71343)
  The Big Bopper (1958)

## *Motion Picture Monsters*

- "Addams Groove"
  (Capitol CS 44794)
  M. C. Hammer (1991)

- "Bo Meets the Monster"
  (Checker 1313)
  Bo Diddley (1958)

- "The Creature"
  (Flying Saucer 501)
  Buchanan and Ancell (1957)

- "Frankenstein"
  (Epic 10967)
  The Edgar Winter Group (1973)

- "Frankenstein of '59"
  (Novelty 301)
  Buchanan and Goodman, with Count Dracula (1959)

- "Frankenstein Returns (Part Two)"
  (Novelty 301)
  Buchanan and Goodman, with Count Dracula (1959)

- "King Kong–Part One"
  (Atlantic 3295)
  The Jimmy Castor Bunch (1975)

- "Monster Mash"
  (Garpax 44167)
  Bobby "Boris" Pickett and the Crypt-Kickers (1962)

- "Monsters' Holiday"
  (Garpax 44171)
  Bobby "Boris" Pickett and the Crypt-Kickers (1962)

- "Nightmare on My Street"
  (Jive 1124)
  D.J. Jazzy Jeff and the Fresh Prince (1988)

- "Theme from *Jaws*"
  (MCA 40439)
  John Williams (1975)

- "Theme from *King Kong* (Part One)"
  (20th Century 2325)
  Love Unlimited Orchestra (1977)

- "Thriller"
  (Epic 04364)
  Michael Jackson (1984)

## Snakes and Spiders

- "Rattlesnake Shake"
  (Reprise 860)
  Fleetwood Mac (1969)

- "The Snake"
  (Soul City 767)
  Al Wilson (1968)

- "Snake Charmer"
  (Federal 12336)
  The Puddle Jumpers (1958)

## Superstition and Bad Luck

- "Bad Luck"
  (Ariola 7611)
  Atlanta Disco Band (1976)

- "Bad Luck (Part One)"
  (Philadelphia International 3562)
  Harold Melvin and the Blue Notes (1975)

- "Bad Moon Rising"
  (Fantasy 622)
  Creedence Clearwater Revival (1969)

- "Born Under a Bad Sign"
  (Stax 217)
  Albert King (1967)

- "Good Luck Charm"
  (RCA 47-7992)
  Elvis Presley (1962)

- "I Ain't Superstitious"
  (Chess 1544)
  Howlin' Wolf (1961)

- "Superstition"
  (Tamla 54226)
  Stevie Wonder (1972)

- "Touch a Four-Leaf Clover"
  (A&M 2580)
  Atlantic Starr (1983)

## *Television Monsters*

- "The Blob"
  (Columbia 41250)
  The Five Blobs (1958)

- "Morgus the Magnificent"
  (Vin 1313)
  Morgus and The Ghouls (1959)

- "Out of Limits"
  (Warner Brothers 5391)
  The Marketts (1963)

## *Werewolves*

- "Fool Moon Fire"
  (Backstreet 52200)
  Walter Egan (1983)

- "Werewolf"
(Polydor 14221)
The Five Man Electrical Band (1974)

- "Werewolf"
(Dolton 16)
The Frantics (1960)

- "Werewolves of London"
(Asylum 45472)
Warren Zevon (1978)

## *Witches and Witchcraft*

- "Bewitched"
(RCA 8434)
Frankie Randall (1964)

- "Marie Laveau"
(RCA 10496)
Bobby Bare (1973)

- "Seasons of the Witch"
(Atco 6632)
Vanilla Fudge (1968)

- "Swamp Witch"
(MGM 14496)
Jim Stafford (1973)

- "The Witch"
(Probe 480)
The Rattles (1970)

- "The Witch"
(Jerden 810)
The Sonics (1966)

- "Witch Queen of New Orleans"
(Epic 10749)
Redbone (1971)

- "The Witch's Promise"
(Reprise 899)
Jethro Tull (1970)

- "Witchcraft"
(RCA 8243)
Elvis Presley (1963)

- "Witch Woman"
  (Asylum 11008)
  The Eagles (1972)

## Zombies, Ghouls, and Banshees

- "Eye of the Zombie"
  (Warner Brothers 28657)
  John Fogerty (1986)

- "Midnight Stroll"
  (Norgolde 103)
  The Revels (1959)

## Selected Discography of Albums and Compact Discs with Halloween Themes

- *Elvira Presents Haunted Hits: The Greatest Rock 'n' Roll Horror Songs of All Time!* (Ri-71492). Santa Monica, California: Rhino Records, 1988. Features Sheb Wooley, Dave Edmunds, The Jayhawks,The Ran-dells, LaVern Baker, The Cramps, The Tubes, and Screamin' Jay Hawkins.

- The Ghouls. *Dracula's Deuce* (ST 2215). Los Angeles, California: Capitol Records, n.d.

- Dickie Goodman. *Dickie Goodman's Greatest Hits* (RNLP 811). Santa Monica, California: Rhino Records, 1983.

- Screamin' Jay Hawkins. *Frenzy* (ED 104). London: Edsel Records, 1982.

- *I Was a Teenage Brain Surgeon!* (Hee). London: Hee Records, n.d. Features The Emersons, Jimmy Dee, Round Robin, Bobby Please, Bobby Bare, The Hollywood Flames, and Billy DeMarco with Count Dracula.

- Henry Mancini. *Mancini's Monster Hits* (RCA Victor CD 60577-2RV). New York: RCA Victor Corporation, 1990.

- Bobby "Boris" Pickett and the Crypt-Kickers. *The Original Monster Mash* (Deram CD 844-147-2). New York: Polygram Records, Inc., 1991 (c. 1962).

- Sam The Sham and the Pharaohs. *Their Second Album.* (E 4314). Hollywood, California: MGM Records, 1965.

- Alan Warner (comp.). *Monster Rock 'n' Roll Show* (DZS 050). Northridge, California: DCC Compact Classics, 1990. Features Bo Diddley, The Revels, Buchanan and Goodman, The Duponts, Johnny Fuller, Redbone, Johnny Otis, Howlin' Wolf, and Morgus and The Ghouls.

- John Williams. *Dracula* (MCA 3166). Universal City, California: MCA Records, 1979.

## REFERENCES

Addams, Charles. *My Crowd: The Original Addams Family and Other Ghoulish Creatures.* New York: Fireside Books/Simon and Schuster, 1991 (c.1970).
Antonicello, Louis. "Zacherle," *Goldmine*, No. 214 (October 7, 1988), pp. 67, 84.
Benton, Mike. *The Illustrated History of Horror Comics.* Dallas, Texas: Taylor Publishing, 1991.
Borst, Ronald V. *Graven Images: The Best of Horror, Fantasy, and Science Fiction Film Art.* New York: Grove Press, 1992.
Cicotte, Susan. "Screamin' Jay Hawkins," *DISCoveries*, III (October 1990), p. 24.
Cooper, B. Lee. "Having a Screaming Ball in Dracula's Hall," *Popular Music and Society*, XV (Spring 1991), pp. 103-105.
Cox, Stephen. *The Munsters: Television's First Family of Fright.* Chicago: Contemporary Books, 1989.
DeLuca, David. "The Mad, Mad Daddy of Cleveland Radio," *Cleveland Magazine*, (September 1984), pp. 82-85, 151-153.
Doherty, Thomas. "The Horror Teenpics," in *Teenagers and Teenpics: The Juvenilization of American Movies in the 1950s* (Boston: Unwin Hyman, 1988), pp. 142-178.
Douglas, Drake. *Horrors!* Woodstock, New York: Overlook Press, 1989 (c. 1967).
Flynn, John L. *Cinematic Vampires: The Living Dead on Film and Television from the Devil's Castle (1896) to Bram Stoker's Dracula (1992).* Jefferson, North Carolina: McFarland and Company, Inc., 1992.
Gelb, Jeff (ed.). *Shock Rock.* New York: Pocket Books, 1992.
Gifford, Denis (comp.). *Mad Doctors, Monsters, and Mummies: Lobby Cards Postcards from Hollywood Horrors!* London: H.C. Blossom, 1991.
Hill, Randal C. "Bobby 'Boris' Pickett," *Goldmine*, No. 220 (December 30, 1988), p. 25.
Jancik, Wayne. "John Zacherle—Dinner with Drac," in *One-Hit Wonders* (New York: Billboard Books, 1990), p. 42.
King, Stephen. *Danse Macabre.* New York: Everest House, 1981.
Larson, Gary. *The PreHistory of the Far Side: A 10th Anniversary Exhibit.* Kansas City, Missouri: Andrews and McMeel, 1989.
Matthews, Bunny. "New Orleans Ain't Afraid of No Ghosts," *Wavelength*, No. 48 (October 1984), pp. 16-19, 28.

Mercer, Kobena. "Monster Metaphors: Notes on Michael Jackson's 'Thriller,'" *Screen*, XXVII (January/February 1986), pp. 26-43.

Milberg, David A. "Oldies But Ghoulies: A Brief History of Halloween's Greatest Hits," *DISCoveries*, No. 65 (October 1993), pp. 125-127.

Neale, Steve. "Halloween: Suspense, Aggression, and the Look," *Framework*, XIV (Spring 1981), pp. 25-29.

Rathgeb, Douglas L. "Bogeyman from the ID: Nightmare and Reality in *Halloween* and *A Nightmare on Elm Street*," *Journal of Popular Film and Television*, XIX (Spring 1991), pp. 36-43.

Schultze, Quentin J., Roy M. Anker, James D. Batt, William D. Romanowski, John W. Worst, and Lambert Zuidervaart. "The Ghoul in the Closet: Understanding Horror Pictures," in *Dancing in the Dark: Youth, Popular Culture, and the Electronic Media* (Grand Rapids, Michigan: William B. Eerdmans Publishing Company, 1991), pp. 232-249.

Sevastakis, Michael. *Songs of Love and Death: The Classical American Horror Film of the 1930s*. Westport, Connecticut: Greenwood Press, 1993.

Shannon, Bob and John Javna. "Monster Mash—Bobby 'Boris' Pickett and The Crypt-Kickers," in *Behind the Hits: Inside Stories of Classic Pop and Rock and Roll* (New York: Warner Books, 1986), p. 115.

Skal, David J. *The Monster Show: A Cultural History of Horror*. New York: W.W. Norton and Company, 1993.

Spignesi, Stephen J. *The Shape Under the Sheet: The Complete Stephen King Encyclopedia*. Ann Arbor, Michigan: Popular Culture, Ink., 1991.

Stone, Gregory P. "Halloween and the Mass Child," *American Quarterly*, XI (Fall 1959), pp. 372-379.

Telotte, J. P. "Through a Pumpkin's Eye: The Reflexive Nature of Horror," in *American Horrors: Essays on the Modern American Horror Film*, edited by Gregory A. Waller (Urbana: University of Illinois Press, 1987), pp. 114-128.

Watson, Elena M. *Television Horror Movie Hosts: 68 Vampires, Mad Scientists, and Other Denizens of the Late-Night Airwaves Examined and Interviewed*. Jefferson, North Carolina: McFarland and Company, Inc., 1991.

Wilson, Gahan. . . . *And Then We'll Get Him!* New York: Richard Marek Publishers, 1978.

Wilson, Gahan. *Gahan Wilson's America*. New York: Simon and Schuster, 1985.

# Chapter 9

# Horror Films

## *SOUNDTRACK SOUNDS*

Alan Warner, *The Monster Rock 'n' Roll Show* (DZS-050). Northridge, California: DCC Compact Classics, Inc., 1990. 17 Songs.

My review copy of *The Monster Rock 'n' Roll Show* CD arrived on October 31, 1990. What a delightful Halloween treat! Creator/producer Alan Warner has compiled a unique collection of 17 classic monster, science fiction, and voodoo-related recordings and linked them with vintage radio commercials from several horror and sci-fi motion pictures. The audio collage works wonderfully.

The cumulative song/movie trailer image that emerges is for the most part a reprise of 1955-1963 pre-Beatlemania, pre-Vietnam, pre-psyche-delic, pre-Watergate America. Harmless fun and farce dominate. Memories of Boris Karloff, Bela Lugosi, and even Casper the Friendly Ghost rumble forth. The predictable nostalgia tunes on the album are: "Monster Mash" (1962), "Midnight Stroll" (1959), "Haunted House" (1959), "Castin' My Spell" (1959), and "The Purple People Eater" (1958). Surprise song inclusions are: "Bo Meets the Monster" (1958) by Bo Diddley, "Frankenstein of '59" (1959) by Buchanan and Goodman, "Franken-

---

The compact disc review by B. Lee Cooper was originally published as "Having a Screaming Ball in Dracula's Hall," *Popular Music and Society*, XV (Spring 1991), pp. 103-105. Reprint permission granted by the author, Editor R. Serge Denisoff, and Bowling Green State University Popular Press. The essay titled "Popular Music, Youth Culture, and Monsters: Adaptations of Horror Themes in American Commercial Recordings, 1956-1991," is scheduled to be published in *Popular Culture in Libraries*. Reprint permission granted by the author, Editor Frank W. Hoffmann, and The Haworth Press.

stein's Den" (1958) by The Hollywood Flames, "Screamin' Ball (at Dracula Hall)" (1958) by The Duponts, "Feast of the Mau Mau" (1969) by Screamin' Jay Hawkins, and "Morgus the Magnificent" (1959) by Morgus and the Ghouls. The highlighted films are universally atrocious–and hilarious. They range from *The Astro-Zombies, The Thing That Couldn't Die, The Amazing Colossal Man*, and *The Mummy* to *Blood of Dracula, 4-D Man,* and *I Was a Teenage Werewolf.*

The producer labels *The Monster Rock 'n' Roll Show* as ". . . a crazed excursion into monster mayhem!" But this 1990 compilation does not surpass the exceptional 1988 Rhino Records release *Elvira Presents Haunted Hits: The Greatest Rock 'n' Roll Horror Songs of All Time!* The curvaceous Mistress of the Dark presents a much broader selection of haunted (and haunting) tunes ranging from 1950s classics such as "The Blob" (1958), "I Put a Spell on You" (1956), and "The Creature" (n.d.) to contemporary rockers including "I Was a Teenage Werewolf" by The Cramps, "Dead Man's Party" by Oingo Boingo, and "Ghostbusters" by Ray Parker Jr. Elvira also features both motion picture and television horror songs. The small screen themes included are "Out Of Limits," "The Addams Family," and "Twilight Zone."

Between *The Monster Rock 'n' Roll Show* and *Elvira Presents Haunted Hits*, one would assume that every hoodoo, voodoo, horror, Frankenstein-mummy-Dracula-werewolf-witch-warlock-Martian invader-space fantasy record ever made had been located. Not so! In fact, so many major scary melodies are omitted that a third compilation is still needed. Perhaps that gothic wizard Ray B. Browne will authorize The Popular Press to issue its first compact disc. The title might be "Wild Bill Schurk Unearths Ghosts, Gory Goblins, and Gruesome Ghouls: A Bowling Green Collection of Dracula Discs and Vampire Vinyl." Among the recordings that should be featured on this new compilation are:

1. "Bad to the Bone" (1982) by George Thorogood and the Destroyers
2. "Black Magic Woman" (1970) by Santana
3. "Crawlin' King Snake" (1949) by John Lee Hooker
4. "The Creature" (1957) by Buchanan and Ancell
5. "Eye of the Zombie" (1986) by John Fogerty
6. "Fool Moon Fire" (1983) by Walter Egan
7. "Frankenstein" (1973) by The Edgar Winter Group
8. "The Haunted House of Rock" (1983) by Whodini
9. "I Put a Spell on You" (1968) by Creedence Clearwater Revival
10. "Jack the Ripper" (1963) by Link Wray
11. "King Kong–Part One" (1975) by The Jimmy Castor Bunch
12. "Love Potion No. 9" (1959) by The Clovers

13. "Monsters' Holiday" (1962) by Bobby "Boris" Pickett and The Crypt-Kickers
14. "Nightmare on My Street" (1988) by D.J. Jazzy Jeff and the Fresh Prince
15. "Omar the Vampire" (1975) by The Hamburger Brothers
16. "The Purple People Eater Meets the Witch Doctor" (1958) by The Big Bopper
17. "Riders in the Sky (A Cowboy Legend)" (1949) by Vaughn Monroe and His Orchestra
18. "Superstition" (1972) by Stevie Wonder
19. "Swamp Witch" (1973) by Jim Stafford
20. "Thriller" (1984) by Michael Jackson
21. "Vampire" (1963) by The Bel-Aires
22. "Voodoo" (1975) by Screamin' Jay Hawkins
23. "Werewolf" (1960) by The Frantics
24. "Werewolves of London" (1978) by Warren Zevon
25. "Who Do You Love?" (1964) by The Sapphires

Fans of novelty recordings, students of popular culture, and film soundtrack analysts will enjoy and benefit from Alan Warner's *Monster Rock 'n' Roll Show*. There is no other comedy/horror/sci-fi audio resource on the market that can match the multimedia approach of this DCC Compact Classics production. No Halloween party should be without this playful, playable recording.

## YOUTH CULTURE AND MONSTERS

During the Eisenhower Administration, the sociological, economic, and demographic phenomenon of the youth culture made its influence felt throughout the United States. Mass media responded swiftly. Discretionary dollars of youthful consumers were especially significant in stimulating the production of age-targeted print, audio, and video commodities. Gothic horror writers Mary Shelley, Bram Stoker, Robert Louis Stevenson, and Edgar Allan Poe and horror film stars Boris Karloff, Lon Chaney Jr., Bela Lugosi, and King Kong provided the popular culture foundation for burgeoning youth interest in monsters during the 1950s and after. Commercial recordings, the bastion of adolescent influence since rock 'n' roll emerged, have reflected the continuing fascination of American youngsters with images, characters, sounds, and situations related to the horror genre. This study examines 35 years of songs–from "I Put a Spell on You" by Screamin' Jay Hawkins (1956) to "The Addams Groove" by

Hammer (1991)–and suggests that comedy rather than terror is the key attracting element among youthful listeners. More than 150 recordings are cited within the text, and an extensive reference list of 200 books and articles is also provided.

From the Wicked Witch who sought to fatten Hansel and Gretel before devouring them, to the Terrible Troll that dwelt beneath the bridge in "The Three Billy Goats Gruff," horror stories have been a staple of childhood fantasy. The annual charade of Halloween night reinforces joyful fright. Ghosts prowl from house to house threatening make-believe mayhem; skeletons dance gleefully on elementary schoolroom walls, and neighbors sport fiendish masks, cloaks, and funny rubber monster hands designed to unnerve even the most experienced trick-or-treaters. Newsstands bristle with horrific periodicals such as *Tales from the Crypt* comics and *Famous Monsters of Filmland* journals, while bookstores abound with scary volumes by Stephen King. Adolescent television film viewing runs the gamut from monster classics such as *King Kong* (1933), *Frankenstein* (1931), *Dracula* (1931), and *The Wolf Man* (1941) to more recent horror flicks including *Halloween* (1978), *Alien* (1979), *Amityville Horror* (1979), *Friday the 13th* (1980), *A Nightmare on Elm Street* (1984), and *The Addams Family* (1991). Cable television has capitalized on youthful fascination with ghouls, goblins, and vampires to make late-night weekend programming a continuing collage of Friday the 13th, Mardi Gras, insane asylums, Halloween, graveyards, and sinister laboratories where mad scientists concoct lethal potions and create abnormal beings to conquer the world. Even daily comic pages in local newspapers feature sardonic observations from the macabre characters of Olson and Kelso's "Horrorscope" to Gary Larson's "Far Side."

Many hypotheses have been advanced concerning youthful involvement with horror. Few writers acknowledge the most uncomplicated reason, though. It is simply fun to be frightened for a moment. The unsettling instant is a magnificent, electric jolt from the predictable present. Visions of confronting a one-eyed creature, of being captured by a gigantic demon, or of opening the tomb of a cursed mummy constitute harmless childhood escapes from daily chores, repetitive schoolwork, or other mundane household experiences. This is not to deny the potential creedence of numerous psychoanalytic theories concerning youthful fascination with terror. It simply acknowledges that American popular culture has made horror a universally acceptable feature of childhood. The following pages examine five decades of audio terror. True to the nature of its youthful audience, popular recordings utilizing the horror genre are typically brief, lively, animated, humorous, absurd, disrespectful toward adult authority, multimedia in characterization, and generally without redeeming aesthetic or social value. To adult listeners, these records are at best silly novelty songs and at worst mindless nonsense. Nevertheless, the ubiquity of monster themes in popular recordings is undeniable. Seeking patterns within the panoply of such recordings helps to clarify the youthful perspective on horror imagery.

> I took my baby to a horror show,
> That's the only place she wants to go.
> She thinks that Dracula is so divine,
> She wants to go steady with Frankenstein.
> She's mad about the monster from outer space,
> She thinks that he's got the cutest face.
> Everytime I try to hold her hand,
> She says she'd rather have a Martian man.
> My baby loves the monster movies . . .

—"Horror Movies"

> I heard her cry,
> The reactor flared.
> She grew and grew,
> I freaked and stared.
> Attack of the fifty-foot woman,
> Our love was at an end.
> All she did to get her kicks,
> Was step on all the men.
> I had to run to save my skin . . .

—"Attack of the Fifty-Foot Woman"

> Then I heard a noise,
> It sounded like great big feet.
> Then I thought about this monster,
> That craved on human meat.
> Was it the creature from the black lagoon?
> Was it the creature called Frankenstein?
> Was it the creature called Wolfman?
> Well, then it must have been that . . . Thing!

—"The Creature"

## THE ROOTS
## OF ROCK 'N' HORROR RECORDINGS

Between 1931 and 1956, horror was primarily a field of adult consumption. Drawn largely from Gothic literature and romantic poetry, the bizarre figures created by Mary Shelley, Bram Stoker, and Robert Louis Stevenson stalked into the American cinema. *Frankenstein* (1931), *Dracula* (1931), *The Mummy* (1932), and *The Werewolf of London* (1935) were films that became the visual essence of early twentieth-century terror. The stars of these horror pictures–Boris Karloff, Bela Lugosi, Henry Hull, and Lon Chaney Jr.–became monster legends. For a quarter century the ideas of suspense, blood-curdling fear, and back-from-the-grave tension were embodied in scenes, characterizations, and plots from these classic characters.

In 1956 significant changes began to occur in monster movies. Actually, greater changes were occurring in the audiences for horror films. The demographic bubble of post-World War II customers began to dominate Saturday matinee theatre business. The response of Universal Pictures and American International in Hollywood, Hammer Films in Great Britain, and the fledgling Toho Studios in Japan was to produce and distribute numerous horror/monster/science fiction films for the expanding adolescent ticket-buying market. These efforts included such diverse releases as *The Creature Walks Among Us* (1956), *Godzilla–King of the Monsters* (1956), *It Conquered The World* (1956), *Blood of Dracula* (1958), *Rodan the Flying Monster* (1957), *Dracula* (1958), *The Fly* (1958), *How to Make a Monster* (1958), and *Revenge of Frankenstein* (1958). During the same period, Hollywood permitted its small screen rival to utilize the classic black-and-white Karloff/Lugosi/Chaney films to fill late evening or weekend programming slots. Once such televised terror was judged to be acceptable, the gates were open for new programming ranging from *The Twilight Zone* (1959-1964) to *The Addams Family* (1964-1966), from *The Outer Limits* (1963-1965) to *The Munsters* (1964-1966).

The emergence of the horror genre in American mass media has been well chronicled. Literature, pulp magazines, comic books, films, radio programs, and television shows have been cited, examined, compared and contrasted, praised or condemned, and categorized for future reference. Audiences for multimedia horror imagery have been investigated by age, gender, and race; they have been psychoanalyzed, socially criticized, and morally discredited. In short, only the most naive doctoral candidate would attempt to pursue an A-to-Z literature search on the hefty field of horror criticism. The monumental volume of commentaries on Dracula alone is enough to stagger all but the most devoted vampirophiles.

What is missing from the study of the late twentieth-century horror motif in America? Somehow, the adaptation of monsters to musical imagery has escaped the notice of most researchers, writers, and social analysts. If there were only one or two modern songs that borrowed ideas from Gothic scenes, then such scholarly silence on lyrical information would be understandable. But when discographic evidence reveals that there is a 35-year treasure trove of lyrical attitudes, observations, stories, images, ideas, and feelings drawn directly from and clearly related to the horror genre, it is unthinkable that researchers would continue to ignore tunes of terror. Even a preliminary excursion into the realm of recent commercial recordings reflects audience acceptance of monster heroes and villains, of Gothic situations and scenery, of suspense/surprise/fright as wonderful illusion, and of being "scared" as a stimulating, joyful event. Rather than being defined as delinquents, deviants, deadheads, dopers, drunks, or demons, America's youthful record-buying audience for horror-related vinyl and cassette tapes should be viewed as fun-seeking adolescents who assess the escapism of horror as culturally reasonable, personally enjoyable, and communal. From Edgar Allan Poe to Stephen King, horror resonates with potential for improving perceptions of self, others, and an unknown future. The strength to accept aliens, the confidence to defy authority, and the courage to promote change within ethical boundaries are valuable lessons to be learned from any popular culture source.

## *The Singers on Horror Recordings*

You hear him howlin' around your kitchen door,
You'd better not let him in.
Little old lady got mutilated late last night,
Werewolves of London again. . . . . . .

He's the hairy-handed gent,
Who ran amok in Kent,
And lately he's been overheard in Mayfair.
You'd better stay away from him,
He'll rip your lungs out, Jim,
I'd like to meet his tailor. . .

—"Werewolves of London" (1978)

Frankenstein was first in line,
And the wolf man came up next.
Dracula was a'doin' his stuff,
A breathin' down my neck.

Jump back, make tracks,
Here comes the hunchback,
Better get outa his way.
Fee fee, fi fi, fo fo, fum,
It was a monster's holiday.

—"(It's a) Monster's Holiday" (1974)

All you would-be monsters come on in,
Boris is gonna show you how to monster swim.
It's something like the Zombie,
But not so slow.
A lot like the Gravediggers,
But not so low.
Can't do the Monkey,
Or even the Dog,
They've both been eaten by the Blob . . .

—"The Monster Swim" (1964)

### Chronology of Selected Mass-Media Resources
### Featuring Horror Sounds and Personalities
### Used in Commercial Recordings, 1931-1991

| Year | Motion Pictures | Radio Programs | Television Shows |
|------|-----------------|----------------|------------------|
| 1931 | Dracula<br>Frankenstein | The Shadow<br>(1931-1956) | |
| 1932 | Mummy<br>White Zombie | | |
| 1933 | Ghoul<br>Invisible Man<br>King Kong | | |
| 1935 | Bride of Frankenstein<br>Werewolf of London | | |
| 1936 | | The Hermit's Cave<br>(1936-19??) | |
| 1938 | | The Mercury Theatre<br>on the Air<br>(1938-1940) | |
| 1939 | | Lights Out<br>(1939-1950) | |
| 1941 | Hunchback of Notre Dame<br>Son of Frankenstein | | |

| Year | Motion Pictures | Radio Programs | Television Shows |
|------|-----------------|----------------|------------------|
| 1942 | Ghost of Frankenstein | Suspense (1942-1962) | |
| 1943 | Frankenstein Meets the Wolf Man Return of the Vampire | Superstition (1943-1946) | |
| 1944 | House of Frankenstein Mummy's Curse | The Strange Dr. Weird (1944-1947) | |
| 1945 | House of Dracula | | |
| 1947 | Abbott and Costello Meet Frankenstein | | |
| 1949 | | | Lights Out (1949-1952) |
| 1950 | | Escape (1949-1954) | |
| 1951 | The Thing | | Tales of Tomorrow (1951-1953) |
| 1953 | Beast from 20,000 Fathoms House of Wax War of the Worlds | | |
| 1954 | Creature from the Black Lagoon Phantom of the Rue Morgue Them! | | |
| 1955 | Abbott and Costello Meet the Mummy Revenge of the Creature | | Alfred Hitchcock Presents (1955-1964) |
| 1956 | Forbidden Planet Godzilla–King of the Monsters Invasion of the Body Snatchers | | |
| 1957 | Amazing Colossal Man Curse of Frankenstein Hunchback of Notre Dame I Was a Teenage Werewolf Rodan–The Flying Monster | | |
| 1958 | Attack of the 50-Foot Woman The Blob Dracula The Fly I Married a Monster from Outer Space Monster on the Campus | | |

| Year | Motion Pictures | Radio Programs | Television Shows |
|------|-----------------|----------------|------------------|
| 1959 | Gigantis–The Fire Monster<br>Teenagers from Outer Space | | One Step Beyond<br>(1959-1961) |
| 1960 | Brides of Dracula<br>Little Shop of Horrors<br>Psycho | | Thriller<br>(1960-1962) |
| 1961 | Curse of the Werewolf<br>Pit and the Pendulum | | |
| 1963 | The Birds | | Outer Limits<br>(1963-1965) |
| 1964 | Evil of Frankenstein | | Addams Family<br>(1964-1966)<br>Munsters<br>(1964-1966) |
| 1966 | | | King Kong<br>(1966-1969) |
| 1968 | Night of the Living Dead<br>Rosemary's Baby | | |
| 1970 | | | Rod Serling's Night<br>Gallery<br>(1970-1973) |
| 1972 | | | Gargoyles |
| 1973 | The Exorcist | | Frankenstein |
| 1974 | Texas Chainsaw Massacre<br>Young Frankenstein | | Dracula<br>Kolchak: The Night<br>Stalker<br>The Strange Case<br>of Dr. Jekyll<br>and Mr. Hyde |
| 1975 | Jaws<br>Rocky Horror Picture Show | | |
| 1976 | King Kong<br>The Omen | | |
| 1978 | Halloween<br>Invasion of the Body<br>Snatchers | | Count Dracula<br>Devil Dog |
| 1979 | Alien<br>Amityville Horror<br>Dawn of the Dead<br>Dracula<br>The Fog<br>Love at First Bite<br>Nosferatu the Vampire | | |

| Year | Motion Pictures | Radio Programs | Television Shows |
|------|-----------------|----------------|------------------|
| 1980 | Altered States<br>Friday the 13th<br>The Shining | | |
| 1981 | An American Werewolf<br>in London<br>The Howling | | |
| 1982 | The Thing | | |
| 1983 | The Hunger | | |
| 1984 | Ghostbusters<br>A Nightmare on Elm<br>Street | | |
| 1985 | Silver Bullet | | |
| 1987 | Lost Boys | | |
| 1988 | Alien Nation<br>Elvira—Mistress of the Dark | | |
| 1989 | The Fly II<br>Pet Sematary | | |
| 1991 | The Addams Family<br>Cape Fear<br>Silence of the Lambs | | Dark Shadows |

The Beatles adapted their name from Buddy Holly's group, The Crickets; the Rolling Stones borrowed their moniker from the title of a popular Muddy Waters' song. Many artists who perform horror tunes elect their group names or individual pseudonyms to identify their commitment to demonic lyrical faire. Of course, others just enjoy utilizing a weird or creepy sobriquet. Among the more fascinating creations are: The Zombies, Screaming Lord Sutch, Count Dracula, Vampire State Building, The Crypt-Kickers, The Five Blobs, Green Slime, Morgus and the Ghouls, Jack the Ripper, Igor and the Maniac, Tony's Monstrosities, Ho Ho Laughing Monster, Ding and Bat, King Horror, The Diablos, and The Grateful Dead.

Beyond horror-related group names, there are a variety of peripheral performers, not necessarily singers, who have stimulated public interest in audio ghoulishness. Pete "Mad Daddy" Meyers of Cleveland radio station WHK-AM stirred up a bubbling pot of wavy gravy and utilized his haunting laughter to promote macabre music and nightly mayhem during the late 1950s. Wolfman Jack Smith, whose legend was enhanced by The Guess Who tune "Clap for the Wolfman" (1974), employed a growling tone to spin pop songs for a popular New York radio station. He also recorded an album titled *Wolfman Jack* (Wooden Nickel Records, 1972) that featured tunes such as "Hoodooin' of Miss Fanny DeBerry," "Evil Woman," and "Hey Wolfman." Monster movie programming on late-night television has invariably featured a spectrum of striking characters with personas related to the horror medium. One of Cleveland's raucous midnight hosts was named Ghoulardi, while Los Angeles horror film addicts were entertained by the voluptuous Mistress of the Dark–Elvira. The latter also recorded a song titled "Full Moon" for her anthology *Elvira Presents Haunted Hits* (Rhino Records, 1988). The earliest recorded salute to a local television personality is the New Orleans classic "Morgus the Magnificent" (1959). This tongue-in-cheek performance, attributed to Morgus and the Three Ghouls on the Vin label, was actually performed by several notable Crescent City rockers–Frankie Ford, Mac Rebennack (a.k.a. Dr. John), Jerry Byrne, and The Huey Smith band.

The three most famous exponents of horror tunes are inevitably more laughable than frightening, though. It is ironic that each parlayed a single song into an entire career of ghoulish delight. These premiere recording demons are John "The Cool Ghoul" Zacherle, Bobby "Boris" Pickett, and Jalacy "Screamin' Jay" Hawkins. Zacherle hosted horror movies for Philadelphia television station WCAU during the late fifties under the relatively passive pseudonym "Roland." Translating the horror medium from film to vinyl was especially successful for Zacherle, whose "Dinner with Drac" (1958) rose to Number 6 on the *Billboard* charts during a 13-week run of sales. After his brief singing success, Zacherle returned to disc jockey work for New York radio station WPLJ-FM. But "Dinner with Drac" returns each Halloween as an acclaimed novelty monster hit. Pickett, backed by The Crypt-Kickers (Leon Russell, Johnny MacCrea, Rickie Page, and Gary Paxton), produced a similarly famous and more frequently charted tune titled "Monster Mash" (1962). The original release hit Number 1 on the *Billboard* charts curing a 14-week run; it resurfaced again in December 1962, yet again in August 1970, and made a final chart appearance for 20 weeks in May 1973. "Monster Mash" may be the most recognizable of all novelty horror tunes. The undeniable king of voodoo/horror/macabre singers is the deep-voiced Screamin' Jay Hawkins. From the original impact of his drunken, shouting record "I Put a Spell on You" (1956) through other minor successes with "Little Demon" (1956), "Alligator Wine" (1958), and "Feast of the Mau Mau" (1969), this bizarre singer has conjured a performing career of sustained frenzy. His stage ritual includes emerging from a fog-enshrouded coffin, flaying his arms to extend his floor-length black and red cape, talking to a skull, and elevating his voice to levels that would challenge an Atlantic coastal foghorn. Hawkins' Dracula persona is especially fearsome when combined with the wild gestures, speed-driven lyrics, grunts, groans, and moans, and the rolling eyes of a man who appears to be truly possessed. Zacherle, Pickett, and Hawkins embody the essence of horror recording during its golden age.

## Songs of Horror

The Zombies were having fun,
The party had just begun.
The guests included Wolfman,
Dracula and his son.

—"Monster Mash" (1962)

We don't go out to roll and rock,
We get our kicks from "The House Of Shock."
He's got shaggy hair,
And a graveyard stare,
Vampire blood spilled everywhere.
That's . . . Morgus the Magnificent!

—"Morgus the Magnificent" (1959)

Waiting for an invitation to arrive,
Going to a party where no one's still alive . . .
It's a dead man's party
Who could ask for more?
Everybody's comin',
Leave your body at the door.

—"Dead Man's Party" (n.d.)

There is a distinction that can be made between songs of terror and fright and monster-related horror tunes. This bipolar pattern is significant to understanding the difference between popular music realism in commenting on human acts of violence, mayhem, and murder and the fantasy of youth culture horror recordings. Traditionally, song lyrics have employed biblical or zoological images to communicate the essence of fear, threat, and evil incarnate. The Satanic theme is particularly common between 1956 and 1991. Such diverse artists as Merle Haggard, Golden Earring, Bobby Vee, Terry Gregory, Van Halen, and Gene Vincent have issued recordings with titles such as "Dealing with the Devil" (1982), "The Devil Made Me Do It" (1983), "Devil or Angel" (1960), "I Never Knew the Devil's Eyes Were Blue" (1982), "Runnin' with the Devil" (1978), and "Race with the Devil" (1956). Reptiles tend to dominate the lyrical fright scene. Performers such as Screamin' Jay Hawkins, Howlin' Wolf, and Al Wilson wailed songs like "Alligator Wine" (1958), "New Crawlin' King Snake" (1966), and "The Snake" to communicate human meanness, evil, and propensity toward lethal behavior.

Metaphors and anthropomorphic imagery aside, violence and fearsome characters are a staple of commercial American recordings. Descriptions of individuals who are "Evil" (1969) and "Bad to the Bone" (1982) are common. Malevolent males are depicted in "Bad, Bad Leroy Brown" (1973), "Big Boy Pete" (1960), "Mack the Knife" (1959), "Maxwell's Silver Hammer" (1969), "Ramblin' Gamblin' Man" (1958), and "Smackwater Jack" (1971); fierce and ferocious females are described in "Devil Woman" (1962, 1976), "Lizzie Borden" (1962), "Louisiana Anna" (1983), "Lucretia MacEvil" (1970), "Lucy and the Stranger" (1982), "Marie Laveau" (1973), "Mary Lou" (1959), "Polk Salad Annie" (1969), and the "Swamp Witch" (1973). The madness and mayhem attributed to such individuals is often related to personal delusion. Superstition can be a powerful agent in prompting unexplainable behavior or in determining bad moods. Curses, spells, or even elixirs are lyrical imperatives for unnatural or unpredictable performances. This phenomena is detailed in lyrics from "Bad Moon Rising" (1969), "Black Magic Woman" (1970), "Born Under a Bad Sign" (1967), "Castin' My Spell" (1959), "Got My Mojo Working"(1956), "I Ain't Superstitious" (1961), "Love Potion No. 9" (1959), "Superstition" (1972), "Under Your Spell Again" (1965), "Voodoo" (1975), "Who Do You Love" (1964), "Witch Queen of New Orleans" (1971), and "Witchy Woman" (1972).

### Selected Illustrations of Horror Songs that Parody Melodies and Rhythms of *Billboard*-Charted Hit Songs, 1961-1964

| Horror Song and Artist | Hit Song and Artist |
|---|---|
| "Let's Twist Again" John Zacherle | "Let's Twist Again (Mummy Time Is Here)" Chubby Checker (1961) |
| "Gravy (with Some Cyanide)" John Zacherle | "Gravy (for My Mash Potatoes)" Dee Dee Sharp (1962) |
| "Weird Watusi" John Zacherle | "Wah Watusi" The Orlons (1962) |
| "The Monster Swim" Bobby "Boris" Pickett and the Rolling Stones | "S-W-I-M" Bobby Freeman (1964) |

Unlike tunes of bedevilment or psychotic malevolence, horror songs, though highly variable in theme and content, tend to be especially identifiable through comic delivery. Parody is common. So is the introduction of random absurdity. The blending of characters and creatures from horror genre with contemporary social events (dining and dancing or distinct political situations) is a standard lyrical practice. Just as the shouted command "Hi Ho, Silver!" has forever transformed a generation's association with the *William Tell Overture*, music themes from fright classics hold continuing sway over imaginations and memories long after specific visual patterns have subsided. "The Addams Family (Main Title)" (1964) by Vic Mizzy will survive even the recent "Addams Groove" (1991) challenge by Hammer. Other readily identifiable horror themes include "Ghostbusters" (1984), "The Munsters" (1964), "Out of Limits" (1963), "Theme from *Jaws*" (1975), "Theme from *King King* (Part One)," "Tubular Bells" (1974) from *The Exorcist*, and "Twilight Zone" (1959).

Themes from soundtracks are sometimes adapted as background music for novelty horror creations. But the nominal honoring of classic horror creatures remains the central identifying factor. It is suspicious, though, that so many monsters appear to share with their teenage audience a strong penchant for dancing. Bobby "Boris" Pickett and the Crypt-Kickers released recordings lauding the following graveyard shuffles: "Monster Mash" (1962), "Monster Mash Party" (1962), "Monster Minuet" (1962), "Monster Motion" (1962), "The Monster Swim" (1964), "Sinister Stomp" (1962), "Skully Gully" (1962), "Transylvania Twist" (1962), and "The Werewolf Watusi" (1964). Both preceding and following this early 1960s deluge, many other performers sought to define dance macabre in rock 'n' roll terms. John Zacherle promoted "Let's Twist Again (Mummy Time Is Here)" (n.d.) and "Weird Watusi" (n.d.); The Ran-Dells described a "Martian Hop" (1963); The Revels described dead men doing the "Midnight Stroll" (1969); and Johnny Winter concocted the "Voodoo Twist" (1964). The DuPonts were apparently correct. Everyone can enjoy a "Screamin' Ball (at Dracula Hall)" (1958).

Monsters, both humanoid and alien, remain the focus for horror humor in recorded song. Mixing science fiction with Gothic fantasy has proven to be successful for both motion picture moguls and contemporary recording artists from the 1950s to the present. Examples of such lyrical blending include "The Purple People Eater" (1958), "The Purple People Eater Meets the Witch Doctor" (1958), "The Eggplant That Ate Chicago" (1966), "The Green Slime" (1969), "Slime Creatures from Outer Space" (1985), and "Attack of the Radio Active Hamsters from a Planet Near Mars" (1989). Penned by pop composer Burt Bacharach, "The Blob"

(1958) is perhaps the epitome of combined sci-fi/horror humor songs. Nevertheless, the classic monsters–Frankenstein, Dracula, the Mummy, King Kong, the Werewolf (or Wolf Man), plus the famous finned 1950s Creature from the Black Lagoon–remain interchangeable personas on novelty horror discs. Salutes to the green menace from the Black Lagoon include "The Creature" (1957), "Meet the Creature" (1957), "The Creature from the Black Lagoon" (n.d.), and "The Monster Gets Mark" (1990). Similar praises are provided for the giant Simian resident of Skull Island in "King Kong" (n.d.), "King Kong–Part One" (1975), "King Song (Your Song)" (1976), and "Kong" (1977). While the Mummy and Dracula are mentioned in numerous horror recordings, they are featured in only a few titles: "The Mummy" (1959), "Me and My Mummy" (1962), "Dinner with Drac" (1958), "Vampire" (1963), and "Omar the Vampire" (1975). The Monster created by galvanic shock is depicted in "Frankenstein's Den" (1958), "Frankenstein Of '59," "Frankenstein Returns" (1959), and the instrumental rocker "Frankenstein" (1973). The snarling, howling victim of lycanthropy is included in numerous song titles over the past 35 years. These include: "Werewolf" (1960), "Werewolf" (1974), "Werewolves of London" (1978), "Fool Moon Fire" (1983), "I Was a Teenage Werewolf" (n.d.), and "Wolfman" (1990).

### Chronology of Selected Commercial Recordings with Lyric References to Horror-Related Characters and Themes, 1956-1991

| Year | Title | Artist |
|------|-------|--------|
| 1956 | I Put a Spell on You | Screamin' Jay Hawkins |
| 1957 | The Creature | Buchanan and Ancell |
| 1958 | The Blob | Five Blobs |
| | Dinner with Drac | John Zacherle |
| | Frankenstein's Den | Hollywood Flames |
| | The Purple People Eater | Sheb Wooley |
| | The Purple People Eater Meets the Witch Doctor | Joe South |
| | Screamin' Ball (at Dracula Hall) | Duponts |
| 1959 | Frankenstein of '59 | Buchanan and Goodman, with Count Dracula |
| | Frankenstein Returns (Part II) | Buchanan and Goodman |
| | Haunted House | Johnny Fuller |
| | Midnight Stroll | Revels |
| | Morgus the Magnificent | Morgus and the Ghouls |
| | The Mummy | McFadden and Dor |
| | Twilight Zone | Neil Norman and His Cosmic Orchestra |

| 1960 | Werewolf | Frantics |
| 1961 | I Ain't Superstitious | Howlin' Wolf |
| 1962 | Monster Mash | Bobby "Boris" Pickett |
| | Monster's Holiday | Bobby "Boris" Pickett |
| 1963 | Out of Limits | Marketts |
| | Spooky Movies | Gary Paxton |
| | Vampire | Bel-Aires |
| 1964 | The Addams Family (main title) | Vic Mizzy |
| | Haunted House | Jumpin' Gene Simmons |
| | The Munsters | Vic Mizzy |
| | Who Do You Love? | Sapphires |
| 1965 | I Put a Spell on You | Nina Simone |
| 1966 | The Eggplant That Ate Chicago | Dr. West's Medicine Show and Junk Band |
| 1967 | Born Under a Bad Sign | Albert King |
| 1968 | I Put a Spell on You | Creedence Clearwater Revival |
| 1969 | Feast of the Mau Mau | Screamin' Jay Hawkins |
| | The Green Slime | Green Slime |
| | I Put a Spell on You | Crazy World of Arthur Brown |
| 1971 | Witch Doctor of New Orleans | Redbone |
| 1972 | Superstition | Stevie Wonder |
| 1973 | Frankenstein | Edgar Winter Group |
| | Monster Mash | Bobby "Boris" Pickett |
| | Swamp Witch | Jim Stafford |
| 1974 | Clap for the Wolfman | Guess Who |
| | Werewolf | Five Man Electrical Band |
| 1975 | King Kong (Part One) | Jimmy Castor Bunch |
| | Omar the Vampire | Hamburger Brothers |
| | Voodoo | Screamin' Jay Hawkins |
| 1976 | King Kong (Your Song) | Bobby "Boris" Pickett and Peter Ferara |
| 1977 | Kong | Dickie Goodman |
| | Theme from King Kong, Part 1 | Love Unlimited Orchestra |
| 1978 | Werewolves of London | Warren Zevon |
| 1982 | Bad to the Bone | George Thorogood and the Destroyers |
| 1983 | Fool Moon Fire | Walter Egan |
| 1984 | Ghostbusters | Ray Parker, Jr. |
| | Thriller | Michael Jackson |

| 1985 | Slime Creatures from Outer Space | Weird Al Yankovic |
|------|----------------------------------|-------------------|
| 1986 | Eye of the Zombie | John Fogerty |
| 1988 | Nightmare on My Street | D.J. Jazzy Jeff and the Fresh Prince |
| 1989 | Attack of the Radioactive Hamsters from a Planet Near Mars | Weird Al Yankovic |
| 1990 | The Monster Gets Mark | Henry Mancini Pops Orchestra |
| 1991 | Addams Groove | Hammer |

The magnitude of recordings confronting horror themes exceeds any artificial bounds of terror taxonomy. The use of Vincent Price's spoken rhyme of ghoulish dread in Michael Jackson's "Thriller" (1984) is a clear salute to Price's Bram Stoker/Edgar Allan Poe adaptations of the 1950s and 1960s. Ghosts and the demonic possession of physical structures are heralded in the two charted versions of "Haunted House" (1959, 1964). The melding of the Yuletide season and the gathering of a ghoulish gaggle of fiends, foes, and forbidden spirits is lauded in "Monsters' Holiday" (1962). The sounds of midnight madness and dread of the undead are featured on John Fogerty's startling "Eye of the Zombie" (1986). Finally, the rejection of cut-and-slash terror of the Freddie Krueger variety is voiced by D. J. Jazzy Jeff and the Fresh Prince in "Nightmare on My Street" (1988).

## Search for Meaning in Horror Songs

A dinner was served for three,
At Dracula's house by the sea.
The hors d'oeuvres were fine,
But I choked on my wine,
When I learned that the main course was me . . .
                                        —"Dinner with Drac" (1958)


It wasn't a cream, man,
This guy was for real.
I said, "Freddie [Krueger], there's been an awful mistake here."
No further words and then I darted upstairs,
Crashed through my door,
Then jumped on my bed,
Pulled the covers up over my head,
And said, "Oh please, do somethin' with Fred!"
He jumped on my bed,

Went through the covers with his claws,
Tried to get me.
But my alarm went off.
Then silence . . .

—"Nightmare on My Street" (1988)


Heard strange noises comin' from a house on the hill,
So I crept up to the window and looked over the sill.
My heart almost stopped,
I nearly died of fright,
By the dim candlelight I saw the strangest sight.
There was Frankenstein and Dracula and Wolfman, too,
Dancin' with some zombies,
What a ghastly crew.
The old ugly vampire was doin' the hop,
Everything was rockin' at the monsters' hop . . .

—"The Monster Hop" (n.d.)


Duality haunts all studies of the horror genre. First, there is considerable disagreement among scholars concerning the line that separates horror from science fiction. Thomas Doherty has noted that the more identifiably human the beast, the more authentic is the horrific force. Thus, giant insects, gelatinous blobs, reptile-based life-forms, hideous aliens, uncontrolled robots, and even radiation-provoked mutants are less frightening than werewolves (so-called "shape changers"), vampires, humanly assembled humans, zombies, mummies, or other accursed demons. Throughout this study and in all of the recordings sampled above, the suspension of reality required to accept Frankenstein and Dracula is assumed to be no less significant than that necessary for the acceptance of the Fly, giant marauding ants, or the wrath of Rodan, Godzilla, and Gorgo. Monsters are monsters.

The second dichotomy of the horror genre is much more significant to an interpretation concerning the lyrical adaptation of monster themes and characters. Stated most simply, several film scholars discriminate "good horror" from "bad horror" according to a bimodal aesthetic/moral/sociopolitical spectrum. Though too complex to detail here, the light vs. dark character of specific fright melodramas hinges on such polarized perspectives as:

| Good Horror | Bad Horror |
|---|---|
| atmospheric suspense | lurid sensationalism |
| seduction | rape |
| titillation | pornography |
| surprise | shock |
| moral neutrality | overt criminality |
| fantasy | hallucination |
| magic | voodoo |
| illusion of terror | random violence |
| dream | nightmare |
| sensitizing story | desensitizing actions |
| personal | voyeurism |
| silence | noise |
| formula and style | tricks and gimmicks |
| uplifting | debasing |
| standard language | foul language |
| inventive | destructive |

Although it is difficult to explain (especially to those who are unfamiliar with the entire field of horror fiction and film produced over the past six decades), the subtlety of dramatization in classic horror films such as *Frankenstein* (1931), *Dr. Jekyll and Mr. Hyde* (1941), *Invasion of the Body Snatchers* (1956), and *The Birds* (1963) has been dramatically eroded in the brutalizing splatter movies of the past two decades. The outright meanness, sadomasochism, vulgar exorcisms, mayhem, and nihilism of films such as *The Texas Chainsaw Massacre* (1974) and *I Spit on Your Grave* (1980) is ludicrous. This is not to imply that contemporary horror classics such as *Silence of the Lambs* (1991), *Misery* (1990), *Cape Fear* (1991), or *Alien* (1979) are in any way inferior to 1930s or 1940s films. It simply acknowledges that demons such as Freddie Krueger, Jason Voorhees, or the Boogie Man in *Halloween* (1978) are less socially redeemable, more radically murderous, and invariably more exploitational than more suggestive, suspenseful horror personas.

Commercial recordings overwhelmingly reflect youthful enthusiasm for "good horror" films, with particular affinity for classic monsters and oversized insects, large birds, and retaliating reptiles. Rather than overtly condemning the "stalk 'em and slice 'em up" films, though, the practice of topical avoidance occurs. Only "Nightmare on My Street" (1988) challenges the too frightening aspect of contemporary "bad horror." In this regard, Robert Louis Stevenson's chemically schizophrenic Dr. Jekyll and Mr. Hyde, though a key thematic character in film, has been much less frequently utilized in song lyrics. However, the still mysterious but real-life London murderer Jack the Ripper has a lengthy discographic history. Songs detailing the knife-wielding maniac's brief reign of terror include: "Jack the Ripper" (1963, 1990), "Hands of the Ripper" (n.d.), and "The Ripper" (1980, 1992). As illustrated before, though, the most violent, murder-prone characters in contemporary lyrics are human characters and not monsters of the horror genre. They are generally fabrications of Jim Croce, Carol King, or other contemporary composers drawing ideas from historical experiences rather than film-based characters.

The ultimate irony is that film characters once deemed too horrible for adolescent viewing, too demonic for transmission into the American living room, have been transformed into permanent comic relief symbols through the medium of recorded music. The bumbling laboratory assistant Ygor ("Igor" on most records), the absentminded or humorously overintense Doctor Frankenstein, and even the hapless Monster are situation comedies awaiting appropriate lyrical settlings. The roots of rock 'n' horror recordings are not limited to the 1930s films of Karloff, Lugosi, and Chaney, either. Nor are they locked in the 1960s revivals by Vincent Price, Peter Cushing, and Christopher Lee. Clearly, they bear little or no relationship whatsoever to the splatter movies of the 1970s and 1980s. The foundations for commercially recorded horror themes are largely based upon the juvenilization of terror that occurred throughout the 1950s and into the early 1960s. Specifically, radio and television programs hosted by vampire-voiced gatekeepers such as "Mad Daddy" Meyers, Ghoulardi, Roland, and Morgus the Magnificent were central to establishing overtly laughable horror. Spinoffs from traditional terror themes into comic situations on television (*The Addams Family* and *The Munsters*) were logical expansions of such big-screen comedy films and cartoons as *Abbott and Costello Meet Frankenstein* (1948), *Mummies, Dummies* (1948) with The Three Stooges, *Master Minds* (1949) with The Bowery Boys, *Abbott and Costello Meet the Invisible Man* (1951), *Bela Lugosi Meets a Brooklyn Gorilla* (1952), *Termites from Mars* (1952) featuring Woody Woodpecker, *Abbott and Costello Meet Dr. Jekyll and Mr. Hyde* (1953), *The Bowery Boys Meet the Monsters* (1954), *Abbott and Costello Meet the Mummy* (1955), *Woodpecker from Mars* (1956) featuring Woody Woodpecker, *Invasion of the Saucer Men* (1957), *Flying Saucer Daffy* (1958) with The

Three Stooges, *Billy the Kid vs. Dracula* (1965), and *Jesse James Meets Frankenstein's Daughter* (1965).

Finally, the off-the-wall 1950s and 1960s productions of formula-driven alien invasion shows, giant bird/ant/praying mantis films, and Dracula/Frankenstein haunts produced a feeling of perpetual humor toward the stock movie characters. Lyrics reflected this sense through dance tunes, dating situations, party scenes, and even Christmas gatherings where stock monsters were honored guests rather than dreaded intruders. Role reversal ruled. Songs of horror became tunes of comic relief. Authentic horror—nuclear annihilation, other forms of military madness, or individual actions by maniacs and mobsters—was not seriously considered in commercial song lyrics until post-1965. But numerous horror recordings from 1956 through 1991 remain consistent according to themes, characters, audiences, and point of view. "They did the mash, the Monster Mash . . . and it caught on in a flash!" Bobby "Boris" Pickett was more perceptive than anyone ever suspected.

# REFERENCES

Addams, Charles. *My Crowd: The Original Addams Family and Other Ghoulish Creatures*. New York: Fireside Books/Simon and Schuster, 1991.

Almost Slim. "Roll 'n' Rock At the House of Shock," *Wavelength*, I (October 1981), pp. 44.

Antonicello, Lou. "John Zacherle: Your Favorite Monster of Ceremonies," *Rockin' 50s*, 8 (October, 1987), pp. 4-5.

Ayles, Allen, Robert Adkinson, and Nicholas Frey (eds.). *The House of Horror: The Story of Hammer Films*. London: Lorrimer Publishing, Ltd., 1973.

Aylesworth, Thomas G. *Monsters from the Movies*. Philadelphia: Lippincott Books, 1972.

Benton, Mike. *The Illustrated History of Horror Comics*. Dallas, Texas: Taylor Publishing, 1991.

Blair, John, Art Turco, and Michael C. Rogers. "Flying Saucers to Star Wars: An Interview with Dickie Goodman," *Record Exchanger*, V (Summer 1977), pp. 20-23.

Bookhardt, Eric D. "That Voodoo That We Do," *Wavelength*, LXXI (September 1986), pp. 26-27.

Bottigheimer, Ruth B. (ed.). *Fairy Tale and Society: Illusion, Allusion, Paradigm*. Philadelphia: University of Pennsylvania Press, 1986.

Bowles, Stephen E. "*The Exorcist* and *Jaws*: Techniques of the New Suspense Film," *Literature/Film Quarterly*, IV (Summer 1976), pp. 196-214.

Brosnan, John. *The Horror People*. New York: New American Library, 1977.

Brustein, Robert. "Reflections on Horror Movies," *Partisan Review*, XXV (Spring 1958), pp. 288-296.

Butler, Ivan. *Horror in the Cinema*. New York: Warner Books, 1970.

Campbell, Joseph and Bill Moyers. *The Power of Myth*. Garden City, New York: Doubleday and Company, Inc., 1988.

Carter, Margaret L. (ed.). *Dracula: The Vampire and the Critics*. Ann Arbor, Michigan: UMI Research Press, 1988.

Carter, Margaret L. (ed.). *The Vampire in Literature: A Critical Bibliography*. Ann Arbor, Michigan: UMI Research Press, 1989.

Cawelti, John G. *Adventure, Mystery, and Romance: Formula Stories As Art and Popular Culture*. Chicago: University of Chicago Press, 1976.

Clarens, Carlos. *An Illustrated History of the Horror Film*. New York: Capricorn Books, 1967.

Coleman, Rick. "Morgus Lives?" *Wavelength*, No. 72 (October 1986), p. 5.

Colman, Stuart. "Screamin' Jay Hawkins: Clown Prince of Rock 'n' Roll," in *They Kept on Rockin': The Giants of Rock 'n' Roll* (Poole, Dorset, England: Blandford Press, 1982), pp. 82-89.

Conner, Jeff. *Stephen King Goes to Hollywood*. New York: New American Library, 1987.

Cooper, B. Lee. "Beyond *Flash Gordon* and *Star Wars*: Science Fiction and History Instruction," *Social Education*. XLII (May 1978), pp. 392-397.

Cooper, B. Lee. "The Image of the Outsider in Contemporary Lyrics," *Journal of Popular Culture*, XII (Summer 1978), pp. 168-178.

Cooper, B. Lee. *Popular Music Perspectives: Ideas, Themes, and Patterns in Contemporary Lyrics*. Bowling Green, Ohio: Bowling Green State University Popular Press, 1991.

Cooper, B. Lee. "Rhythm 'n' Rhymes: Character and Theme Images from Children's Literature in Contemporary Recordings, 1950-1985," *Popular Music and Society*, XIII (Spring 1989), pp. 53-71.

Costello, Jeff. "Screamin' Jay Hawkins Interview," *DISCoveries*, III (October 1990), pp. 24-27.

Culhane, John. *Special Effects in the Movies: How They Do It*. New York: Ballantine Books, 1981.

Daniels, Les. *Living in Fear: A History of Horror in the Mass Media*. New York: Charles Scribner's Sons, 1975.

DeLuca, David. "The Mad, Mad Daddy of Cleveland Radio," *Cleveland Magazine*, (September 1984), pp. 82-85, 151-153.

Derry, Charles. *Dark Dreams: A Psychological History of the Modern Horror Film*. New York: A. S. Barnes and Company, 1977.

Derry, Charles. "More Dark Dreams: Some Notes on the Recent Horror Film," in *American Horrors: Essays On the Modern American Horror Film*, edited by Gregory A. Waller (Urbana: University of Illinois Press, 1987), pp. 162-174.

Dettman, Bruce and Michael Bedford. *The Horror Factory: The Horror Films of Universal, 1931-1955*. New York: Gordon Press, 1976.

Dickstein, Morris. "The Aesthetics of Fright," *American Film*, V (September 1980), pp. 32-37, 56-59.

Dillard, R.H.W. *Horror Films*. New York: Monarch Press, 1976.

Doherty, Thomas. *Teenagers and Teenpics: The Juvenilization of American Movies in the 1950s.* Boston: Unwin Hyman, 1988.

Dowdy, Andrew. *The Films of the Fifties: The American State of Mind.* New York: William Morrow and Company, Inc., 1973.

Dynamo, Skinny. "Buchanan and Goodman," *Now Dig This,* XXXVI (March 1986), p. 14.

Evans, Walter. "Monster Movies and Rites of Initiation," *Journal of Popular Film,* IV, No. 2 (1975), pp. 124-142.

Evans, Walter. "Monster Movies: A Sexual Theory," *Journal of Popular Film,* II. No. 4 (1973), pp. 353-365.

Everson, William K. *Classics of the Horror Film: From the Days of the Silent Film to the Exorcist.* Secaucus, New Jersey: The Citadel Press, 1974.

Faull, Trev. "Screaming Lord Sutch," *Record Collector,* No. 50 (October 1983), pp. 20-23.

Fieffer, Jules. *The Great Comic Book Heroes.* New York: Dial Press, 1965.

Florescu, Radu. *In Search of Frankenstein.* Boston: New York Graphic Society, 1975.

Fowler, Douglas. "*Alien, The Thing,* and the Principles of Terror," *Studies in Popular Culture,* IV (Summer 1981), pp. 16-23.

Frank, Alan. *The Horror Film Handbook.* Totowa, New Jersey: Barnes and Noble, 1982.

Garner, Jack. "The Addams Family," *Lansing* (Michigan) *State Journal,* November 21, 1991), p. 4.

Gifford, Dennis. *A Pictorial History of the Horror Movies.* London: Hamlyn Publishing Group, Ltd., 1973.

Gilbert, James. *A Cycle of Outrage: America's Reaction to the Juvenile Delinquent in the 1950s.* New York: Oxford University Press, 1986.

Giles, Dennis. "Conditions of Pleasure in Horror Cinema," in *Planks of Reason: Essays on the Horror Film,* edited by Barry Keith Grant (Metuchen, New Jersey: Scarecrow Press, 1984), pp. 38-52.

Girgus, Sam. *The American Self: Myth, Popular Culture, and the American Ideology.* Albuquerque: University of New Mexico Press, 1980.

Glut, Donald F. *Classic Monster Movies.* Metuchen, New Jersey: Scarecrow Press, 1978.

Glut, Donald F. *The Dracula Book.* Metuchen, New Jersey: Scarecrow Press, 1975.

Glut, Donald F. *The Frankenstein Legend.* Metuchen, New Jersey: Scarecrow Press, 1973.

Goldstein, Richard. "The Horror! The Horror!" *Village Voice,* (November 27, 1984), p. 77.

Grant, Barry Keith (ed.). *Planks of Reason: Essays on the Horror Film.* Metuchen, New Jersey: Scarecrow Press, 1984.

Grixti, Joseph. *Terrors of Uncertainty: The Cultural Contexts of Horror Fiction.* London: Routledge Books, Ltd., 1989.

Haining, Peter. *Terror! A History of Horror Illustrations from the Pulp Magazines.* New York: A & W Visual Library, 1976.

Haining, Peter (ed.). *The Ghouls: Horror Stories That Became Great Films*. New York: Stein and Day, 1971.

Heller, Terry. *The Delights of Terror: An Aesthetics of the Tale of Terror*. Urbana: University of Illinois Press, 1987.

Hill, Randal C. "Bobby 'Boris' Pickett," *Goldmine*, No. 220 (December 30, 1988), p. 25.

Hoffmann, Frank W. and William G. Bailey, "Monster Movies," in *Art and Entertainment Fads* (Binghamton, New York: The Haworth Press, 1990), pp. 189-191.

Hoppenstand, Gary and Ray B. Browne (eds.). *The Gothic World of Stephen King: Landscape of Nightmares*. Bowling Green, Ohio: Bowling Green State University Popular Press, 1987.

Horsting, Jessie. *Stephen King at the Movies*. New York: Starlog, 1986.

Hughes, Mike and Tom Schmitz, "Da-Da Da-Dum (Click, Click)," *Lansing (Michigan) State Journal*, (November 21, 1991), p. 5.

Hughes, Winifred. *The Maniac in the Cellar: Sensation Novels of the 1860s*. Princeton, New Jersey: Princeton University Press, 1980.

Huss, Roy and T. J. Ross (eds.). *Focus on the Horror Film*. Englewood Cliffs, New Jersey: Prentice-Hall, Inc. 1972.

Hutchinson, Tom. *Horror and Fantasy in the Cinema*. London: Studio Vista, 1974.

Kawin, Bruce F. *Telling It Again and Again: Repetition in Literature and Film*. Ithaca, New York: Cornell University Press, 1972.

Keller, David H. *Life Everlasting and Other Tales of Science, Fantasy, and Horror*. Westport, Connecticut: Hyperion Press, 1974.

London, Rose. *Zombie: The Living Dead*. New York: Bounty Books, 1976.

Luciano, Patrick. *Them Or Us: Archetypal Interpretations of Fifties Alien Invasion Films*. Bloomington: Indiana University Press, 1987.

Maha, Ed. *Horrors from Screen to Scream*. New York: Avon Books, 1975.

Mank, Gregory William. *It's Alive! The Classic Cinema Saga of Frankenstein*. New York: A.S. Barnes and Company, 1981.

Marsden, Michael T., John G. Nachbar, and Sam L. Grogg, Jr. (eds.). *Movies As Artifacts: Cultural Criticism of Popular Film*. Chicago: Nelson-Hall, Inc., 1982.

Martin, Linda and Kerry Segrave. *Anti-Rock: The Opposition to Rock 'n' Roll*. Hamden, Connecticut: Archon Books, 1988.

McCarthy, Todd and Charle Flynn (eds.). *Kings of the Bs—Working Within the Hollywood System: An Anthology of Film History and Criticism*. New York: E.P. Dutton and Company, Inc., 1975.

McCarty, John. *Splatter Movies: Breaking the Last Taboo of the Screen*. New York: St. Martin's Press, 1984.

McConnell, Frank D. "Rough Beasts Slouching," *Kenyon Review*, I (Summer, 1970), pp. 109-120.

McConnell, Frank D. "Song of Innocence: *The Creature from the Black Lagoon*," *Journal of Popular Film*. II (Summer, 1973), pp. 15-28.

McGee, Mark T. *Fast and Furious: A History of American-International Pictures*. Jefferson, North Carolina: McFarland Books, 1984.

Mercer, Kobena. "Monster Metaphors: Notes on Michael Jackson's 'Thriller,' " *Screen*. XXVII (January-February, 1986), pp. 26-43.

Murphy, Brian. "Monster Movies: They Came from Beneath the Fifties," *Journal of Popular Film*. I (Winter, 1972), pp. 31-44.

Nye, Russel. *The Unembarrassed Muse: The Popular Arts in America*. New York: Dial Press, 1970.

Pickard, P.M. *I Could a Tale Unfold: Violence, Horror, and Sensationalism in Stories for Children*. London: Tavistock Books, 1961.

Pirie, David. *A Heritage of Horror: The English Gothic Cinema, 1946-1972*. New York: Avon Books, 1974.

Pirie, David. *The Vampire Cinema*. London: Galley Press, 1977.

Prawer, S.S. *Caligari's Children: The Film as a Tale of Terror*. New York: Oxford University Press, 1980.

Preiss, Byron (ed.). *The Ultimate Dracula*. New York: Dell Publishing, 1991.

Preiss, Byron (ed.). *The Ultimate Frankenstein*. New York: Dell Publishing, 1991.

Preiss, Byron (ed.). *The Ultimate Werewolf*. New York: Dell Publishing, 1991.

Punter, David. *The Literature of Terror: A History of Gothic Fictions from 1765 to the Present Day*. New York: Longman Books, 1980.

Rea, Steven X. "They Only Came Out at Night," *Waxpaper*, IV (April, 1979), pp. 4-7.

Rockett, W.H. "The Door Ajar: Structure and Convention in Horror Films Would Terrify," *Journal of Popular Film and Television*, X (Fall, 1982), pp. 130-136.

Rose, Mark. "Monster," in *Alien Encounters: Anatomy of Science Fiction* (Cambridge, Massachusetts: Harvard University Press, 1981), pp. 176-195.

Rovin, Jeff. *The Encyclopedia of Monsters*. New York: Facts on File, 1989.

Saleh, Dennis. *Science Fiction Gold: Film Classics of the Fifties*. New York: Comma Books, 1979.

Schultze, Quentin J., Roy M. Anker, James D. Batt, William D. Romanowski, John W. Worst, and Lambert Zuidervaart. *Dancing in the Dark: Youth, Popular Culture, and the Electronic Media*. Grand Rapids, Michigan: William B. Eerdmans Publishing Company, 1991.

Shephard, Leslie (ed.). *The Book of Dracula*. New York: Wings Books, 1991.

Shulins, Nancy. "Ooooh, That's Scary: Popular Culture Embraces Bone-Chilling Characters," *Lansing (Michigan) State Journal*, (March, 1991), p. 1D.

Silver, Alain, and James Ursini. *The Vampire Film*. New York: A.S. Barnes and Company, 1975.

Slusser, George. "Fantasy, Science Fiction, Mystery, Horror," in *Shadows of the Magic Lamp: Fantasy and Science Fiction in Film*, edited by George Slusser and Eric S. Rabkin (Carbondale: Southern Illinois University Press, 1985), pp. 208-230.

Smith, Wes. "The Wolfman," in *The Pied Pipers of Rock 'n' Roll: Radio Deejays of the 50s and 60s* (Marietta, Georgia: Longstreet Press, Inc., 1989), pp. 249-288.

Sontag, Susan. "The Imagination of Disaster," *Commentary*, XL (October 1965), pp. 42-48.

Soren, David. *The Rise and Fall of the Horror Film: An Art Historical Approach to Fantasy Cinema*. Columbia, Missouri: Lucas Books, 1977.

Stanley, John. *Revenge of the Creature Features Movie Guide: An A to Z Encyclopedia to the Cinema of the Fantastic* (third revised edition). Pacifica, California: Creatures at Large Press, 1988.

Tatar, Maria. *The Hard Facts of the Grimms' Fairy Tales*. Princeton, New Jersey: Princeton University Press, 1987.

Telotte, J.P. *Dreams of Darkness: Fantasy and the Films of Val Lewton*. Urbana: University of Illinois Press, 1985.

Tosches, Nick. "Screamin' Jay Hawkins: Horror and the Foot-Shaped Ashtray," in *Unsung Heroes of Rock 'n' Roll: The Birth of Rock 'n' Roll in the Dark and Wild Years Before Elvis* (New York: Charles Scribner's Sons, 1984), pp. 120-127.

Tropp, Martin. *Mary Shelley's Monster: The Story of Frankenstein*. Boston: Houghton Mifflin Company, 1971.

Twitchell, James B. *Dreadful Pleasures: An Anatomy of Modern Horror*. New York: Oxford University Press, 1985.

Twitchell, James B. "Frankenstein and the Anatomy of Horror," *Georgia Review*, XXXVII (Spring 1983), pp. 41-78.

Twitchell, James B. *The Living Dead: A Story of the Vampire in Romantic Literature*. Durham, North Carolina: Duke University Press, 1981.

Twitchell, James B. *Preposterous Violence: Fables of Aggression in Modern Culture*. New York: Oxford University Press, 1989.

Underwood, Peter (ed.). *The Vampire's Bedside Companion*. London: Leslie Frewin, Ltd., 1975.

Underwood, Tim and Chuck Miller (eds.). *Bare Bones: Conversations on Terror with Stephen King*. New York: McGraw-Hill Book Company, 1988.

Underwood, Tim and Chuck Miller (eds.). *Fear Itself: The Horror Fiction of Stephen King*. New York: New American Library, 1982.

Varnado, S.L. *Haunted Presence: The Numinous in Gothic Fiction*. Tuscaloosa: University of Alabama Press, 1987.

Vaughn, Susan. "Monster Movies?" *School Library Journal*, (October 1971), pp. 73-85.

Waller, Gregory A. (ed.). *American Horrors: Essays on the Modern American Horror Film*. Urbana: University of Illinois Press, 1987.

Waller, Gregory A. *The Living and the Undead: From Stoker's Dracula to Romero's Dawn of the Dead*. Urbana: University of Illinois Press, 1986.

Warren, Bill. *Keep Watching the Skies! American Science Fiction Movies of the Fifties: Volume One, 1950-1957*. Jefferson, North Carolina: McFarland and Company, 1982.

Waters, Harry F. "A Monster Revival," *Newsweek*, CXVII (January, 1991), pp. 58-59.

Wilson, Gahan. *Gahan Wilson's America*. New York: Simon & Schuster, 1985.

Winter, Douglas E. *Stephen King: The Art of Darkness* (revised and expanded). New York: New American Library, 1986.

Wood, Robin and Richard Lippe (eds.). *American Nightmare: Essays on the Horror Film*. Toronto: Festival of Festivals, 1979.

Wright, Gene. *Horrorshows: The A to Z of Horror in Film, TV, Radio, and Theatre*. New York: Facts on File, 1986.

# Chapter 10

# Humor

## *ROOTS OF ROCK HUMOR*

*50 Coastin' Classics* (Rhino CD R2-71090). By The Coasters (Santa Monica, California: Rhino Records, 1992). Two Discs, with Historical Booklet. 18 songs.

Popular music scholars and rock journalists alike are expanding their search for the roots of rock 'n' roll. Blues specialists laud the contributions of performers from Robert Johnson to Muddy Waters; country music afficianados point to foundation figures such as Moon Mullican and Hank Williams, along with Bill Haley's Saddlemen; and gospel enthusiasts contend that the rise of doo-wop and soul was portended in the emotional harmonies of The Soul Stirrers. The most forceful and convincing "roots" arguments, of course, center on the vibrant rhythm 'n' blues music that filtered through various urban enters (New Orleans, Kansas City, Chicago, New York City, Los Angeles, Houston, and Detroit) from 1940 into the early 1950s. R&B heroes who became models for early rock 'n' rollers include Roy Brown, Amos Milburn, Wynonie Harris, and Arthur Crudup. But who provided the artistic guidance for rock 'n' roll's comic performers such as The Jayhawks, The Olympics, and, most important of all, The Coasters?

Between 1949 and 1968 one comic ensemble act dominated American recorded humor. When The A-Sharp Trio and The Robins finally emerged as The Coasters in 1956, rock 'n' roll discovered its funny bone. Actually,

The three reviews in this chapter are scheduled to be published in *Popular Music and Society*. The essay appeared as "Sultry Songs as High Humor," *Popular Music and Society*, XXVII (Spring 1993), pp. 71-85. Reprint permission granted by the author, Editor R. Serge Denisoff, and Bowling Green State University Popular Press.

black ghetto styles, radio broadcast programs, and various youth culture fantasies of the 1950s and early 1960s found commercial success via short stories articulated by a vocal team that variously featured Carl Gardner, Leon Hughes, Billy Guy, Bobb Nunn, Obie "Young" Jessie, Cornell Gunter, Will "Dub" Jones, and Earl "Speedo" Carroll. These black men eventually became rock royalty when they were enshrined in The Rock 'n' Roll Hall of Fame in 1987. But the sources of their musical magic were as unique as they were. The Coasters were undoubtedly aware of both Fats Waller and Louis Jordan and His Tympany Five; they had performed with Esther Phillips; they had experienced countless R&B giants on radio and records. Yet it was three white men–Johnny Otis, Jerry Leiber, and Mike Stoller–who shaped the style and substance of their professional recording careers. This was genuine integration. It was cooperation rather than manipulation. It was the same kind of black-and-white musical madness that made Stax Records of Memphis so distinctive during the 1960s.

*50 Coastin' Classics* is truly a celebration of cross-cultural collaboration. The stage-smart Coasters and the street-smart Leiber and Stoller provided the ATCO label with 18 "Hot 100" *Billboard* songs between 1956 and 1964. They also accomplished something else that is rarely acknowledged. Just as Chuck Berry, they captured American popular culture in lyric, phrasing, language, and theme. The moon-June-spoon pabulum of 1940s popular songs was not replaced in the mid-1950s by intense cerebral lyric commentary; instead, mythic courtship themes were bent to approximate real life dilemmas–many funny, frustrating, and far out–of adolescent dating and mating. Irreverence bristled from "Charlie Brown" (1959); economic hardship echoed throughout "Wake Me, Shake Me" (1960) and "Shoppin' for Clothes" (1960); parental tyranny blossomed in "Yakety Yak" (1958). The popular culture was broadly exploited in other Coasters' tunes as well. "Little Egypt" (1961) was a burlesque of burlesque; "Along Came Jones" (1959) satirized movie serials; and "Searchin'" (1957) laughingly utilized radio and television detectives Boston Blackie, Sam Spade, Joe Friday, Bulldog Drummond, and Charlie Chan to track down a missing sweetheart.

The Coasters did not just sing songs; they told tales. Their records were skits set to music. This format was carefully staged and rehearsed by Leiber and Stoller, but artfully performed by the gleeful jesters themselves. The heritage for such oral amusement is at the heart of America's popular culture. Vaudeville, burlesque, silent movies, and early radio and television programs launched hundreds of off-the-wall models including Jack Benny and Rochester, Groucho Marx, George Burns, Spike Jones and His City Slickers, Amos 'n' Andy, and a plethora of soap opera and detective story heroes and heroines. The Coasters adapted these comic styles and adopted humorous characterizations at will. "Charlie Brown" (1959) begins with a funky nursery rhyme recitation; "The Shadow Knows" (1958) acknowledges an audio debt to Lamont Cranston; and "Bad Detective" (1964), "Searchin'" (1957), "Riot in Cell Block #9" (1954), and "Framed" (1954) lampoon numerous serials such as "Gangbusters," "Dragnet," and "Boston Blackie." In today's climate of political correctness, of course, the raucous interchanges delivered in "Smokey Joe's Cafe" (1955), "Young Blood" (1957), "Three Cool Cats" (1959), and "Wait a Minute" (1961) might be condemned as too racist, too sexist, or too socially and spiritually demeaning.

Fortunately, the humor of The Coasters is as universal and timeless as that of Mae West, W.C. Fields, and Bo Diddley ("Say Man"). One should not be surprised, either, that country music comedian and social satirist Ray Stevens has mimicked the recitation style and even copied material from The Coasters. Just listen to his renditions of "Santa Claus Is Watching You" (1962) and "Along Came Jones" (1969).

This magnificent Rhino collection features a truly remarkable span of recorded excellence. Wisely, the early Spark recordings of The Robins lead off the collection—"Riot in Cell Block #9" (1954), "Framed" (1954), and "Smokey Joe's Cafe" (1955). Then the ATCO Coaster classics march forward—"Young Blood" (1957), "That Is Rock and Roll" (1959), and "Poison Ivy" (1959). Special treats include three rare Date label releases—"Soul Pad" (1967), "Down Home Girl" (1967), and "D.W. Washburn" (1968)—plus a previously unissued, somewhat raunchy tune titled "Shake 'Em Up and Let 'Em Roll" (recorded in 1968). An informative booklet, featuring a fine group biography by Robert Palmer, a songography interview with both Leiber and Stoller, a full sessionography compiled by Mike Stoller, and a raft of B&W photographs of The Coasters accompanies the two compact disc set. (A bibliography of recent Coasters' studies is provided at the conclusion of this review. No print references are listed in the Rhino booklet.)

Just as the sly humor of Hank Ballard's Midnighters and Billy Ward's Dominoes spawned both reissues and response recordings, the influence of The Coasters among both contemporaries ("Western Movies" by The Olympics) and future rock stars is worth noting. Perhaps the wild men and wiley women at Rhino will someday consider issuing a compilation titled *Coasters' Classics Copied.* Such an anthology would feature prominent music stars including the Rolling Stones ("Down Home Girl"), Bad Company ("Young Blood"), Jim Croce ("Searchin'"), The Monkees ("D.W. Washburn"), Burton Cummings ("Framed"), and Delbert McClinton ("One

Kiss Led to Another," and "(When She Wants Good Lovin') My Baby Comes to Me." For now, though, *50 Coastin' Classics* is more than enough enjoyment.

> *Sgt. Pepper's* (Rhino CD R2-70371). By Big Daddy. Santa Monica, California: Rhino Records, Inc., 1992.

Big Daddy, Rhino's revisionist rock 'n' roll revivalists, has built a reputation for restyling 1980s hits into 1950s formats. The challenge of revisiting The Beatles' most influential album—especially during the twenty-fifth anniversary year of its release—might be daunting to some musicians. But not to Big Daddy. The eight-man band produces a distinctively humorous and musically innovative retrospective of *Sgt. Pepper's Lonely Hearts Club Band*.

Charted performances of *Sgt. Pepper* tunes include Elton John's "Lucy in the Sky with Diamonds" (1975) and Joe Cocker's "With a Little Help from My Friends" (1968). But nothing can match Big Daddy's off-the-wall rhythmic innovations. Imagine The Coasters ("Charlie Brown" and "Young Blood") singing *Sgt. Pepper's* introductory theme in doo-wop harmony; think of Johnny Mathis ("Chances Are") crooning "With a Little Help from My Friends"; consider Jerry Lee Lewis ("Whole Lotta Shakin' Goin' On") rockin' through "Lucy in the Sky with Diamonds"; ponder Dion and the Belmonts ("The Wanderer" and "Drip Drop") producing a finger-snapping treatment on "Fixing a Hole"; or speculate on Paul Anka ("Diana") applying a mock-calypso style to "She's Leaving Home." Frightening, isn't it? But the disc features even more surprising arrangements! Consider "When I'm Sixty-Four" interpreted by The Dominoes ("Sixty-Minute Man"), "Lovely Rita" lauded by Elvis Presley ("His Latest Flame"), and "A Day in the Life" hiccuped by Buddy Holly ("Peggy Sue" and "Oh Boy").

Nothing could be more enjoyable, more entertaining, or more potentially educational than demonstrating how humorously pop melody patterns can vacillate. Laughter and learning can go hand-in-hand with Big Daddy's sly, syncopated approach to revealing rock's rhythm roots.

## *POLITICAL SATIRE*

> *Fools on the Hill* (Capitol Steps CSCD 1011). By The Capitol Steps. Alexandria, Virginia: Capitol Steps Records, 1992.

Just mention musical political satire, and Mark Russell immediately comes to mind. Yet since 1984, a 17-member ensemble troupe of glib and gifted House and Senate Aides have been performing and recording the richest, raunchiest, and most rhythmic political parodies imaginable. The Capitol Steps are genuine Washington insiders. They are merciless, witty, sharp-tongued critics of waste, womanizing, wrangling, and wanton wickedness in the U.S. Government. Republicans and Democrats alike receive lyrical lashings. Nothing in politics escapes this team of pop parody masters. While Bill Strauss and Elaina Newport craft character-assassinating lyrics, Bo Ayars plots the nifty musical arrangements.

Although the stinging verbal barbs are wonderful, the breadth of music adapted for the satirical attacks distinguishes this group. The melodies are familiar, and add to the muckraking madness. *Fools on the Hill* features parodies of signature recordings by The Beatles, Paul Anka, David Bowie, Lee Greenwood, Tammy Wynnette, and Country Joe McDonald. But there are also selections stolen from Stephen Sondheim and Leonard Bernstein, Richard Rodgers and Oscar Hammerstein, and Gilbert and Sullivan. For spice, the Capitol Steps even parody "Rubber Ducky" (renamed "Rubber Checky" in a bouncy attack on Congressional overdrafts) and "Supercalifragilisticexpialidocious" (recycled as "Superfranticunproductivenothinglegislation"). Finally, Alan Sherman's laughable camp song "Hello Muddah, Hello Fadduh" is given a Middle East slant as "Hello Mullah, Hello Fattah."

The scope of satirical slashing in the 23 songs on this compact disc is breathtaking. "Stand by Your Klan" excoriates David Duke's political wizardry; "Ground Control to Jedi Brown" lampoons Governor Jerry as a bizarre California oddity; "Bill 'n' Dan's Draft Dodgin' Rag" undresses the Clinton and Quayle military dolls; "Sound of Tsongas" is a tribute to Paul's oh-so-boring political lectures, "Favored Right Wing" reveals fundamental problems about Pat Buchanan's political puffery; and "If I Weren't a Rich Man" debunks the common man/pork-rind pleadings of George Herbert Walker Bush. Beyond political personalities, The Capitol Steps assail computerized sex in "Yuppie Love," attack journalistic sensationalism in "When They're Fishing in *The Star*," and assault Japanese buy-out/takeover endeavors in "I, Yokohama." From Mario Cuomo ("Shamlet") to Pee Wee Herman ("Lirty Dies: Skex Sandals"), from junk bond dealers ("Mike Milken") to superpatriot rednecks ("God Bless My Chevrolet"), no one escapes the musical mirth. What fun!

## SUGGESTIVE LYRICS

Conventional wisdom suggests that censorship thwarts creativity. When artists are aware of possible suppression, the chilling effect of a repressive atmosphere narrows productivity. This has not been true in the realm of commercial recording. Politicians, clergymen, journalists, and women's groups have fired salvo after salvo at sexist lyrics and sensuous themes in contemporary songs. Nothing works, though. Singers avoid censorship landmines by modifying images, substituting words, and making newer and better jokes about sexual relations. Listening audiences delight in innovations, innuendoes, and imaginary situations. Censors can only cringe. Morality and aesthetics carry virtually no weight in popular music. Worse yet, free speech contentions protect not only the talented and inventive wordsmith, but also the bawdy bozo and the mean-spirited, arrogant woman-basher.

The most fascinating aspect of commercial recording strategies toward censorship challenges is . . . how lyricists connive to beat the system. Rather than exploring every issue of lyric controversy—racism, politics, drugs, violence, murder, and so on—this study focuses solely on sex themes in popular songs. The essay examines five categories of censorship dodges: (1) clothing styles and physical attributes are explored as suggestive external elements; (2) word substitutions and nonlyrical aural insinuations are noted as sensual audio manipulations; (3) comic images and playful sexual commentaries are assembled in lecherous situations; (4) high emotions and passions allow men and women to abandon control of their inhibitions; and (5) bragging, boasting men and women pursue lives that become outrageous sexual escapades.

## *External Elements As Sexual Manifestations*

Direct sexual comments may be forbidden on recordings, but innuendoes and passionate speculations are common in popular lyrics. Initial attraction is often fueled by either sexy clothing styles or distinctive physical attributes. Cloaked in highly suggestive observations, numerous recordings have utilized creative, sometimes comic, settings that highlight specific body parts. The focus on physique—90 percent of the time on the female form—makes lyrical lechery successful. Censors tend to look for single-word offenses. But general references to contemporary clothing, whether revealing bathing suits or form-fitting sweaters, are judged as reasonable.

Cheap or expensive, gaudy or sophisticated, contemporary styles are frequent sources of lyric commentary. Wilson Pickett lauds "Mini-Skirt Minnie" (1969), while Isreal Tolert extols a "Big Leg Woman (with a Short Short Mini Skirt)" (1970). The early 1970s resurgence of short shorts was heralded by Salvage's "Hot Pants" (1971), Bobby Byrd's "Hot Pants—I'm Coming, I'm Coming, I'm Coming" (1971), and James

Brown's "Hot Pants (She Got to Use What She Got, to Get What She Wants)" (1971). The sexy image of fishnet hose have a lengthy lyrical heritage. Slim Harpo appreciates them in "Tip on In" (1967), as does Morris Day in "Fishnet" (1988). Skimpy beachwear is another commonly observed phenomenon. Recorded imagery ranges from Brian Hyland's shy young lady in the "Itsy Bitsy Teenie Weenie Yellow Polka Dot Bikini" (1960) to The Rip Chords' more bold young woman in a "One Piece Topless Bathing Suit" (1964). Other suggestive commentaries are featured in Mitch Ryder's "Devil with a Blue Dress On" and "Good Golly Miss Molly" (1966), David Dundas's "Jeans On" (1977), and Joe Cocker's shameless striptease soliloquy "You Can Leave Your Hat On" (1986).

Clothing masks the human frame. Singers and songwriters often go beyond external covering to praise both visible and invisible physical traits. Once again, suggestive phrasing beats banning, yet still communicates sexual themes in undisguised clarity. Although many gender-conscious commentators would undoubtedly label these lyrical perspectives as hopelessly sexist, the songs are unabashedly comic. Queen adores "Body Language" (1982); The Bar-Kays claim "She Talks to Me with Her Body" (1983); and Con Funk Shun and Syl Johnson laud "Ms. Got-the-Body" (1983) and "Ms. Fine Brown Frame" (1982). Shapely legs, thighs, and hips are the most frequently mentioned attractions for women watchers. The Electric Boys are wild about girls who are "All Lips 'n' Hips" (1990); Rod Stewart raves about "Hot Legs" (1978); ZZ Top fantasizes about "Legs" (1984); Elvis Presley ogles a "Long Legged Girl (with the Short Dress On)" (1967); and the All Points Bulletin Band praises "Sexy Ways—Pretty Legs" (1976). The lower portion of the female torso is a focal area for humorous attention. Beyond the numerous versions of Cajun comic Rockin' Sidney's "My Toot-Toot," there are many salutes to well-rounded derrieres—both large and small. Carl Carlton encourages women to "Swing That Sexy Thing" (1983); James and Bobby Purify marvel at dancing girls who can "Shake a Tail Feather" (1967) to gain male attention; and the raucous SirMixaLot expresses admiration for chunky bottoms in "Baby Got Back" (1992). Finally, the bustline is noted by Carl Carlton in "She's a Bad Mama Jama (She's Built, She's Stacked)" (1981). Finally, the entire female frame is sketched mathematically in The Showmen's "39-21-46" (1966).

## Audio Manipulation and Word Substitution

The ability of singers to communicate sensual themes without offending either moralistic critics or community standards censors often rests on misdirection. That is, the intended sexual suggestion must be masked, muffled, and manipulated. There is also a sense of in-crowd secrecy, with performer/audience complicity in a very funny, very sexy joke system. Much of this essay explores such diversions. In standard examinations of classic literature, allegories, metaphors, and various forms of imagery are readily anticipated. Songwriters and singers benefit from the fact that most censorship efforts focus solely on direct verbal statements that can be clearly heard and universally understood. No one who has listened to Mick Jagger, Jimmy Reed, most heavy metal music, garage band recordings, or bootleg concert tapes would ever describe these sounds as . . . clear. Thus, the beat-the-censor issue on sex themes is often achieved through linguistic disguise. But there is also a shrewdness among adaptive lyricists that allows overly suggestive words and images to be replaced (some might say "bowdlerized") by less offensive terminology. Word substitution may either soften meaning or heighten the "secret" humor shared between the artist and the knowledgeable listener.

Millie Jackson and 2 Live Crew thrive on specificity, directness, and sexual shock. So do many 1950s rhythm 'n' blues singers and many more contemporary rappers. But commercial recording success in the realm of depicting male-female relationships demands subtltey. Imagination becomes a key element. The incomprehensible lyrics of The Kingsmen's "Louie Louie" (1963) prompted a popular mythology that grew from airplay analysis to motion picture fame in *Animal House*. While speculation fueled the sexual imagery myth about "Louie Louie," suggestive titles such as "Last Night" (1961) and "Raunchy" (1957) made instrumental recordings by The Mar-Keys and Bill Justis seem mysteriously risqué. David Rose's version of "The Stripper" (1962) plays on the history of traditional burlesque sounds to promote nonlyrical suggestions of Sally Rand's peekaboo nudity. Combining heavy breathing with not-too-veiled invitations for sensual companionship, Sylvia and Donna Summer feature seductive monologues on "Pillow Talk" (1973) and "Love to Love You Baby" (1975).

Word substitution is a strategy utilized to overcome objections to direct sexual images through the utilization of nonvolatile terms. Little Richard's "Tutti Frutti" (1955) and Chick Willis's "Stoop Down Baby" (1972) achieved radio airplay as a result of such word replacement. More major lyric alteration occurred in Joe Turner's "Shake, Rattle, and Roll" (1954) as it became a major popular hit in 1954 for Bill Haley and the Comets. The same type of story-line revision was applied to Smiley Lewis's "One Night" (1956) before it reached nationwide hit status in 1958 for Elvis Presley. The most frequently cited lyric change illustration is related to the Hank Ballard and the Midnighters' classic "Work with Me Annie"

(1954). This tune went through two lyric conversions. First, Etta James crafted a revised recording entitled "The Wallflower" (1954); then Georgia Gibbs softened the Ballard lyric even more to produce "Dance with Me Henry" (1955).

Clearly, the range of words or terms that allude to sex exceed description here. Intercourse has been defined as the "Wild Thing" (1988), a woman's fanny is "My Toot-Toot" (1985) and a penis is "My Ding-a-Ling" (1992). Yet each of these songs were hits for Tone-Loc, Rockin' Sidney, and Chuck Berry. The humor of trying to explain the meanings of "party," "make it," "work out," "ride," "ball," "rock," "roll," or "dance" as synonyms for sex is one way to comprehend the creativity of lyricists in confounding censors.

## Suggestive Situations

Critics of contemporary lyrics tend to overlook the sexual content of popular music from the 1920s, 1930s, and 1940s. From show tunes to pop ballads, such canny wordsmiths as Cole Porter and crafty singers such as Frank Sinatra spun tales that made censors blush. However, their sly humor bartered banning away. Eddie Cantor laughed through warnings about a bridegroom's zeal in "Makin' Whoopee" (1929); Ben Bernie nervously pleaded "Let's Misbehave" (1928); Paul Whiteman's Orchestra chuckled along with music fans on "Let's Do It (Let's Fall in Love)" (1929); Robert Johnson expressed the mock frustration of a forgotten lover in "Terraplane Blues" (1936); and Frank Sinatra urged the object of his affection to indulge in "All of Me" (1948). Chilly external conditions are juxtapositioned with passionate internal options in Vaughn Monroe's "Let It Snow! Let It Snow! Let It Snow!" (1945) and on the Johnny Mercer/Margaret Whiting duet "Baby, It's Cold Outside" (1949).

Comic imagery in sexual situations is a particularly popular phenomenon. Transmission of venereal disease is hinted at in The Coasters' "Poison Ivy" (1959) and Bachman-Turner Overdrive's "You Ain't Seen Nothin' Yet" (1974). Penis envy is explored in Bullmoose Jackson's "Big Ten-Inch Record" (1953), Albert King's "Crosscut Saw" (1967), and Chuck Berry's "My Ding-a-Ling" (1972). Evenings of passion too hot to detail are depicted by the Big Bopper's "Chantilly Lace" (1958), in The Four Seasons' "December, 1963 (Oh, What a Night)" (1975), in Bob Seger's "The Horizontal Bop" (1980), by The Dells' "Oh, What a Night" (1969), in The Clovers' "One Mint Julep" (1952), in Chuck Berry's "Reelin' and Rockin'" (1972), and by The Drifters' "Such a Night" (1954).

Many songs describe women as so tempting as sex objects that men—even married men—cannot be blamed for pursuing them. Little Richard contends "The Girl Can't Help It" (1957). Singers often seem unable to specifically identify the source of sexual attraction. Such situations are illustrated in Chuck Jackson and Maxine Brown's "Something You Got" (1965), The Accents' "Wiggle Wiggle" (1958), Marv Johnson's "You Got What It Takes' (1959), and Hot Chocolate's "You Sexy Thing" (1975). While a few women exert physical control over zealous suitors–as in the Georgia Satellites' "Keep Your Hands to Yourself" (1986) and Denise LaSalle's "My Tu-Tu" (1985), many others are much more sexually accommodating. The Weather Girls are praying for a major climatic change in "It's Raining Men" (1983). More direct invitations are provided by Grace Jones in "Pull Up to the Bumper" (1981), in Anita Ward's "Ring My Bell" (1979), by B.B. King's "Sweet Little Angel" (1956), by Joe Turner's "TV Mama" (1954), and in Captain and Tennille's "You Never Done It Like That" (1978). Nevertheless, a frustrated Joe Tex feels obligated to scream "I Gotcha" (1972). The comedy of macho sex drives is featured in Marty Robbins' "Jumper Cable Man" (1981), Sam Cooke's "Little Red Rooster" (1963), the Rolling Stones' "Start Me Up" (1981), and Elvis Presley's "Steamroller Blues" (1973). The ultimate novelty song about male sensual egotism is Right Said Fred's "I'm Too Sexy" (1991).

Playfully suggestive songs stand the test of time. The revivals of "Makin' Whoopee" (1965) by Ray Charles and "Baby, It's Cold Outside" (1962) by Ray Charles and Betty Carter illustrate the continuity of this situational humor. Timing rather than either place or season is often the source of sensual commentary. Post-midnight meetings augur well for all-night bedroom adventures. Eric Clapton lets it all hang out "After Midnight" (1970); Al Hibbler has similar plans "After the Lights Go Down Low" (1956); Wilson Pickett urges his lady friend to wait "In the Midnight Hour" (1965) when his love comes tumbling down; and Ray Charles screams that "(Night Time Is) The Right Time" (1959) to be with the one you love. Naturally, there is much advice available about wooing and winning attractive women. Roy Head urges would-be Romeos to "Treat Her Right" (1965), while The Cornelius Brothers and Sister Rose suggest that if gentlemen "Treat Her Like a Lady" (1971), then she will give in to them. The unpredictability of male-female relationships is portrayed lyrically through varying plans, expectations, and indecisive actions. Love seemingly never proceeds smoothly. Slim Harpo attempts to assume control in "Baby Scratch My Back" (1966); The Pointer Sisters ponder "Should I Do It" (1982); Slim Harpo examines the merchandise prior to seeking the opportunity to "Tip on In" (1967); and Ray Charles is frustrated and confused by all women in "What'd I Say?" (1959).

Postmarital escapades and multiple-dating relationships are common sources of lyrical review—with a tongue-in-cheek style, of course. Infidelity poses an alimony dilemma in the Dr. John and Rickie Lee Jones revival of "Makin' Whoopee!" (1991). Anger over a cheating female is expressed by Albert King in "Laundromat Blues" (1966), by Johnnie Taylor in "Who's Making Love" (1968), and by Bobby Marchan in "There's Something on Your Mind" (1960). Male philandering is hauntingly challenged in The Pointer Sisters whispered version of "How Long (Betcha' Got a Chick on the Side)" (1975). Many songs echo the pleas, promises, and passion of Derek's "Back Door Man" (1969). Sagas of macho males and mean mistreatin' mamas are undeniably staples among sex-related songs.

## Beyond Control

Passionate feelings and excessive sexual behaviors are frequently depicted in popular recordings. Singers usually justify impetuous actions by defining their emotional condition as . . . beyond control. Just like a rampant forest fire fanned by high winds, lyricists utilize the image of a blazing inferno to describe maximum emotional involvement, zeal, and euphoria. The Boys Band plead "Don't Stop Me Baby (I'm on Fire)" (1982); The Ohio Players and The Pointer Sisters emphasize the dilemma of losing emotional control in lyrically different versions of "Fire" (1974; 1978); and Jose Feliciano echoes The Doors classic request—come on, baby, "Light My Fire" (1968). Whether actual body heat or just imagined high temperature, sexual attraction is frequently assessed as the direct opposite of a cold chill. Peggy Lee revived Little Willie John's signature song and etched several warm historical images with "Fever" (1958). Meanwhile, Foreigner warned female fans that they are "Hot Blooded" (1978); Loverboy proclaimed total admiration for "Hot Girls in Love" (1983); and the always outspoken Millie Jackson presented a steamy case for "Hot! Wild! Unrestricted! Crazy Love" (1986).

The sense of losing all rational power has also been a description for young love. And when sex is involved, this irrationality is compounded by the desire for unknown physical pleasures. Robert Palmer depicts a person who is "Addicted to Love" (1986), while The Chambers Brothers freely acknowledge "I Can't Turn You Loose" (1968). Lyrical testimonials to emotional unraveling are too numerous to mention. A few illustrations include "Breathless" (1958) and "Great Balls of Fire" (1957) by Jerry Lee Lewis, "I'm So Excited" by The Pointer Sisters (1982); "Passion" (1980) by Rod Stewart; "Start Me Up" (1981) by the Rolling Stones; and "Urgent" (1981) by Foreigner. From zealous exclamations such as "Sock It to Me, Baby!" (1967) by Mitch Ryder to purring, gasping, cooing fantasy in "Pillow Talk" (1973) by Sylvia, losing control is depicted as a basic human trait.

Moving beyond physical attraction, hormones, adrenaline, and the addictive nature of sexual interaction, there is a humor-laden set of songs that appear to make passion a Jekyll-and-Hyde option. Love becomes chemistry. Sex is the result of carefully administered potions, spells, and aphrodisiacs. The advantage of such strange elixirs is discussed by Tone-Loc in "Funky Cold Medina" (1989), by The Clovers in "Love Potion No. 9" (1959), and by Dennis Edwards in "(You're My) Aphrodisiac" (1984). Voodoo and conjured magic also yield control over loved ones in "Castin' My Spell" (1959) by Johnny Otis and "I Put a Spell on You" (1956) by the self-proclaimed high priest of mojo madness, Screamin' Jay Hawkins.

Amateur experimentation with sex is yet another common element in popular songs. Whether fumbling and overtly humorous, as in Jim Stafford's laughable "Spiders and Snakes" (1973), or painfully mechanical, as in Bob Seger's backseat learning of "Night Moves" (1976), these escapades are invariably funny. The loss of virginity for both males and females through random sexual experiences is considered in retrospect by Cher in "Gypsies, Tramps, and Thieves" (1971), by B.J. Thomas in "I Recall a Gypsy Woman" (1981), and by Dusty Springfield in "Son-of-a Preacher Man" (1968). Only with maturity does passion begin to yield to reason.

### Tall Tales

The more extravagant the behavior, the more captivating the character depicted in the lyric. Sexuality may be illustrated by physical attributes, by emotional volatility, or by dominance over members of the opposite sex. Fascination with the antics of a Mississippi Queen, a Lovin' Dan, or a free-speaking Tone-Loc causes grins, giggles, and guffaws. While immorality is not necessarily honored, individual arrogance and social rebellion are admired. The lyrical ingenuity that permits sexual tales to be publicly broadcast titillates listeners and expands the realm of popular discussion. Prostitutes demonstrate insight and social perspective, as Creole Lady Marmalade laughs about her straight-arrow white clients. A wily mother cynically blasts the hypocritical mentality found in Harper Valley. Virility, confidence, experience, and slight hints of violence also make a cadre of bragging, boasting males attractive in lyrics. Underlying all of these images, though, is a distinct comic perspective.

Jimmy Reed asks the most painful question of male subservience—"Baby What You Want Me to Do?" (1960). The Georgia Satellites are instructed in no uncertain terms to "Keep Your Hands to Yourself"

(1986). Bettye Swann is just as direct in saying "Don't Touch Me" (1969) if you don't love me. Jean Knight sings "don't mess with 'My Toot-Toot'" (1985), while Bulldog encounters a one word negative response–"No" (1972). But the ultimate woman in control is Meatloaf's unwilling mate in "Paradise by the Dashboard Light" (1978). Jeannie C. Riley blows the whistle on the Peyton Place-like behavior of the deviant denizens attending the "Harper Valley P.T.A." (1968). Two of the most powerful, wildest women on record are depicted by Maria Muldaur in "Midnight at the Oasis" (1974) and by LaBelle in "Lady Marmalade" (1975).

Male dominance is probably the most common source of comic recording. Braggadocio is always funny. The Black Crowes assert that they are "Hard to Handle" (1991). Clarence Carter claims extravagant sexual staying power in "Sixty-Minute Man" (1973). Assertion of sexual control proves "I'm a Man" (1955) to Bo Diddley. The same power over women is asserted by The Buchanan Brothers in "Medicine Man" (1969), by Peter Gabriel in "Sledgehammer" (1986), by Elvis Presley in "Steamroller Blues" (1973), and by Tone-Loc in "Wild Thing" (1988). Lecherous warnings–or invitations–are also framed by Cream in "Sunshine of Your Love" (1968) and by Jerry Lee Lewis in "Whole Lotta Shakin' Goin' On" (1959).

Multiple tune tall tales examining sexual adventures are clearly related to stories communicated in singular recordings. The roots of such extended escapades may be found in the raucous ideas stated in recordings such as "Come a Little Bit Closer" (1964) by Jay and the Americans, "Hard to Handle" (1968) by Otis Redding, "Lady Godiva" (1966) by Peter and Gordon, "Lady Marmalade" (1975) by LaBelle, "Long Tall Sally" (1956) by Little Richard, "One Mint Julep" (1952) by The Clovers, "Santa Baby" (1953) by Eartha Kitt, "Skinny Legs and All" (1967) by Joe Tex, "Sweet Rhode Island Red" (1974) by Ike and Tina Turner, "Telephone Man" (1977) by Meri Wilson (1977), and "Wild Thing" (1988) by Tone-Loc. The distinction gained by a few songs, however, is that they have extended audio existences via either repetition (frequent commercial revivals) or multiple responses (answer songs). Not unlike soap operas, a few stories of passion, playfulness, potency, and pregnancy capture audience attention and retain interest over an extended time period.

Long before Chuck Berry hit the national charts with the slightly off-color, mildly suggestive audience participation tune "My Ding-a-Ling" (1972), the song had become a Crescent City regional standard. New Orleans song wizard Dave Bartholomew launched the joking description of protecting the male sex organ with "My Ding-a-Ling" (1952). Within the next two years three related recordings appeared—Dave Bartholomew's "Little Girl Sing Ting-a-Ling" (1953), The Bees' "Toy Bell" (1954), and The Spiders' "The Real Thing" (1954). After Chuck Berry's 1972 revival of Bartholomew's song, a female singer recording under the pseudonym Miss Chuckle Cherry issued a ding-a-ling answer entitled "My Pussycat" (1972).

A folk song of duration beyond definition is "Frankie and Johnny." Love and infidelity have sparked version after version of this cheating and killing song. The tune is far less suggestive than "My Ding-a-Ling," but much more violent than "Chantilly Lace." Promiscuity triggers murder. Among the artists who have explored the "Frankie and Johnny" tale since 1955 are Johnny Cash, Brook Benton, Sam Cooke, The Greenwood County Singers, Elvis Presley, Sylvia Robbins, Kay Starr, Johnny Sea, Ben Sherwin, The Greenwoods, The Serendipity Singers, and The Kingston Trio.

During the early 1950s, two rhythm 'n' blues songs lauded the sexual adventures of a prodigious suitor and a young woman with few scruples. Ironically, Lovin' Dan and Annie were never lyrically linked. But their exploits echoed in vinyl throughout the decade. "Sixty-Minute Man" (1951) by The Dominoes was a story of sexual athleticism that might have ended as a chuckle with "Can't Do Sixty No More" (1952) by The Du-Droppers. But additional stories of Lovin' Dan's antics stretched over the next two decades. Recordings extending the promiscuous pursuits included "Dancin' Dan" (1956) by The Cadets, "Don't Stop Dan" (1954) by The Checkers, "The Hatchet Man" (1955) by The Robins, and "Sixty-Minute Man—Part Two" (1970) by Rufus Thomas.

The most frequently noted sexual tall tale is drawn from The Midnighters' "Work With Me Annie" (1954). This Hank Ballard tune was sanitized by Etta James under the title "The Wallflower" (1954) and further popularized by Georgia Gibbs as "Dance with Me Henry" (1955). But the lecherous content of the original song nurtured a variety of story-expanding discs. Examples of this theme development included "Annie Don't Love Me No More" (n.d.) by The Hollywood Flames, "Annie Had a Baby" (1954) by The Midnighters, "Annie Kicked the Bucket" (n.d.) by The Nu-Tones, "Annie Met Henry" (1955) by The Cadets, "Annie Pulled a Hum-Bug" (1954) by The Midnights, "Annie's Answer" (1954) by Hazel McCallum and The El Doradoes, "Annie's Aunt Fanny" (1954) by The Midnighters, "Eat Your Heart Out Annie" (n.d.) by The Jordimars, "Henry's Got Flat Feet" (1955) by The Midnighters, "Hey, Henry!" (1955) by Etta James, "I'm the Father of Annie's Baby"—(n.d.) by Danny Taylor, and "My Name Ain't Annie" (1955) by Linda Hayes and the Platters.

## *Conclusion*

Explorations of sexual behaviors and sex-related themes are undeniably common in song lyrics. This pattern is consistent throughout the past 50 years. Efforts to eliminate or dramatically curb sexual references have been universally unsuccessful. In fact, the more stringent censors have become in respect to banning specific words, phrases, and topics, the more creative lyricists and singers have become in revising, rephrasing, or masking the nature of their communication. Sexual commentary in lyrics continues unabated.

The goal of this study is not to justify or defend lyrical obscenity. The author is often distressed by the uninventive, repetitive, antifemale commentaries mouthed by Van Halen, 2 Live Crew, and numerous other heavy metal bands and boorish male rappers. Neither ribald humor nor aesthetic license are served by recordings such as "Me So Horny" (1989), "Black and Blue" (1988), "I Wanna Sex You Up" (1991), and "I Want Your Sex" (1987), but these songs should be allowed to find their own routes into well-deserved obscurity. Direct attacks by censors, no matter how justified, only tend to heighten interest among those who well-meaning music critics wish to shelter.

Bawdy lyrics can be genuine fun. The heritage of Louis Jordan, Bullmoose Jackson, Hank Ballard, Champion Jack Dupree, and The Dominoes deserves to be honored. The wit of these R&B titans translates well into the popular tales of the Big Bopper, Joe Tex, and The Coasters. Even songs from the prerock era—"Makin' Whoopee!" and "Terraplane Blues," for instance—are as meaningful, laughable, and enduring today as they were more than 50 years ago. Suggestive songs are here to stay. Bonnie Raitt captured the essence of selling sultry songs to a popular music audience in a passage from a recent hit. She noted, "Let's give them something to talk about/a little mystery to figure out."

## REFERENCES

Allen, Harry. "Tone-Loc," *Musician*, No. 128 (June 1989), pp. 19-22, 30.
Booth, Dave "Daddy Cool." "Joe Tex," *Soul Survivor*, No. 2 (Spring 1985), pp. 4-8.
Bridges, John and R. Serge Denisoff. "Changing Courtship Patterns in the Popular Song: Horton and Carey Revisited," *Popular Music and Society*, X (Fall 1986), pp. 29-45.
Bronson, Fred. *The Billboard Book of Number One Hits* (revised and enlarged edition). New York: Billboard Publications, Inc.

Carey, James T. "Changing Courtship Patterns in the Popular Song," *American Journal of Sociology*, LXXIV (May 1969), pp. 720-731.

Clark, Alan. "The Coasters," in *Rock and Roll Legends–Number Four* (West Covina, California: Leap Frog Productions) pp. 14-18.

Clarke, Donald. "The Coasters," *The Penguin Encyclopedia of Popular Music* (London: Viking/Penguin Books, 1989), p. 252.

"The Coasters," *The Golden Age*, No. 18 (1988), pp. 12-20.

Colman, Stuart. "The Coasters: That Is Rock 'n' Roll," in *They Kept On Rockin':* *The Giants of Rock 'n' Roll* (Poole, Dorset, England: Blandford Press, 1982), pp. 95-97.

Cooper, B. Lee. "Lovin' Dan and Lady Marmalade Are Doin' the Wild Thing: Sex and Song Lyrics, 1940-1990" (Mimeographed essay presented at the Annual Meeting of the Midwest Popular Culture Association in Indianapolis, Indiana in October, 1991).

Cooper, B. Lee. "Lust, Levity, and Legalism: Popular Songs and Censorship, 1940-1990" (Mimeographed essay and audio tape presented at the Annual Convention of the American Culture Association in New Orleans, Louisiana in April, 1992).

Cooper, B. Lee. "Personal Relationships, Love, and Sexuality," in *A Resource Guide To Themes in Contemporary American Song Lyrics, 1950-1985* (Westport, Connecticut: Greenwood Press, 1986), pp. 131-181.

Cooper, B. Lee. "Sex, Songs, and Censorship: A Thematic Taxonomy of Popular Recordings For Music Librarians and Sound Recording Archivists," *Popular Culture in Libraries*, in press.

Cooper, B. Lee. "Sultry Songs and Censorship: A Thematic Discography For College Teachers," *International Journal of Instructional Media*, XX, No. 2 (1993), pp. 181-194.

Cooper, B. Lee and Wayne S. Haney. *Response Recordings: An Answer Song Discography, 1950-1990*. Metuchen, New Jersey: Scarecrow Press, Inc. 1990.

Cramlington, Tom (comp.). "The Coasters on London Records," *Now Dig This*, No. 16 (July 1984), p. 8.

Cray, Ed (comp.), *The Erotic Muse: American Bawdy Songs* (second edition). Urbana: University of Illinois Press, 1991.

Davis, Sheila. "Pop Lyrics: A Mirror and a Molder of Society," *ETC: A Review of General Semantics*, XLII (Summer, 1985), pp. 167-169.

Delle, Bill. "Annie (and Henry) Records," *Wavelength*, No. 91 (May 1988), p. 34.

Denisoff, R. Serge. *Inside MTV*. New Brunswick, New Jersey: Transaction Books, 1991.

DeVoss, David. "Aural Sex: The Rise of Porn Rock," *Human Behavior*, V (July 1976), pp. 64-68.

Doggett, Peter. "The Coasters," *Record Collector*, No. 26 (October 1981), pp. 13-18.

Espositio, Jim. "Donna Summer and Sex Rock," *Oui*, V (September 1976), pp. 86-88, 100-104.

Evans, Simon. "Working with Annie . . .," *Blues and Rhythm*, No. 69 (May 1992), pp. 8-11.

Firminger, John. "Platter Chatter: The Big Bopper," *Now Dig This*, No. 95 (February 1991), pp. 18-21

Frith, Simon and Angela McRobbie. "Rock and Sexuality," in *On Record: Rock, Pop, and The Written Word*, edited by Simon Frith and Andrew Goodwin (New York: Pantheon Books, 1990), pp. 371-389.

Gaar, Gillian G. "Censorship Yesterday and Today–As American As Apple Pie?" *Goldmine*, No. 276 (February 1991), pp. 48, 50.

Gaar, Gillian G. *She's a Rebel: The History of Women in Rock and Roll*. Seattle, Washington: Seal Press, 1992.

Goldberg, Danny. "Popular Music Under Siege: The Censorship Wars," *Civil Liberties*, No. 367 (Summer 1989), pp. 1, 4-5.

Goldberg, Marv and Mike Redmond. "The Cornell Gunter Story," *Record Exchanger*, No. 13 (June 1973), pp. 4-10.

Graebner, William. "The Erotic and Destructive in 1980s Rock: A Theoretical and Historical Analysis," *Tracking*, (Winter 1988), pp. 8-20.

Grendysa, Peter. " 'Louie Louie': Not Dirty at All," *Goldmine*, No. 168 (January 2, 1987), p. 6.

Grendysa, Peter. "Sneakin' Back," *Bim Bam Boom*. No. 11 (1973), pp. 40-41.

Grendysa, Peter. "You've Heard That Song Before: Record Censorship and Hysteria," *Goldmine*, No. 155 (July 4, 1986), p. 73.

Griggs, Bill. "Spotlight on the Big Bopper," *Rockin' 50s*, No. 10 (February 1988), pp. 8-14.

Hardy, Phil and Dave Laing. "The Coasters," in *The Faber Companion to 20th-Century Popular Music* (London: Faber and Faber, 1990), pp. 152-153.

Hoffmann, Frank. *Intellectual Freedom and Censorship*. Metuchen, New Jersey: Scarecrow Press, Inc., 1989.

Horton, Donald. "The Dialogue of Courtship in Popular Songs," *American Journal of Sociology*. LXII (May 1957), pp. 569-578.

Huffman, James R. and Julie L. Huffman. "Sexism and Cultural Lag: The Rise of the Jailbait Song, 1955-1985," *Journal of Popular Culture*, XXI (Fall 1987), pp. 65-83.

Isler, Scott. "Parent Terror–Insidious Rock Lyrics: The Inquisition Begins," *Musician*, No. 86 (December 1985), pp. 50-62.

Jancik, Wayne. *The Billboard Book of One-Hit Wonders*. New York: Billboard Books, 1990.

Knight, Tim. "Big Bopper: From Head Waiter to Rock 'n' Roll Hero," *Goldmine*, No. 223 (February 19, 1989), pp. 12-13, 29.

Lance, Larry M. and Christina Y. Berry. "Has There Been a Sexual Revolution? Human Sexuality in Popular Music, 1968-1977," *Journal of Popular Culture*, 19 (Summer 1985), pp. 65-73.

Linder, Robert A. "Censorship Is Not the Answer," *Billboard*, XCVII (April 13, 1985), p. 10.

Logsdon, Guy (comp.). *The Whorehouse Bells Were Ringing and Other Songs Cowboys Sing*. Urbana: University of Illinois Press, 1989.

Martin, Linda and Kerry Segrave. *Anti-Rock: The Opposition to Rock 'n' Roll*. Hamden, Connecticut: Archon Books, 1988.

McDonald, James R. "Censoring Rock Lyrics: A Historical Analysis of the Debate," *Youth and Society*, XIX (March 1988), pp. 294-313.

Melton, Peter. "Censored! An Overview of the History of Banned and Censored Records in America," *Goldmine*, No. 276 (February 22, 1991), pp. 113-116.

Millar, Bill. "At Smokey Joe's Cafe," *The History of Rock*, No. 15 (1982), pp. 294-297.

Millar, Bill. *The Coasters*. London: Star/W.H. Allen and Company, Ltd., 1974.

Moonoogian, George. "Oh, That Annie!" *Record Exchanger*, No. 23 (1977), pp. 20-21.

Moonoogian, George and Chris Beachley. "Lovin' Dan: A Look Thirty Years Later–Does He Have 59 to Go?" *It Will Stand*, No. 20 (1980), pp. 4-7.

Newman, Ralph M. "Whose Ding-a-Ling?" *Bim Bam Boom*, No. 9 (1973), pp. 16-17.

Nite, Norm N. "The Coasters," in *Rock On: The Illustrated Encyclopedia of Rock 'n' Roll–The Solid Gold Years* (New York: Thomas Y. Crowell Company, 1974), pp. 126-129.

Oak, Giles. *Devil's Music: A History of the Blues* (revised edition). London: British Broadcasting Corporation, 1983.

Prinsky, Lorraine E. and Jill Leslie Rosenbaum. "Leer-ics or Lyrics: Teenage Impressions of Rock 'n' Roll," *Youth and Society*, XVIII (June 1987), pp. 384-397.

Robinson, Glen O. "The FCC and the First Amendment: Observations on 40 Years of Radio and Television Regulation," *Minnesota Law Review*, LII (November 1967), pp. 67-163.

Roland, Tom. *The Billboard Book of Number One Country Hits*. New York: Billboard Books, 1991.

Root, Robert L. Jr. *The Rhetorics of Popular Culture: Advertising, Advocacy and Entertainment*. Westport, Connecticut: Greenwood Press, 1987.

Rosenbaum, Jill and Lorraine Prinsky. "Sex, Violence, and Rock 'n' Roll: Youths' Perceptions of Popular Music," *Popular Music and Society*, XI (Spring 1987), pp. 79-89.

Ruby, Jay. "Censorship, Nudity, and Obscenity in American Popular Music," in *The Rock Giants*, edited by Pauline Rivelli and Robert Levin (New York: World Publishing Company, 1970), pp. 3-6.

Samuels, Shepard H. "Dirty Words on Radio," *Wavelength*, No. 90 (April 1988), p. 27.

Sandmel, Ben. "Whose Toot-Toot?" *Wavelength*, No. 56 (June 1985), pp. 24-28.

Savage, Jon. "The Enemy Within: Sex, Rock, and Identity," in *Facing The Music*, edited by Simon Frith (New York: Pantheon Books, 1988), pp. 131-172.

Scott, Steve. "The Big Bopper," *Record Collector*, No. 116 (April, 1989), pp. 82-83.

Shannon, Bob and John Jauna. *Behind the Hits: Inside Stories of Classic Pop and Rock and Roll*. New York: Warner Books, 1986.

Shor, Russ. "Racy Race Records and Bawdy Bucolic Ballads," *Goldmine*. No. 52 (September, 1980), p. 181.

Simels, Steve. "*Review of Loc-ed After Dark* by Tone-Loc," *Stereo Review*, LIV (July 1989), pp. 84-85.

Stambler, Irwin. "The Coasters," *The Encyclopedia of Pop, Rock, and Soul*, revised edition (New York: St. Martin's Press, 1989), pp. 134-135.

Stidom, Larry (comp.). *Izatso?! Larry Stidom's Rock 'n' Roll Trivia and Fact Book*. Indianapolis, Indiana: L. Stidom, Publisher, 1986.

Tamarkin, Jeff. "The Censorship Debate: Four Opinions [Frank Zappa, Jennifer Norwood, Dave Marsh, and Pat Boone]," *Goldmine*, No. 276 (February 22, 1991), pp, 52-54, 112, 126.

Thompson, Stephen I. "Forbidden Fruit: Interracial Love Affairs in Country Music," *Popular Music and Society*, XIII (Summer 1989), pp. 23-37.

Tosches, Nick. *Country: Living Legends and Dying Metaphors in America's Biggest Music* (revised edition). New York: Charles Scribner's Sons, 1985.

Tosches, Nick. *Unsung Heroes of Rock 'n' Roll: The Birth of Rock 'n' Roll in the Dark and Wild Years Before Elvis*. New York: Charles Scribner's Son, 1984.

Weisman, Eric Robert. "Wine, Women, and Song: Frank Sinatra and the Rhetoric of Whoopee," *Pennsylvania Speech Communication Annual*, XXXII (1976), pp. 67-79.

Whitburn, Joel (comp.). *Pop Memories, 1890-1954: The History of American Popular Music*. Menomonee Falls, Wisconsin: Record Research, Inc., 1986.

Woodford, Chris. "Don't Mess with My Toot-Toot!" *Now Dig This*, No. 31 (October 1985), p. 25.

Woodford, Chris. "Who Are the Coasters?" *Now Dig This*, No. 108 (March 1992), pp. 5-7.

Young, Charles M. "My Talk with Tipper [Gore]," *Musician*, No. 106 (August 1987), pp. 21-26, 56, 113-114.

Zucker, Mark J. "The Saga of Lovin' Dan: A Study in the Iconography of Rhythm and Blues Music of the 1950s," *Journal of Popular Culture*, XVI (Fall 1982), pp. 43-51.

Chapter 11

# Legends

## *ROCK BIOGRAPHIES*

*Rock Lives: Profiles and Interviews.* By Timothy White. New York: Henry Holt and Company, 1990. Illustrated. 807 pp.

Critics will undoubtedly view this biographical survey in different ways. Some will see *Rock Lives* as a Burma Shave sign tour along rock's meandering highway. As the reader cruises along, Timothy White initially calls attention to Chuck Berry, Ray Charles, Little Richard, and Elvis Presley. As the literary accelerator moves toward the floorboard, the names of Bob Dylan, Stevie Wonder, Jim Morrison, and Pete Townshend whiz by. And toward the road's end, the reader concludes the scenic chase with Bono Vox, The Beastie Boys, Jon Bon Jovi, and the artist formerly known as Prince.

Another way to understand White's anthology is to accept the Faustian interpretation that he offers in his "Introduction." The author speculates about the success of various popular performers being linked to an "other-worldly tutor" and to a "secret handshake with the Angel of Death." (p. xix) This metaphor of dealing with Satan plays especially well in White's analyses of haunted bluesman Robert Johnson, a performer who sang "Hellhound on My Trail" and "Me and the Devil Blues" after a midnight conversation with Lucifer at a darkened crossroad. Similar parallels are explored for such diverse artists as Jerry Lee Lewis and "Prince." White even concludes his book by quoting Voltaire: "You must have the Devil in you to succeed in any of the arts" (p. 780).

These reviews by B. Lee Cooper have been published in *Blue Suede News, Popular Culture in Libraries*, and *Popular Music and Society*. Reprint permission has been granted by the author, Editor Frank Hoffmann, and The Haworth Press, and Editor R. Serge Denisoff and Bowling Green State University Popular Press.

This reviewer perceives *Rock Lives* as a tour de force of White's own career as journalist, critic, and fascinated observer. The author is evolving a philosophic statement about the meaning of life by examining particular segments of rock artists' existences. Candor and hype, comedy and tragedy lurk throughout the hefty volume. Although arranged in a roughly chronological format featuring "Pioneers" (Professor Longhair, Buddy Holly, and Sam Cooke), "Pilgrims" (John Lennon, Mick Jagger, and Aretha Franklin), and "Progeny" (Michael Jackson, John Mellencamp, and Bruce Springsteen), the essays and interviews actually originated at varying times within the framework of White's own prolific literary career. Unlike brash fellow rock commentator Dave Marsh, White is both reflective and cautious when noting that ". . . rock and roll has less to do with rebellion than with an exquisite self-absorption in which there is no tug of war, only a swift, steady pull" (pp. xviii-xix). The author, after more than 20 years of stargazing, assesses the rock galaxy with both wonder and puzzlement.

The 59 vignettes assembled for *Rock Lives* are provocative, well-written and highly subjective. One might quarrel with the tripartite book structure, especially since White lists Bill Haley as a "Pilgrim" rather than a "Pioneer." A more serious difficulty with a study that seeks to present a comprehensive profile is omission. White misses the boat by failing to include Carl Perkins, Roy Orbison, Hank Ballard, B.B. King, Bo Diddley, Fats Domino, Hank Williams, Neil Young, Smokey Robinson, Marvin Gaye, Jackie Wilson, Elton John, Hank Williams Jr., Allen Toussaint, Quincy Jones, and a boatload of 1980s performers—including Madonna. Despite these flaws, this volume represents the best of rock biography available today. It is oral history via interview; music history via biography; and journalistic history via reflection.

## SONGWRITERS

*Not Fade Away: A Comparison of Jazz Age with Rock Era Pop Song Composers.* By Walter Rimler. Ann Arbor, Michigan: Pierian Press, 1984. Illustrated. 221 pp.

Walter Rimler's study offers a challenging, controversial, critical analysis of the songs produced by composers of the 1930s and 1940s and by songwriters of the 1960s and 1970s. Borrowing his text's title from the familiar Buddy Holly tune, Rimler searches for those distinctive melodic and lyrical elements that make certain tunes emerge as pop hits and then allow them to endure the test of time to become popular standards. *Not*

*Fade Away* features a carefully honed commentary on two generations of composing talent. To represent the most gifted theater and show-tune writers Rimler has selected George Gershwin, Jerome Kern, Cole Porter, Richard Rodgers, Irving Berlin, and Harold Arlen. The works of these six masters are judged against the compositions of John Lennon, Paul McCartney, George Harrison, Bob Dylan, Mick Jagger, Keith Richards, Paul Simon, Carole King, Eddie Holland, Lamont Dozier, and Brian Holland. The latter group obviously represents The Beatles, the Rolling Stones, and the Motown Sound, as well as the individual artistry of Bob Dylan, Carole King, and Paul Simon (sans Art Garfunkel).

Despite the lack of scholarly notation within the text and the absence of both a bibliography and a discography, this study is as authoritative as it is provocative. Rimler notes that the earlier generation (Gershwin, Kern, and company) demonstrated greater productive longevity, more complex musical structure, better quality of lyric, more intricate theme patterns, and more sophistication and humor than the 1960s folks (Dylan, King, and company). This sounds suspiciously like the drivel many youngsters hear from their parents: "The music of our youth was wonderful and melodic; your music is loud, lewd, crude, and senseless." Rimler's analysis is several cuts above this kind of carping, mindless criticism. First, the author is enormously knowledgeable about all forms and styles of popular music from 1920 to the present; second, he is sensitive to the writing goals of both generations of writers; and third, he even argues with himself ("Afterword," pp. 207-209) about the possibility that his thesis concerning the decline of quality in contemporary lyric writing may be incorrect. This kind of introspection adds to the credibility of his well-argued work.

While there is much to recommend about this book—the well-crafted mini-biographies of the 17 composers being investigated, the concise commentaries on songwriting communities (New York City, London, and Detroit), song-producing partnerships (from Richard Rogers and Lorenz Hart to The Beatles), and songwriters as performers—most readers will strain to challenge Rimler's contention that the old songs are qualitatively better than the new ones. Is he mistakenly comparing apples and oranges, or pears and pizza? Too many knowledgeable musical scholars—such as Wilfrid Mellers in *Twilight of the Gods: The Music of The Beatles* (1973) and Terence J. O'Grady in *The Beatles: A Musical Evolution* (1983)—have successfully demonstrated the richness, creativity, and artistic validity of contemporary music. Too much has been written—by David Pichaske in *A Generation in Motion: Popular Music and Culture in the Sixties* (1979) and by Jerome L. Rodnitzky in *Minstrels of the Dawn: The Folk-Protest Singer as a Cultural Hero* (1976)—about the fine poetry and trenchant social commentary of modern songs to accept Rimler's thesis that modern lyrics are haphazard, self-serving, and often incoherent. How can one assemble a representative list of contemporary songwriting giants without including Hank Williams, Chuck Berry, Neil Diamond, Smokey Robinson, Stevie Wonder, Pete Townshend, and many, many others? How can one overlook the work of great collaborating pop music duos such as Jerry Leiber and Mike Stoller or Felice and Boudleaux Bryant?

Walter Rimler writes clearly, illustrates his positions well, and makes a convincing case that the rigors of writing for Broadway and movie musicals sharpened the wits of the older generation of songwriters. He contends that the problem of early burnout due to instant fame, huge wealth, and worldwide recognition makes contemporary song writers self-indulgent, lazy, and incapable of expanding their own talent and artistry. *Not Fade Away* is a book that deserves to be read and reread by serious students of American music and culture. It is entertaining, enlightening, disturbing, engaging, and valuable.

### *ALAN FREED*

*Big Beat Heat: Alan Freed and the Early Years of Rock and Roll.* By John A. Jackson. New York: Schirmer Books, 1991. Illustrated. 400 pp.

Farmingdale, Long Island public school teacher John A. Jackson has really done his homework on *Big Beat Heat.* This study utilizes previously unreleased testimony by Alan Freed before the 1960 House subcommittee on legislative oversight, interview recollections provided by several Freed family members, legal advice from Justice Joseph Stone of the New York City Criminal Court (retired) on the infamous 1959 payola investigation, and music history advice and analyses from George Moonoogian, Rick Coleman, Marv Goldberg, Mike Redmond, and William F. Griggs. The author has also consulted an impressive number of government documents, rock-era books and articles, and historic television and radio program tapes. No other study on Alan Freed comes close to this one in respect to detail, documentation, and breadth of perspective.

Jackson's work is primarily a chronological review of Freed's life beginning with the ill-fated Moondog Coronation Ball of March 21, 1952. The commentary extends from his associations with Cleveland's WJW radio executives, promoter Lew Platt, and record-store owner Leo Mintz through his involvements with New York City's WINS station, his spectacular Holiday Rock 'n' Roll Stage Shows at the Brooklyn Paramount, to the extended payola smear period, and concludes with his lonely death on January 20, 1965. The photographs in this volume are spectacular, drawn from Freed family albums, the National Television Archives (courtesy of John Cavello), and newspaper files.

The extensive research assembled for this volume neither lionizes nor defames Alan Freed. Instead Jackson casts the enigmatic disc jockey as a victim of his own personal excesses (enormous ego, cigarettes, and liquor), a small fish in a tough, shark-infested business-enterprise pool, an unwitting pawn in a political chess-game, and an off-the-wall enthusiast for unknown black singers and 1950s rhythm 'n' blues. The author identifies a variety of complex governmental and entrepreneurial drives that tossed Freed's fragile character and feckless career about before simply discarding him. Dick Clark, Morris Levy, and several of Freed's contemporaries demonstrated high-level savvy and avoided the pitfalls of becoming scapegoats or sacrificial lambs. It is too bad that Jackson failed to focus more intimately on Cleveland's 1950s radio scene, where wizard Bill Randle, wily Wes Hopkins, and wacky Pete "Mad Daddy" Meyers offer superb comparative images to Freed's Roman candle existence.

The triumph of rock 'n' roll over Tin Pan Alley, over ASCAP, over hundreds of white pop-crooners, and over segregationists of all political, economic, and social stripes was not achieved by those of pure heart. That reality has been documented by Nick Tosches and Peter Guralnick. *Big Beat Heat* humanizes the mythic figure of Alan Freed, outlines his financial irresponsibility and self-destructive habits, but accurately champions the wild-eyed enthusiasm he generated as he fostered the rise of doo-wop ballads, R&B classics, rockabilly tunes, and the eccentric and electric evangelism of Little Richard. This book is heavy on history, light on music, but marvelous on the arcane intricacies of the recording industry during the pre-Beatles period.

## *AHMET ERTEGUN*

*Music Man: Ahmet Ertegun, Atlantic Records, and the Triumph of Rock 'n' Roll.* By Dorothy Wade and Justine Picardie. New York: W. W. Norton and Company, Inc., 1990. Illustrated. 303 pp.

This brief volume examines the professional career of Turkish-born Ahmet Ertegun, the wily music entrepreneur who launched Atlantic Records in 1947. Utilizing interviews with several key recording industry leaders—Seymour Stein, Jerry Wexler, Tom Dowd, Herb Abramson, David Geffen, and Morris Levy, the authors present a journalistic account of Ertegun's rise from a Harlem hobbyist to "the greatest rock 'n' roll mogul in the world." Facts do not lie. Neither do record sales. The fascinating tale of Ertegun's artistry stretches from the early 1950s (Ruth Brown, Joe Turner, LaVern Baker, and Ray Charles) to the 1970s and late 1980s (Led Zeppelin, the Rolling Stones, Foreigner, and Genesis). Crafty showman, masterful manipulator, and ingenious surveyor of musical talent and commercial trends, Ertegun surely deserves a laudatory biography.

The strength of *Music Man* can be found in the rich writing style of the authors. From individual word choice to the context of examining issues of contention among the powerful personalities probed in this investigation, Wade and Picardie are superb. While acknowledging Ertegun's genius, the necessary luck and diligent work of his colleagues is also hailed. Probing both big names (Mick Jagger, Phil Collins, Jerry Leiber, and Hy Weiss) along with relatively obscure Atlantic insiders (Miriam Bienstock and Mica Ertegun) produces a feel not only for specific events, but also for the evolution of Ertegun's less publicized career components. The tale of Atlantic Records is framed in respect to various tensions: artistry vs. accountancy, cooperation vs. competition, and Harlem harmonies vs. heavy metal. These dichotomies are themselves fractured into varying challenging forces as the music industry advances through four decades. The shortcomings of *Music Man* are in many ways tied to the book's strengths. Wade and Picardie have attempted to encompass too much in a single volume. Even their valuable interview perspective falls short because too many topics are approached, then abandoned. The authors lose their focus on Ertegun as they scramble to explain Mafia connections and organized crime involvements, payola scandals, black backlash politics and the intricacies of label diversification. The central story flounders, although Ertegun pops up again and again. A more successful approach might have centered on Atlantic's commitment to contemporary music, and the sociological, political, and economic factors that led The Drifters, Wilson Pickett, Cream, Buffalo Springfield, Sonny and Cher, Aretha Franklin, AC/DC, Phil Collins, and INXS to fall under Ertegun's command—or spell.

Although song titles appear in several sections of the text, one doubts that Wade and Picardie are actually familiar with Atlantic's classic tunes. Too bad. Even the revelations about Phil Collins admiring R&B, about Foreigner's Mick Jones appreciating Solomon Burke and Arthur Alexander, and about the already well-publicized devotion of Mick Jagger to both Chess and Atlantic black stars lack meaning without identifying specific song influences. Brief references to Motown's pop revolution as compared to the more blatantly black sounds on noncrossover stars signed by Atco,

Stax, and Atlantic require much greater analysis in regard to record chart assessment and enduring song influence. It is hard to believe that Aretha Franklin, Otis Redding, Percy Sledge, and other soul giants who influenced Michael Bolton, Joe Cocker, The Commitments, and thousands of other performers could be diminished by a monetary bow to Berry Gordy Jr.

Beyond the historic musical contributions of Atlantic, a tribute to Ahmet Ertegun should have included a lengthy discography of his favorite songs. So much effort is devoted to defining his sensitivity, his wealth of music knowledge, and his perception of hit melodies and infectious rhythms, the reader longs to know what this "Music Man" considered to be preeminent. A wonderful disc display should have covered each decade from the 1940s thru the 1980s, with Ertegun identifying his Atlantic favorites plus those songs from other labels that he most admired.

*Music Man*, along with Charlie Gillett's *Making Tracks*, Robert Palmer's *Baby, That Was Rock 'n' Roll*, and Peter Guralnick's *Sweet Soul Music*, offer wonderful introductions to the world of Atlantic Records. However, the definitive history of this spectacular label still awaits a literary troubadour.

## *PHIL SPECTOR*

*Collecting Phil Spector: The Man, the Legend, the Music.* By John J. Fitzpatrick and James E. Fogerty. St. Paul, Minnesota: Spectacle Press, 1991. Illustrated. 128 pp.

The rock era has been shaped by many persons who are neither singers nor instrumentalists, lyricists nor composers. From disc jockeys such as Alan Freed and Dick Clark to prominent record company executives such as Berry Gordy, John Hammond, and Ahmet Ertegen, industry talent-brokers have functioned as guides to the world of popular music. Producer Phil Spector is undeniably a huckster, hype-merchant, and egomaniac. He is also one of those rare record producers who, like George Martin, has established an identifiable niche for himself as a legendary musical entrepreneur. Love him or hate him, no student of contemporary popular music can ignore his remarkable impact and lasting influence.

*Collecting Phil Spector* is a thoroughly researched, beautifully illustrated review of Spector's professional activities and musical achievements. In addition to a thorough bibliography of Spector-related books and articles, the authors provide exceptional lists of print resources on The Crystals, Darlene Love, The Righteous Brothers, The Ronettes, Ronnie

Spector, and even The Teddy Bears (pp. 89-95). The "Discography," fronted by exquisite color reproductions of 112 Spector-related album covers and picture sleeves, is clearly structured and meticulously detailed (pp. 82-88, 96-123). This volume is a collector's dream. But it is also the type of reference work that should be housed in every academic music library and sound recordings archive in the United States and Great Britain.

John J. Fitzpatrick and James E. Fogerty offer a concise, well-reasoned overview of their subject's career. From the 1960s girl group phenomena to the bombastic "wall of sound," from the distinctive rock 'n' roll Christmas album to the emergence of The Righteous Brothers' "blue-eyed soul" sound, all familiar bases are touched. New territory is explored, though, in the examination of Spector-related influences on The Beatles (especially George Harrison and John Lennon,) the Rolling Stones, Sonny and Cher, The Ramones, Bruce Springsteen, Bette Midler, and Billy Joel. Ignoring biographical controversies, the authors establish musical authority as the guiding rationale for their work. They explain, "Spector's personal and professional idiosyncracies have become as much a focus of media attention as his music. . . . Preoccupation with Spector's eccentricities has been allowed by some analysts, however, to overshadow the reason for his fame. Make no mistake–Phil Spector's powerful music is the reason for his enduring celebrity" (p. 8). This handsome, carefully indexed, fact-filled study is sure to help both critics and fans alike focus on vinyl triumphs rather than personal vanity. *Collecting Phil Spector* is a milestone publication.

## FRANK SINATRA

*Sinatra: The Man and His Music–The Recording Artistry of Francis Albert Sinatra, 1939-1992.* By Ed O'Brien and Scott P. Sayers Jr., Austin, Texas: TSD Press, 1992. Illustrated. 304 pp.

This volume is a Sinatra lover's dream come true! In updating and expanding their 1980 *Sinatra Sessions*, Ed O'Brien and Scott Sayers have assembled a beautifully illustrated, clearly printed, and factually authoritative discographic tribute to "The Voice," "The Chairman of The Board," and "Ol' Blue Eyes." *Sinatra* features: (1) recording dates, master numbers, arrangers, conductors, and locations for every Sinatra recording session (from February 3, 1939 to August 27, 1991); (2) a complete alphabetical listing of all commercially released Sinatra song titles (from "A Baby Just Like You" and "A Cottage for Sale" to "Yours Is.My Heart Alone" and "Zing Went the Strings of My Heart"); (3) an alphabetized listing of all unissued Sinatra tracks; (4) recording information on all Sinatra V-Disc sessions; (5) a chronological listing of all Sinatra songs featured on motion picture soundtracks (from "I'll Never Smile Again" in the 1941 film *Las Vegas Nights* to "Hello Young Lovers" in the 1991 movie *Jungle Fever*); (6) a history of Sinatra albums and singles that charted in either *Billboard* or *Cash Box*; (7) Sinatra Grammy nominations and awards; (8) unused cover art for proposed Sinatra projects; and (9) rare black-and-white photographs of Sinatra in concert and in the recording studio.

This work is unabashedly laudatory. It highlights the longevity and productivity of a popular music legend. What is totally absent, unfortunately, is any sense of critical analysis or historical commentary. One might incorrectly conclude that each Sinatra recording is absolutely perfect or that he never encountered anything less than ideal arrangements, orchestrations, or studio recording quality. It would be particularly sad to think that the two authors do not chuckle about Frank's uncharacteristically futile attempts to cover Jim Croce's "Bad, Bad Leroy Brown" (he recorded two different versions on December 10, 1973 and October 13, 1974) and Otis Williams and the Charms' "Two Hearts, Two Kisses" (recorded by Sinatra on March 7, 1955). Similarly, it is regrettable that only broadstroke testimonial information is provided when comparative chart-performance statistics might have been beneficial in defining Sinatra's long-term influence. Granted, Sinatra lacks the singer/songwriter credentials of many prominent contemporary recording stars—Paul Simon, "Prince," Stevie Wonder, Smokey Robinson, Paul McCartney, and Bruce Springsteen. But it would be invaluable to compare him to other classic American song stylists such as Bing Crosby and Louis Armstrong, Tony Bennett and Elvis Presley, and Ray Charles and James Brown.

Such a concluding "Coda" in the O'Brien and Sayers effort would have made this study a truly landmark resource. No music library or sound recording archive should miss this reasonably–priced, definitive discography. Sinatra worshipers now have access to a new bible. Popular music historians face the task of defining a vocal talent that spans seven decades of fame and fortune in an industry that is known more for one-hit wonders than for multiyear recording successes.

## JACKIE WILSON

*Jackie Wilson–Mr. Excitement* (Rhino CD R2-7O775). Santa Monica, California: Rhino Records, Inc., 1992. Three Compact Discs, plus Illustrated Booklet.

Defining Jackie Wilson as "Mr. Excitement" is not inaccurate. It is simply too confining. Wilson's performing experience included church roots (The Ever Ready Gospel Singers), street vocal group harmony (The Thrillers), obscure solo ventures (under the pseudonym "Sonny Wilson"), performances with a first-rate rhythm 'n' blues singing group (Billy Ward and the Dominoes), and, finally, a spectacular independent career as a rock 'n' roll, R&B, pop, and soul legend. From 1951 through 1975, he produced a remarkable array of hit recordings. The genre variations in Jackie Wilson's songs rival the breadth of material tackled by the greatest of rock's early stylists—Ray Charles, Jerry Lee Lewis, Little Richard, and Elvis Presley. The distinction between Wilson and these others is two-fold: his magnificent vocal range and his dynamic stage presence. Any nickname for Wilson's abilities and achievements should reflect these traits.

Achieving mainstream popularity, currently labeled as "crossover recognition" by record chart analysts, was the goal of many 1950s artists. Among the white performers pursuing this elusive goal, Bobby Darin proved to be highly successful at marketing himself simultaneously as a rock 'n' roller ("Splish Splash"), an R&B shouter ("What'd I Say"), a pop tune revivalist ("Lazy River"), as well as a theatre music interpreter ("Mack the Knife"). Jackie Wilson's vocal talents far exceeded those of Bobby Darin, though. Wilson tackled traditional ethnic tunes ("Danny Boy") as well as classical format songs ("Night" and "Alone at Last") with immense vigor. He ignited both blues ballads ("Doggin' Around") and rockin' numbers ("Lonely Teardrops" and "Reet Petite"). But he was at his very best on dance-oriented tunes ("Baby Workout" and "Shake! Shake! Shake!") that permitted him to demonstrate his acrobatic prowess as a mighty motion man. During the 1960s he also teamed with other artists on some uniquely soulful material. He worked with Linda Hopkins ("Shake a Hand"), LaVern Baker ("Think Twice"), and Count Basie ("Chain Gang"). Jackie Wilson charted 47 hits in *Billboard*'s R&B category, and 54 hits on the "Hot 100" listing. These striking figures do not include his highly successful three-year stint as lead singer with The Dominoes, either.

Tracing the influences on Jackie Wilson's singing style and professional recording career is a complex matter. His broad repertoire of songs indicates his personal interest in Al Jolson, Mario Lanza, and Hoagy Carmichael. Tutelage by Billy Ward undoubtedly introduced him to many classic pop recordings. From his Detroit roots Wilson encountered Little Willie John, Hank Ballard, and Clyde McPhatter. He also met many composers, arrangers, and music industry personnel that shaped his lengthy career. These contacts included Billy Davis, Rose Marks, Al Green, Berry

Gordy, Nat Tarnapol, Dick Jacobs, and Milton Delugg. Artists that were influenced by seeing Jackie Wilson perform constitute a who's who of rock–Elvis Presley, Gladys Knight, B.B. King, Smokey Robinson, Aretha Franklin, and Dionne Warwick. The stage presence of Michael Jackson is an incarnation of Jackie Wilson (and, probably, James Brown as well). Tributes to Wilson include Van Morrison's "Jackie Wilson Said (I'm in Heaven When You Smile)" and The Commodores' "Nightshift." Even more impressive are the laudable reinterpretations of several of Wilson's classic tunes–"Lonely Teardrops" by Brian Hyland (1971), "To Be Loved" by Michael Henderson (1979), "Doggin' Around" by Klique (1983), and "(Your Love Keeps Lifting Me) Higher and Higher" by Rita Coolidge (1977).

Rhino's *Mr. Excitement* anthology provides a chronological journey from "St. Louis Blues" (1957) to "Don't Burn No Bridges" (1975). Jackie Wilson's audio triumphs are well-represented, along with many lesser-known, but similarly interesting recordings. This three-CD box set contains a thoughtfully organized career history drafted by *Chicago Soul* author Robert Pruter. Full discographic information is also featured in the illustrated booklet. (A bibliography of recent studies on Jackie Wilson is listed below.) A number of fine black-and-white photographs of Wilson and his prodigious record album output are included as well. No R&B fan should miss this exceptional compilation. Similarly, music librarians and sound recording archivists ought to add this marvelous longitudinal study to their collections.

## *JERRY LEE LEWIS*

*Rockin' My Life Away: Listening to Jerry Lee Lewis.* By Jimmy Guterman. Nashville, Tennessee: Rutledge Hill Press, 1991. Illustrated. 233 pp.

The thesis of *Rockin' My Life Away* is clear: "Jerry Lee Lewis lived his life through his music; we can understand his life only through his music" (p. 27). What does this imply? The Ferriday, Louisiana fireball has never been hailed as a composer. Unlike youth-culture troubadour Chuck Berry, social critic Bruce Springsteen, human development analyst Paul Simon, or cultural commentator Bob Dylan, Jerry Lee Lewis has always been a song stylist rather than a lyric originator. Nevertheless, Jimmy Guterman has skillfully argued that song selection, stylistic adaptation, and lyric manipulation constitute the distinctive oral history of rockin' Jerry Lee. In addition, the inability of wives, managers, and producers to harness the performer's ferocious energies and to reduce his insecurities probably cost Jerry Lee the opportunity to join his popular music heroes—Al Jolson, Jimmie Rodgers, and Hank Williams—as one of America's premier song interpreters.

Guterman's tale is essentially a chronological review of Jerry Lee Lewis as public performer and studio artist. Childhood experiences, incidents of drug and alcohol abuse, parental misunderstandings, failed marriages, and other personal events are briefly noted; however, both historical events and personal problems are filtered through the mysterious psyche of a talented but troubled piano player. Signature events such as the Vietnam War, John F. Kennedy's assassination, Woodstock, and the Reagan-Bush era mean little within the intellectual orbit of Jerry Lee. Guterman contends that any form of standard biographical format cannot approach this mythic musical force that, along with Elvis Presley and Little Richard, launched the rock 'n' roll mystery upon American popular culture.

The literary challenge facing Guterman was staggering. The story of Jerry Lee Lewis' life has been told by Robert Cain (*Whole Lotta Shakin' Goin' On*–1981), Alan Clark (*Jerry Lee Lewis*–1980), Myra Lewis and Murray Silver (*Great Balls of Fire! The Uncensored Story of Jerry Lee Lewis*–1982), and Nick Tosches (*Hellfire: The Jerry Lee Lewis Story*–1982). Similarly, lengthy discographic studies have been authored by Colin Escott (*Jerry Lee Lewis: The Killer*–1986/1987), Wim de Boer (*Breathless: The Jerry Lee Lewis Long Play Album Guide*–1983), and Richard Weize (*A Preliminary Jerry Lee Lewis Discography, 1963-1977*–1986/1987). But *Rockin' My Life Away* breaks new, intriguing ground. Guterman probes the nature of Jerry Lee's personality through his rebellious interactions with musicians, producers, audiences, and recording industry managers in both live and studio performances. With the guile of Sherlock Holmes, the tenacity of Columbo, and the insight of Perry Mason, the author produces a fascinating profile of rock's bad boy.

*Rockin' My Life Away* goes well beyond the oft-repeated Jerry Lee Lewis myths in exploring recent American popular music. The Sun Records mystique of developing talent is broadly challenged; Guterman asserts that Sam Phillips merely inherited gifted artists, allowed them free reign in his laissez-faire Memphis studios, and then either sold them (Elvis Presley), mismanaged them (Jerry Lee Lewis), or saw them gain national fame with other recording companies (Roy Orbison, Charley Rich, and Johnny Cash). The power and distinctiveness of Carl Perkins' rockabilly style is consistently heralded, while the commercial sellout by Elvis is soundly condemned. The production techniques of both Sun and Smash Records are explored to demonstrate the repetition techniques employed in Jerry Lee's recording sessions–a fact that gives lie to the frequent tales of single-take perfection on key rocking tunes.

From the handsome multicolored dust jacket to the variety of black-and-white photographs within the text, from the thoughtful album list (pp. 209-219) to the thorough "Index" (pp. 217-223), Guterman has crafted a valuable, distinctive volume. The only omission from this study that might enable a reader to comprehend the magnitude of Jerry Lee's hit power is an appendix chronologically listing all of "The Killer's" charted U.S. singles. Such a list would support the author's assertion that Jerry Lee's impact on pop, R&R, and country music was both significant and long-term. This volume should be acquired by record collectors, rock 'n' roll fans, ethnomusicologists, sound recording archivists, and cultural historians. It will leave readers . . . BREATHLESS!

## *PAUL McCARTNEY*

*Paul McCartney: From Liverpool to Let It Be.* By Howard A. DeWitt. Fremont, California: Horizon Books, 1992. Illustrated. 276 pp.

Howard A. DeWitt is a rare breed in the field of popular music scholarship. He combines impressive academic credentials and extensive post-secondary school teaching experience with frequent international investigations of rock 'n' roll history and active concert promotion of classic blues performers. When not laboring in the classroom, DeWitt can be found speaking at a Beatlefest convention, hosting a television show, attending a concert with legendary bluesman Jimmy McCracklin, lecturing at a Popular Culture Association session, interviewing Battle Creek, Michigan friends of Del Shannon, or drafting articles for *DISCoveries* or *Blue Suede News*. The love of music, all forms of contemporary recorded sound, resonates throughout DeWitt's writings. While some authors devote their lifetimes to examining individual figures (Frank Sinatra, Louis Armstrong, or Hank Williams) and thereby lose perspective on broader social and musical trends, this writer seizes varying dominant performers as focal points to analyze and assess the dynamic vistas of the contemporary recording industry and modern musical history. DeWitt's previous booklength studies are gems. He has examined *Van Morrison: The Mystic's Music* (1983), *Jailhouse Rock: The Bootleg Records of Elvis Presley* (1983), *Chuck Berry: Rock and Roll Music* (1985), and *The Beatles: Untold Tales* (1985). This new analysis of Paul McCartney further demonstrates the author's insight into the uncontrollable world of rock images and recording realities.

*Paul McCartney* is a biographical journey that highlights the uneasy mix of musicianship, friendship, and business. Different audiences will appreciate different aspects of the analysis. DeWitt is a revisionist in his perspective on the composing prowess of Paul and John Lennon. Rather than adhering to the "playful, silly little love songs" McCartney and "serious, hard-edged social commentary" Lennon stereotypes, DeWitt defines each man as a shifting, growing, self-contained, creative force. The dynamics of personal enlightenment and professional change—which occurred in the lives of George Harrison and Ringo Starr as well—culminated in the demise of The Beatles and the parallel rise of four separate and unequal post-1970 celebrity careers. Paul's aesthetic, organizational, financial, and legal acumen prompted him to assert hegemony among the Fab Four in 1968. However, no internal leadership could halt the impending breakup. Too many centrifugal personal concerns, social issues, business conflicts, and media-contrived frictions overwhelmed the Liverpool group. Ultimately, Paul flew off to chart a continuing commercial recording career with Linda Eastman, Wings ("Band on the Run"), James Bond ("Live and Let Die"), Stevie Wonder ("Ebony and Ivory"), and Michael Jackson ("Say Say Say"). Shrewd entrepreneurial judgment and pop recording savvy has served McCartney well throughout his splendid career.

Beyond a fascinating and perceptive biographical history, DeWitt provides numerous black-and-white photographs of McCartney, an "Appendix" containing tips on collecting rare Beatles' recordings on the Apple label, a detailed song-by-song analysis of the *White Album*, and an annotated "Bibliography" of literary resources consulted and various individuals interviewed (including Clive Epstein, Charlie Lennon, Bob Wooler, Eddie Hoover, and many others). A thorough "Index" is also provided.

The undeniable strength of this study is the scholarly objectivity (though not detachment) of the author and the fascinating motivational insights into the mid-career behavior of the Fab Four and their worldwide audience. DeWitt is especially critical of ax-grinding journalists who continually created mischief and fostered personal conflicts throughout The Beatle's recording empire. The missing link in this otherwise exemplary biography, of course, is direct contact with its subject. Failing to submit the entire hypothesis to Paul McCartney's scrutiny and critical commentary means that all of the other oral history sources in the study remain unchallenged (though not necessarily inaccurate). One hopes that DeWitt will ship a complimentary copy to Linda and Paul as a calling card.

No Beatles fan should miss this study. Similarly, popular culture scholars should acquire this volume to explore the unpredictable interplay of commerce, artistry, multimedia advertising, broadcast and literary journalism, and individual personalities. DeWitt's detailed diagnosis of The Beatles in conflict clearly illustrates why "We Can Work It Out," "All You Need Is Love," and "Come Together" were impossible late 1960s goals for John, Paul, George, and Ringo.

# REFERENCES

Aquila, Richard. *That Old Time Rock and Roll: A Chronicle of an Era, 1954-1963*. New York: Schirmer Books, 1989.

"The Blues and Soul Hall of Fame: Number Eleven–Jackie Wilson," *Blues and Soul*, No. 579 (February 5-18, 1991), pp. 21-23.

Clark, Alan (comp.). *Legends of Sun Records*. West Covina, California: Alan C. Lungstrum/National Rock and Roll Archives, 1986.

Clark, Alan (comp.). *Legends of Sun Records–Number Two*. West Covina, California: Alan C. Lungstrum/National Rock and Roll Archives, 1992.

Clark, Alan (comp.). *Rock and Roll Legends–Number One*. West Covina, California: Alan C. Lungstrum/Leap Frog Productions, 1981.

Clark, Alan (comp.). *Rock and Roll Legends–Number Two*. West Covina, California: Alan C. Lungstrum/Leap Frog Productions, 1982.

Clark, Alan (comp.). *Rock and Roll Legends–Number Three*. West Covina, California: Alan C. Lungstrum/Leap Frog Productions, 1982.

Clark, Alan (comp.). *Rock and Roll Memories–Number One*. West Covina, California: Alan C. Lungstrum/National Rock and Roll Archives, 1987.

Clark, Alan (comp.). *Rock and Roll Memories–Number Two*. West Covina, California: Alan C. Lungstrum/National Rock and Roll Archives, 1987.

Clark, Alan (comp.). *Rock and Roll Memories–Number Three*. West Covina, California: Alan C. Lungstrum/National Rock and Roll Archives, 1988.

Clark, Alan (comp.). *Rock and Roll Memories–Number Four*. West Covina, California: Alan C. Lungstrum/National Rock and Roll Archives, 1989.

Clark, Alan (comp.). *Rock and Roll Memories–Number Five*. West Covina, California: Alan C. Lungstrum/National Rock and Roll Archives, 1990.

Clark, Alan (comp.). *Rock and Roll Memories–Number Six*. West Covina, California: Alan C. Lungstrum/National Rock and Roll Archives, 1991.

Clark, Alan (comp.). *Rock and Roll Memories–Number Seven*. West Covina, California: Alan C. Lungstrum/Leap Frog Productions, 1992.

Clarke, Donald (ed.). *The Penguin Encyclopedia of Popular Music*. New York: Viking Penguin, Inc., 1989.

Cohn, Nik. *Ball the Wall: Nik Cohn in the Age of Rock*. London: Picador Books, 1989.

Colman, Stuart. *They Kept on Rockin': The Giants of Rock 'n' Roll*. Poole, Dorset, England: Blandford Press, 1982.

Cordell, John A. (comp.). "Jackie Wilson Discography," *Record Profile Magazine*, No. 4 (February-March 1984), pp. 61-62.

Cotten, Lee. *Shake, Rattle, and Roll–the Golden Age of American Rock 'n' Roll: Volume One–1952-1955*. Ann Arbor, Michigan: Pierian Press, 1989.

DeCurtis, Anthony, James Henke, and Holly George-Warren (eds.). *The Rolling Stone Illustrated History of Rock and Roll* (fully revised and updated). New York: Random House, 1992.

Elson, Howard. *Early Rockers*. New York; Proteus Books, 1982.

Ennis, Philip H. *The Seventh Stream: The Emergence of Rock 'n' Roll in American Popular Music*. Hanover, New Hampshire: Wesleyan University Press, 1992.

Garofalo, Reebee and Steve Chapple. "From ASCAP to Alan Freed: the Pre-History of Rock 'n' Roll," in *American Popular Music—Volume Two: The Age of Rock*, edited by Timothy E. Scheurer (Bowling Green, Ohio: Bowling Green State University Popular Press, 1989), pp. 63-72.

Giddins, Gary. "Jolson's Greatest Heir," in *Rhythm-A-Ning: Jazz Tradition and Innovation in the 80s*. (New York: Oxford University Press, 1985), pp. 146-152.

Griggs, Bill. "Spotlight on Jackie Wilson (Part One)," *Rockin' 50s*, No. 26 (October 1990), pp. 8-15.

Griggs, Bill. "Spotlight on Jackie Wilson (Part Two)," *Rockin' 50s*, No. 27 (December 1990), pp. 7-13.

Guralnick, Peter. *Feel Like Going Home: Portraits in Blues and Rock 'n' Roll*. New York: Outerbridge and Dienstfrey, 1971.

Guralnick, Peter. *Listener's Guide to the Blues*. New York: Facts On File, 1982.

Guralnick, Peter. *Lost Highway: Journeys and Arrivals of American Musicians*. Boston: David R. Godine, 1979.

Hannusch, Jeff (a.k.a. Almost Slim). *I Hear You Knockin': The Sound of New Orleans Rhythm and Blues*. Ville Platte, Louisiana: Swallow Press, 1985.

Hardy, Phil and Dave Laing. *The Faber Companion to 20th-Century Popular Music*. London: Faber and Faber, 1990.

Jackson, John A. *Big Beat Heat: Alan Freed and the Early Years of Rock and Roll*. New York: Schirmer Books, 1991.

Jacobs, Dick, as told to Tim Holmes. "Jackie Wilson—Taking It Higher: A Producer Remembers 'Mr. Excitement,'" *Musician*, No. 111 (January 1988), pp. 21-26, 97-98.

Jones, Wayne. *Rockin', Rollin', and Rappin'*. Fraser, Michigan: Goldmine Press, 1980.

Joyce, Frank. "Jackie Wilson: Lonely Teardrops," in *The First Rock and Roll Confidential Report: Inside The Real World of Rock and Roll*, edited by Dave Marsh, with Lee Ballinger, Sandra Choron, Wendy Smith, and Daniel Wolff (New York: Pantheon Books, 1985), pp. 40-41.

Keegan, Kevin. "Above Jacob's Ladder: A Tribute to Jackie Wilson," *Record Profile Magazine*, No. 4 (February-March 1984), pp. 8-11, 26-27, 59-61.

Kiefer, Kit (ed.). *They Called It Rock: The Goldmine Oral History of Rock 'n' Roll, 1950-1970*. Iola, Wisconsin: Krause Publications, 1991.

Lazell, Barry, Dafydd Rees, and Luke Crampton (eds.). *Rock Movers and Shakers: An A To Z of the People Who Made Rock Happen*. New York: Billboard Publications, Inc., 1989.

Loder, Kurt. "Jackie Wilson: 1934-1984," *Rolling Stone*, No. 417 (March 15, 1984), p. 44.

Lydon, Michael. *Boogie Lightning*. New York: Dial Press, 1974.

Lydon, Michael. *Rock Folk: Portraits from the Rock 'n' Roll Pantheon*. New York: Dial Press, 1971.

McEwen, Joe. "Jackie Wilson," in *The Rolling Stone Illustrated History of Rock and Roll* (revised edition), edited by Jim Miller (New York: Rolling Stone Press/Random House, 1980), pp. 117-119.

Naha, Ed (comp.). *Lillian Roxon's Rock Encyclopedia* (revised edition). New York: Grosset and Dunlap, Inc., 1978.

Newman, Ralph M. and Alan Kaltman. "Lonely Teardrops: The Story of a Forgotten Man," *Time Barrier Express*, No. 24 (April-May 1979), pp. 29-32.

Nickols, Pete. "Jackie Wilson," *Record Collector*, No. 56 (April 1984), pp. 15-18.

Nite, Norm N. (comp.). *Rock on Almanac: The First Four Decades of Rock 'n' Roll–A Chronology*. New York: Harper and Row, 1989.

Nite, Norm N., with Ralph M. Newman (comps). *Rock On–The Illustrated Encyclopedia of Rock 'n' Roll: Volume Two–The Years of Change, 1964-1978* (updated edition). New York: Harper and Row, 1984.

Nite, Norm N., with Charles Crespo (comps.). *Rock On–The Illustrated Encyclopedia of Rock 'n' Roll: Volume Three–The Video Revolution, 1978 to the Present*. New York: Harper and Row, 1985.

Ochs, Michael. *Rock Archives: A Photographic Journey Through the First Two Decades of Rock and Roll*. New York: Doubleday and Company, Inc., 1984.

Palmer, Robert. *Baby, That Was Rock and Roll: The Legendary Leiber and Stoller*. New York: Harcourt Brace Jovanovich, 1978.

Pareless, Jon and Patricia Romanowski (eds.). *The Rolling Stone Encyclopedia of Rock and Roll*. New York: Rolling Stone Press/Summit Books, 1983.

Pruter, Robert. "Jackie Wilson," *Chicago Soul* (Champaign-Urbana: University of Illinois Press, 1991), pp. 267-279.

Pruter, Robert. "Jackie Wilson: His Chicago Years," *Goldmine*, No. 192 (December 4, 1987), pp. 30, 34.

Pruter, Robert. "Jackie Wilson: The Most Tragic Figure in Rhythm 'n' Blues," *Goldmine*, No. 294 (November 1, 1991), pp. 10-18.

Richardson, Clive. "Hot Gospel," *The History of Rock*, No. 17 (1982), pp. 330-332.

Settle, Ken. "Jackie Wilson: A Celebration of Dignity," *Goldmine*, No. 82 (July 17, 1982), p. 79.

Settle, Ken. "Jackie Wilson: The 'Showman' Is Laid to Rest," *Goldmine*, No. 94 (March 2, 1984), pp. 7-8.

Shaw, Arnold. "Interview with Jackie Wilson," *Honkers and Shouters: The Golden Years of Rhythm and Blues* (New York: Collier Books, 1978), pp. 441-445.

Stamble, Irwin. "Jackie Wilson," *The Encyclopedia of Pop, Rock, and Soul*, revised edition (New York: St. Martin's Press, 1989), pp. 742-743.

Stierle, Wayne. "Ertegun and Wexler: The First Rock and Roll Songwriters," *DISCoveries*, II (July 1989), pp. 100-101.

Wade, Dorothy and Justine Picardie. *Music Man: Ahmet Ertegun, Atlantic Records, and The Triumph of Rock 'n' Roll*. New York: W.W. Norton and Company, Inc., 1990.

Welding, Pete and Toby Byron (eds.). *Bluesland: Portraits of Twelve Major American Blues Masters*. New York: Dutton/Penguin Books, 1991.

Whitburn, Joel (comp.). *Pop Memories, 1890-1954: The History of American Popular Music*. Menomonee Falls, Wisconsin: Record Research, Inc., 1986.

Whitburn, Joel (comp.). *Top Pop Singles, 1955-1990*. Menomonee Falls, Wisconsin: Record Research, Inc., 1991.

White, Timothy. "Jerry Wexler: The Godfather of Rhythm and Blues," *Rolling Stone*, No. 331 (November 27, 1980), pp. 48-52, 74-81.

White, Timothy. *Rock Lives: Profiles and Interviews*. New York: Henry Holt and Company, 1990.

Chapter 12

# Marriage

## *WEDDING SONGS*

*Rockin' and Rollin' Wedding Songs* (Two volumes—Compact Discs R2-70588/9). Compiled by Michael Ochs, with sound produced for CD by Bill Ingot and booklet notes written by Richard Henderson. Santa Monica, California: Rhino Records, Inc., 1992.

The Rhino Records wild men (plus Brigid Pearson) are at it again! Not satisfied with issuing *Baseball's Greatest Hits* (R2-70710), *The Dr. Demento 20th Anniversary Collection* (R2-70743) of bizarre novelty tunes, *The Best of "Louie Louie"* (R2-70187), and a berserk collection of off-color R&B tunes titled *Risqué Rhythm* (R2-70570), the Santa Monica music maestros have now turned their attention to matrimonial melodies. Twenty-eight tunes are assembled on two compact discs under the title *Rockin' and Rollin' Wedding Songs*. The cover photos for these discs feature two different wedding parties, each portraying a bride and groom preparing to take their vows while skating at a 1950s roller rink. For the Rhino crews, this is standard satirical characterization for all dignified, solemn occasions. After all, they could have featured a portly parson in a purple bowling shirt pronouncing wedding vows at Strike-O-Rama Lanes in Cleveland.

This anthology is a mixed bag of predictable nuptial nostalgia and unanticipated marital mayhem. "Chapel of Love" (1964) by The Dixie

The compact disc review by B. Lee Cooper is scheduled to be published in *Popular Music and Society.* Reprint permission granted by the author, Editor R. Serge Denisoff, and Bowling Green State University Popular Press. The essay by B. Lee Cooper was originally published as "Marriage, Family Life, and Divorce" in *A Resource Guide to Themes in Contemporary Song Lyrics, 1950-1985* (Westport, Connecticut: Greenwood Press, 1986), pp. 81-100. Reprint permission granted by the author and Greenwood Press.

Cups, "To the Aisle" (1957) by The Five Satins, "Hey Paula" (1962) by Paul and Paula, and "Wedding Bell Blues" (1969) by The 5th Dimension prompt warm pop-music memories. For R&B fans and connoisseurs of classic doo-wop singing styles, "Wedding Boogie" (1950) by The Johnny Otis Orchestra, "Church Bells May Ring" (1956) by The Willows, "The Wedding" (1955) by The Solitaires, and "Three Steps from the Altar" (1961) by Shep and the Limelites will be particularly pleasing. Raucous humor is also presented on "If You Want to Be Happy" (1963) by Jimmy Soul, "Babalu's Wedding Day" (1959) by The Eternals, and "Big Bopper's Wedding" (1958) by The Big Bopper. Finally, a number of tunes ranging from minor pop hits—"I'm Gonna Get Married" (1959) by Lloyd Price and "Down the Aisle of Love" (1958) by The Quin-Tones—to unheard of uncharted melodies—"Here Comes the Bride" (1967) by Prince Buster, "Girl I Want to Marry You" (1968) by Jay and the Techniques, "I Wish That We Were Married" (1962) by Ronnie and the Hi-Lites, and "Wedding Bells" (1958) by Tiny Tim and the Hits—complete this strolling-to-the-altar audio collection.

These two discs feature a fascinating array of sounds. The material is creatively packaged. The liner notes are insufferably cute, but bulging with facts and insights about both the familiar and obscure singers. Discographic information provided is both thorough and accurate. What else could anyone ask of two volumes of *Rockin' and Rollin' Wedding Songs*? Plenty! First, the random song grouping on each disc is horrible, especially when four doo-wop tunes appear in succession on volume one, and three more are lumped together in volume two. A chronological pattern beginning with the 1950 Johnny Otis song and moving forward to the mid-1970s might inadvertently produce such back-to-back genre duplication, but it would still be better than the haphazard playlist presented here. Second, the use of more familiar (i.e., "hit") versions of individual songs should have been a priority on this kind of popular anthology. The Diamonds clanging pop rendition of "Church Bells May Ring" (1956) should have upstaged The Willows' shuffling R&B recording; and songwriter Paul Stookey's own "Wedding Song (There Is Love)" should have been anthologized rather than Toni Tennille's competent but uncharted version. Third, if the title *Rockin' and Rollin'* is actually intended to denote the rebellious, upbeat format of wedding songs to be presented, then the compiler misses the target by featuring such overly orchestrated, schmaltzy recordings as "For Me and My Gal" (1973) by Nilsson and "Band of Gold" (1955) by Don Cherry. How could Freddy Cannon's boom-boom version of "For Me and My Gal" (1961) escaped capture for this anthology? Or perhaps *Rockin' and Rollin'* is simply designed to define the time period between 1950 and 1975. In that case, the inclusion of Don Cherry's recording is reasonable, but several other omissions become much more glaring. For instance, the 1950s alone featured a bevy of bride-and-groom show tunes, pop ballads, and R&B comedy numbers that were more popular than many of the songs contained in the Rhino set. Among the overlooked gems are "Aba Daba Honeymoon" (1951) by Carleton Carpenter and Debbie Reynolds, "Get Me to the Church on Time" (1956) by Julius LaRosa, "Go on with the Wedding" (1956) by Patti Page, "Hawaiian Wedding Song" (1959) by Andy Williams, "(I'm Always Hearing) Wedding Bells" (1955) by Eddie Fisher, "Love and Marriage" (1955) by Frank Sinatra, "One Mint Julep" (1952) by The Clovers, "Rock and Roll Wedding" (1956) by Sunny Gale, "Somebody Bad Stole De Wedding Bell" (1954) by Eartha Kitt, "Wedding Bells (Are Breaking Up That Old Gang of Mine)" (1954) by The Four Aces, and "Where Were You (On Our Wedding Day)?" (1959) by Lloyd Price.

The final reservations that one might register about *Rockin' and Rollin' Wedding Songs* relate to the failure of either Michael Ochs or Richard Henderson to acknowledge and assess the expansive nature of marriage-related themes contained in post-World War II popular songs. Rather than detailing the recording careers of The Platters, Al Green, or Tiny Tim ("... not the uke-playing chap who married Miss Vicki on the *Tonight Show*"), the compilers should have explained alternative song options, as well as the availability of premarital admonition tunes. Why not expand the search for a lifetime romantic commitment so clearly voiced in "Wedding Bell Blues" (1969) by adding songs such as "Please Set a Date" (1978) by George Thorogood, "Different Drum" (1967) by Linda Ronstadt, or "Keep Your Hands to Yourself" (1986) by The Georgia Satellites? How about examining the nature of advice from others about impending wedding plans? The Rhino discs offer sage suggestions on "If You Wanna Be Happy" (1963) and "I'm Gonna Get Married" (1959), but unwisely ignore such broadly popular lyrical commentaries as "Shop Around" (1960) by The Miracles, "Take Time to Know Her" (1968) by Percy Sledge, and "Someone Saved My Life Tonight" (1975) by Elton John.

The 28 tunes found in the Rhino collection of wedding songs are undeniably enjoyable. Both CDs are worth owning. But the real merit of such theme-driven anthologies is always related to the artistic perception of compilers in structuring and rationalizing song order. Beyond the music, skillful organization attracts buyers. Disc jockeys, wedding reception hosts, students of American culture, researchers in sociology, and dozens of other categories of potential customers for *Rockin' and Rollin' Wedding Songs* would be more likely to purchase a better organized, more histori-

cally accurate, and more clearly theme-oriented set of songs. The concluding portion of this review features a selected discography of marriage-related recordings that should be considered for volumes three, four, and
five of Rhino's extended collection of Wedding Songs discs.

## Selected Chronological Discography of Wedding Songs, 1945-1990

- "The Girl That I Marry"
  (Columbia 36975)
  Frank Sinatra (1946)

- "Wedding Bells (Are Breaking Up That Old Gang of Mine)"
  (Mercury 8069)
  Steve Gibson (1948)

- "The Wedding Song"
  (RCA Victor 9035)
  Irving Fields (1948)

- "Marriage Vow"
  (RCA 48-0056)
  Hank Snow (1949)

- "Wedding Bells"
  (MGM 10401)
  Hank Williams (1949)

- "Wedding Bells Will Soon Be Ringing"
  (Capitol 40224)
  Margaret Whiting and Jimmy Wakely (1949)

- "The Wedding of Lili Marlene"
  (Decca 24706)
  The Andrews Sisters (1949)

- "Aba Daba Honeymoon"
  (Mercury 5586)
  Dick Haymes and Kitty Kallen (1950)

- "Marrying for Love"
  (RCA 47-3922)
  Perry Como (1950)

- "Wedding Boogie"
  (Savoy 764)
  The Johnny Otis Orchestra (1950)*

- "The Wedding Samba"
  (Decca 24841)
  The Andrews Sisters and Carmen Miranda (1950)

- "Aba Daba Honeymoon"
  (MGM 30282)
  Carleton Carpenter and Debbie Reynolds (1951)

- "I Went to Your Wedding"
  (RCA Victor 4835)
  Steve Gibson and the Red Caps, with Damita Jo (1952)

- "One Mint Julep"
  (Atlantic 963)
  The Clovers (1952)

- "Our Honeymoon"
  (Columbia 21008)
  Carl Smith (1952)

- "I'm Walking Behind You"
  (RCA Victor 5293)
  Eddie Fisher (1953)

- "Marriage of Mexican Joe"
  (Abbott 141)
  Carolyn Bradshaw (1953)

- "Somebody Bad Stole De Wedding Bell"
  (RCA Victor 5610)
  Eartha Kitt (1954)

- "Wedding Bells (Are Breaking Up That Old Gang of Mine)"
  (Decca 29123)
  The Four Aces (1954)

- "Wedding Bells Are Ringing in My Ears"
  (Lost Nite 323)
  The Angels (1954)

- "Band of Gold"
  (Columbia 40597)
  Don Cherry (1955)*

- "(I'm Always Hearing) Wedding Bells"
  (RCA 6015)
  Eddie Fisher (1955)

- "Love and Marriage"
  (Capitol 3260)
  Frank Sinatra (1955)

- "Marry the Man"
  (Columbia 4-40407)
  Rosemary Clooney and Jose Ferrer (1955)

- "The Wedding"
  (Old Town 1014)
  The Solitaires (1955)*

- "Church Bells May Ring"
  (Mercury 70835)
  The Diamonds (1956)

- "Church Bells May Ring"
  (Melba 102)
  The Willows (1956)*

- "Get Me to the Church on Time"
  (RCA 6567)
  Julius LaRosa (1956)

- "Go on with the Wedding"
  (Decca 29776)
  Kitty Kallen and Georgie Shaw (1956)

- "Rock and Roll Wedding"
  (RCA 6479)
  Sunny Gale (1956)

- "The Wedding"
  (Cadence 1273)
  The Chordettes (1956)

- "I Want to Marry You"
  (Fee Bee 221)
  The Dell-Vikings (1957)*

- "Kisses Sweeter Than Wine"
  (Roulette 4031)
  Jimmie Rodgers (1957)

- "Third Finger–Left Hand"
  (Columbia 40956)
  Eileen Rodgers (1957)

- "To the Aisle"
  (Ember 1019)
  The Five Satins (1957)*

- "Wedding Ring"
  (Kapp 194)
  Russ Hamilton (1957)

- "Betty and Dupree"
  (Atlantic 1168)
  Chuck Willis (1958)

- "Big Bopper's Wedding"
  (Mercury 71375)
  The Big Bopper (1958)*

- "Down the Aisle of Love"
  (Hunt 321)
  The Quin-Tones (1958)*

- "A House, a Car, and a Wedding Ring"
  (Checker 906)
  Dale Hawkins (1958)

- "Just Married"
  (Columbia 41143)
  Marty Robbins (1958)

- "Let the Bells Keep Ringing"
  (ABC-Paramount 9907)
  Paul Anka (1958)*

- "Put a Ring on My Finger"
  (Columbia 41222)
  Les Paul and Mary Ford (1958)

- "The Wedding"
  (Mercury 71382)
  June Valli (1958)

- "Wedding Bells"
  (Roulette 4123)
  Tiny Tim and the Hits (1958)*

- "Babalu's Wedding Day"
  (Hollywood 70)
  The Eternals (1959)*

- "Bells, Bells, Bells (The Bell Song)"
  (Swan 4036)
  Billy and Lillie (1959)*

- "Chapel of Dreams"
  (Gone 5069)
  The Dubs (1959)

- "Hawaiian Wedding Song"
  (Cadence 1358)
  Andy Williams (1959)

- "I'm Gonna Get Married"
  (ABC-Paramount 10032)
  Lloyd Price (1959)*

- "Mary Lou"
  (Roulette 4177)
  Ronnie Hawkins (1959)

- "Peggy Sue Got Married"
  (Coral 62134)
  Buddy Holly and the Crickets (1959)

- "We Told You Not to Marry"
  (Glover 201)
  Titus Turner (1959)

- "Where Were You (on Our Wedding Day)"
  (ABC-Paramount 9997)
  Lloyd Price (1959)

- "Down the Aisle"
  (Ace 583)
  Ike Clanton (1960)

- "Shop Around"
  (Tamla 54034)
  The Miracles (1960)

- "Wedding Day"
  (RCA 47-7745)
  Ray Peterson (1960)

- "For Me and My Gal"
  (Swan 4083)
  Freddy Cannon (1961)

- "I Hear Bells (Wedding Bells)"
  (ABC-Paramount 10248)
  The Dell-Vikings (1961)*

- "It's Gonna Work Out Fine"
  (Sue 749)
  Ike and Tina Turner (1961)

- "Make Believe Wedding"
  (Era 3057)
  The Castells (1961)

- "Three Steps from the Altar"
  (Hull 747)
  Shep and the Limelites (1961)*

- "The Wedding"
  (Columbia 42148)
  Anita Bryant (1961)

- "When We Get Married"
  (Heritage 102)
  The Dreamlovers (1961)*

- "Hey, Paula"
  (Philips 40084)
  Paul and Paula (1962)*

- "I Wish We Were Married"
  (Joy 260)
  Ronnie and the Hi-Lites (1962)*

- "Most People Get Married"
  (Mercury)
  Patty Page (1962)

- "Ruby Ann"
  (Columbia 42614)
  Marty Robbins (1962)

- "Wedding Bells"
  (Chess 1835)
  Billy Stewart (1962)

- "Down the Aisle (Wedding Bells)"
  (Newtown 5777)
  Patti LaBelle and the Blue Belles (1963)

- "(I Cried at) Laura's Wedding"
  (Jamie 1260)
  Barbara Lynn (1963)

- "If You Wanna Be Happy"
  (S.P.Q.R. 3305)
  Jimmy Soul (1963)*

- "Little Band of Gold"
  (Joy 274)
  James Gilreath (1963)

- "Not Too Young to Get Married"
  (Philles 113)
  Bob B. Soxx and the Blue Jeans (1963)

- "(Today I Met) The Boy I'm Gonna Marry"
  (Philles 111)
  Darlene Love (1963)

- "The Wedding Song"
  (Chelsea 103)
  The Fabulaires (1963)

- "Chapel Of Love"
  (Red Bird 001)
  The Dixie Cups (1964)*

- "Matchmaker Matchmaker"
  (RCA 47-8448)
  Ethel Ennis (1964)

- "White on White"
  (United Artists 685)
  Danny Williams (1964)

- "You Never Can Tell"
  (Chess 1906)
  Chuck Berry (1964)

- "I'm Henry VIII, I Am"
  (MGM 13367)
  Herman's Hermits (1965)

- "Makin' Whoopee"
  (ABC 10609)
  Ray Charles (1965)

- "Marry Me"
  (Jomada 600)
  Johnny Daye (1965)

- "The Wedding"
  (Mercury 72332)
  Julie Rogers (1965)

- "Band of Gold"
  (Imperial 66165)
  Mel Carter (1966)

- "Bus Stop"
  (Imperial 66186)
  The Hollies (1966)

- "Eleanor Rigby"
  (Capitol 5715)
  The Beatles (1966)

- "Husbands and Wives"
  (Smash 2024)
  Roger Miller (1966)

- "If I Were a Carpenter"
  (Atlantic 2350)
  Bobby Darin (1966)

- "Wouldn't It Be Nice?"
  (Capitol 5706)
  The Beach Boys (1966)*

- "Different Drum"
  (Capitol 2004)
  Linda Ronstadt and the Stone Poneys (1967)

- "Here Comes the Bride"
  (RCA Album)
  Prince Buster (1967)*

- "Marryin' Kind of Love"
  (Kapp 805)
  The Critters (1967)

- "Wedding Bell Blues"
  (Verve 5024)
  Laura Nyro (1967)

- "Wedding Gown for Sale"
  (Warner Brothers 7004)
  Don Crawford (1967)

- "With This Ring"
  (Musicor 1229)
  The Platters (1967)*

- "Girl I Want to Marry You"
  (Smash Album)
  Jay and the Techniques (1968)*

- "If I Were a Carpenter"
  (Motown 1124)
  The Four Tops (1968)

- "The Marriage Bit"
  (Columbia 44563)
  Lefty Frizzell (1968)

- "Take Time to Know Her"
  (Atlantic 2490)
  Percy Sledge (1968)

- "Worst That Could Happen"
  (Buddah 75)
  The Brooklyn Bridge (1968)

- "Cherry Hill Park"
  (Columbia 44902)
  Billy Joe Royal (1969)

- "Wedding Bell Blues"
  (Soul City 779)
  The 5th Dimension (1969)*

- "Wedding Cake"
  (MGM 14034)
  Connie Francis (1969)

- "Band of Gold"
  (Invictus 9075)
  Freda Payne (1970)

- "If I Were a Carpenter"
  (Columbia 45064)
  Johnny Cash and June Carter (1970)

- "Marry Me"
  (Republic 1409)
  Ron Lowry (1970)

- "We've Only Just Begun"
  (A&M 1217)
  The Carpenters (1970)

- "Marriage Has Ruined More Good Love Affairs"
  (Decca 32778)
  Jan Howard (1971)

- "Rings"
  (Entrance 7500)
  Cymarron (1971)

- "That's the Way I've Always Heard It Should Be"
  (Elektra 45724)
  Carly Simon (1971)

- "Wedding Song (There Is Love)"
  (Warner Brothers 7511)
  Paul Stookey (1971)

- "Wedlock Is a Padlock"
  (Hot Wax 7007)
  Laura Lee (1971)

- "Wedding Song (There Is Love)"
  (MGM 14431)
  Petula Clark (1972)

- "Chapel of Love"
  (Atlantic 2980)
  Bette Midler (1973)

- "For Me and My Gal"
  (RCA Album)
  Nilsson (1973)*

- "Wedding Bells"
  (Mercury 73381)
  Frank Zappa, with Ruben and the Jets (1973)

- "Let's Get Married"
  (Hi 2262)
  Al Green (1974)*

- "Marry Me Again"
  (A&M 1636)
  April Stevens (1974)

- "Wedding Bells"
  (Monument 8597)
  Billy Swan (1974)

- "The Wedding Song"
  (Chicago Fire 7402)
  Ral Donner (1974)

- "Little Band of Gold"
  (Columbia 10121)
  Sonny James (1975)

- "Someone Saved My Life Tonight"
  (MCA 40421)
  Elton John (1975) (1975)

- "Wedding Song (There Is Love)"
  (A&M Album)
  Captain and Tennille (1975)*

- "Golden Ring"
  (Epic 50235)
  George Jones and Tammy Wynette (1976)

- "Baby Please Set a Date"
  (Rounder Album)
  George Thorogood and the Destroyers (1978)

- "Love, Love, Love/Chapel of Love"
  (Warner Brothers 8610)
  Sandy Posey (1978)

- "Paradise by the Dashboard Light"
  (Epic 50588)
  Meatloaf (1978)

- "Wedding Song (There Is Love)"
  (Ariola 7726)
  Mary MacGregor (1978)

- "You'll Accomp'ny Me"
  (Capitol 4904)
  Bob Seger (1980)

- "All My Rowdy Friends (Have Settled Down)"
  (Elektra 47191)
  Hank Williams, Jr. (1981)

- "Husbands and Wives"
  (Warner Brothers 49825)
  David Frizzell and Shelly West (1981)

- "Just Married"
  (RCA 13095)
  Louise Mandrell and R.C. Bannon (1983)

- "Let's Pretend We're Married"
  (Warner Brothers 29548)
  Prince (sic) (1983)

- "Our Wedding Band"
  (RCA 13095)
  Louis Mandrell and R.C. Bannon (1983)

- "Wedding Bells"
  (Moonshine 3019)
  Margo Smith (1983)

- "White Wedding (Part One)"
  (Chrysalis 42697)
  Billy Idol (1983)

- "Band of Gold"
  (Epic 04423)
  Charly McClain (1984)

- "Size Seven Round (Made of Gold)"
  (Epic 04876)
  George Jones and Lacy J. Dalton (1985)

- "I Knew the Bride (When She Used to Rock and Roll)"
  (Columbia 05570)
  Nick Lowe and His Cowboy Outfit (1986)

- "Keep Your Hands to Yourself"
  (Elektra 69502)
  The Georgia Satellites (1986)

- "She Thinks That She'll Marry"
  (MTM 72076)
  Judy Rodman (1986)

- "Savin' the Honey for the Honeymoon"
  (Capitol 44007)
  Sawyer Brown (1987)

- "Makin' Whoopee!"
  (Warner Brothers 22976)
  Dr. John, featuring Rickie Lee Jones (1989)

---

\* Songs featured on the 1992 Rhino set of *Rockin' and Rollin' Wedding Songs*.

## MARRIAGE, FAMILY LIFE, AND DIVORCE

For singers of the 1950s, love and marriage were inevitably linked. Vocalists of both sexes acknowledged this. Frank Sinatra and Dinah Shore depicted the unity of courtship and marital bliss as a horse-and-carriage relationship in their separate renditions of "Love and Marriage" (1955). Two years later Jimmie Rodgers expanded this dualistic theme to include the growth of an extremely large family–all because his sweetheart/wife had "Kisses Sweeter Than Wine" (1957). Beyond mythical tales of happily-ever-after lives for newlyweds, however, there are numerous songs that depict realistic strains that inevitably occur within marital relationships. Jealousy resulting from real or imagined incidents, singular sexual indiscretions, or frequent acts of cheating and infidelity are chronicled in tunes such as "Lyin' Eyes" (1975), "Smoke from a Distant Fire" (1977), and "Take a Letter, Maria" (1969). Although spouses often elect to forgive and forget the indiscretions of a mate in order to sustain a marriage, there are numerous songs that describe the pain of permanent separation and the finality of divorce. Many of the same emotions expressed in premarital "lost love" tunes sung by unmarried men and single women are even more deeply echoed in songs describing the end of a marriage, the dissolution of a family, and the loneliness of starting over without a partner.

Marriage is often a highly fantasized event. It is seen as a moment of personal exhilaration that propels a groom "From a Jack to a King" (1962). It can also be the fulfillment of a long-time dream, as in "(Today I Met) The Boy I'm Gonna Marry" (1963), "Hey Paula" (1962), "Betty and Dupree" (1958), and "Band of Gold" (1955). Yet there are also skeptics and jokers observing the institution of marriage along with the idealistic romantics. Some tunes urge caution in selecting a mate–"Shop Around" (1960), "If You Wanna Be Happy" (1963), "If I Were a Carpenter" (1966), "Take Time to Know Her" (1968), and "Someone Saved My

Life Tonight" (1975); other recordings are openly whimsical toward the marital state—"One Mint Julep" (1952), "It's Gonna Work Out Fine" (1961), "You Never Can Tell" (1964), "I'm Henry VII, I Am" (1965), and "Let's Pretend We're Married" (1983); and a few songs either balk at marriage in general—"Different Drum" (1967), "That's the Way I've Always Heard It Should Be" (1971), and "The Right Thing to Do" (1973)—or express selfish opposition to an impending wedding—"Wedding Bells (Are Breaking Up That Old Gang of Mine)" (1954), "Go on with the Wedding" (1956), "(I Cried At) Laura's Wedding" (1963), and "Worst That Could Happen" (1968).

Despite the varying feelings described above, The Dreamlovers' plans for "When We Get Married" (1961) are transformed from a wish into reality once the determination "I'm Gonna Get Married" (1959) is finally secured. Examples of wedding songs abound. Among the most popular during the past three decades are: "(I'm Always Hearing) Wedding Bells" (1955), "Church Bells May Ring" (1956), "Get Me to the Church on Time" (1956), "To the Aisle" (1956), "Big Bopper's Wedding" (1958), "Down the Aisle of Love" (1958), "Hawaiian Wedding Song" (1959), "Down the Aisle" (1960), "For Me and My Gal" (1961), "Down the Aisle (Wedding Bells)" (1963), "Chapel of Love" (1964), "The Wedding" (1965), "We've Only Just Begun" (1970), and "The Wedding Song (There Is Love)" (1971). As a footnote, Frank Sinatra comments that although the first encounter with marital bliss may be wonderful, even a return engagement at a chapel's steps can be personally fulfilling. He proclaims that love is even lovelier "The Second Time Around" (1961).

Reactions to married life vary in popular songs. Images of wives as lifelong companions, lovers, and selfless friends abound. Examples of such recordings are "Kisses Sweeter Than Wine" (1957), "Little Green Apples" (1968), "Friend, Lover, Woman, Wife" (1969), "My Woman, My Woman, My Wife" (1970), "Good-Hearted Woman" (1976), "Devoted to You" (1978), and "Do That to Me One More Time" (1979). Other positive reflections of married life include the melancholy "Honey" (1968) and the anti-materialistic "Ruby Ann" (1962). One highlight of marriage, of course, is the annual celebration of the event as depicted in "Our Anniversary" (1962).

Family life is simple when the unit consists only of a newlywed couple. Once children are added to the domestic scene, parental responsibilities become more complicated. Sly and the Family Stone describe the disunity of sibling rivalry within a household in "Family Affair" (1971). The positive sides of parenting are depicted in terms of fatherly pride in "Mama's Pearl" (1971) and of parents' reflections on the maturing, chaos, and talents of their offspring in "Willie and the Hand Jive" (1958), "Broomstick Cowboy" (1965), "Watching Scotty Grow" (1970), and "Saturday Morning Confusion" (1971). There is sadness, too. The blight of poverty in the lives of the young is depicted in "Rag Doll" (1964), "Poor Man's Son" (1965), "In the Ghetto" (1969), and "Patches" (1970).

A husband and wife must adopt new roles–and new names. The "daddy" and "mommy" labels denote not only family responsibilities but also changes in lifestyle. Images of fathers in popular music are sometimes funny–"Yakety Yak" (1958), "Peek-a-Boo" (1958), and "Summertime Blues" (1958), but generally are strong and serious. Tunes illustrating this latter thought include "Oh! My Pa-Pa" (1953), "My Dad" (1962), "Father Knows Best" (1962), "My Daddy Knows Best" (1963), "Daddy Sang Bass" (1968), "Color Him Father" (1969), "Let Me Be the Man My Daddy Was" (1969), "Daddy Could Swear, I Declare" (1973), and "Leader of the Band" (1981). Sometimes, however, the father's behavior is called into question by youngsters, as in "Papa Was Too" (1966) and "Papa Was a Rolling Stone" (1972). Mothers tend to be described as loving, selfless creatures who are totally devoted to their young ones. Songs stating this conviction are "Mama" (1960, 1966), "For Mama" (1965), "Dreams of the Everyday Housewife" (1968), "Lady Madonna" (1968), "Mama Liked the Roses" (1970), "Mother" (1971), "Mother and Child Reunion" (1972), "I'll Always Love My Mama" (1973), and "Loves Me Like a Rock" (1973).

Parents are also remembered and rated in terms of particular situations. Will they allow frequent dating? Do they acknowledge their child's judgments and opinions as having validity? Are they kind and hospitable to their child's teenage friends? Do they understand key adolescent concerns? Do they set rules fairly? Are they consistent models or hypocrites in respect to the behavioral and ethical standards they demand of their children? These issues are explored in numerous recordings such as "Teenager's Mother (Are You Right?)" (1956), "Mama Said" (1961), "Wolverton Mountain" (1962), "Mama Didn't Lie" (1963), "Mama Don't Allow" (1963), "Mrs. Brown You've Got a Lovely Daughter" (1965), "Skip a Rope" (1967), "1432 Franklin Pike Circle Hero" (1968), "Harper Valley P.T.A." (1968), "Mama Told Me (Not to Come)" (1970), "Sylvia's Mother" (1972), "The Free Electric Band" (1973), and "Your Daddy Don't Know" (1982). In musical terms, the indictment by Loggins and Messina–"Your Mama Don't Dance" (1972)–is symbolic of the generation gap in both age and parental understanding.

Somewhere between the joy of being a bride and a groom and the sorrow of permanent separation and divorce, there lies an unpleasant zone of emotional instability. The path to this area may be lined with imagined acts of unfaithfulness that spark fits of jealousy or with real situations of infidelity that mark the abandonment of crucial marriage vows. In either case, tensions within personal and family relationships can become unbearable. Margo Smith defined the ethical situation clearly in her song "Either You're Married or You're Single" (1983). For some, temptation to cheat on a spouse can be faced and overcome. This is illustrated in "Almost Persuaded" (1966) and "Family Man" (1983); for others, however, there is strong verbal support from the mate that is designed to ensure fidelity to the marriage and to frighten away would-be sources of alienated affection. These recordings include "Leave My Kitten Alone" (1959), "You'll Lose a Good Thing" (1962), "Don't Mess with Bill" (1966), "Him or Me–What's It Gonna Be?" (1967), "Foolish Fool" (1969), "Let's Stay Together" (1971), "He Don't Love You (Like I Love You)" (1975), "You Belong to Me" (1978), and "Stop in the Name of Love" (1983). Despite pleading from a loving spouse, opportunities for sexual indiscretion seem to be never ending. Waitresses, such as the tart at "Smokey Joe's Cafe" (1955), urge men to "Come a Little Bit Closer" (1964). Women who don't mind "Steppin' Out" (1976) on their husbands advertise the fact by keeping their "Backfield in Motion" (1969). Dr. Hook notes that domestic life can be particularly tense "When You're in Love with a Beautiful Woman" (1979). Of course, the suspicions spawned by jealousy over extreme physical attractiveness are not always well-formed or deserved. Yet they exist. The disruptive power of jealousy is thoroughly articulated in songs such as "Hey! Jealous Lover" (1956), "Silhouettes" (1957), "Chip-Chip" (1961), "Suspicion" (1964), "Don't Answer the Door" (1966), "The Chokin' Kind" (1969), "Suspicious Minds" (1969), and "How Long (Betcha' Got a Chick on the Side)" (1975).

Infidelity, the pursuit of forbidden fruit, the desire to have an "Outside Woman" (1974) or a "Back Door Man" (1969), is too strong, too exhilarating for many married people. Cheating occurs. These acts of betrayal are described in varying tones of guilt, pleasure, and suspicion about the behavior of the marriage partner in numerous recordings. Among the most popular illustrations are "Tonight You Belong to Me" (1956), "Lipstick on Your Collar" (1959), "I'm Gonna Move to the Outskirts of Town" (1961), "I've Got News for You" (1961), "Smokey Places" (1961), "Walk on By" (1961, 1964), "Your Cheatin' Heart" (1962), "Frankie and Johnny" "Steal Away" (1964), "The Cheater" (1966), "Somebody Has Been Sleeping in My Bed" (1967), "Woman, Woman," (1967), "Delilah" (1968), "I Heard It Through the Grapevine" (1968), "Midnight Confessions" (1968), "Who's Making Love" (1968), "Ruby, Don't Take Your Love to Town"

(1969), "Your Husband–My Wife" (1969), "(If Loving You Is Wrong) I Don't Want to Be Right" (1972), "Me and Mrs. Jones" (1972), "Third Rate Romance" (1975), "Torn Between Two Lovers" (1976), "Lucille" (1977), "Smoke from a Distant Fire" (1977), "Trying to Love Two" (1977), "Man on Your Mind" (1982), "The Other Woman" (1982), "Holding Her and Loving You," (1983), and "Midnight Fire" (1983). Popular songs even document the varying reactions of those involved in love triangles. Betrayed wives voice reactions in "To the Other Woman (I'm the Other Woman)" (1970) and "Angel in Your Arms" (1977); a betrayed husband reacts in "Take a Letter, Maria" (1969); and the objects of extramarital affection even respond in "Clean Up Woman" (1971) and "She's Got the Papers (But I Got the Man)" (1981).

On many occasions, marriages are saved because jealousy subsides and is replaced by renewed trust. Similarly, sexual adventurism ceases to be enjoyable, thrilling, or rewarding and cheating finally stops. The difficulties of marital life remain, but the couple survives intact. But popular songs also address the reality of separation and divorce. Actually, singers and songwriters address two themes. First, they cover the facts of legal separation—"Alimony" (1959), "D-I-V-O-R-C-E" (1968), and "With Pen in Hand" (1968), or the physical disappearance of a mate and parent—"Hit the Road Jack" (1961), "For Lovin' Me" (1965), "Go Now!" (1965), "By the Time I Get to Phoenix" (1967), "You Better Sit Down Kids" (1967), "Leaving on a Jet Plane" (1969), "Got to See If I Can't Get Mommy (to Come Back Home)" (1970), "Your Daddy Don't Live in Heaven (He's in Houston)" (1981). But more important, they depict the differing emotional reactions to the collapse of a supposed-to-be lifetime relationship. There are appeals for resolution of differences based upon the belief that life without the loved one would be meaningless. These include "Hey, Girl" (1963), "I've Been Loving You Too Long (To Stop Now)" (1965), "Let's Hang On!" (1965), "Ain't Too Proud to Beg" (1966), "I Can't Turn You Loose" (1968), "Breaking Up Is Hard to Do" (1975), and "Break It to Me Gently" (1982). But the die is usually cast by this time. The signs of "Love on the Rocks" (1980) are symbolized in dozens of behavioral and attitudinal shifts. Both members of a dissolving marriage articulate feelings such as those contained in "What's the Reason I'm Not Pleasing You" (1957), "So Sad (To Watch Good Love Go Bad)" (1960), "Where Did Our Love Go" (1964), "You've Lost That Lovin' Feelin'" (1964), "You Keep Me Hangin' On" (1966), "Time Was" (1969), "(I Know) I'm Losing You" (1970), and "You Don't Bring Me Flowers" (1978).

Although the final separation might be summed up in objective terms such as "We Just Disagree" (1977), deep emotional links sometimes echo

"I Can't Stop Loving You" (1962). Attempts to renew contacts or reveries about the former relationship prompt images such as those expressed in "Since I Don't Have You" (1959), "All Alone Am I" (1962), "Memphis" (1964), "Crying Time" (1965), and "One Less Bell to Answer" (1970). However, some feel that enough is enough. Once a relationship has ended in emotional pain, it would be foolish to attempt to fan the flame again. Julie London states this position clearly in "Cry Me a River" (1955), as does Fats Domino in "I Hear You Knocking" (1961).

## REFERENCES

Betrock, Alan. *Girl Groups: The Story of a Sound.* New York: Delilah Books, 1982.

Gaar, Gillian G. *She's a Rebel: The History of Women in Rock and Roll.* Seattle, Washington: Seal Press, 1992.

Greig, Charlotte. *Will You Still Love Me Tomorrow? Girl Groups From the 50s On.* London: Virago Press, 1989.

Hibbard, Don J. and Carol Kaleialoha. *The Role of Rock: A Guide to the Social and Political Consequences of Rock Music.* Englewood, New Jersey: Prentice-Hall, Inc., 1983.

Greil, Marcus. "The Girl Groups," in *The Rolling Stone Illustrated History of Rock and Roll* (fully revised and updated), edited by Anthony DeCurtis and James Henke, with Holly George Warren (New York: Random House, 1992), pp. 189-191.

Redmond, Mike. "Crying in the Chapel," *Record Exchanger,* IV (1975), pp. 26-27.

Whitburn, Joel (comp.). *Top Country Singles, 1944-1988.* Menomonee Falls, Wisconsin: Record Research, Inc., 1989.

Whitburn, Joel (comp.). *Top Pop Singles, 1955-1993.* Menomonee Falls, Wisconsin: Record Research, Inc., 1994.

Chapter 13

# Motion Pictures

*Risky Business: Rock in Film.* By R. Serge Denisoff and William D. Romanowski. New Brunswick, New Jersey: Transaction Books, 1991. 768 pp.

R. Serge Denisoff is a colossus in the realm of popular music analysis. He has authored hundreds of book reviews, record commentaries, and scholarly essays. He has edited the academic journal *Popular Music and Society* since 1971. Finally, his booklength publications are indicative of the breadth of his musical interest: *Great Day Coming: Folk Music and the American Left* (Penguin, 1971); *Sing a Song of Social Significance* (Popular Press, 1972); *The Sounds of Social Change: Studies in Popular Culture*, with Richard A. Peterson (Rand McNally, 1972); *Solid Gold: The Popular Record Industry* (Transaction Books, 1975); *Waylon: A Biography* (University of Tennessee Press, 1983); *Tarnished Gold: The Record Industry Revisited*, with the assistance of William L. Schurk (Transaction Books, 1986); and *Inside MTV* (Transaction Books, 1988). Only Charlie Gillett (*The Sound of the City: The Rise of Rock and Roll*, Pantheon, rev. ed., 1983) and Simon Frith *(Sound Effects: Youth, Leisure, and the Politics of Rock 'n' Roll*, Pantheon, 1981) can compare to Denisoff in providing insight into the sociology of music since 1950. Other writers—Nick Tosches and Peter Guralnick, for instance—may provide more passion, but none have the breadth of perception that typifies Denisoff's thoughtful commentaries. Opinionated, critical, scholarly, thorough, and somewhat mysterious as a public persona, the Bowling Green State University professor is always worth reading. Denisoff's co-author on *Risky Business* is a young doctoral candidate who teaches at Calvin College in Grand Rapids, Michigan. He

This study by B. Lee Cooper is scheduled to be published under the title "Popular Music/Popular Film: A Review Essay and Bibliography" in *Popular Culture in Libraries*. Reprint permission granted by the author, Editor Frank Hoffmann, and The Haworth Press.

has written several fine journal essays and is the co-author of a superb study titled *Dancing in the Dark: Youth, Popular Culture, and the Electronic Media* (William B. Eerdman, 1991).

Borrowing their book title from the 1983 Tom Cruise film, Denisoff and Romanowski define the task of predicting audience responses to soundtrack-driven motion pictures as a very "risky business." Sociological analysis, marketing and promotion techniques, technological innovations, and demographic calculations undergird their chronological tale (1954-1990) of the search for media synergy. The authors define this complex term succinctly: "Practitioners used the concept to describe the interplay between organisms that increases their ability to achieve an effect of which each is individually incapable. More simply, synergy increases each component's effectiveness in reaching a mutually desirable goal" (p. 10). The movie industry needed to utilize the record industry's most popular product—rock songs—to overcome the challenge of television in the late 1950s. The adaptations of pop tunes to motion picture plots is the phenomena examined throughout *Risky Business*. The greed, poor judgment, miscalculations, luck, swindling, political machinations, propaganda techniques, successes, failures, and embarrassments that abound in rock-related filmmaking are elaborately (and often humorously) detailed. Pursuing a chronological format, the authors spin a story that is worthwhile reading—even at a hefty 768 pages. The anecdotal illustrations are delightful and insightful. The tales of record company executives and film board chairmen originally rejecting ideas such as pairing Jennifer Warnes and Joe Cocker to do "Up Where We Belong" on the 1982 *An Officer and a Gentleman* soundtrack abound (p. 507). The detailed investigations into early 1950s events, myths, and personalities also prompt new perspectives. Denisoff and Romanowski trace the zig-zag trail of Bill Haley and the Comets' anthem "Rock Around the Clock" (pp. 11-61) and pay special attention to the generational volcano that launched the youthful Elvis Presley as rock 'n' roll's King over the more elderly Haley, the wrong-race-but-multitalented Chuck Berry, and the wild-and-woolly Jerry Lee Lewis. The footnote documentation is particularly thorough, with more than 120 citations per chapter. The authors rely heavily on trade journals (*Billboard* and *Variety*), newspapers and magazines (*The New York Times, Village Voice, Rolling Stone, Newsweek,* and *Time*), and a few specialty publications (*Film Journal* and *American Film*). The book features a wonderfully detailed Index (pp. 753-768) as well.

What sets this text apart from all other rock film studies is thoroughness. Ironically, the hallmark of the authors' efforts also becomes the only source of criticism. Denisoff and Romanowski address each and every soundtrack-driven motion picture produced since the early 1950s. They explain the sources of tunes utilized in particular films, reiterate and assess critical reviews and other responses to individual motion pictures, provide magnificent synopses of the plots, characters, and stars of specific films, and place soundtracks in a context of immediate influence, innovation, and ultimate impact on the movie industry. What is missing? Perhaps more page space. For some strange reason, the text ends with a tiny, incomplete Bibliographical Notes (pp. 749-751) section that contrasts sharply with the minute detail presented in the footnote pages. Even more bewildering is the lack of any discography. With access to Bowling Green State University's excellent Sound Recordings Archive, it seems impossible that the vinyl and compact disc history of soundtracks has been omitted. This reviewer's suspicion is that the Transaction Books' editors snorted, "No, we can't put another sixty pages in this study. You've got to consolidate the bibliography and drop the record list altogether." Whatever the reason, it is a sad omission. A landmark study, *Risky Business* should be solid from stem to stern, from text/ footnotes to bibliography/discography.

## *MOTION PICTURE BIBLIOGRAPHY*

### *General Motion Picture Studies and Rock Film Guides*

- Bangs, Lester. "Introduction to Rock Cinema '78," *Phonograph Record Magazine*, VIII (May-June 1978), pp. 12-13.

- Beauchamp, Phil. "Black Vocal Groups in Motion Pictures," *Time Barrier Express*, No. 22 (March-April 1977), pp. 6-11.

- Belz, Carl. "Act Naturally: The Rise of the Rock and Roll Movie," in *The Story of Rock*, second edition (New York: Harper and Row, 1972), pp. 14-18.

- Bentley, Bill. "New Orleans Goes to Hollywood," *Wavelength*, No. 45 (July 1984), pp. 16-18.

- Blair, John. "Early Rock Cinema, 1956-1960," *Goldmine*, No. 40 (September 1979), pp. 8-12A.

- Bordman, Gerald. "Rock and Roll; Pitch and Toss," in *American Musical Comedy: From Adonis to Dreamgirls* (New York: Oxford University Press, 1982), pp. 178-190.

- Brady, Barry. *Reelin' and Rockin': The Golden Age of Rock 'n' Roll Movies*. Australia: The Printing Place, Ltd., 1982.

- Brown, Ashley. "Rock Spreads Its Wings," *The History of Rock*, No. 11 (1982), pp. 201-203.

- Bull, Debby. "Reeling and Rocking," *Rolling Stone*, No. 468 (February 27, 1986), pp. 53-54.

- Burt, Rob. *Rock and Roll: The Movies*. New York: Sterling Publishing Company, 1986.

- Burt, Rob. *Rockerama: 25 Years of Teen Screen Idols*. New York: Delilah Books, 1983.

- Cagin, Seth and Philip Dray. *Hollywood Films of the Seventies: Sex, Drugs, Violence, Rock 'n' Roll, and Politics*. New York: Harper and Row, 1984.

- Cajiao, Trevor. "Classic Film Footage on Video: Rock 'n' Roll–The Greatest Years," *Now Dig This*, No. 81 (December 1989), pp. 24-25.

- Cohen, Mitch. "Rockcinema–The First 21 Years, 1955-1976," *Phonograph Record Magazine*, VI (August 1976), pp. 1, 36-43.

- Cross, Robin. *2000 Movies: The 1950s*. New York: Arlington House, 1988.

- Darling, Cary. "Rock Movies Grow Up," *Billboard*, (August 2, 1980), pp. 3, 4, 10.

- Dellar, Fred (comp.). *New Musical Express Guide to Rock Cinema*. Middlesex, England: Hamlyn Paperbacks, 1981.

- Denisoff, R. Serge and William D. Romanowski, "The Pentagon's Top Guns: Movies and Music," *Journal of American Culture*, XII (Fall 1989), pp. 67-78.

- Desplas, John. "Rock Films: Suffering in Style," *Wavelength*, I (June 1981), pp. 35-36.

- Doherty, Thomas. *Teenagers and Teenpics: The Juvenilization of American Movies in the 1950s*. Boston: Unwin Hyman Books, 1988.

- Dowdy, Andrew. "Beats, Bikers, and Rebellious Youth," in *The Films of the Fifties: The American State of Mind* (New York: William Morrow and Company, 1975), pp. 130-158.

- Edgerton, Gary R. (ed.). *Film and the Arts in Symbiosis: A Resource Guide*. Westport, Connecticut: Greenwood Press, 1988.

- Ehrenstein, David and Bill Reed. *Rock on Film*. New York: Delilah Books, 1982.

- Evans, Mark. "The Emergence of Pop Music," in *Soundtrack: The Music of the Movies* (New York: Hopkinson and Blake, 1975), pp. 190-210.

- Flinn, Carol. "Male Nostalgia and Hollywood Film Music: The Terror of the Feminine," *Canadian University Music Review*, X, No. 2 (1990), pp. 19-26.

- Fong-Torres, Ben. "Rock on Reels: Doin' The Hollywood Hustle," *Rolling Stone*, (April 20, 1978), pp. 45-46.

- Friendly, David T. "Music Can Make The Movie," *Detroit* (Michigan) *News*, (November 25, 1986), pp. 1, 2C.

- Furcolow, John. "Marriage Made in Hollywood Heaven: Filmmakers Hit Right Combination By Adding Dose of Rock 'n' Roll," *Lexington* (Kentucky) *Herald-Leader*, (July 1-0, 1985), pp. 1, 12D.

- Gaar, Gillian G. "Rock Soundtracks: A 30-Year Tradition and Going Strong," *Goldmine*, No. 233 (June 30, 1989), pp. 91-93.

- Graff, Gary. "When Song Meets Movie, Sparks (And Dollars) Fly," *Detroit* (Michigan) *Free Press*, (August 31, 1986), pp. 1, 6C.

- Grant, Barry K. "The Classic Hollywood Musical and the 'Problem' of Rock 'n' Roll," *Journal of Popular Film and Television*, XIII (Winter 1986), pp. 195-205.

- Harrington, Richard. "The Saga of the Sound Track," *Washington Post*, (January 12, 1986), p. 1, 10, 11K.

- Hoffman, Frank W. and William G. Bailey. *Arts and Entertainment Fads*. Binghamton, New York: The Haworth Press, 1990.

- Hogg, Brian. "Psych-Out!" *Record Collector*, No. 135 (November 1990), pp. 18-20.

- Holden, Stephen. "How Rock Is Changing Hollywood's Tune," *The New York Times*, (July 16, 1989), p. 1H.

- Holden, Stephen. "Movies, Music, and Money: Who's on First?" *High Fidelity*, XXX (October 1980), p. 108.

- Jackson, John. "1950's Visual," *Rockin' 50s*, No. 6 (June 1987), pp. 6-7.

- Jackson, John. "1950's Visual," *Rockin' 50s*, No. 8 (October 1987), pp. 6-7.

- Jackson, John. "1950's Visual," *Rockin' 50s*, No. 10 (February 1988), pp. 6-7.

- Jackson, John. "Rock 'n' Roll Movies of 1957," *Rockin' 50s*, No. 2 (October 1986), p. 8.

- Jefferson, Margo. "Rock and Reel: Today's Biggest Movie Stars Are Sound Tracks," *Vogue*, CLXXVIII (January 1988), pp. 42-43.

- Jenkinson, Philip and Alan Warner. *Celluloid Rock: Twenty Years of Movie Rock*. London: Lorrimer Publishing, 1974.

- Jinkins, Shirley and Michael H. Price. "Country At the Movies," *Country Sounds*, I (June 1986), pp. 18, 26-27, 53.

- Keith, Don Lee. "New Orleans Music in Film," *Wavelength*, No. 13 (November 1981), pp. 35-36.

- Kelly, William P. "Running on Empty: Reimagining Rock and Roll," *Journal of American Culture*, IV (Winter 1981), pp. 152-159.

- Kirby, Kip. "Hollywood Finally Flashes That Proud Soundtrack Smile," *Billboard*, (November 23, 1985), pp. 6, 11, 13, 15.

- Marcus, Greil. "Rock Films," in *The Rolling Stone Illustrated History of Rock and Roll* (revised edition), edited by Jim Miller (New York: Random House/Rolling Stone Press Book, 1980), pp. 390-400.

- Marsh, Dave. "Schlock Around The Clock," in *Fortunate Son* (New York: Random House, 1985), pp. 151-162.

- Martin, Linda and Kerry Segrave. *Anti-Rock: The Opposition to Rock 'n' Roll*. Hamden, Connecticut: Archon Books, 1988.

- McCarthy, Todd and Charles Flynn (eds.), *King of the Bs—Working Within the Hollywood System: An Anthology of Film History and Criticism*. New York: E.P. Dutton and Company, Inc., 1975.

- McGee, Mark Thomas. *The Rock and Roll Movie Encyclopedia of the 1950s*. Jefferson, North Carolina: McFarland and Company, Inc., 1990.

- McGuigan, Cathleen and Peter McAlevey. "Rock Music Goes Hollywood," *Newsweek*, CV (March 11, 1985), p. 78.

- McLafferty, Gerry. *Elvis in Hollywood: Celluloid Sell-Out*. New York: State Mutual Book and Periodical Service, 1989.

- Meeker, David. *Jazz in the Movies: A Guide to Jazz Musicians, 1917-1977*. New Rochelle, New York: Arlington House, 1977.

- Meredith, Louis. "Musicals on Video," *Stereo Review*, XLIX (April 1984), pp. 36-37.

- Meredith, Louis. "The Sound of Movies: A Critic's Choice of Ten Top Sonic Spectaculars," *Stereo Review*, XLIX (November 1984), pp. 56-57.

- Miller, Debby. "Rock Is Money to Hollywood Ears," *Rolling Stone*, No. 407 (October 27, 1983), pp. 102-105.

- Nickols, Pete. "Rock 'n' Roll Movies," *Now Dig This*, No. 59 (February 1988), p. 27.

- Occhiogrosso, Peter. "Reelin' and Rockin'," *American Film*, IX (April 1984), pp. 44-51.

- Prendergast, Roy M. "From 1950 to the Present," in *A Neglected Art: A Critical Study of Music in Films* (New York: New York University Press, 1977), pp. 98-167.

- Resnik, Henry S. "The Rock Pile," *Saturday Review*, XLIV (January 30, 1971), pp. 48-50.

- Richards, Stanley (ed.). *Great Rock Musicals*. New York: Stein and Day, 1979.

- Rockwell, John. "The Sound of Hollywood," in *The Rolling Stone Illustrated History of Rock and Roll* (rev. ed.), edited by Jim Miller (New York: Random House/Rolling Stone Press Book, 1980), pp. 407-414.

- Romanowski, William D. and R. Serge Denisoff. "Money For Nothin' and the Charts For Free: Rock and the Movies," *Journal of Popular Culture*, XXI (Winter 1987), pp. 63-78.

- Sandahl, Linda J. (comp.). *Encyclopedia of Rock Music on Film: A Viewer's Guide to Three Decades of Musicals, Concerts, Documentaries, and Soundtracks, 1955-1986*. Poole, Dorset, England: Blandford Press, 1987.

- Simels, Steve. "Movie Music," *Stereo Review*, XLII (April 1987), pp. 59-61, 114.

- Simels, Steve. "Rock Goes to the Movies," *Stereo Review*, XL (June 1978), pp. 82-85

- Smith, Monty. "Rock 'n' Role: A Concise History of the Big Beat on the Big Screen," in *New Musical Express Guide to Rock Cinema*, compiled by Fred Dellar (Middlesex, England: Hamlyn Paperbacks, 1981), pp. 9-21.

- Smolian, Steven (comp.). *A Handbook of Film, Theater, and Television Music on Record, 1948-1969: Alphabetical Listing*. New York: Record Undertaker, 1970.

- Smolian, Steven (comp.). *A Handbook of Film, Theater, and Television Music on Record, 1948-1969: Index*. New York: Record Undertaker, 1970.

- Stacy, Jan and Ryder Syvertsen. *Rockin' Reels: An Illustrated History of Rock and Roll Movies*. Chicago: Contemporary Books, Inc., 1984.

- Staehling, Richard. "From *Rock Around the Clock* to *The Trip*: The Truth About Teen Movies," in *King of the Bs*, edited by Todd McCarthy and Charles Flynn (New York: E.P. Dutton and Company, 1975), pp. 220-251.

- Struck, Jurgen. *Rock Around the Cinema: Spielfilme, Dokumentationen, Video-Clips*. Reinbeck: Rowohlt, 1985.

- Tannenbaum, Bob. "Soundtracks Thrived in Summer of '85: Arranged Marriages Between Movies and Rock 'n' Roll Produced Spectacular Results," *Rolling Stone*, No. 461 (November 21, 1985), pp. 15-17.

- Upton, Rich. "Just Four of the 101 Ways to Screw Up a Soundtrack," *DISCoveries*, I (December 1988), p. 41.

- Upton, Rich. "Love and Hate . . . Soundtracks," *DISCoveries*, I (May-June 1988), p. 27.

- Upton, Rich. "Soundtracks: Who's in Charge Here? Or, Why Don't They Let Me Do This?" *DISCoveries*, I (October 1988), p. 41.

- Upton, Rich. "What Makes a Soundtrack Collectible?" *Goldmine*, No. 158 (August 15, 1986), p. 72.

- Woffinden, Bob. "Rock At the Drive-In," *The History of Rock*, No. 11 (1982), pp. 206-210.

- Zoglin, Richard. "Hollywood Catches the Rock Beat: Some Tracks Have Become the Key to Orchestrating a Box Office Hit," *Time*, CXXIII (March 26, 1984), p. 72.

### *Movie Posters and Film Memorabilia*

- Betrock, Alan. *The I Was a Teenage Juvenile Delinquent Rock 'n' Roll Beach Party Movie Book: A Complete Guide to the Teen Exploitation Film, 1954-1969*. New York: St. Martin's Press, 1986.

- Betrock, Alan (comp.). *Rock 'n' Roll Movie Posters*. New York: Shake Books, 1979.

- Clark, Alan (comp.). *Rock and Roll in the Movies—Number One*. West Covina, California: Alan Lungstrum, 1987.

- Clark, Alan (comp.). *Rock and Roll in the Movies—Number Two*. West Covina, California: Alan Lungstrum, 1987.

- Clark, Alan (comp.). *Rock and Roll in the Movies—Number Three*. West Covina, California: Alan Lungstrum, 1988.

- Clark, Alan (comp.). *Rock and Roll in the Movies—Number Four*. West Covina, California: Alan Lungstrum, 1989.

## *Commentaries on Specific Motion Pictures*

- Bangs, Lester. "*The Last Waltz*: A Film By Martin Scorsese," *Phonograph Record Magazine*. VIII (May-June 1978), pp. 13, 16, 18ff.

- Blair, John. "A Focus on *Carnival Rock*," *Goldmine*, No. 55 (December 1980), pp. 170-171.

- Blair, John. "Rock and Roll Cinema: A Focus on *Rock, Baby, Rock It*," *Goldmine*, No. 41 (October 1979), p. 9.

- Bowles, Stephen E. "*Cabaret* and *Nashville*: The Musical As Social Comment," *Journal of Popular Culture*, XII (Winter 1978), pp. 550-556.

- Cajiao, Trevor. "*Great Balls of Fire*," *Now Dig This*, No. 72 (March 1989), pp. 4-5.

- Carpenter, John. "*Love Me Tender*," *Now Dig This*, No. 22 (January 1985), pp. 17-20.

- Cooper, B. Lee. "Review of 41 Original Hits From the Soundtrack of *American Graffiti*," in *Images of American Society in Popular Music* (Chicago: Nelson-Hall, Inc., 1982), pp. 196-198.

- Coppage, Noel. "And Then There's *Nashville*," *Stereo Review*, XXXV (October 1975), pp. 55-56.

- Cott, Jonathan. "A Hard Day's Knights," in *The Beatles Reader*, edited by Charles P. Neises (Ann Arbor, Michigan: Pierian Press, 1984), pp. 157-163.

- Curtis, James M. "From *American Graffiti* to *Star Wars*," *Journal of Popular Culture*, XIII (Spring 1980), pp. 590-601.

- Denisoff, R. Serge. "*A Hard Day's Night* in Hell: *Sid and Nancy*," *Popular Music and Society*, XIII (Fall 1989), pp. 63-73.

- Denisoff, R. Serge and William Romanowski. "Katzman's *Rock Around the Clock*: A Pseudo-Event?" *Journal of Popular Culture*, XXIV (Summer 1990), pp. 65-78.

- Denisoff, R. Serge. "The 'Misadventures' of a Rock Film: *Eddie and the Cruisers*," *Popular Music and Society*, XII (Fall 1988), pp. 39-56.

- Denisoff, R. Serge. "Review of *The Big Chill*," *Popular Music and Society*, XIII (Spring 1989), pp. 115-118.

- Denisoff, R. Serge. "Review of *The Girl Can't Help It*," *Popular Music and Society*, XIII (Spring 1989), pp. 105-111.

- Denisoff, R. Serge. "Review of *Streets of Fire*," *Popular Music and Society*, XIII (Spring 1989), pp. 103-105.

- Desplas, John. "*La Bamba*–Song and Dance," *Wavelength*, No. 82 (August 1987), pp. 6-7.

- Goldberg, Michael. "Monterey Pop: The Dawning of An Age," *Rolling Stone*, No. 501 (June 4, 1987), pp. 116-120.

- Griffin, Sid. "*American Hot Wax*," *Phonograph Record Magazine*, VIII (May-June 1978), p. 18.

- Griggs, Bill. "Buddy Holly Lives!" *Record Digest*, I (August 1, 1978), pp. 5-6.

- Griggs, Bill. "Great Balls of Fire," *Rockin' 50s*, No. 19 (August 1989), pp. 4-5.

- Griggs, Bill. "*La Bamba*–The Movie," *Rockin' 50s*, No. 8 October 1987), p. 17.

- Hasbany, Richard. "*Saturday Night Fever* and *Nashville*: Exploring the Comic Mythos," *Journal of Popular Culture*, XII (Winter 1978), pp. 557-571.

- Holden, Stephen. "Paul Simon Tells His Story: On Film and Vinyl," *Rolling Stone*, No. 328 (October 16, 1980), pp. 54-55.

- Jackson, John. "1950's Visual," *Rockin' 50s*, No. 1 (August 1986), pp. 6-7. (Review of *Jamboree*).

- Jackson, John. "1950's Visual," *Rockin' 50s*, No. 2 (October 1986), pp. 6-7. (Review of *The Girl Can't Help It*).

- Jackson, John. "1950's Visual," *Rockin' 50s*, No. 3 (December 1986), pp. 6-7. (Review of *Rock Around the Clock*).
- Jackson, John. "1950's Visual," *Rockin' 50s*, No. 4 (February 1987), pp. 6-7. (Review of *Rock, Rock, Rock*).
- Jackson, John. "1950's Visual," *Rockin' 50s*, No. 5 (April 1987), pp. 6-7. (Review of *Don't Knock the Rock*).
- Jackson, John. "1950's Visual," *Rockin' 50s*, No. 7 (August 1987), pp. 6-7. (Review of *Go, Johnny, Go*).
- Jackson, John. "1950's Visual," *Rockin' 50s*, No. 9 (December 1987), pp. 6-7. (Review of *Rock, Baby, Rock It*).
- Jackson, John. "1950's Visual," *Rockin' 50s*, No. 12 (June 1988), pp. 8-9. (Review of *Let the Good Times Roll*).
- Kelly, William P. "More Than a Woman: Myth and Mediation in *Saturday Night Fever*," *Journal of American Culture*, II (Summer 1979), pp. 235-247.
- Luijters, Guss and Gerard Timmer (trans. Josh Pachter). *The Girl Can't Help It* (1956), in *Sexbomb: The Life and Death of Jayne Mansfield* (Secaucus, New Jersey: Citadel Press, 1988), pp. 52-53.
- Marsh, Dave. "*This Is Elvis*: The Once and Forever King," *Rolling Stone*, No. 344 (May 28, 1981), pp. 46-49.
- Meltzer, R. "*Rock 'n' Roll High School*: 'The Greatest Rock-and-Roll 35 mm'er in Close to a Goddam Decade!,'" *Waxpaper*, IV (May 4, 1979), pp. 12-14.
- Meredith, Louis. "Hail! Hail! Chuck Berry!" *Stereo Review*, LIII (June 1988), p. 149.
- Nassour, Ellis and Richard Broderick. *Rock Opera: The Creation of Jesus Christ Superstar from Record Album to Broadway Show to Motion Picture*. New York: Hawthorn Books, 1973.
- Nunn, Roger. "Celluloid Rock: *Go, Johnny, Go*," *Now Dig This*, No. 61 (April 1988), pp. 12-13.
- Plasketes, George. "Great Balls of Fire!" *Popular Music and Society*, XIII (Fall, 1989), pp. 75-80.
- Plasketes, George M. "*La Bamba*: Rock Resurrection in the Me Decade," *Popular Music and Society*, XII (Fall 1988), pp. 111-116.
- Pond, Steve. "*Eddie and The Cruisers*: Hollywood Rips Off Bruce," *Rolling Stone*, No. 405 (September 29, 1983), pp. 57, 62-63.

- Robbins, Ira. "The Who Movie: *Kids Are Alright* Director Jeff Stein Tells TP All About It," *Trouser Press*, No. 37 (April 1979), pp. 16-19.

- Rollin, Roger B. "Robert Altman's *Nashville*: Popular Film and the American Character," *South Atlantic Bulletin*, XLII (November 1977), pp. 41-50.

- Sodowsky, Alice, Roland Sodowsky, and Stephen Witte. "The Epic World of *American Graffiti*," in *Movies As Artifacts: Cultural Criticism of Popular Film*, edited by Michael T. Marsden, John G. Nachbar, and Sam L. Grogg, Jr. (Chicago: Nelson-Hall, Inc., 1982), pp. 217-222.

- Whitesell, Rick. "The 34th Elvis Presley–*This Is Elvis*," *Goldmine*, No. 56 (January 1981), p. 19.

### Rock Film Composers

- Cresser, Wayne. "Ry Cooder: Scoring Big in the Movies," *Goldmine*, No. 193 (January 1, 1988), pp. 20, 106.

- Goodfriend, James. "Randy Newman's Movie Music," *Stereo Review*, XLIII (December 1979), pp. 72-73.

- Mitchell, Elvis. "Cooder Been a Contender," *Film Comment*, XXII (March-April 1986), pp. 76-77.

- Scherman, Tony. "Ry Cooder's Crossroads Blues," *Rolling Stone*, (October 10, 1985), pp. 55-59.

- Upton, Rich. "The Film Scores of Randy Newman," *Goldmine*, No. 146 (February 28, 1986), p. 60.

### Awards and Honors for Film Music

- Pollock, Bruce. "Awards Index," in *Popular Music, 1980-1984: Volume 9* (Detroit, Michigan: Gale Research Company, 1986), pp. 297-298.

- Shapiro, Nat and Bruce Pollock, "Awards Index," in *Popular Music, 1920-1979–A Revised Cumulation: Volume Three* (Detroit, Michigan: Gale Research Company, 1985), pp. 2713-2720.

- Whitburn, Joel. "Academy Award Winners–Best Song," and "Grammy Award Winners–Record of the Year/Song of the Year," in

*Pop Singles Annual, 1955-1990* (Menomonee Falls, Wisconsin: Record Research, Inc., 1991), pp. 702-703 and 704-705.

## *Bibliographies, Discographies, and Filmographies*

- Aros, Andrews A. *Elvis: His Films and Recordings*. Diamond Bar, California: Applause Publications, 1980.

- Berry, Chuck. "Discography/Filmography," in *Chuck Berry—The Autobiography* (New York: Harmony Books, 1987), pp. 334-341.

- Brady, Barry. "Blue Suede Views: A Rock 'n' Roll Filmography," in *Reelin' and Rockin': The Golden Age of Rock 'n' Roll Movies* (Australia: The Printing Place, Ltd., 1982), pp. 61-65.

- Burns, Gary. "Film and Popular Music," in *Film and the Arts in Symbiosis: A Resource Guide*, edited by Gary R. Edgerton (Westport, Connecticut: Greenwood Press, 1988), pp. 217-242.

- Christensen, Roger and Karen Christensen (comps.). *Christensen's Ultimate Movie, TV, and Rock 'n' Roll Directory* (third edition). San Diego: Cardiff-By-The-Sea Press, 1988.

- Chu, John and Elliot Cafritz. *The Music Video Guide*. New York: McGraw-Hill Book Company, 1986.

- Cooper, B. Lee. "Motion Picture and Television Soundtrack Music," in *The Popular Music Handbook: A Resource Guide for Teachers, Librarians, and Media Specialists* (Littleton, Colorado: Libraries Unlimited, 1984), pp. 150-155.

- Doggett, Peter. "British Beat on Film," *Record Collector*, No. 135 (November 1990), pp. 10-13.

- Doggett, Peter. "Elvis' Film Soundtracks," *Record Collector*, No. 12 (August 1980), pp. 27-32.

- Hammontree, Patsy Guy. "Filmography," in *Elvis Presley: A Bio-bibliography* (Westport, Connecticut: Greenwood Press, 1985), pp. 240-260.

- Harris, Steve. "Film Music," in *Film, Television, and Stage Music on Phonograph Records: A Discography* (Jefferson, North Carolina: McFarland and Company, Inc., 1988), pp. 7-274.

- Harry, Bill. *Beatlemania: The History of the Beatles on Film*. London: Virgin Book, 1984.

- Hart, Paul. "A Guide to Short Beatles Films," *Record Profile Magazine*, No. 7 (September-October 1984), pp. 20-23.

- Heatly, Michael. "Presley on Film," *The History of Rock*, No. 11 (1982), pp. 211-214.

- Hendler, Herb. "Important Films in the Rock Era," in *Year by Year in the Rock Era: Events and Conditions Shaping the Rock Generations That Reshaped America* (Westport, Connecticut: Greenwood Press, 1983), pp. 285-292.

- Hoffmann, Frank and B. Lee Cooper. "Films," in *The Literature of Rock II* (Metuchen, New Jersey: Scarecrow Press, Inc., 1986), pp. 881-889.

- Karnback, James. "Rock 'n' Roll Film Directory," in *Contemporary Music Almanac 1980/81*, compiled by Ronald Zalkind (New York: Schirmer Books, 1980), pp. 804-816.

- Lax, Roger and Frederick Smith. *The Great Song Thesaurus* (second edition, updated and expanded). New York: Oxford University Press, 1989.

- Leibowitz, Alan. "Movie Soundtrack Recordings," in *The Record Collector's Handbook* (New York: Everest House, 1980), pp. 97-103.

- Lichter, Paul. "Discography and Films," in *The Boy Who Dared to Rock: The Definitive Elvis* (Garden City, New York: Dolphin Books, 1978), pp. 199-298.

- Limbacher, James L. *Film Music: From Violins to Video*. Metuchen, New Jersey: Scarecrow Press, 1974.

- Limbacher, James L. *Keeping Score: Film Music*. Metuchen, New Jersey: Scarecrow Press, 1981.

- Lynch, Dennis. "James Bond: Double Naught Music," *Goldmine*, No. 115 (December 21, 1984), pp. 48-56.

- Macken, Bob, Peter Fornatale, and Bill Ayres (comps.). "Rock-Oriented Films–A Chronological Listing By Release Date," in *The Rock Music Source Book* (Garden City, New York: Anchor Books, 1980), pp. 592-593.

- Marsh, David. "Rock 'n' Roll Films" and "Ten Best/Ten Worst Rock 'n' Roll Films," in *Contemporary Music Almanac 1980/81*, compiled by Ronald Zalkind (New York: Schirmer Books, 1980), pp. 797-803.

- Matthew-Walker, Robert. "Appendix I–Filmography," in *Elvis Presley: A Study in Music*. (London: Omnibus Press, 1983), pp. 119-134.

- McGee, Mark Thomas. *The Rock and Roll Movie Encyclopedia of the 1950s*. Jefferson, North Carolina: McFarland and Company, Inc., 1990.

- Osborne, Jerry (edited by Ruth Maupin). *The Official Price Guide to Movie/TV Soundtracks and Original Cast Albums*. New York: House of Collectibles, 1991.

- Osborne, Jerry and Bruce Hamilton (comps.). *Movie/TV Soundtracks and Original Cast Albums Price Guide*. Phoenix, Arizona: O'Sullivan, Woodside and Company, 1981.

- Pitts, Michale R. and Louis Harrison Jr. (comps.). *Hollywood on Record: The Film Stars' Discography*. Metuchen, New Jersey: Scarecrow Press, 1978.

- Rose, Edward (comp.). *Soundtrack Record Collectors' Guide*. Minneapolis, Minnesota: Dored Company, 1978.

- Russell, Wayne. "Gene Vincent at the Movies," *Goldmine*, No. 91 (December 1983), p. 187.

- Sandahl, Linda J. *Rock Films: A Viewer's Guide to Three Decades of Musicals, Concerts, Documentaries, and Soundtracks, 1955-1986*. New York: Facts on File, 1987.

- Shore, Michael (comp.). *Music Video: A Consumer's Guide*. New York: Ballantine Books, 1987.

- Smolian, Steven (comp.). *A Handbook of Film, Theater, and Television Music on Record, 1948-1969*, (Two Volumes). New York: The Record Undertaker, 1970.

- Thomas, Tony. *Music for the Movies*. New York: A.S. Barnes, 1973.

- Tobler, John and Richard Wootton. "Filmography," in *Elvis: The Legend and the Music* (New York: Crescent Books, 1983), pp. 182-183.

- Trudeau, Noah Andre. "The Bond Cycle," *High Fidelity*, XXXV (August 1985), pp. 47-48, 80.

- Van Hollebeke, Jim. "Elvis Presley: A Guide to the Films of Elvis," *Goldmine*, No. 105 (August 3, 1984), pp. 6-16.

- Warner, Alan. *Who Sang What on the Screen*. London: Angus and Robertson, 1986. (c. 1984)

- Westcott, Steven D. (comp.). *A Comprehensive Bibliography of Music for Film and Television.* Detroit, Michigan: Information Coordinators, 1985.

- Zmijewsky, Steven and Boris Zmijewsky. *Elvis: The Films and Career of Elvis Presley.* Secaucus, New Jersey: Citadel Press, 1983.

## Unpublished Film Studies

- Redd, Lawrence N. "The Impact of Radio, Motion Pictures, and Television on the Development of Rhythm and Blues, and on Rock and Roll Music" (Unpublished Masters Thesis at Michigan State University, 1971).

- Slater, Thomas J. "Rock Music, Youth, and Society: The Uses of Rock Music in the Movies, 1955-1981" (Mimeographed paper presented at the 12th Annual Convention of the Popular Culture Association in Louisville, Kentucky on April 14, 1982).

# Chapter 14

# Multiculturalism

## *CLASSICAL MUSIC INFLUENCES*

*Rockin' the Classics and Classicizin' the Rock: A Selectively Annotated Discography—First Supplement.* Compiled By Janell R. Duxbury. Westport, Connecticut: Greenwood Press, 1991. 168 pp.

University of Wisconsin at Madison Technical Services Librarian Janell R. Duxbury has devoted two volumes to make a single point: The influence of the European classics on American rock music is pervasive and continuing. Rather than hearing "Bumble Boogie" (Rimsky-Korsakov influence), "Nut Rocker" (Tchaikovsky influence), "A Fifth of Beethoven" (Ludwig influence), and "Rock Me Amadeus" (Mozart influence) as interesting anomalies, Duxbury obviously senses that there is a direct linear relationship between Western art music and many, many contemporary popular recordings. She first made her case in 1985 via *Rockin' the Classics and Classicizin' the Rock* and has since reinforced her position in 1991 with the *First Supplement.*

The only hesitation that one feels about endorsing Duxbury's scholarship stems from the fact that it lacks sufficient balance and perspective. The recognition of nonclassical African and Caribbean rhythms as roots of rock tempos is either severely muted or totally absent. The acknowledgement of black folk-elements in numerous popular melodies and lyrics is not mentioned. And the marvelous artistic creativity of Chuck Berry, Paul Simon, Bonnie Raitt, Bruce Springsteen, Stevie Wonder, and hundreds of other U.S., British, and Australian pop singers/songwriters seems sub-

These five reviews by B. Lee Cooper are scheduled to be published in *Popular Music and Society* and *Popular Culture in Libraries*. Reprint permission granted by the author, Editor R. Serge Denisoff, and Bowling Green State University Popular Press, and Editor Frank Hoffmann and The Haworth Press.

sumed by the erroneous contention that The Beatles, Jeff Beck, or Lindsey Buckingham are totally and exclusively dependent on Bach, Brahms, and Beethoven.

Duxbury's two volumes are invaluable resources for identifying classical music borrowings and adaptations in contemporary songs. But the wacky humor of Spike Jones' mutilating "The William Tell Overture," the irony of Chuck Berry appealing for Beethoven to roll over and tell Tchaikovsky that rock music has arrived, and the unceremonious seizure of Bach's "Minuet in G" by The Toys says much more about modern music than Duxbury is able to communicate. An authentically popular music is unabashedly an amalgam of highbrow and lowbrow, of classic and folk/blues/country, and of stylish, stylized, and stolen tunes and lyrics. A strong dose of Michael Bane, Charlie Gillett, Peter Guralnick, Lawrence Redd, Jerome Rodnitzky, and Nick Tosches should accompany any perusal of *Rockin' the Classics*. In the meantime, do not expect to encounter too many articles focusing on classical nuances found in the recordings of Little Richard, Jerry Lee Lewis, Lee Dorsey, Big Mama Thornton, James Brown, Lou Ann Barton, Don and Dewey, or Mitch Ryder and the Detroit Wheels.

## RHYTHM 'N' BLUES ROOTS

*The Rocking 40's* (Hoy Hoy CD 40-S-O1). Compiled by Morgan Wright. Brattleboro, Vermont: Hoy Hoy Compact Discs, 1992.

*What Was the First Rock 'n' Roll Record?* By Jim Dawson and Steve Propes. Boston: Faber and Faber, 1992. 201 pp. Paperback.

*Record Collector* Editor Peter Doggett recently wrote, "Rock in 1993 is so fragmented, so divided into rival rebel camps, that it's impossible to agree where the centre of the music is today, let alone where it's come from." Concerning the pursuit of rock's rhythmic roots, Doggett's frustration is obvious. He laments, "Every contemporary music fan worships different gods; and my deities are likely to be your devils." Heavy metal enthusiasts and rap music supporters, for instance, revel in being ahistorical. Nevertheless, a significant portion of the pop music pantheon—lovers of Elvis Presley and Otis Redding, fans of Aretha Franklin and Bonnie Raitt, and followers of Led Zeppelin and the Rolling Stones—hark back to early 1950s America to locate the roots of rock. Morgan Wright, Jim Dawson, and Steve Propes argue that such conventional wisdom ignores the authentic 1940s foundation of the rock 'n' roll empire.

Morgan Wright has assembled a superb collection of 22 rhythm 'n' blues tunes to illustrate that African-American boogie was the authentic cornerstone of the rock revolution. Ranging from the Pete Johnson and Big Joe Turner rendition of "That's All Right Baby" (1938) to Doc Sausage's recording of "Sausage Rock" (1950), Wright demonstrates how the hard-driving rock idiom was born. From suggestive lyrics to honking saxophones, from piano boogie woogie to heavy drum support, black music is undeniably a catalyst. Among the most enlightening tracks are "Rock Awhile" (1949) by Goree Carter and His Hepcats, "I Want to Rock and Roll" (late 1940s) by Scatman Crothers, and "Rockin' the House" (1947) by Memphis Slim and His House Rockers. Other artists included in *The Rocking 40's* are The Wynonie Harris All Stars, Amos Milburn, Tommy Brown, The Freddie Mitchell Orchestra, The Buster Bennett Band, Luke Jones with Joe Alexander's Highlanders, Roy Brown and His Mighty Men, Cleo Brown, Joe Brown and His Kool Kats, Albert Ammons, Joe Lutcher and His Society Cats, Melvin "Sax" Gill, and Louis Jordan and His Tympany Five. Wright stands firm on his conviction that Elvis Presley's success was strictly imitation, not creative innovation. R&B singers had already articulated the patois, while their rockin' instrumental supporters had launched the big beat long before Alan Freed, Elvis, Colonel Parker, or Dick Clark sold the myth of white rock 'n' roll.

Jim Dawson and Steve Propes use literary persuasion rather than audio illustration to document their pursuit of *What Was the First Rock 'n' Roll Record?* They formulate an entertaining, provocative, fact-filled examination of 50 recordings released between 1944 and 1956. Unfortunately, their anthology does not answer the question stated in the book's title. But Dawson and Propes provide an array of fascinating clues to this ongoing debate. Actually, this volume combines the historical perspective of Nick Tosches' *Unsung Heroes of Rock 'n' Roll* (1984) with the kind of music trivia contained in Bob Shannon and John Javna's *Behind the Hits* (1986). The result is enlightening. The authors explore a strange concoction of 1940s tunes including "The Honeydripper," "House of Blue Lights," "That's All Right," "Open the Door, Richard," and "Good Rockin' Tonight"; they mix these numbers together with several early 1950s releases including "The Fat Man," "Rollin' and Tumblin'," "I'm Movin' On," "Rocket 88," and "Sixty-Minute Man"; and they complete their antique vinyl gumbo with such mid-1950s rockin' classics as "I've Got a Woman," "Bo Diddley," "Maybellene," "Tutti Frutti," "Blue Suede Shoes," and "Heartbreak Hotel." From Joe Liggins, Big Boy Crudup, and Wynonie Harris through Fats Domino, Muddy Waters, and Jackie Brenston to Chuck Berry, Little Richard, and Elvis Presley, Dawson and Propes chase the elu-

sive question: What was the first genuine rock 'n' roll record? The conclusion is obvious: No one really knows.

The strength of this detailed discographic investigation is found in the
piecemeal approach to audio archeology. Clearly, individual records are
the fundamental building blocks of the rock era. While egos, greed, hype,
and backstabbing (whether racial, royalty based, or copyright related)
have been endemic problems within the recording industry, the transcen-
dent magic of popular songs clearly outweighs all commercial or bureaucratic negatives. Dawson and Propes note time and again the simple facts
of rock's roots: a honking saxophone, a pumping piano, a sexy male or
female singer, an uncomplicated lyric line about love gained or love lost,
or an outrageously humorous story. Nowhere does God transmit a sancti-
fied rock 'n' roll decalogue to any single performing prophet. The high
priests of rock are invariably self-anointed. John Lee Hooker, Louis Jordan, and Stick McGhee join Wild Bill Moore, Jimmy Preston, and Bill
Haley in leading America's postwar youth away from big-band pop
sounds and toward the promised land of rock 'n' roll. No one knew where
the journey would end. Clearly, no one ever suspected in 1953 that 40
years later Michael Jackson, Madonna, "Prince," and Bruce Springsteen
would be continuing the tradition of irreverence, humor, car songs, dance,
sex, and rhythm that began with Clyde McPhatter, Hank Ballard, LaVern
Baker, Johnny Otis, and The Crows.

Popular music fans should purchase *The Rocking 40's* (available from
Hoy Hoy Distributors, RR1, P.O. Box 90, Suite 3, Hoosick Falls, New
York 12090), listen to the magic of rockin' postwar R&B, and then read the
fascinating Dawson and Propes sleuth book. Other recommended readings
on the roots of rock 'n' roll include *Feel Like Going Home: Portraits in
Blues and Rock 'n' Roll* (1971) by Peter Guralnick, *Honkers and Shouters:
The Golden Years of Rhythm and Blues* (1978) by Arnold Shaw, *Rock Is
Rhythm and Blues: The Impact of Mass Media* (1974) by Lawrence N.
Redd, and *Unsung Heroes of Rock 'n' Roll: The Birth of Rock 'n' Roll in
the Dark and Wild Years Before Elvis* (1984) by Nick Tosches.

It is too bad that The Piltdown Men recorded in 1960. For rock fans and
pop paleontologists such as Wright, Dawson, and Propes, the ideal title for
the first rock 'n' roll record would have been "Brontosaurus Stomp."

## *BLUES HEROES*

*Encyclopedia of the Blues*. By Gerard Herzhaft (Translated by Bri-
gitte DeBord). Fayetteville, Arkansas: University of Arkansas Press,
1992. Illustrated. 513 pp.

French discographer and music historian Gerard Herzhaft has assembled a fact-filled salute to contributors to the African-American blues genre. This authoritative encyclopedia not only features alphabetically-arranged biographical sketches, but also provides a thorough "Bibliography" (pp. 401-406), a "Select Discography" (pp. 407-429), an annotated review of individual tunes that have become "Blues Standards" (pp. 435-478), a songography of "Blues Artists and Their Instruments" (pp. 479-493), and a comprehensive "Index" (pp. 495-513). This volume surpasses all previous efforts, including Sheldon Harris' monster study *Blues Who's Who* (1979).

Herzhaft is a gifted analyst, with a flair for drafting clear, concise sketches. His interpretations of Little Joe Blue, Lonnie Brooks, Robert Cray, and Little Walter are pointed and precise. He is thoughtfully deferential toward mythical blues giants like Howlin' Wolf, Muddy Waters, John Lee Hooker, and B.B. King. But Herzhaft maintains the spirit of an ethnic blues purist as he segregates nearly all white performers from black recording artists. This is a tragic flaw in his otherwise exemplary analysis. While accepting Johnny Otis as a "white Negro," Herzhaft relegates Eric Clapton, Stevie Ray Vaughan, Roy Buchanan, John Hammond, Mike Bloomfield, Paul Butterfield, and other white and British American bluesmen to second-class status. Too bad. Herzhaft is even less charitable toward such talented white women blues singers as Bonnie Raitt, Marcia Ball, and Lou Ann Barton. What a shame.

There are several other surprises in *Encyclopedia of The Blues* aside from the author's aversion to white blues stars. First, rock 'n' roll legends and soul stars are well-represented among the blues pantheon. Herzhaft includes Chuck Berry, Ray Charles, Bo Diddley, Fats Domino, Screamin' Jay Hawkins, Syl Johnson, Little Richard, and even Ann Peebles. Second, several major black female artists with reasonable blues credentials are either downplayed or overlooked. These ladies include Etta James, Irma Thomas, Tina Turner, and the splendid Alligator Records' blues trio Saffire. Finally, an even larger number of black bluesmen are also either downplayed or ignored. These artists include Little Willie John, James Booker, Huey Smith, James Brown, Otis Redding, Nappy Brown, and Lou Rawls.

Despite philosophical peculiarities or omissions of particular blues artists, Herzhaft deserves high praise for his compilation efforts. For too many years only the most vapid rock stars appeared in pop music encyclopedias; it is delightful to encounter a biographical directory that acknowledges so many key blues contributors to American cultural and musical history. Don't miss this book!

## HEAVY METAL BANDS

*Headbangers: The Worldwide Megabook of Heavy Metal Bands*. By Mark Hale. Ann Arbor, Michigan: Popular Culture, Ink., 1993. Illustrated. 542 pp.

Popular Culture, Ink., headquartered in Ann Arbor, is an internationally acclaimed publisher of music books. What began as a Beatles memorabilia and reference specialty-house has expanded and diversified to include valuable volumes on The Beach Boys, Elvis Presley, the Rolling Stones, The Everly Brothers, Michael Jackson, and Chuck Berry. Publisher Tom Schultheiss directs the production of exhaustive, in-depth chronologies (*A Day in the Life: The Beatles Day-By-Day, 1962-1979*), discographies (*The Illustrated Discography of Hot Rod Music, 1961-1965*), bibliographies (*Yesterday's Papers: The Rolling Stones in Print, 1963-1984*), and encyclopedias (*Who's Who in New Wave Music: An Illustrated Encyclopedia, 1976-1982*). Popular Culture, Ink. studies are matchless contributions to the systematic examination of current performers and contemporary music trends. The most recent publication, however, marks their initial involvement in heavy metal music. *Headbangers* explores a segment of the contemporary audio landscape that most scholars and reference librarians seldom consider. Heavy metal is . . . a truly different creature.

The triumph of rock/soul/pop music in the United States during the last half of the twentieth century can be explained commercially, culturally, and demographically. At first, young rock artists and R&B groups were satisfied just to make a buck. Then the goal of career longevity emerged. Once Elvis Presley, The Platters, Chuck Berry, and The Everly Brothers demonstrated that the one-hit-wonder tag was unwarranted for rock performers, the next plateau of success became the ability of artists to attract record-buying interest from more divergent groups of fans. The issue of crossover, praised by music industry moguls and condemned by stylistic purists, was mastered by Aretha Franklin, Ray Charles, and a number of talented Motown groups. Once commercial stability and cultural diversity had been achieved, the only remaining question was: How long can they last? Eric Clapton, Tina Turner, Mick Jagger, Paul Simon, and hundreds of other beyond thirty-years-of-age artists are still attracting new young fans, while sustaining their older supporters. B.B. King, Stevie Wonder, The Grateful Dead, Joe Cocker, and Linda Ronstadt have demonstrated ever-broadening demographic support, creative growth, and fascinating skill at combining their 1950s and 1960s rhythms with an 1980s and 1990s look and sound.

*Headbangers* provides an encyclopedic review of the international field of heavy metal bands from the late 1970s up to the present. While hard rock roots (Deep Purple, Led Zeppelin, Grand Funk Railroad, and Cream) are readily acknowledged, author Mark Hale emphasizes the true champions of musical metal—Judas Priest, Motorhead, Iron Maiden, Def Leppard, Whitesnake, Saxon, Anthrax, Metallica, Megadeth, and Slayer. This spectacular volume is superior to all other major surveys, including *Encyclopedia Metallica* (1983), *The International Encyclopedia of Hard Rock and Heavy Metal* (1983), and *HMAZ: The Ultimate Heavy Metal Encyclopedia* (1985). Each entry includes detailed band personnel information, precise listings of demo tracks and album releases, and perceptive editorial comments about metal styles. Terrific black-and-white photographs and thorough indexes punctuate this remarkable salute to the monsters of metal mayhem.

Hale's "Introduction" (pp. xiii-xxii) explains why heavy metal music marks a significant departure from rock/soul/pop. There is no interest in traditional commercial success, little option for popular crossover, and virtually no chance for achieving any demographic spread. While rock continues to celebrate sex, drinking, romantic love, and teenage defiance of parental and school authority, heavy metal blasts forth antisocial themes including nuclear holocaust, torture, evil, death, and insanity. While Aerosmith, Bad Company, the Rolling Stones, and ZZ Top may be loud, the giants of heavy metal are R-E-A-L-L-Y L-O-U-D, if not downright deafening. Finally, while rock continues to produce love songs, nostalgia themes, and novelty numbers, heavy metal blazes ever-darkening audio trails—sci-fi fantasy, sword-and-sorcery, blood-and-thunder, sadism, masochism, speed-metal, death-metal, thrash-metal, L.A. sleaze/glam, Euro-metal, and funk-metal. It is ironic and troubling that metal and rap have become the musics of choice for alienated white and black male teens. Viewing females as objects for arrogant sexual exploitation and mainstream society as total hypocrisy unites these two otherwise disparate musical styles.

*Headbangers* is an unparalleled effort at defining and illustrating the evolution of a distinctive genre of American music. No heavy metal fan should miss this outstanding encyclopedia. Students of popular culture, music reference librarians, and researchers in American and European musical culture will also benefit from this exceptional compilation.

## *MUSICAL DIVERSITY*

*All Music Guide.* Edited by Michael Erlewind and Scott Bultman. San Francisco, California: Miller Freeman, Inc., 1992. 1176 pp.

This spectacular guide to compact discs, albums, and cassette tapes is an essential purchase for popular music fans. Eighty competent music reviewers, critics, and journalists have provided the expertise to analyze personnel and recorded material from 26 different music categories. Among these genres are rock/pop/soul, easy listening, rap, blues, cajun/ zydeco, gospel, country/western, folk, classical, reggae, and jazz. Specialty fields are also covered. The diverse mix includes soundtracks/cast recordings, women's music, gay music, Christmas, children's music, environmental, and sound effects. Individual entries within the stylistic chapters are arranged alphabetically by artist. Each citation features a brief history of the performer, plus an annotated list of key recordings. The precision of each entry is understandable and required in a volume that covers the entire musical waterfront. Beyond segmented biographies and recording lists, the lengthy jazz section also features concise "music maps" that provide chronological explorations of jazz drumming, jazz piano, jazz bass and double bass, jazz conga and bongo, jazz flute, jazz guitar, and jazz saxophone. A thorough "Index" (pp. 1148-1176) provides quick, easy access to any performer mentioned in the text.

In a social and political environment where diversity and multiculturalism have become battleground terms, the *All Music Guide* is an olive branch of worldwide twentieth century sound recordings. More than just a disc catalog, more than just a biographical encyclopedia, and more than just an exploration of a particular style of playing or singing, this book is a music fan's smorgasbord, a disc jockey's handy tool, and a music reference librarian's dream. For sound recording archivists who will appreciate the magnitude of the 23,000 albums listed in the 1992 Miller Freeman text, the news for the future is even better. An *All Music Guide* database, containing over 100,000 albums and reviews, will be available in 1993 as a consumer CD-ROM for computer users, and as an on-line discographic service in record stores across the country. (For additional information, contact the editors at 315 Marion Avenue in Big Rapids, Michigan 49307. FAX 616-796-3060.)

The shortcomings and omissions in this mammoth masterpiece are remarkably few. In respect to popular recordings, the realm of comedy/ novelty discs is regrettably absent. Too bad! Allan Sherman, Stan Freberg, "Weird Al" Yankovic, Homer and Jethro, Nervous Norvus, and Buchanan and Goodman deserve public recognition. Fortunately, Spike Jones and Louis Jordan are listed. A second problem is the puny attempt to provide a bibliography for this superb text.

Such a fine reference guide and discography should feature a first-rate list of popular music print resources–20 to 25 pages at least–instead of a weak, two-page Books on Music afterthought. No doubt this volume will prosper in academic and public libraries, in music departments, at commercial radio stations, and on the bookshelves of cultural elitists, nostalgia buffs, and headbangers alike. David A. Milberg's commentaries on "Christmas" recordings (pp. 610-620) are indicative of the thorough yet readable, definitive yet humorous views that make this eclectic effort so rewarding.

# REFERENCES

Bashe, Philip. *Heavy Metal Thunder: The Music, Its History, Its Heroes*. Garden City, New York: Dolphin Books/Doubleday and Company, Inc., 1985.

Behague, Gerard H. (ed.). *Music and Black Ethnicity: The Caribbean and South America*. New Brunswick, New Jersey: Transaction Publishers, 1994.

Bindas, Kenneth J. (ed.). *America's Musical Pulse: Popular Music in Twentieth-Century Society*. Westport, Connecticut: Praeger Books, 1992.

Broughton, Viv. *Black Gospel: An Illustrated History of the Gospel Sound*. Poole, Dorset, England: Blandford Press, 1985.

Broven, John. *South to Louisiana: The Music of the Cajun Bayous*. Gretna, Louisiana: Pelican Publishing Company, 1983.

Citron, Stephen. *Noel and Cole: The Sophisticates*. New York: Oxford University Press, 1993.

Cohn, Lawrence. *Nothing But the Blues: The Music and the Musicians*. New York: Abbeville Press, 1993.

Collier, James Lincoln. *Jazz: The American Theme Song*. New York: Oxford University Press, 1993.

Cusic, Don. *The Sound of Light: A History of Gospel Music*. Bowling Green, Ohio: Bowling Green State University Popular Press, 1991.

Denisoff, R. Serge and Richard A. Peterson (eds.). *The Sounds of Social Change: Studies in Popular Culture*. Chicago: Rand McNally and Company, 1972.

Denselow, Robin. *When the Music's Over: The Story of Political Pop*. London: Faber and Faber, 1990.

Duxbury, Janell R. "Shakespeare Meets the Backbeat: Literary Allusion in Rock Music," *Popular Music and Society*, XII (Fall 1988), pp. 19-23.

Eisen, Jonathan (ed.). *The Age of Rock: Sounds of the American Cultural Revolution*. New York: Vintage Books, 1969.

Eisen, Jonathan (ed.). *The Age of Rock 2: Sights and Sounds of the American Cultural Revolution*. New York: Vintage Books, 1970.

Ellison, Mary. *Lyrical Protest: Black Music's Struggle Against Discrimination*. New York: Praeger Books, 1989.

Erlewine, Michael and Scott Bultman (eds). *All Music Guide*. San Francisco: Miller Freeman, Inc., 1992.

Finn, Julio. *The Bluesman: The Musical Heritage of Black Men and Women in the Americas*. Brooklyn: Interlink, 1992.

Gaar, Gillian G. *She's a Rebel: The History of Women in Rock and Roll*. Seattle: Seal Press, 1992.

Garofalo, Reebee (ed.). *Rockin' the Boat: Mass Music and Mass Movements*. Boston: South End Press, 1992.

George, Nelson. *The Death of Rhythm and Blues*. New York: Pantheon Books, 1988.

Giddins, Gary. *Rhythm-a-Ning: Jazz Tradition and Innovation in the 80s*. New York: Oxford University Press, 1985.

Giddins, Gary. *Riding on a Blue Note: Jazz and American Pop*. New York: Oxford University Press, 1981.

Goddard, Peter and Philip Kamin (comps.). *Shakin' All Over: The Rock 'n' Roll Years in Canada*. Toronto: McGraw Hill Ryerson, Ltd., 1989.

Goodall, H.L., Jr. *Living in the Rock 'n' Roll Mystery: Reading Context, Self, and Others as Clues*. Carbondale: Southern Illinois University Press, 1991.

Gould, Philip. *Cajun Music and Zydeco*. Baton Rouge: Louisiana State University Press, 1992.

Governar, Alan. *Meeting the Blues: The Rise of the Texas Sound*. Dallas, Texas: Taylor Publishing Company 1988.

Guralnick, Peter. *Sweet Soul Music: Rhythm and Blues and the Southern Dream of Freedom*. New York: Harper and Row, 1986.

Harris, Michael W. *The Rise of Gospel Blues: The Music of Thomas Andrew Dorsey in the Urban Church*. New York: Oxford University Press, 1992.

Heilbut, Anthony. *The Gospel Sound: Good News and Bad Times* (revised and updated edition). New York: Limelight Editions, 1985.

Hemming, Roy and David Hajdu. *Discovering Great Singers of Classic Pop: A New Listener's Guide to the Sounds and Lives of Top Performers and Their Recordings, Movies, and Video*. New York: Newmarket Press, 1991.

Herzhaft, Gerard (translated by Brigette DeBord). *Encyclopedia of the Blues*. Fayetteville, Arkansas: University of Arkansas Press, 1992.

Hirshey, Herri. *Nowhere to Run: The Story of Soul Music*. New York: Da Capo Press, 1994.

Hoffmann, Frank (comp.). *The Literature of Rock, 1954-1978*. Metuchen, New Jersey: Scarecrow Press, Inc., 1981.

Hoffmann, Frank and B. Lee Cooper (comps.). *The Literature of Rock II, 1979-1983* (two volumes). Metuchen, New Jersey: Scarecrow Press, Inc., 1986.

Hoffmann, Frank and B. Lee Cooper (comps.). *The Literature of Rock III, 1984-1990* (two volumes). Metuchen, New Jersey: Scarecrow Press, Inc., 1995.

Kiefer, Kit (ed.). *They Called It Rock: The Goldmine Oral History of Rock 'n' Roll, 1950-1970*. Iola, Wisconsin: Krause Publications, 1991.

Lewis, George H. (ed.). *All That Glitters: Country Music in America*. Bowling Green, Ohio: Bowling Green State University Popular Press, 1993.

Lomax, Alan. *The Land Where the Blues Began*. New York: Pantheon Books, 1993.

Loza, Steven. *Barro Rhythm: Mexican American Music in Los Angeles*. Urbana: University of Illinois Press, 1993.

Malone, Bill C. *Country Music U.S.A.* (revised edition). Austin: University of Texas Press, 1985.

Malone, Bill C. *Southern Music–American Music*. Lexington: University of Kentucky Press, 1979.

Melhuish, Martin. *Heart of Gold: 30 Years of Canadian Pop Music*. Toronto: Canadian Broadcasting Corporation, 1983.

Middleton, Richard. *Pop Music and the Blues: A Study of the Relationship and Its Significance*. London: Victor Gollancz, Ltd., 1972.

Mulvaney, Rebekah Michele. *Rastafari and Reggae: A Dictionary and Source Book*. Westport, Connecticut: Greenwood Press, 1990.

Oakley, Giles. *The Devil's Music: A History of the Blues* (revised edition). London: British Broadcasting Corporation, 1983.

Oliver, Paul (ed.). *The Blackwell Guide to Blues Records*. Cambridge, Massachusetts: Basil Blackwell, Inc., 1989.

Oliver, Paul. *Songsters and Saints: Vocal Traditions on Race Records*. New York: Cambridge University Press, 1984.

Otis, Johnny. *Upside Your Head: Rhythm and Blues on Central Avenue*. Hanover, New Hampshire: Wesleyan University Press/University Press of New England, 1993.

Palmer, Robert. *Deep Blues*. New York: Viking Press, 1981.

Peretti, Burton W. *The Creation of Jazz: Music, Race, and Culture in Urban America*. Urbana: University of Illinois Press, 1992.

Pruter, Robert. *Chicago Soul*. Champaign-Urbana: University of Illinois Press, 1991.

Reagon, Bernice Johnson (ed.). *We'll Understand It Better By and By: Pioneering African American Gospel Composers*. Washington, DC: Smithsonian Institution Press, 1992.

Rimler, Walter. *Not Fade Away: A Comparison of Jazz Age with Rock Era Pop Song Composers*. Ann Arbor, Michigan: Pierian Press, 1984.

Rose, Tricia. *Black Noise: Rap Music and Black Culture in Contemporary America*. Hanover, New Hampshire: Wesleyan University Press, University Press of New England, 1994.

Rosenberg, Neil V. *Bluegrass: A History*. Urbana: University of Illinois Press, 1985.

Rosenthal, David H. *Hard Bop: Jazz and Black Music, 1955-1965*. New York: Oxford University Press, 1992.

Santelli, Robert. *The Big Book of the Blues: A Biographical Encyclopedia*. New York: Penguin Books, 1993.

Scheurer, Timothy E. (ed.). *American Popular Music–Volume Two: The Age of Rock*. Bowling Green, Ohio: Bowling Green State University Popular Press, 1989.

Schoener, Allen (ed.). *Harlem on My Mind: Cultural Capitol of Black America, 1900-1968*. New York: Random House, 1968.

Scott, Frank and the staff of Down Home Music (comps.). *The Down Home Guide to the Blues*. Chicago: A Cappella Books, 1991.

Shannon, Bob and John Jauna. *Behind the Hits: Inside Stories of Classic Pop and Rock and Roll*. New York: Warner Books, 1986.

Shaw, Arnold. *Honkers and Shouters: The Golden Years of Rhythm and Blues*. New York: Collier Books, 1978.

Spender, Jon Michael. *Blues and Evil*. Knoxville: University of Tennessee Press, 1993.

Spender, Jon Michael (ed.). *The Emergency of Black and the Emergence of Rap*. Durham, North Carolina: Duke University Press, 1991.

Stambler, Irwin (comp.). *The Encyclopedia of Pop, Rock, and Soul* (revised edition). New York: St. Martin's Press, 1989.

Stanley, Lawrence A. (ed.). *Rap: The Lyrics*. New York: Penguin Books, 1992.

Tichi, Cecelia. *High Lonesome: The American Culture of Country Music*. Chapel Hill: University of North Carolina Press, 1994.

Tosches, Nick. *Country: Living Legends and Dying Metaphors in America's Biggest Music* (revised edition). New York: Charles Scribner's Sons, 1985.

Tosches, Nick. *Unsung Heroes of Rock 'n' Roll: The Birth of Rock 'n' Roll in the Dark and Wild Years Before Elvis*. New York: Charles Scribner's Sons, 1984.

Tucker, Stephen R. "Pentecostalism and Popular Culture in the South: A Study of Four Musicians," *Journal of Popular Culture*. XVI (Winter 1982), pp. 68-80.

VanDerMerwe, Peter. *Origins of the Popular Style: The Antecedents of Twentieth-Century Popular Music*. Oxford, England: Clarendon Press, 1989.

Walser, Robert. *Running with the Devil: Power, Gender, and Madness in Heavy Metal Music*. Hanover, New Hampshire: Wesleyan University Press, University Press of New England, 1993.

Ward, Ed, Geoffrey Stokes, and Ken Tucker. *Rock of Ages: The Rolling Stone History of Rock and Roll*. New York: Rolling Stone Press/Summit Books, 1986.

Weinstein, Deena. *Heavy Metal: A Cultural Sociology*. New York: Lexington Books, 1991.

Wilson, Charles R. and William Ferris (eds.). *Encyclopedia of Southern Culture*. Chapel Hill: University of North Carolina Press, 1989.

Chapter 15

# Railroads

"How would you describe the American railroad system to a Martian?"

My son wiggled uncomfortably in his classroom chair, looking intently at his desktop and only slowly raising his gaze to meet the teacher's eyes.

"Well Michael? If a traveler from outer space asked you to explain railroads to him, how would you begin?"

Although the question seemed absurd to him, Mike finally tackled the topic. "I'd tell the Martian that trains were transportation vehicles for people and freight. I'd also say that people still sing about them even if they are vanishing."

The junior high school teacher was obviously surprised by the second part of this answer. The entire class, sensing her sudden bewilderment, giggled. Mike turned red in embarrassment. Then he took the offensive. "You guys know what I mean. The good old days of railroading are long gone. There's no more John Henry or Casey Jones, no more smoke-belching steamers, and no train-riding hobos or gamblers. But for some reason guys like Kenny Rogers and Johnny Cash keep singing songs about railroads as if they were still around."

## CHANGE AND TRAIN-RELATED IMAGES

Despite my son's assertion to the contrary, railroads are still in existence. But social, economic, and technological changes during the past 60 years have greatly diminished their role in American life. What should be of particular interest to students of popular culture, however, is the continuing use of various train-related images in modern song lyrics. From the Civil War until the end of World War II, steam-powered engines played an

This essay by B. Lee Cooper was originally published as "Shifting Images of Transportation Technology and American Society in Railroad Songs," *International Journal of Instructional Media*, X, No. 2 (1982-1983), pp. 131-146. Reprint permission granted by the author, Editor Phillip J. Sleeman, and Baywood Publishing Company.

integral role in the transportation, industrialization, and urbanization of the United States. An array of popular stories and social images emerged, depicting the exploits of engineers, other trainmen, and travelers during this 80-year period. However, since 1945 the railroad world has changed dramatically. Employee unionization, diesel engines, and the introduction of interstate highway systems and jet-propelled aircraft have drastically altered the scope of railroading activities. But the images of earlier transportation experiences persist. And nowhere is this more evident than in the field of popular music. History students can gain much by exploring the varying images of trains and train-related incidents in song lyrics. A central question for classroom investigation is: How do popular songs of the mid-twentieth century utilize railroad imagery to depict changes in contemporary American culture?

Although the automobile has undeniably received a considerable amount of lyrical attention, composers and crooners have also focused their commentaries on steamboats ("Proud Mary"), airplanes ("Jet Airliner"), trucks ("Convoy"), sailing vessels ("The Sloop John B"), buses ("Thank God and Greyhound"), and spaceships ("Jupiter C"). Yet no area of public and commercial transportation has a longer or richer tradition of melodious eulogy than the American railroad system. For several decades bluegrass pickers, country and western performers, folk singers, and bluesmen (and blueswomen, too) have sung about railroads. The country tunes of Jimmie Rodgers ("Waitin' for a Train," "Hobo Bill's Last Ride," "Brakeman's Blues," and "Old Number Five") and Hank Snow ("Golden Rocket," "Fireball Mail," and "City of New Orleans") have been echoed in the blues realm by Big Bill Broonzy ("This Train"), Howlin' Wolf ("Smokestack Lightnin'"), Leadbelly ("Rock Island Line"), and Son House ("Empire State Express"). Nearly all the performing giants of early and mid-twentieth-century folk, bluegrass, country and western, and blues singing recorded lyrical commentaries about trains. In fact, the variety singers who have dealt with railroading themes (Pete Seeger, Lester Flatt and Earl Scruggs, Mississippi John Hurt, Blind Willie McTell, Woody Guthrie, Bukka White, and others) is exceeded only by the contrasting images and conflicting tales that they presented concerning America's train culture. On one hand, locomotive transportation was depicted as scenic, cheap, readily available, romantic, individualistic, and a constant source of personal freedom and geographical mobility. On the other hand, trains were described as noisy and ugly, prone to crashes and untimely delays, physically dangerous to humans and animals, sources of choking smoke, fire hazards, and potential vehicles for familial separation and human misery.

Although popular singers from 1946 to the present continued to incorporate train themes into their songs, their lyrics portrayed some very significant shifts in railroad imagery. In order to illustrate these shifts within a lyrical spectrum of more than 300 train songs, a thematic guideline was created to demonstrate common characteristics. The seven basic image categories that were developed are outlined in the table below. Each category is followed by a list of specific identifying characteristics.

### Train-Related Themes and Images in Popular Song Lyrics, 1920-1980

#### Historical Perspectives

1. Report of a Train Wreck or Railroad Accident
2. Biographical Review of a Prominent Railroading Figure
3. Recognition of the National or Regional Significance of a Specific Railroad Line
4. Nostalgic Yearning for the Conditions of an Earlier Age or Social Style
5. Comment on the Economic Role of a Railroad within a Community
6. Observation About the Evolution of Transportation Technology

#### Social Mobility

1. Shift from Poverty to Wealth
2. Personal Sense of Social Change
3. Desire to Increase Personal Opportunity
4. Expansion of Freedom
5. Interest in New Relationships and Novel Socioeconomic Settings
6. Decline in Social Status
7. Escape from Domineering Parents or from a Nagging Wife or Husband

#### Geographical Mobility

1. Movement from Rural Setting to Urban Environment
2. Shift from East Coast to West Coast
3. Migration from Southern States to Northern States
4. Return to Southern Home from Northern Area
5. Return from West Coast to the South or East Coast
6. Flight from Complex City Life to a More Simple Rural Existence
7. Departure from a Loved one
8. Return to a Loved One

#### Employment Situations

1. Search for New Employment Opportunities and Challenges
2. Explanation of the Occupational Roles of Engineers, Brakemen, Porters, Ticket Agents, and Other Railroad Employees
3. Escape from Unproductive Job Situations or Feelings of Occupational Boredom
4. Migration from Place to Place, from Job to Job
5. Runaway from Home to Seek Economic Opportunity and Personal Independence

### Heroes and Heroic Achievements

1. Models of Behavior for Hard Work and Responsible Social Behavior
2. Examples of Extreme Heroism in Difficult (or Apparently Impossible) Situations

### Metaphors for Life Situations

1. Journey from Life to Death or from Earth to Heaven
2. Transformation from Evil and Captivity to Good and Freedom
3. Achievement of Wealth and Success
4. Trains as Women, Nations, or Living Legends
5. Railroads as Paths to Freedom for Prisoners, Lost Souls, Youngsters, Henpecked Husbands, Mistreated Women, and Other Wanders
6. Symbols of National Prominence, Individual Courage, or Historic Development

### Rhythm Patterns

1. Source of Musical Cadence in a Song
2. Element in Human Pulse and Rhythm of Life
3. Sound Which Beckons an Individual to Escape from Drudgery of Current Existence in Search of a New Life

The seven themes created for this study warrant additional explanation. The following pages expand upon the brief outlines of characteristics that were provided in the table and also add specific song illustrations to illuminate the meaning of each category for teaching purposes.

## *Historical Perspectives*

The high profile of railroads in commercial recordings prior to World War II can be partially attributed to the high frequency with which dramatic songs lyricized actual historical incidents. "One of the most popular kinds of railroad songs has been the train-wreck ballad, of which some two dozen have been preserved on record," notes folksong scholar Norm Cohen. He continues,

> Most of these ballads describe historically verified accidents, ranging in date from "The Wreck on the C & O," which occurred near Hinton, West Virginia, on October 23, 1890, to "Wreck of the C & O Sportsman," which occurred in the same part of the country approximately forty years later. . . . Doubtless the best known are the favorites, "Casey Jones" and "Wreck of the Southern Old 97," recounting accidents of April 30, 1900, near Vaughan, Mississippi, and September 27, 1903, near Danville, Virginia, respectively. (p. 185)

Numerous recordings capture other elements of train-related history. Construction of railway lines ("John Henry," "Nine-Pound Hammer," and "Drill, Ye Tarriers Drill"), reports of train robbers, ("Let Jesse Rob the Train" and "Railroad Bill"), and even stories denouncing the practice of interstate toll charges ("Rock Island Line") are presented as historical observations, although the songwriters and singers occasionally embellish the heroics of laborers, bandits, or engineers. Perhaps the most humorous popular recording to recount a two-rail social furor was The Kingston Trio's revival of the 1948 protest song "M.T.A." The melody for this song was borrowed from "The Wreck of Old 97." Beyond America's northern border, the historical development of locomotive transportation has been skillfully depicted in Gordon Lightfoot's "Canadian Railroad Trilogy."

## Social Mobility

Hank Snow, Bukka White, and dozens of other singers wrote and performed songs that depicted trains as vehicles providing avenues of escape from rural poverty; from nagging parents, bossy wives, or interfering mothers-in-law; from prisons of the mind, body, or spirit; and from the drudgery of a boring job. Although the majority of railroad wanderers reported in popular lyrics tend to be male, it is undeniable that women in search of new lives were also frequent users of steam or diesel-driven transportation. The movement toward greater personal freedom, a new social status, more income potential, and other positive gains is depicted in: "Me and Bobby McGee," "I'm Movin' On," "Folsom Prison Blues," "Midnight Train," "The Gambler," and "Train, Train."

## Geographical Mobility

It is difficult to differentiate geographical from social mobility. The links, real and potential, between vertical shifts in status and horizontal moves from one region to another are obvious. The railroad functioned as a highly visible, available, inexpensive, and frequently used source of migration by rural dwellers to the centers of urban life in New Orleans, Chicago, Detroit, New York, and elsewhere throughout the United States. Among the songs that illustrate geographical mobility are: "The Atlanta Special," "Trains and Boats and Planes," "Freight Train," "Cannon Ball," "City of New Orleans," and "Long Twin Silver Line." But Americans also used the train to return home–either in triumph or as a worldly-wise, but financially disabled prodigal son (or daughter). This theme shows up in: "Homeward Bound," "Midnight Train to Georgia," "I'm Coming Home," and "Hey, Porter."

## Employment Situations

Numerous songs contain references to railroad employees; some describe their occupational functions in great detail. Most of the time, however, the porter, ticket agent, engineer, or other train workers serve as sympathetic ears for a troubled traveler or as a source of frustration for a would-be rider. As long as railroads were viewed as functional sources of geographical relocation and social mobility, the gatekeepers of locomotive life were central figures in the process of departure. Migrants were uneven in their assessment of railroad personnel. However, whether the commentator is an unconcerned observer of railroad life, a potential or in-route passenger, or a railroad employee, the descriptions of railroad roles are informative. These songs include: "Hey, Porter," "The Wreck of Old 97," "Brakeman's Blues," "Conductor Took My Baby to Tennessee," "Crazy Engineer," "Drill, Ye Tarriers, Drill," "Good Conductor," "Hold That Train Conductor," "I've Been Workin' on the Railroad," "Mr. Brakeman Let Me Ride Your Train," "Spike Driver Blues," and "Ticket Agent Blues."

## Heroes and Heroic Achievements

Heroic images often emerge from the commission of antisocial or illegal activities. In the realm of railroad songs, Buck Owens' tribute to a premier nineteenth-century outlaw—"Let Jesse Rob the Train"—illustrates this situation. This kind of salute has also been accorded to "Railroad Bill," who is said to have been Morris Slater, a negro outlaw who terrorized Alabama and Florida from 1984 to 1897. On the other hand, the two most noted heroic figures of lyrical railroad lore are the brave but doomed engineer "Casey Jones" and the steam-drill-hating powerhouse tracklayer "John Henry." Other examples of heroism or actions of heroic dimensions in lyrics are illustrated in "Ben Dewberry's Final Run" and "The Wreck of Old 97."

## Metaphors for Life Situations

The most prominent illustrations of train metaphors are found in songs that portray escapes to freedom from either physical or spiritual captivity. These songs include: "Midnight Special," "Folsom Prison Blues," "Friendship Train," "Love Train," and "Peace Train." Transformations from earthly existence to heavenly afterlife are illustrated in: "People Get Ready," "This Train," "Hobo on a Freight Train to Heaven," "If I Got My Ticket, Lord," and "Slow Train." The complex nature of human relations is metaphori-

cally depicted in: "Train of Thought" and "Heart Like Railroad Steel."
Brett Williams has noted with particular interest the tendency of musicians
to portray both positive (motherhood, loving wife, beautiful bride, stable
family center) and negative (flighty female, cheating tramp, prostitute,
unfaithful wife, and nagging mother-in law) female images in railroad
songs. Among the tunes illustrating this trend are: "Empire State Express,"
"Brakeman's Blues," "Train of Thought," and "Train of Love."

### *Instrumentation*

Trains are sound machines. Numerous singers allude to engines bells,
whistles, clanging wheels, and other distinctive audio elements. J. M.
Eleasor, a writer who complained to a railroad company about the switch-
yard cacophony outside of his motel room, captured the sounds produced
by a slow-moving switcher and its endlessly shifting boxcars,

> Why is it that your switch engine has to ging and dong and fizz and
> spit and clang and bang and buzz and hiss and bell and wail and pant
> and rant and howl and yowl and grate and grind and pull and bump and
> click and clank and chug and moan and hoot and toot and crash and
> grunt and gasp and moan and whistle and squeak and squak and blow
> and jar and jerk and rasp and jingle and twange and rumble and jangle
> and ring and clatter and yelp and howl and hum and snarl and puff and
> growl and thump and boom and clash and jolt and jostle and screech
> and snort and slam and throb and crink and quiver and rumble and roar
> and rattle and yell and smoke and smell and shriek like hell all night
> long? (p. 6)

Other examples of railroad sounds converted to rhythm sources and
audio stimuli for human reactions include: "Wabash Cannonball," "I Heard
That Lonesome Whistle," "Folsom Prison Blues," "Train Whistle Blues,"
and "Lonesome Whistle Blues." The rhythm of train's helped to shape the
guitar-playing style of "Johnny B. Goode," while the distant screech of a
locomotive whistle tempts both men and women to wander and roam.

## *SONGS WITH TRAIN-RELATED THEMES*

The seven train-related themes identified previously are illustrated in
the songs listed below. In order to establish historical perspective, the
tunes are divided into three unequal time periods during the sixty years

under investigation. These periods are: 1920-1945, 1946-1960, and 1961-1980. Some tunes originating in the 1920s, 1930s, and early 1940s, were successfully revived by artists during succeeding decades. Such cultural transmission suggests either the strength of folk images contained in a particular lyric or the commercial acuity of a particular singer (or his manager, arranger, or producer). In some cases, both elements function simultaneously to generate song revivals. The extended table below offers a selected list of train songs and recording artists divided chronologically into the three periods identified above.

### *1920-1945*

- "Ben Dewberry's Final Run"
  (Bluebird 5482)
  Jimmie Rodgers (1927)

- "Casey Jones"
  (Okeh 40038)
  Fiddlin' John Carson and His Virginia Reelers (1923)

- "Chattanooga Choo Choo"
  (Bluebird 11230)
  Glenn Miller and His Orchestra (1941)

- "Chicago Bound Blues"
  (Paramount 12056)
  Ida Cox (1923)

- "Fireball Mail"
  (Okeh 6685)
  Roy Acuff (1942)

- "Freight Train Blues"
  (Paramount 12211)
  Trixie Smith (1938)

- "Hobo Bill's Last Ride"
  (Victor 22421)
  Jimmie Rodgers (1929)

- "John Henry"
  (Vocalion 1474)
  Furry Lewis (1929)

- "Long Train Blues"
  (Brunswick 7205)
  Robert Wilkins (1929)

- "Mail Train Blues"
  (Okeh 8345)
  Sippie Wallace (1926)

- "New River Train"
  (Herwin 75506)
  Vernon Dalhart (1925)

- "On the Atchison, Topeka, and the Santa Fe"
  (Decca 23436)
  Judy Garland and the Merry Macs (1945)

- "Panama Limited Blues"
  (Vocalion 1009)
  Ada Brown (1926)

- "Railroad Bill"
  (Okeh 45425)
  Frank Hutchison (1924)

- "Railroad Blues"
  (Paramount 12262)
  Trixie Smith (1925)

- "Railroadin' and Gambling"
  (Bluebird 8325)
  Uncle Dave Macon (1938)

- "The Southern Cannon Ball"
  (Victor 23811)
  Jimmie Rodgers (1931)

- "Spike Driver Blues"
  (Okeh 8692)
  Mississippi John Hurt (1928)

- "Ticket Agent Blues"
  (Decca 7078)
  Blind Willie McTell (1935)

- "Wabash Cannonball"
  (Victor 23731)
  The Carter Family (1932)

- "Waitin' for a Train"
  (Victor V-4001 4)
  Jimmie Rodgers (1928)

- "Waitin' for the Train to Come In"
  (Columbia 36867)
  Harry James and Kitty Kallen (1945)
- "The Wreck of the Virginian Train"
  (Champion 15467)
  John Hutchens (1927)

## *1946-1960*

- "Black Train Blues"
  (Vocal Ion 05588)
  Bukka White (1950)
- "Click-Clack"
  (Swan 4001)
  Dickey Doo and the Don'ts (1958)
- "The Devil's Train"
  (Columbia 37822)
  Roy Acuff (1947)
- "Down by the Station"
  (Capitol 4312)
  The Four Preps (1960)
- "Down Home Special"
  (Checker 850)
  Bo Diddley (1957)
- "Fast Freight Blues"
  (Josie 828)
  Sonny Terry (1958)
- "Folsom Prison Blues"
  (Sun 232)
  Johnny Cash (1956)
- "Freight Train"
  (Mercury 71102)
  Rusty Draper (1957)
- "Harmonica Train"
  (Jackson 2302)
  Sonny Terry and His Night Owls (1952)
- "Hey, Porter"
  (Sun 221)
  Johnny Cash (1955)

- "I'm Movin' On"
  (RCA Victor 21-0328)
  Hank Snow (1950)

- "Johnny B. Goode"
  (Chess 1691)
  Chuck Berry (1958)

- "Lonesome Train"
  (Modern 888)
  Johnny Moore's Three Blazers (1951)

- "Mama from the Train"
  (Mercury 70971)
  Patti Page (1956)

- "Mean Old Train"
  (Gotham 515)
  John Lee Hooker (1953)

- "Midnight Cannonball"
  (Atlantic 1069)
  Joe Turner (1955)

- "Mystery Train"
  (Sun 223)
  Elvis Presley (1955)

- "Rock Island Line"
  (London 1650)
  Lonnie Donnegan (1956)

- "Smokestack Lightnin' "
  (Chess 1618)
  Howlin' Wolf (1956)

- "Toot, Toot, Tootsie (Good-Bye)"
  (MGM 10548)
  Art Mooney (1949)

- "Train Fare Home"
  (Aristocrat 1306)
  Muddy Waters (1948)

- "The Wreck of Old 97"
  (RCA Victor 20-4095)
  Hank Snow (1951)

## *1961-1980*

- "Chattanooga Choo Choo"
  (Butterfly 1205)
  Tuxedo Junction (1978)

- "The City of New Orleans"
  (Reprise 1103)
  Arlo Guthrie (1972)

- "Engine Engine No. 9"
  (Smash 1983)
  Roger Miller (1965)

- "Folsom Prison Blues"
  (Columbia 44513)
  Johnny Cash (1968)

- "Friendship Train"
  (Soul 35068)
  Gladys Knight and the Pips (1969)

- "The Gambler"
  (United Artists 1250)
  Kenny Rogers (1979)

- "Homeward Bound"
  (Columbia 43511)
  Simon and Garfunkel (1966)

- "I'm Movin' On"
  (Smash 1813)
  Matt Lucas (1963)

- "King's Special"
  (ABC 11280)
  B. B. King (1970)

- "Last Train to Clarksville"
  (Colgems 1001)
  The Monkees (1966)

- "Let Jesse Rob the Train"
  (Warner Brothers 49118)
  Buck Owens (1979)

- "Locomotive Breath"
  (Chrysalis 2110)
  Jethro Tull (1976)

- "Long Train Runnin'"
  (Warner Brothers 17698)
  The Doobie Brothers (1973)

- "Long Twin Silver Line"
  (Capitol 4836)
  Bob Seger (1980)

- "Love Train"
  (Philadelphia International 3524)
  The O'Jays (1973)

- "Lover Please"
  (Mercury 71941)
  Clyde McPhatter (1962)

- "Marrakesh Express"
  (Atlantic 2652)
  Crosby, Stills, Nash, and Young (1969)

- "Midnight Special"
  (Imperial 66087)
  Johnny Rivers (1965)

- "Midnight Train to Georgia"
  (Buddah 383)
  Gladys Knight and the Pips (1973)

- "Orange Blossom Special"
  (Columbia 43206)
  Johnny Cash (1965)

- "Peace Train"
  (A & M 1291)
  Cat Stevens (1971)

- "People Get Ready"
  (ABC-Paramount 10622)
  The Impressions (1965)

- "Southbound Train"
  (Atlantic 2892)
  Graham Nash and David Crosby (1972)

- "I Took the Last Train"
  (Elektra 45500)
  David Gates (1978)

- "Train of Thought"
  (MCA 40245)
  Cher (1974)

- "Train, Train"
  (Atco 7207)
  Blackfoot (1979)

- "Trains and Boats and Planes"
  (Scepter 12153)
  Dionne Warwick (1966)

- "Trouble in Mind"
  (Colpix 175)
  Nina Simone (1961)

## *Summary*

The table below summarizes some general conclusions of this preliminary investigation of audio instructional resources.

### Shifting Patterns in Train-Related Themes and Images in Lyrics of Popular Songs

| Themes and Images | 1920-1945 | 1946-1960 | 1961-1980 |
|---|---|---|---|
| A. Historical Perspectives | Great emphasis on personal experiences and historical events | Reduced emphasis on reports of train wrecks and activities of railroad characters | Historical railroad events and train personnel regarded as sources of nostalgia |
| B. Social Mobility | High degree of rail travel | Moderate rail travel | Sharp decline in rail use |
| C. Geographical Mobility | Same as above | Same as above | Same as above |
| D. Employment | Many illustrations of rail-related jobs mentioned | Reduced number of rail-related jobs mentioned | Greatly reduced number of rail-related jobs mentioned |
| E. Heroes and Heroic Activities | High number of heroes and heroic illustrations | Reduced number of heroic images and unique achievements | Rail heroes viewed as antique characters |
| F. Metaphors for Life Situations | High number used | Moderate number used | High number used |
| G. Instrumentation | Acoustic guitar or harmonica used to imitate trains | Continued use of guitar and harmonica | Electric guitar, drum, and other instruments used |

Beyond the mere identification of different thematic trends in train songs, the following speculative statements seem warranted:

1. The increase of private automobile travel on interstate highways and the growth of airline, bus, and other forms of relatively inexpensive commercial travel alternatives have contributed to the steady decline of public contact with railroads over the past three decades. The lyrics of popular songs since 1950 illustrate a parallel decline in the real elements of railroad contact in terms of individual perspectives: experience with historical events (train wrecks); personal, social, and geographical mobility; employment situations; and the admiration for living railroad heroes.

2. Public interest in technological nostalgia, combined with the use of folk images that are reinforced by childhood toys and grandparents' stories, have fostered an increased use of train-related metaphors in contemporary songs.

3. The traditional railroad song, along with new tunes that contain train-related images, will probably continue to be a staple of American music and popular culture during the next 20 years.

Obviously, each history teacher will want to organize the train songs listed above in his or her own personal instructional format. For this reason, no specific classroom approach has been mandated. The major difficulty in implementing this oral history review of railroad imagery is locating and taping the necessary recordings. Although there are several fine anthology albums of train songs presently on the market and students can usually provide recordings of mid-1970s vintage for classroom use, there is one collegiate resource area designed specifically to assist teachers in assembling taped audio instructional materials. The Audio Center in the William T. Jerome Library at Bowling Green State University in Ohio is dedicated to collecting, cataloging, and circulating all types of recorded materials. All of the songs mentioned in this study can be obtained in any sequence desired by sending a blank cassette or reel-to-reel tape to the following address:

Mr. William L. Schurk
Sound Recordings Archivist
The William T. Jerome Library
Bowling Green State University
Bowling Green, Ohio 43403

## REFERENCES

Botkin, B. A. and Alvin F. Harlow (eds.). *A Treasury of Railroad Folklore: The Stories, Tall Tales, Traditions, Ballads and Songs of the American Railroad Man*. New York: Bonanza Books, 1953.

Beck, James H. (ed.). *Rail Talk: A Lexicon of Railroad Language*. Gretna, Nebraska: James Publications, 1978.

Carpenter, Ann Miller. "The Railroad in American Folksong, 1865-1920," in *Diamond Bessie and the Shepherds*, edited by Wilson M. Hudson (Austin: Texas Folklore Society, 1972), pp. 103-119.

Carter, Gerald C. "The Real John Henry Stands Up," *Michigan Academician*, XVIII (Summer 1986), pp. 329-337.

Cohen, Norm, with music edited by David Cohen. *Long Steel Rail: The Railroad in American Folksong*, Urbana: University of Illinois Press, 1981.

Cooper, B. Lee. "Oral History, Popular Music, and American Railroads, 1920-1980," *Social Studies*, LXXIV (November/December 1983), pp. 223-231.

Cooper, B. Lee. "Transportation System," in *A Resource Guide to Themes in Contemporary American Song Lyrics, 1950-1985* (Westport, Connecticut: Greenwood Press, 1986), pp. 235-252.

Dew, Lee A. "The Locomotive Engineer: Folk Hero of The 19th Century," *Studies in Popular Culture*, I (Winter 1977), pp. 45-55.

Eleaser, J.M. "Boys Are That Way," *Living in South Carolina*, XXII (September 1980), p. 6.

Green, Archie. "John Henry Revisited," *JEMF Quarterly*, XIX (Spring 1983), pp. 12-31.

Lyle, Katie Letcher. *Scalded to Death by the Steam: Authentic Stories of Railroad Disasters and the Ballads That Were Written About Them*. Chapel Hill, North Carolina: Algonquin Books, 1983.

Manning, Ambrose. "Railroad Work Songs," *Tennessee Folklore Society Bulletin*, XXIII (June 1966), pp. 41-47.

McPherson, James Alan and Miller Williams (eds.). *Railroad: Trains and Train People in American Culture*. New York: Random House, 1976.

Miller, Arthur H., Jr. "Trains and Railroading, "in *Handbook of American Popular Culture—Volume Three*, edited by M. Thomas Inge (Westport, Connecticut: Greenwood Press, 1981), pp. 497-515.

Oliver, Paul. "Railroad Bill," *Jazz and Blues*, I (May 1971), pp. 12-14.

Oliver, Paul. "Rock Island Line," *Music Mirror*, IV (January 1957), pp. 6-8.

Parks, Jack. "The Lure of the Railroad," *Country Music*, II (February 1974), pp. 32-34, 68-71.

Townley, Eric. "Jazz, Blues, and U.S. Railroads," *Storyville*, No 68 (December 1976/January 1977), pp. 55-58.

Williams, Brett. *John Henry: A Bio-Bibliography*. Westport, Connecticut: Greenwood Press, 1983.

Chapter 16

# Regional Music

## *GEOGRAPHY OF SOUND*

*The Sounds of People and Places: Readings in the Geography of American Folk and Popular Music.* Edited by George O. Carney. Lanham, Maryland: University Press of America, Inc., 1987. Illustrated. 339 pp.

This collection of 16 essays on the geography of American music offers a variety of valuable insights into the spatial nature of audio-oriented popular culture. George O. Carney, a teaching specialist in historical and cultural geography and a dedicated student of twentieth-century music, folk architecture, and historic preservation, has pioneered this scholarly investigation of the geography of music. From his Oklahoma State University vantage point, he has explored the diffusion of country, folk, bluegrass, and pop music via radio broadcasting, performer migration, and other geographically defined means of cultural exchange. Most of Carney's own landmark essays from the *Journal of Cultural Geography* and the *Journal of Geography* are reprinted in this collection. Also included in the volume are superb studies on Woody Guthrie's dust bowl music themes by James Curtis, on the geographic diffusion and spatial impact of gospel quartet singing by A. Doyne Horsley, on the cultural origins and shifting locus of rock 'n' roll's roots by Larry Ford, on field recording of traditional American music by Christopher Lornell, and on old-time fiddling in big sky country by John M. Crowley. The often-quoted essay "Country Music: A Reflection of Popular Culture" by

---

Five of these nine reviews by B. Lee Cooper were originally published in *Popular Music and Society.* Reprint permission granted by the author, Editor R. Serge Denisoff, Managing Editor Pat Browne, and Bowling Green State University Popular Press.

Charles F. Gritzner and a perceptive new commentary on "The Miami Sound: A Contemporary Latin Form of Place-Specific Music" by James R. Curtis and Richard F. Rose round out the anthology.

In recent years the study of popular music has been divided among biographers (hack hypsters vs. contemporary historians) and socioeconomic analysts. These bipolar publishing tendencies have obscured more educationally beneficial options in examining the nature and meaning of contemporary music. Carney's work attempts to provide a corrective jolt to this literary trend. His questions are wonderfully fundamental, though admittedly skewed toward time, place, and physical movement. The weak link for both Carney and his biographical/socioeconomic competitors is message. Very few scholars are able to amass the necessary volume of lyrical information to make generalizations across musical genre lines about the meaningful subcultures being depicted. Yet it is the personal hopes and fears, the them-and-us images, and the here-and-there social and physical change commentaries that must be at the heart of authentic cultural study. In his introductory essay "The Roots of American Music," Carney delves into pre-1955 black and country music as a complex information system of biography, religion, history, politics, ecology, and patriotism. He even demonstrates a sensitivity to ethnic identity by briefly exploring the sociological issues of exclusion, assimilation, and inclusion. But few of the other essays progress as far toward seeking distinctive cultural definitions via popular music. No matter, though. This is primarily a geographical tutorial guide of music, and as such, it is brilliant. Carney and his contributors deserve rich praise.

*The Sounds of People and Places* is required reading for cultural anthropologists, American Studies specialists, ethnomusicologists, popular music fans, and—of course—all geographers. Hopefully Carney, Gritzner, Curtis, Ford, and other writers assembled here will turn their geography of music analyses to new questions after 1988. Why has Australia been so successful in producing popular music performers who succeed in the United States? Why have England, France, and Japan been so interested in reissuing early American recordings? How and where did American blues recordings make their way from the United States into British culture prior to 1964? How did specific cities such as Houston, Texas; Macon, Georgia; and Jackson, Mississippi contribute to the rise of rock era music during the 1950s and 1960s? Hopefully as Carney plans his next Reader he will begin to explore some of the lyric-based cultural interpretations that make David Pichaske's *A Generation in Motion: Popular Music and Culture in the Sixties* (Schirmer, 1979) so valuable. But for now, this volume is a wonderful addition to the field of both geography and popular music teaching.

## *MEMPHIS, TENNESSEE*

*Sweet Soul Music: Rhythm and Blues and the Southern Dream of Freedom.* by Peter Guralnick. New York: Harper and Row, 1986. Illustrated. 438 pp.

Peter Guralnick writes like Aretha Franklin sings—with power, self-confidence, emotion, and poetry. It is ironic that a Boston-based white journalist should be the premier analyst and historian of black music's most potent period, 1954-1976. *Sweet Soul Music* is the third key study that Guralnick has produced. In 1971 he explored the lives of several rockabilly and blues musicians in *Feel Like Going Home*; in 1979 he investigated the journeys of selected country and blues singers in *Lost Highway.* For his latest book Guralnick spent five years crisscrossing the United States conducting over 100 personal interviews (Estelle Axton, Solomon Burke, Isaac Hayes, Chips Moman, Rufus Thomas, Phil Walden, and Jerry Wexler), examining previous studies by the foremost soul music students (Cliff White, Bill Millar, Gerri Hirshey, Charlie Gillett, Joe McEwen, and Stanley Booth), and listening to records and tapes of the best black vocalists of the soul era (Sam Cooke, Ray Charles, Otis Redding, James Brown, and Aretha Franklin). Combining the skills of an oral historian and a most perceptive sociologist, Guralnick draws this mass of material together into a fascinating tale of talent, triumph, tumult, and tragedy.

The central theme of *Sweet Soul Music* is that rhythm and blues matured and prospered within a southern soul triangle (Memphis, Tennessee; Macon, Georgia; and Muscle Shoals, Alabama) through the cooperative efforts of black singers and black and white musicians, entrepreneurs, and disc jockeys. The rise of the new soul sound paralleled the emergence of the civil rights movement during the 1960s. Not unlike the black man's struggle for social equality and political influence, soul music was dashed against the reefs of dead heroes and ideological extremism late in the 1960s. The deaths of Martin Luther King Jr. and Robert F. Kennedy were events that symbolized politically the same leadership malaise that occurred in the musical world when Sam Cooke, Otis Redding, Jackie Wilson, King Curtis, and Joe Tex disappeared. Lost leadership produced a hardening of production formula lines, a loss of creativity, a tension between formerly cooperative black and white artists and businessmen, and an end to the golden era of black music chart dominance. This concise description is overly simplified. Guralnick's brilliant, detailed interpretation is not.

Complexity of ideas and clarity of writing make this study unique among popular music critiques. Guralnick documents the shifting sensitivities to self among such diverse performers as Sam Cooke, Ray Charles, James Browne, and Solomon Burke; he illustrates how conflicting personalities and musical preferences among decision makers such as Jerry Wexler and Ahmet Ertegun at Atlantic Records or Jim Stewart and Steve Cropper at Stax Records strengthened rather than diminished the emerging soul-sound movement; he depicts the total personal involvement of artists and producers in seven-days-a-week, morning-'til-night record making and performing; he describes the chance events and pure luck that marked successes within various southern soul production-efforts; and finally he notes the difficulty of sustaining freedom of musical development as a few small, creative companies expanded into conglomerate status. Guralnick's eye for new images never rests. Even when he is overwhelmed by his own love of an artist or a particular style, he is able to step back intellectually in order to gain a less emotional, more analytical perspective.

What does Guralnick's study say to students of contemporary American culture? Plenty. First, while Motown's Berry Gordy Jr. brilliantly adapted the burgeoning Detroit sound (Smokey Robinson, The Supremes, Marvin Gaye, and Stevie Wonder) to attract the dollars of the white record-buying audience, a more regionally driven sound emerged from the blending of distinctively black musical elements—R&B and gospel—by an integrated group of stylistic experimenters and small-business entrepreneurs below the Mason-Dixon line. Motown's assimilation spawned The Temptations and a vinyl pop form that is still celebrated in nostalgia movies such as *The Big Chill*; Stax, Volt, Fame, and other southern soul labels launched a more emotive art form that enlivened the integrity of black Americans and dramatically enriched the musical heritage of the world. Humorously, all of this occurred during the rise and heyday of The Beatles and the Rolling Stones. To the credit of both of these British groups (and many of their U.K. contemporaries such as Eric Burdon, Joe Cocker, and even Welsh pop performer Tom Jones) they openly acknowledged American black music as the source of their first musical ideas.

A second point from Guralnick's cultural commentary is that the South has been and will probably continue to be a bastion of American musical creativity (if not always sales success). Traditional black blues notwithstanding, the independence and bullheadedness of many redneck rockers and soulful shouters continues to fuel the popular music field. Whether outrageous country offerings by Hank Williams Jr. and numerous Austin-based outlaws, or rock 'n' blues sounds by Stevie Ray Vaughan, The Fabulous Thunderbirds, and other bands, the big noise from Dixie continues. But it has yet to be seen if any new James Browns or Otis Reddings will leap out of Macon, Georgia. The paths to superstardom today for blacks appear to be relatives (Michael Jackson from the Jackson Five and Whitney Houston from Cissy Houston and Dionne Warwick), dogged longevity (Patti LaBelle and Tina Turner), or sheer genius (Ray Charles and Stevie Wonder).

The final mark of excellence in *Sweet Soul Music* is the author's balanced perspective. Guralnick is a gifted stylist with a keen eye for irony. In compiling this oral history, he is always aware of both conflicting interpretations and also of factual omissions. Fortunately for the reader Guralnick is often able to fill in the blanks with additional oral pursuits or by his own wily speculations. It is especially refreshing to have a writer initiate his study with the admission that many of his preresearch assumptions were proven invalid by the information acquired. In addition to a confessional introduction, Guralnick treats the reader to a midstream analysis of his personal commitment to soul music and his difficulty in objectifying his own position. The historian in Guralnick wins out, fortunately, and his work is marvelous.

Are there any serious shortcomings in this text? Not really. Guralnick provides a thorough general bibliography with attention to specialized articles on individual soul artists. His selected discography is less comprehensive, but beautifully annotated. It is hard to imagine how Guralnick could have enhanced his analysis other than by doubling the size of his work through developing a fully contrasting evolutionary profile of Detroit's black music steamroller with full biographical commentaries on Stevie Wonder, Diana Ross, Marvin Gaye, The Four Tops, and Motown's other giants. Maybe Guralnick will treat us to this material—or possibly a study on the musical roots of Sly Stone; "Prince"; Earth, Wind, and Fire and other non-Motown, non-southern black artists—in volume two.

*Sweet Soul Music* is nearly flawless. It is a book to be treasured by music fans, by oral historians, by business development students, by black studies specialists, and by rock journalists.

*White Boy Singin' the Blues: The Black Roots of White Rock*. By Michael Bane. New York: Penguin Books, 1982. 269 pp.

Several books and essays published during the past decade have chastized white recording artists for stealing tunes from black performers and then building successful pop music careers on the shoulders of unacknowledged African-American singers and composers. Michael Bane offers a thoughtful corrective interpretation to this half-true portrayal about the nature of the contemporary music industry. His arguments are honest, earthy, and cogent. He examines such complex elements as interaction, synthesis, cooperation, and reaction in areas of human relations and economic enterprise. *White Boy Singin' the Blues* is undeniably a paean to black musical creativity. It is also a first-rate elaboration of mutual misunderstandings and exchanges between the black and white cultures in America. But most of all this book tells the story of how the blues and country music became rock—the sound of our time.

Michael Bane has compiled a lengthy list of literary credits. His articles have been published in the *Charlotte Observer, The Village Voice,* and *Rolling Stone*; he has served as editor and contributing columnist for *Country Music* magazine; and he has produced two book-length popular music studies: *The Outlaws* (1978) and *Who's Who in Rock* (1981). From the historical perspective established in this study, though, the most important qualification that Bane possesses for examining the evolutionary and geographical development of contemporary music is his Memphis birthplace. As the author himself asserts,

> We'll be spending a lot of time in Memphis, because it is the single most important city in the history of American popular music, the home of the blues and Beale Street, the home of Elvis Presley and Sun Records, the home of Stax Records and some of the finest soul music of the 1960s. One would be hardpressed to find some area of popular music that wasn't touched by that city—its influence can be felt in today's discos and country honky-tonks. (pp. 17-18)

The majority of Bane's analysis is delivered in a chronological format. He begins with the African heritage of Mississippi Delta tunes, moves to the growth of gospel songs within the context of Bible Belt evangelism, explores the birth of Beale Street blues and black dance, traces the rhythmic interchanges between hillbilly/country and western singers and early blues musicians, studies the emergence of Sun Records and Sam Phillips— and of Elvis Presley and Charlie Rich "singin' nigger stuff" to white audiences, acknowledges the powerful pulse of the Motown era, comments on the impact of Limey rockers (The Beatles, the Rolling Stones, Joe Cocker and Eric Clapton) and the electronic white boys (Paul Butterfield and Mike Bloomfield) who spotlighted the talents of B.B. King, Howlin' Wolf, Muddy Waters, and the powerhouse bluesmen of Chicago, speaks about the ill-fated icons of the late 1960s (Otis Redding, Janis Joplin, and Jimi Hendrix), praises Phil Walden and the explosion of southern rock, and concludes with a 1970s survey of Isaac Hayes, disco, and the urban cowboy reaction. This oversimplified topical recitation is somewhat unfair to Bane. His well-organized text flows with feeling, energy, and insight. The power of his concise statements and strongly-cast images make his book a smooth-reading, distinctive contribution to the literature of rock.

The genuinely eerie aspect about Bane's study is his ability to conjure from a Southerner's perspective the mystery, fear, danger, and suspicion that continues to shroud race relations in the United States. "Rock and roll," observes the author, "was initially more than a white man singing the blues—it was a spark that arced between the two cultures, black and white." Popular music has constantly drawn its authority and dynamic power of renewal from this electric fusion. One of the more fascinating assertions that Bane makes is that there is no such thing as black music. His conception of all post-1950 American popular music—supplementing and broadening the positions presented by Lawrence Redd, Charlie Gillett, and Peter Guralnick—is that the "Top 40" steamroller is fueled by black energy while still functioning in a predominantly white economy.

There are several questions that Bane either fails to ask or neglects to answer fully in this slim volume. Why are The Righteous Brothers ignored as prototypical 1960s white boys singin' the blues? Is white blues stylist John Hammond (who is not even mentioned in the text) a transitional white boy singin' the blues, a preserver or a conserver of the authentic blues heritage, a commercially unsuccessful honky, or simply an insignificant 1960s folk singer gone blues crazy? How do Johnny Otis (pp. 137-138) and George Thorogood (omitted) fit into Bane's Memphis-connection thesis? Are Chicago, New York City, New Orleans, Detroit, Los Angeles and other black population centers consistently second to Memphis during the past three decades in both creative energy and historic relevance to fostering the nationwide rock phenomenon? What should be made of rock's newest generation—from Britain's heavy metal thumpers to America's jazz fusion specialists—as inheritors of the Memphis gospel/blues/R&B seed? Bane touches ever so briefly on some of these issues, but his study would have been much stronger if he had devoted more time to carefully exploring them. For academic readers, the total lack of internal citations and the failure to provide either a bibliography or a discography also creates credibility problems.

Bane has produced a readable, informative, and somewhat disturbing study. His verbal playfulness and lack of footnotes may unintentionally fool some scholars and frustrate others—but this book matches the very best analyses of rock music yet written. *White Boy Singin' the Blues* should be required reading for all students of American popular music and contemporary race relations.

*Rythm Oil: A Journey Through the Music of the American South.* By Stanley Booth. New York: Pantheon Books, 1991. Illustrated. 254 pp.

Georgia-born, Tennessee-enlightened Stanley Booth is a superb, hard-drinking rock journalist. Besides authoring *The True Adventures of the Rolling Stones* (1985), he has crafted essays for *Rolling Stone, Esquire, Eye,* and several other popular magazines. *Rythm Oil,* the fanciful Memphis description for a mojo potion peddled on Beale Street, is a mesmerizing series of previously published biographical sketches and concert reviews about the roots of blues and soul music. The book is a well-balanced triad: a history of southern popular music, a biography of some blues and soul giants, and an autobiography. The unity achieved within the text is both amazing and significant. Booth achieves this flow of facts and ideas by providing highly personalized, perceptive introductory commentaries before each of the 20 chapters in the volume. The total impact is haunting.

Booth is an authentic frontline observer, participant, and critic on several rock 'n' roll battlefields. Memphis is the key war-zone for this Georgia boy turned musical Ernie Pyle. Booth eulogizes old soldiers (Robert Johnson, Furry Lewis, and Mississippi John Hurt), examines Congressional Medal of Honor candidates (Elvis Presley, Otis Redding, and Janis Joplin), and interviews current field commanders (B.B. King, Al Green, Keith Richards, and ZZ Top). What is somewhat unnerving about Booth's longitudinal perspective is that tragic, violent death seems to sweep along in his journalistic wake. He readily admits his own fascination with fallen heroes–from Elvis Presley and Otis Redding to Martin Luther King Jr. and Robert F. Kennedy. Even his beloved Memphis is depicted as an unappreciated urban Phoenix, with an unconquerable (and generally evil) spirit that rises again and again from the dead despite pestilence, social decay, slavery, and even sterilizing urban renewal. Booth's fascination with victims, himself included, would be morbid but for his exceptional wit, literary style, and historical insight.

There are few rock journalists that deserve to be anthologized. Cranky Dave Marsh is one; enthusiastic Jeff "Almost Slim" Hannusch is another; wild Nick Tosches is a third; and persistent Peter Guralnick is a fourth. There are not more than three other writers who can fathom the meaning, the value, and the dark rigors of musical contributions to twentieth-century American culture. Booth does. This book is a treasure.

## NEW ORLEANS, LOUISIANA

*I Hear You Knockin': The Sound of New Orleans Rhythm and Blues.*
By Jeff Hannusch. Ville Platte, Louisiana: Swallow Press, 1985.
Illustrated. 374 pp.

Jeff Hannusch (a.k.a. Almost Slim) has crafted a delightful series of biographical sketches on selected artists, recording company personnel, and radio broadcasting personalities that made New Orleans rhythm and blues a distinctive musical force from the late 1940s until the mid-1970s. The glory years of 1959-1965 are focal points for this study. Nevertheless, the author does justice both to the sunrise performances of the Crescent City sound by saluting Roy Brown, Guitar Slim, and Smiley Lewis and to the sunset artists such as James Booker and Professor Longhair. *I Hear You Knockin'* depicts giants–those of technical prowess and commercial genius (Cosimo Matassa, Johnny Vincent, and Marshall Sehorn), those of producing inventiveness and playing wizardry (Allen Toussaint and Dave Bartholomew), and those of instrumental and vocal magic (Irma Thomas, Lee Allen, Frankie Ford, Chris Kenner, Ernie K-Doe, Jesse Hill, and Lee Dorsey). In all, 31 New Orleans greats are portrayed.

Hannusch writes with obvious love and deep respect, but not without a keen sense of social and musical reality. Since much of his information is drawn from individual interviews, points of personal and professional disagreement crop up throughout the text. Beyond oral testimony, the author acknowledges his debt to previous historical studies by Paul Oliver, John Broven, and Peter Guralnick and to discographic and record-chart data compiled by Joel Whitburn, Ray Topping, Mike Ledbitter, and Neil Slaven. The breadth of characters covered and the exceptional array of photographs assembled by Hannusch make this book a key resource on the personalities that launched and shaped New Orleans R&B.

Although this study was conceived and written in an upbeat fashion, the author provides much more than a who-knew-who-in-New-Orleans per- spective. Hannusch blends the warm reminiscing of artists and producers with the cold facts of American social history following the second World War. For most black artists, music was the key to social, economic, and geographic mobility. Yet it was a volatile genie that once freed could sometimes evaporate or be stolen rather than continuing to fulfill the creative performer's wishes and dreams. The undercurrent themes in *I Hear You Knockin'*–commentaries about nonsuccessful moments, hours, days, months, and years–are crammed with incidents of alcoholism, insan- ity, gambling, malnutrition, drug abuse, poverty, suspicion and mistrust, fraudulent business practices, suicides, syphilis, and segregation. These are heavy problems. Yet as the author notes they are indelible marks on the tempo of musical life in New Orleans.

Despite the many strengths of this study, there are several major and minor shortcomings in Hannusch's first book-length work. First, the author elected to omit a Fats Domino chapter from the book because a close friend will soon be publishing a biography on The Fat Man. This is a crucial error that dramatically weakens the text. Second, other key figures such as Little Richard, Lloyd Price, Dr. John, The Neville Brothers, and Clarence "Frogman" Henry merit far more coverage than Hannusch provides. Third, the "Appendixes" (which feature charted R&B singles from 1949-1971, the names and addresses of important Crescent City R&B Clubs, and a selected discography of reissued R&B albums) contain no specific information about the oral resources and interviews cited throughout the text or about the specific literary resources that were used. Finally, the publisher failed to require the author to assemble an index for *I Hear You Knockin'*. This makes the fact-filled, name-crowded, song-title-studded text impossible to use as a reference for specific questions. Since the author's introduction mentions plans to develop a second volume on this topic, most of these problems will hopefully be corrected.

This book salutes a single city and its sound. Ideally, Almost Slim or some other R&B enthusiast with a penchant for bio-discographic analysis will expand this vision from one city to the entire Southern belt. A survey tracing the evolution of R&B from 1945-1975 in Macon, Jackson, New Orleans, Houston, and Memphis would make fascinating reading. *I Hear You Knockin'* is an excellent primer on the cycle of popular music prominence. The lessons are clear. Music is a tenuous business endeavor, for artist and recording company alike. But genuinely good music remains its own reward—for the performer, the listener, and even future generations. Jeff Hannusch champions the cause of those who are rapidly fading from collective public memory—even though their immortal vinyl contributions remain as examples of their energy, creativity and talent.

*Safe with Me and Irma Thomas Live* (RCS A-1OO4CD). Shreveport, Louisiana: RCS/Paula Records, 1991. 20 Songs.

*"Time Is on My Side": The Best of Irma Thomas—Volume One* (CDP 97988). Hollywood, California: Minit/E.M.I. Records, 1992. 23 Songs.

Irma Thomas is a regional superstar, the universally acclaimed Soul Queen of New Orleans. Yet her national reputation has never matched either her high-profile Crescent City image or the magnetic quality of her sensual performing style. Some of her best songs have been adopted by powerful male artists: "Time Is on My Side" by the Rolling Stones and

"Ruler of My Heart" by Otis Redding (retitled "Pain in My Heart"). The show-stopping recordings from her early years–"It's Raining," "Wish Someone Would Care," and "Break-a-Way"–fell short of Top Ten recognition in both R&B and pop *Billboard* charts. And her adaptations of more classic hit tune material–"It's too Soon to Know," "Maybe," and "I Can't Help Myself"–have never produced public interest beyond her native state.

These two compact discs offer a well-rounded perspective on Irma Thomas's lengthy professional career. The *Best Of . . .* set is the superior product in respect to song selections, total production quality, and perceptive liner notes. *Safe with Me*, the 1991 studio portion of a dual release compact disc, demonstrates the breadth of Thomas's current repertoire, with "Princess LaLa" echoing the singer's high regard for the deep-seated voodoo legends of Creole country. *Irma Thomas Live* is a reprise of her classic 1960s material that was originally recorded on stage in 1979 during a performance at The Kingfish Club in Baton Rouge.

It is a shame that so many spectacular, soulful female artists–Ann Peebles, Lou Ann Barton, Darlene Love, Marcia Ball, Deanna Bogart, Joanna Connor, and (most of all) Irma Thomas–linger in local limelights rather than flourish in the glare of national attention. Of course, Bonnie Raitt, Tina Turner, Aretha Franklin, and a few others have succeeded with a vengeance. But considering the high quality of her songwriters (Allen Toussaint, Jackie DeShannon, Van McCoy, Doc Pomus, and Burt Bacharach), the deep emotion and rhythmic power of her vocal styling, and the spectacular venues where she has recorded (Cosimo Matassa's Studio in Louisiana, Muscle Shoals Sound in Alabama, and Sound Stage Records in Tennessee), it is impossible to explain Irma Thomas's protracted apprenticeship as a popular performer.

## *BOSTON, MASSACHUSETTS*

*Yankee Blues: Musical Culture and American Identity.* By MacDonald Smith Moore. Bloomington: Indiana University Press, 1985. Illustrated. 213 pp.

*Yankee Blues* is a fascinating assessment of sociological and musical change in the United States. MacDonald Smith Moore utilizes the commentaries of Charles Ives and Daniel Gregory Mason to symbolize the attitudes, opinions, and beliefs of several New England composers and music critics of the 1900-1940 period. These classically cultured artists, bound together by Western European literary and musical traditions, were appalled by the emergence of jazz and other modernist music after World War I. The popularity of promoters and composers such as George Gershwin, Aaron Copland, and Ernest Bloch was deemed threatening; the growing influence of younger music critics such as Gilbert Sildes, Carl Von Vechten, and John Hammond was seen as disruptive; and the increasing acclaim secured by Sidney Bechet, Duke Ellington, and Louis Armstrong was unthinkable and unacceptable.

The Yankee music aristocracy decried the mechanistic, materialistic, hedonistic, sensual, and primitive nature of urban jazz and other popular music between the World Wars. The focus of *Yankee Blues* is frustration—the frustration of highbrow Victorian composers who could not impose their collective will on a new generation of musicians that represented vastly diversified ideological, regional, and ethnic (particularly Jewish and Negro) backgrounds. Beyond music, the author captures America's struggle of rising national consciousness in regard to the benefits of genuine cultural pluralism. Through the metaphor of musical evaluation, early twentieth-century thinkers struggled toward the reality of different ideas and different spokesmen as legitimate and creative, rather than false and disruptive.

Revisiting the roots of America's musical transition is intriguing. But does Moore end his saga too soon? Granted, a vast change in style and sound occurred with the emergence and acceptance of ragtime and jazz. But the continuing revolution in contemporary music—the post-World War II triumph of blues, rhythm 'n' blues, rockabilly, rock 'n' roll, and rock—is an even more significant extension of the cultural battle depicted in *Yankee Blues*. The complex bureaucratic, economic, technological, sociological, as well as ideological struggles involved in post-1950 musical change are revealed in several exceptional books and articles. Strangely, they are not mentioned in Moore's lengthy bibliography. They warrant citation as logical intellectual outgrowths of his well-stated and strongly supported premise. These works are:

- Bane, Michael. *White Boy Singin' the Blues: The Black Roots of White Rock* (Penguin, 1982).

- Chapple, Steve and Reebee Garofalo. *Rock 'N' Roll is Here to Pay: The History and Politics of the Music Industry* (Nelson-Hall, 1977).

- Denisoff, R. Serge. *Solid Gold: The Popular Record Industry* (Transaction, 1975).

- Denisoff, R. Serge and Richard A. Peterson (eds.). *The Sounds of Social Change: Studies in Popular Culture* (Rand McNally, 1972).

- Gillett, Charlie. *The Sound of the City: The Rise of Rock and Roll* (Pantheon, 1983).

- Kamin, Jonathan. "Parallels in the Social Reactions to Jazz and Rock," *Journal of Jazz Studies*, II (December 1974), pp. 95-125.

- Peterson, Richard A. and David G. Berger. "Cycles in Symbol Production: The Case of Popular Music," *American Sociological Review*, XL (April 1975), pp. 158-173.

- Pichaske, David. *A Generation in Motion: Popular Music and Culture in the Sixties* (Schirmer, 1979).

- Rodnitzky, Jerome L. *Minstrels of the Dawn: The Folk-Protest Singer as a Cultural Hero* (Nelson-Hall, 1976).

- Shaw, Arnold. *Honkers and Shouters: The Golden Years of Rhythm and Blues* (Collier, 1978).

- Tosches, Nick. *Country: The Biggest Music in America* (Dell, 1977).

- Tosches, Nick. *Unsung Heroes of Rock 'n' Roll: The Birth of Rock 'n' Roll in the Dark and Wild Years Before Elvis* (Scribner's, 1984).

Moore's study is enhanced through the insights in his "Epilogue" (pp. 169-171). Here the author shifts from historical analysis to personal observation. Moore contends, "Prejudice and preference interpenetrate. The critical faculty is manifold. It separates not only wheat from chaff but wines from wines. . . ." True to the scholar's ethic, he urges society to be discriminating but not to discriminate. He even chides those black intellectuals of the 1960s who unwittingly appropriated the redemptive cultural strategy of Ives and Mason by using the aesthetic myth of African-American "soul" to attack white musicians, composers, and critics.

*Yankee Blues* is a vital, valuable monograph. Although difficult reading at times, it is a worthwhile investigation of musical culture and national identity in transition.


## *AUSTIN, TEXAS*

*Meeting the Blues.* By Alan Govenar. Dallas, Texas: Taylor Publishing Company, 1988. Illustrated. 239 pp.

*Meeting the Blues* is designed to be an oral history of the Texas music originated by people who are darker than blue. To assemble this volume folklorist, photographer, and filmmaker Alan Govenar has interviewed hundreds of blues performers; he has secured many personal photographs, performance snapshots, and playbills to illustrate his documentary study; and he has compiled an up-to-date selected blues discography to support his text. This book, structured in a modified encyclopedia format, presents each biographical entry as an open-ended interview session.

Govenar's message is clear. *Texas Blues* is a long-standing cultural phenomenon with a rich heritage. This music has served as the potting soil for the eclectic sounds of the rock era. From R&B to soul, from rockabilly to country rock, the blues rhythm base is undeniable. Beyond the rhythmic contribution, though, lyrics are also an important element in the blues roots. Guitar stylist Albert Collins notes ". . . a lot of people misinterpret the blues. They feel like it's depressing music." To overcome this stereotype, Govenar strives to demonstrate that joy, bragging, enthusiasm, excitement, and success (often sexual, only occasionally economic) are as much a part of blues music as pain, sorrow, and woe.

The documentary strength of Govenar's approach ultimately weakens the quality of his work. Allowing talented bluesmen to play their music is always pure magic. However, as reporters and cultural analysts, these same performers are uneven, sometimes uninformed spokesmen and rambling word-merchants. The sharedness of blues lyrics contrasts with the unfocused reflections presented in *Meeting the Blues*. Two activities should have occurred to overcome this literary problem. Initially, the author should have drafted a brief biographical essay to precede the commentaries of each blues artist. Next, Govenar should have exercised a stronger editorial hand and a more directed interview technique in order to produce maximum insights into the lives and careers of those blues giants that he interviewed.

From its startling orange-blue-yellow-white cover featuring an in-flight-photo of Albert Collins to the two-page photograph of the community of Waco, Texas circa 1939, Govenar is a genius at portraying the varying blues life via visuals. He is the Charles Keil, the Paul Oliver, the Samuel Charters of blues photography. Actually, his role more closely parallels that of Michael Ochs, the compiler of the wonderful *Rock Archives* (Doubleday, 1984). Govenar allows his legends to pose and posture with their guitars, violins, and harmonicas, their microphones and chairs, and their special dressed-to-kill performing attire. But both the more private and the more public images of black life in Texas are much more fascinating. Corona beers, lavishly dressed nightclub women, children in poverty, cotton pickers, prison farm workers and road gangs, storefronts and classic cars, segregated bus terminals and theaters, and dancehall after dancehall are trapped in time.

In addition Govenar includes photos of sheet music, record labels, newspaper clippings, picture discs, promotional circulars, and other poster memorabilia. It is also pleasant to note that along with the black blues legends (T-Bone Walker, B.B. King, and Freddie King) and journeymen performers (Charles Brown, Little Joe Blue, and Lowell Fulson), Govenar includes several white Texas bluesmen (Anson Funderburgh, Delbert McClinton, Johnny Winter, and the steamy brothers Vaughan–Jimmie and Stevie Ray).

*Meeting the Blues* is a timely salute to a particular form of Texas music. It would be delightful if Alan Govenar would now turn his visual attention to the Chicago blues scene and create a similar pictorial tribute to Muddy Waters, Howlin' Wolf, Willie Dixon, Little Walter, Otis Spann, and others. Meanwhile, blues fans should flock to this work. Another audience for this study should be students of black history and the civil rights movement. Nowhere is the integration of culture, music, and people more clearly illustrated than in the chaning blues scene of the Lone Star State.

*Texas Rhythm/Texas Rhyme: A Pictorial History of Texas Music* (second edition). By Larry Willoughby. Austin, Texas: Tonkawa Free Press, 1990. Illustrated. 165 pp.

Throughout the twentieth-century various cities have claimed the title "Music Capital of the United States." Kansas City fostered jazz; Nashville promoted country; Memphis and Chicago championed rhythm 'n' blues; and from St. Louis, New Orleans, New York, and Los Angeles grew varying forms of blues, pop, dance band sounds, doo-wop harmonies, and ethnic beats. Through providing a mobile perspective that roams from Houston to Austin, from San Antonio to Lubbock, Larry Willoughby argues with conviction that the Lone Star State is truly the cradle of contemporary American music. *Texas Rhythm/Texas Rhyme* combines stylistic diversity with individual artistic excellence to prove the claim to national musical dominance.

Willoughby presents a ten-chapter survey of enthusiastic Texas music. Beginning with nineteenth-century roots typified by "The Yellow Rose of Texas," brass bands, and rowdy ragtime, this pictorial history proceeds through singing cowboys (Carl Sprague, Gene Autry, Tex Ritter, and R. Texas Tyler), wailing bluesmen (Mance Lipscomb, Blind Lemon Jefferson, Leadbelly, and Lightnin' Hopkins), western swing artists (Bob Wills, Hank Thompson, and Asleep at the Wheel), jazz performers and big bands (Harry James, Oran "Hop Lips" Page, Jack Teagarden, and Ornette Coleman), rhythm and blues giants (Charlie Christian, Aaron "T-Bone" Walker, Clarence "Gatemouth" Brown, and Little Esther Phillips), rock 'n' roll stars (Janis Joplin, Buddy Holly, and Roy Orbison), and modern country royalty (Willie Nelson, George Jones, Kris Kristofferson, Waylon Jennings, and Barbara Mandrell). The author portrays Austin as the electronic magnate for 1970s, 1980s, and 1990s Texas troubadours of all stripes. Television's "Austin City Limits" has brought national attention to all forms of Texas musical talent. The final section of the volume features an extended photo review of newly emerging singers and pickers.

Willoughby's commentaries are succinct, factual, and informative. But the black-and-white photography is the authentic strength of *Texas Rhythm/Texas Rhyme*. The power of Willoughby's study lies in its shotgun approach to blasting name after name at the target of national musical influence. Diversity ultimately outdoes singular stardom, too. Where else but Texas are dead heroes (Freddie King and Stevie Ray Vaughan) as powerful as living legends (Albert Collins and ZZ Top)? Where else would one expect to encounter Lyle Lovett, Delbert McClinton, Omar and the Howlers, Joe Ely, and The Fabulous Thunderbirds rockin' at middle-of-nowhere county fairs? And where else are top stars (John Denver, Kenny Rogers, Tanya Tucker, Clint Black, and George Strait) and quirky performers (Kinky Friedman, Doug Sahm, Marcia Ball, and Jerry Jeff Walker) so prevalent? Only in a place as big as . . . .

## REFERENCES

Burns, Gary. "Bosstown: Another Look at the 'Boston Sound' of 1968," *Goldmine*, No. 311 (June 26, 1992), pp. 16-34.

Carney, George O. (ed.). *The Sounds of People and Places: A Geography of American Folk and Popular Music* (third edition). Lanham, Maryland: Rowan and Littlefield Publishers, Inc., 1994.

Chase, Gilbert. *America's Music: From the Pilgrims to the Present* (revised third edition). Urbana: University of Illinois Press, 1992.

Cooper, B. Lee and Wayne S. Haney. *Rockabilly: A Bibliographic Resource Guide*. Metuchen, New Jersey: Scarecrow Press, Inc., 1990.

Cummings, Tony. *The Sound of Philadelphia*. London: Methuen, 1975.

DeWitt, Dennis. "Memphis: The Beat That Won't Stop," *Blue Suede News*, No. 18 (1992), pp. 13-14.

Erlewine, Michael and Scott Bultman (eds.). *All Music Guide*. San Francisco: Miller Freeman, Inc., 1992.

Escott, Colin, with Martin Hawkins. *Good Rockin' Tonight: Sun Records and the Birth of Rock 'n' Roll*. New York: St. Martin's Press, 1991.

Goddard, Peter and Philip Kamin (comps.). *Shakin' All Over: The Rock 'n' Roll Years in Canada*. Toronto: McGraw Hill Ryerson, Ltd., 1989.

Gould, Philip. *Cajun Music and Zydeco*. Baton Rouge: Louisiana State University Press, 1992.

Govenar, Alan. *Meeting the Blues: The Rise of the Texas Sound*. Dallas, Texas: Taylor Publishing Company, 1988.

Griggs, Bill. *A "Who's Who" of West Texas Rock 'n' Roll Music*. Lubbock, Texas: William F. Griggs/Rockin' 50s Magazine, 1994.

Hannusch, Jeff (a.k.a. Almost Slim). *I Hear You Knockin': The Sound of New Orleans Rhythm and Blues*. Ville Platte, Louisiana: Swallow Press, 1985.

Lepri, Paul. *The New Haven Sound, 1946-1976*. New Haven, Connecticut: United Printing Services, Inc., 1977.

Loza, Steven. *Barrio Rhythm: Mexican American Music in Los Angeles*. Urbana: University of Illinois Press, 1993.

MacLeod, Bruce A. *Club Date Musicians: Playing the New York Party Circuit*. Urbana: University of Illinois Press, 1993.

Malone, Bill C. *Southern Music–American Music*. Lexington: University Press of Kentucky, 1979.

McDonough, Jack. *San Francisco Rock: The Illustrated History of San Francisco Rock Music*. San Francisco: Chronicle Books, 1985.

McEwen, Joe. "The Sound of Chicago," in *The Rolling Stone Illustrated History of Rock and Roll* (fully revised and updated), edited by Anthony DeCurtis and James Henke, with Holly George-Warren (New York: Random House, 1992), pp. 171-176.

McKee, Margaret and Fred Chisen Hall. *Beale Black and Blue: Life and Music on Black America's Main Street*. Baton Rouge: Louisiana State University Press, 1981.

Melhish, Martin. *Heart of Gold: 30 Years of Canadian Pop Music*. Toronto: Canadian Broadcasting Corporation, 1983.

Miller, Jim. "The Sound of Philadelphia," in *The Rolling Stone Illustrated History of Rock and Roll* (fully revised and updated), edited by Anthony DeCurtis and James Henke, with Holly George-Warren (New York: Random House, 1992), pp. 515-520.

Moore, MacDonald Smith. *Yankee Blues: Musical Culture and American Identity*. Bloomington: Indiana University Press, 1985.

Nolan, Alan. *Rock 'n' Roll Road Trip: The Ultimate Guide to the Sites, the Shrines, and the Legends Across America*. New York: Pharos Books, 1992.

Palmer, Robert. "The Sound of Memphis," in *The Rolling Stone Illustrated History of Rock and Roll* (fully revised and updated), edited by Anthony DeCurtis and James Henke, with Holly George-Warren (New York: Random House, 1992), pp. 266-271.

Patterson, Daniel W. (ed.). *Sounds of the South*. Durham, North Carolina: Duke University Press, 1991.

Perry, Charles. "The Sound of San Francisco," in *The Rolling Stone Illustrated History of Rock and Roll* (fully revised and updated), edited by Anthony DeCurtis and James Henke, with Holly George-Warren (New York: Random House, 1992), pp. 362-369.

Rockwell, John. "The Sound of New York City," in *The Rolling Stone Illustrated History of Rock and Roll* (fully revised and updated), edited by Anthony DeCurtis and James Henke, with Holly George-Warren (New York: Random House, 1992), pp. 549-560.

Rowe, Mike. *Chicago Blues: The City and the Music.* New York: Da Capo Press, Inc., 1975.

Sculatti, Gene and Davin Seay. *San Francisco Nights: The Psychedelic Music Trip, 1965-1968.* New York: St. Martin's Press, 1985.

Shank, Barry. *Dissonant Identities: The Rock 'n' Roll Scene in Austin, Texas.* Hanover, New Hampshire: University Press of New England, 1994.

Smith, Michael P. *A Joyful Noise: A Celebration of New Orleans Music.* Dallas, Texas: Taylor Publishing Company, 1990.

Tracy, Steven C. *Going to Cincinnati: A History of the Blues in the Queen City.* Champaign: University of Illinois Press, 1993.

Vera, Billy. "A Pilgrimage to New Orleans," *Bim Bam Boom,* No. 11 (1973), pp. 30-31.

Ward, Ed. "The Sound of Texas," in *The Rolling Stone Illustrated History of Rock and Roll* (fully revised and updated), edited by Anthony DeCurtis and James Henke, with Holly George-Warren (New York: Random House, 1992), pp. 252-259.

Willoughby, Larry. *Texas Rhythm/Texas Rhyme: A Pictorial History of Texas Music.* Austin: Texas Monthly Press, Inc., 1984.

Wilson, Charles R. and William Ferris (eds.). *Encyclopedia of Southern Culture.* Chapel Hill: University of North Carolina Press, 1989.

Winner, Langdon. "The Sound of New Orleans," in *The Rolling Stone Illustrated History of Rock and Roll* (fully revised and updated), edited by Anthony DeCurtis and James Henke, with Holly George-Warren (New York: Random House, 1992), pp. 37-47.

# Chapter 17

# Rock Journalism

## *"BEST" AND "WORST" RECORDINGS*

*The Worst Rock 'n' Roll Records of All Time: A Fan's Guide to the Stuff You Love to Hate!* By Jimmy Guterman and Owen O'Donnell. New York: Citadel Press, 1991. Illustrated. 252 pp.

*The Best Rock 'n' Roll Records of All Time: A Fan's Guide to the Stuff You Love!* By Jimmy Guterman. New York: Citadel Press, 1992. Illustrated. 205 pp.

In 1978 Paul Gambaccini compiled *Rock Critics' Choice: The Top 200 Albums*; in 1982 Tom Hibbert assembled *The Perfect Collection: The Rock Albums Everybody Should Have*; and in 1989 Dave Marsh produced *The Heart of Rock and Soul: The 1001 Greatest Singles Ever Made*. Not to be outdone, Jimmy Guterman has organized two volumes that theoretically alert music fans to the 100 "worst" and 100 "best" rock 'n' roll records. The author surveys the past four decades—noting special emphasis on the 1970s and the 1980s—to select very good and very bad vinyl products. Among the worst singles he discovers are "My Ding-a-Ling" by Chuck Berry (1972), "I Dig Rock and Roll Music" by Peter, Paul, and Mary (1967), and "Cat's in the Cradle" by Harry Chapin (1974). His selections for worst albums include *Pat Boone* (1957), Bob Dylan *Live at Budokan* (1978), and *Blood, Sweat and Tears* (1969). Among the best singles Guterman lists are "Whole Lotta Shakin' Going On" by Jerry Lee Lewis (1957), "Maggie May" by Rod Stewart (1971), and "When Doves Cry" by the artist formerly known as Prince (1984). The best albums he finds include *Every Picture Tells a Story* by Rod Stewart (1971), *Exile on Main*

---

These reviews by B. Lee Cooper are scheduled to be published in *Popular Music and Society*. Reprint permission granted by the author, Editor R. Serge Denisoff, and Bowling Green State University Popular Press.

*Street* by the Rolling Stones (1972), and *Astral Weeks* by Van Morrison (1968).

Guterman must be joking! These two volumes are the literary equivalent of Orson Welles' report about Martian invaders. It is unforgivable to overlook so many exceptionally good songs–"I Heard It Through the Grapevine," "(I Can't Get No) Satisfaction," "Respect," "Johnny B. Goode," "Hot Blooded," and "In the Midnight Hour"–while honoring so many mediocre tunes. A more serious error is Guterman's unwillingness to define rock 'n' roll as anything more distinctive than music produced after 1955. If the genre of rock 'n' roll is to be distinguished from pop, jazz, country, and soul, then no list of best songs could avoid "Blue Suede Shoes," "Tutti Frutti," "Roll with It," "(We're Gonna) Rock Around the Clock," "Hurts So Good," "Brown Sugar," and "Summertime Blues." Without Joe Cocker, Gene Vincent, Ronnie Hawkins, The Guess Who, Bob Seger, Johnny Rivers, and Jack Scott there is absolutely no credibility to an alleged rock 'n' roll analysis.

A more problematic situation is Guterman's tendency to equate albums with individual songs. It is not that great albums do not exist. But the currency of modern music remains the hit single–not EPs, or even boxed sets. Unfortunately, *Sgt. Pepper* taught too many journalists an erroneous lesson about the so-called concept album. The productive genius of The Beatles is as rare as the thematic balance achieved in their magnificent 1967 LP. But Joel Whitburn's numerous "Hot 100" *Billboard* chart volumes provide an antidote to album-oriented myopia. Guterman's best albums are generally ill-chosen. But the real problem is that the author is searching through the wrong musical medium.

The identification of the worst rock 'n' roll records should have been a tongue-in-cheek operation exploring novelty recordings, answer songs, Christmas tunes, or other bizarre discs. It is ludicrous to condemn songs such as "Jack and Diane," "Ebony Eyes," "The Horizontal Bop," "State of Shock," "The Dangling Conversation," "American Woman," "The Loco-Motion," and "Eve of Destruction." Guterman simply has not listened to enough music to compile a Barry Hansen-type anthology of bad songs. Guterman's chief error is in slamming several good tunes; a Dr. Demento approach is needed to sample, select, and exhibit the most bodacious, crazy, humorous, off-center, rude, obnoxious, poorly conceived, weirdly orchestrated, and awfully produced music from hell.

If the goal of compiling these volumes was (as Guterman contends) to counter rock journalism's hyperbole and to restore sanity, humor, and perspective, then the works are utter failures. They are clearly monuments to self-indulgent speculation. If the goal was to promote controversy for the sake of controversy, then the enterprise is . . . worthless. There is no need to justify or defend the vitality, versatility, or vanity of rock 'n' roll music. Critics will never be assuaged; fans will never be objective. The real value of assembling lists of best, favorite, more influential, or most popular songs is to reflect upon the aesthetic self. Socrates beware. What these twin towers of Guterman's ego say is: "Jimmy needs to listen to more blues, country, jazz, pop, and rockabilly before his musical arteries (and opinions) harden."

## HISTORY OF ROCK AND ROLL

*The Rolling Stone Illustrated History of Rock and Roll* (third edition). Edited by Anthony DeCurtis and James Henke, with Holly George-Warren. New York: Random House, 1992. Illustrated. 710 pp.

Twelve years separate the second and third editions of *The Rolling Stone Illustrated History of Rock and Roll*. The momentous decade of the 1980s witnessed the death of vinyl and the birth of the compact disc, the triumph of music television (MTV) and the abundance of rock sound-tracks, the publicity power of Michael Jackson, Madonna, Prince, and Bruce Springsteen, and the expansion of American popular music as a world-stage phenomenon. All of this is documented in the hefty DeCurtis and Henke volume. The book consists of 94 chapters. These units are crafted by authorities on particular artists or regional music styles. The numerous photographs that support the text are marvelous, and the accompanying discographies for each chapter are concise yet authoritative. If a popular music enthusiast could own only one volume describing the rock era, this would probably be it.

Is there anything to quibble about in this third edition? Certainly. First, it is arrogant and misleading to pretend that any author (even Peter Guralnick, Robert Palmer, Greg Shaw, or Jim Miller) knows everything about a single rock personality or genre. Each chapter in *The Rolling Stone Illustrated . . .* should feature a supportive bibliography listing at least 25 sources. Second, there is too much self-satisfaction among the editors with the writing of old-guard journalists. In the "Doo-Wop" chapter, for example, Barry Hansen should yield his Dr. Demento pen to Anthony J. Gribin and Matthew M. Schiff, authors of *Doo-Wop: The Forgotten Third of Rock 'n' Roll* (1992). Similarly, Jim Miller ought to be replaced by Nick Tosches on the "Jerry Lee Lewis" chapter. Langdon Winner should acknowledge Chas White as the premiere biographer of "Little Richard," and Robert Christgau ought to encourage Howard A. DeWitt to describe "Chuck Berry." It is difficult to conceive that Greil Marcus knows more about "Girl Groups" than Alan Betrock, Gillian Gaar, or Charlotte Greig and equally impossible to believe that Joe McEwen understands "The Chicago Sound" as thoroughly as Robert Pruter. New blood, new ideas, and new interpretations are more than warranted. DeCurtis and Henke were sadly overconservative in their revising and revisioning.

Maintaining historical balance in a longitudinal study is always problematic. Demoting Steely Dan and elevating Madonna makes sense; but eliminating Rod Stewart and Elvis Costello is like omitting Little Richard and Buddy Holly. DeCurtis and Henke must avoid trashing contemporary giants in order to make room for a multicultural, politically correct, linguistically diverse but vapid chapter on "The Global Beat." Even the new "Up From the Underground" chapter is painfully superficial. A more critical discussion of whether rap music is soul writing in the 1990s, or racism and sexism, or even music at all should have ended the volume. No such luck!

The next edition of *The Rolling Stone Illustrated History of Rock and Roll* will appear on CD-ROM at your regional information center in 2004. The chapters on "Madonna," "The Velvet Underground," "Neil Young," "The Solo Beatles," "Phil Spector," "Anarchy in the U.K.," and "Rap and Soul" will be eliminated. New chapters on "The Triumph of Dead Rock 'n' Roll Heroes," "The Balding of Rock Journalism," "The Rock 'n' Roll Presidents," "Novelty Tunes–Louis Jordan, Weird Al Yankovic, and David Letterman," and "Black Dudes with Attitude" will be added. Meanwhile, grab the 1992 edition. It is terrific!

## ROCK WRITERS

*The Penguin Book of Rock and Roll Writing.* Edited by Clinton Heylin. New York: Viking/Penguin Books, Inc., 1992. Illustrated. 682 pp.

This cinderblock-size volume features 80 previously published commentaries written by 59 different rock journalists and musicians, which are randomly arranged into ten sections. Editor Clinton Heylin presents perspectives on rock history, aesthetics, political commentary, touring, fantasy and fiction, the recording industry, and fallen heroes and martyrs. The authors featured in the Penguin collection range from classic critics (Charlie Gillett, Nik Cohn, Jon Landau, Greil Marcus, and Simon Frith) to neophyte observers (Steve Albini, Joe Carducci, Deborah Frost, and Adrian Thrills.) Additional commentaries by Bob Dylan, Lou Reed, Pete Townshend, and Patti Smith are also featured.

The practice of anthologizing rock writing dates back to 1969. In that year Jonathan Eisen assembled 37 essays for *The Age of Rock: Sounds of the American Cultural Revolution*. This stellar collection featured contributions by Nat Hentoff, Hugh Mooney, Stanley Booth, Ralph Gleason, Richard Poirer, Wilfrid Mellers, Robert Christgau, Paul Williams, Gene Lees, Tom Wolfe, and others. In half the number of pages devoted to the Heylin volume, Eisen generated twice the punch. Critical shots were sharper; assessments of individual performers showed more emotion and insight, and the writing styles exhibited were more hard-edged and less cute. Production quality and print size are the only improvements that Heylin's 1992 tome can claim over Eisen's classic 1969 work.

Why is this *Penguin Book of Rock and Roll Writing* so disappointing? There are many reasons. It fails to present the best, most controversial, most provocative essays of those journalists who are included in the study. Simon Frith, for instance, has had much to say about the sloppy nature of "Rock Biography," and some of his constructive criticism should have been highlighted here. Only Joe Carducci spits fire, kicks butts, and names names as a rock literati should. Additionally, Heylin's entire project is called into question by the omission of numerous talented, perceptive, and influential authors. Among those missing in literary action are Michael Bane, R. Serge Denisoff, Colin Escott, Bill Flanagan, Gillian Gaar, Nelson George, Pete Grendysa, Peter Guralnick, Robert Hilburn, Gerri Hirshey, Dave Marsh, Richard Middleton, Philip Norman, Robert Palmer, Bruce Pollock, Nick Tosches, and Ian Whitcomb. Is that all? Nope! Heylin also ignores Stanley Booth, Reebee Garofalo, Peter Hesbacher, Jonathan Kamin, George Lewis, George Moonoogian, Richard Peterson, Robert Pruter, Jerome Rodnitzky, and Jeff Tamarkin. Finally, no bibliography is provided. This is unexcusably criminal in a volume that purports to salute rock writing. Heylin behaves just as a record company executive who issues an artist sampler disc but forgets to provide lists of compact discs by each performer. It is unthinkable that the remarkable works of Escott, Guralnick, and Tosches are not listed as exemplary rock literary pieces.

*The Penguin Book of Rock and Roll Writing* is pleasant reading and does showcase several excellent, traditional interpretations of commercial music from 1950-1990. No one will be offended by any comments in the text. Nevertheless, there must be someone in the contemporary publishing world who admires rock journalism and music criticism enough to foster a cutting-edge anthology. This ain't it, folks!

# REFERENCES

Bane, Michael. *White Boy Singin' the Blues: The Black Roots of White Rock.* New York: Da Capo Press, 1992.

Bangs, Lester (edited by Greil Marcus). *Psychotic Reactions and Carburetor Dung—The Work of a Legendary Critic: Rock 'n' Roll as Literature and Literature as Rock 'n' Roll.* New York: Alfred A. Knopf, Inc., 1988.

Booth, Stanley. *Rythm Oil: A Journey Through the Music of the American South.* New York: Pantheon Books, 1991.

Christgau, Robert. *Any Old Way You Choose It: Rock and Other Pop Music, 1967-1973.* Baltimore, Maryland: Penguin Books, 1973.

Cohn, Nik. *Ball the Wall: Nick Cohn in the Age of Rock.* London: Picador Books, 1989.

Colman, Stuart. *They Kept on Rockin': The Giants of Rock 'n' Roll.* Poole, Dorset, England: Blandford Press, 1982.

Cooper, B. Lee. "Review of *Rock on Almanac* by Norm N. Nite, *The Harmony Illustrated Encyclopedia of Rock* (sixth edition), and *That Old Time Rock and Roll* by Richard Aquila," *Journal of Popular Culture,* XXIV (Summer 1990), pp. 175-177.

DeCurtis, Anthony and James Henke, with Holly George-Warren (eds.). *The Rolling Stone Album Guide.* New York: Random House, 1992.

DeCurtis, Anthony and James Henke, with Holly George-Warren (eds.). *The Rolling Stone Illustrated History of Rock and Roll* (fully revised and updated). New York: Random House, 1992.

Eisen, Jonathan (ed.). *The Age of Rock: Sounds of the American Cultural Revolution.* New York: Vintage Books, 1969.

Eisen, Jonathan (ed.). *The Age of Rock/2: Sights and Sounds of the American Cultural Revolution.* New York: Vintage Books, 1970.

Eisen, Jonathan (ed.). *Twenty-Minutes Fandangos and Forever Changes: A Rock Bazaar.* New York: Vintage Books, 1971.

Flanagan, Bill. *Written in My Soul: Conversations with Rock's Great Songwriters.* Chicago: Contemporary Books, Inc., 1987.

Flippo, Chet. *Everybody Was Kung-Fu Dancing: Chronicles of the Lionized and the Notorious.* New York: St. Martin's Press, 1991.

Fong-Torres, Ben (ed.). *The Rolling Stone Rock 'n' Roll Reader.* New York: Bantam Books, 1974.

Fong-Torres, Ben (comp.). *What's That Sound? The Contemporary Music Scene from the Pages of Rolling Stone.* Garden City, New York: Doubleday Anchor Books, 1976.

Fornatale, Pete. *The Story of Rock 'n' Roll.* New York: William Morrow and Company, 1987.

Frith, Simon. *Music for Pleasure: Essays in the Sociology of Pop.* New York: Routledge, Chapman, and Hall, 1988.

Frith, Simon and Andrew Goodwin (eds.). *On Record: Rock, Pop, and the Written Word.* New York: Pantheon Books, 1990.

Gatten, Jeffery N. (comp.). *The Rolling Stone Index: Twenty-Five Years of Popular Culture, 1967-1991.* Ann Arbor, Michigan: Popular Culture, Ink., 1993.

Giddins, Gary. *Rhythm-a-Ning: Jazz Tradition and innovation in the 80s.* New York: Oxford University Press, 1985.

Giddins, Gary. *Riding on a Blue Note: Jazz and American Pop.* New York: Oxford University Press, 1981.

Gillett, Charlie. *The Sound of the City* (revised edition). London: Souvenir Press, 1983.

Goldman, Albert. *Freakshow.* New York: Atheneum Press, 1971.

Goldman, Albert. *Sound Bites.* New York: Turtle Bat Books, 1992.

Goldstein, Richard. *Goldstein's Greatest Hits: A Book Mostly About Rock 'n' Roll.* Englewood Cliffs, New Jersey: Prentice-Hall, Inc., 1970.

Guralnick, Peter. *Feel Life Going Home: Portraits in Blues and Rock 'n' Roll.* New York: Outerbridge and Dienstfrey, 1971.

Guralnick, Peter. *Lost Highway: Journeys and Arrivals of American Musicians.* Boston: David R. Godine, 1979.

Guralnick, Peter. *Sweet Soul Music: Rhythm and Blues and the Southern Dream of Freedom.* New York: Harper and Row, 1986.

Heylin, Clinton (ed.). *The Penguin Book of Rock and Roll Writing.* New York: Penguin Books, 1992.

Hirshey, Gerri. *Nowhere to Run: The Story of Soul Music.* New York: Penguin Books, 1984.

Landau, Jim. *It's Too Late to Stop Now: A Rock and Roll Journal.* San Francisco: Straight Arrow Books, 1972.

Lazell, Barry, with Dafydd Rees and Luke Crampton (eds.). *Rock Movers and Shakers: An A to Z of the People Who Made Rock Happen.* New York: Billboard Publications, Inc., 1989.

Loder, Kurt. *Bat Chain Puller: Rock and Roll in the Age of Celebrity.* New York: St. Martin's Press, 1990.

Lydon, Michael. *Boogie Lightning.* New York: Dial Press, 1974.

Lydon, Michael. *Rock Folk: Portraits from the Rock 'n' Roll Pantheon.* New York: Dial Press, 1971.

Marcus, Greil. *Lipstick Traces: A Secret History of the Twentieth Century.* Cambridge, Massachusetts: Harvard University Press, 1989.

Marcus, Greil. *Mystery Train: Images of America in Rock 'n' Roll Music* (third revised edition). New York: Plume/Penguin Books, 1990.

Marcus, Greil. *Ranters and Crowd Pleasers: Punk in Pop Music, 1977-1992.* New York: Doubleday, 1993.

Marcus, Greil (comp.). *Rock and Roll Will Stand.* Boston: Beacon Press, 1969.

Marcus, Greil (ed.). *Stranded: Rock and Roll for a Desert Island.* New York: Alfred A. Knopf, Inc., 1979.

Marsh, Dave. *Fortunate Son.* New York: Random House, 1985.

Marsh, Dave. *The Heart of Rock and Soul: The 1001 Greatest Singles Ever Made.* New York: New American Library, 1989.

Marsh, Dave. *Louie Louie: The History and Mythology of the World's Most Famous Rock 'n' Roll Song*. New York: Hyperion Books, 1993.

Marsh, Dave, with Lee Ballinger, Sandra Choron, Wendy Smith, and Daniel Wolff. *The First Rock and Roll Confidential Report: Inside the Real World of Rock and Roll*. New York: Pantheon Books, 1985.

Miller, Jim (ed.). *The Rolling Stone Illustrated History of Rock and Roll*. New York: Random House/Rolling Stone Press, 1976.

Murray, Charles Shaar (edited by Neil Spencer). *Shots from the Hip*. London: Penguin Books, 1991.

Naha, Ed (comp.). *Lillian Roxon's Rock Encyclopedia* (revised edition). New York: Grosset and Dunlap, 1978.

Nash, Alanna. *Behind Closed Doors: Talking with the Legends of Country Music*. New York: Alfred A. Knopf, Inc., 1988.

Norman, Philip. *The Road Goes on Forever: Portraits from a Journey Through Contemporary Music*. New York: Fireside Books, 1982.

Palmer, Robert. *Deep Blues*. New York: Viking Press, 1981.

Pruter, Robert. *Chicago Soul*. Champaign-Urbana: University of Illinois Press, 1991.

Roxon, Lillian. *Lillian Roxon's Rock Encyclopedia*. New York: Universal Library/Grosset and Dunlap, 1969.

Sander, Ellen. *Trips: Rock Life in the Sixties*. New York: Charles Scribner's Sons, 1973.

Santelli, Robert. *Sixties Rock: A Listener's Guide*. Chicago: Contemporary Books, 1985.

Tobler, John (ed.). *Who's Who in Rock and Roll*. New York: Crescent Books, 1991.

Tobler, John and Pete Frame. *Rock 'n' Roll: The First 25 Years*. New York: Exeter Books, 1980.

Wenner, Jann S. *20 Years of Rolling Stone: What a Long, Strange Trip It's Been*. New York: Friendly Press, 1987.

Whitcomb, Ian. *Rock Odyssey: A Musician's Guide to the Sixties*. Garden City, New York: Dolphin Books, 1983.

Whitcomb, Ian (comp.). *Whole Lotta Shakin' : A Rock 'n' Roll Scrapbook*. London: Arrow Books, Ltd., 1982.

White, Timothy. *Rock Lives: Profiles and Interviews*. New York: Holt and Company, 1990.

White, Timothy. *Rock Stars*. New York: Stewart, Tabori, and Chang, 1984.

Williams, Paul. *The Map: Rediscovering Rock and Roll–A Journey*. South Bend, Indiana: And Books, 1988.

Williams, Paul. *Outlaw Blues: A Book of Rock Music*. New York: E.P. Dutton, 1969.

Williams, Paul. *Rock and Roll: The 100 Best Singles*. New York: Carroll and Graf Publishers, Inc., 1993.

Yorke, Ritchie. *Axes, Chops, and Hot Licks: The Canadian Rock Music Scene*. Edmonton: M.G. Hurtig, Publisher, 1971.

Yorke, Ritchie. *The History of Rock 'n' Roll*. New York: Methuen Press, 1976.

# Chapter 18

# Science Fiction

## PART I

"I don't think he ever took a vacation before. And now he's paying $30,000 for just an hour of past/time. Who can figure it?"

The unresponding probe technician dug the heel of his military boot into the gravel walkway, silently sharing his partner's puzzlement. Ordinarily, probe travelers were either rich eccentrics or government-funded research scientists. Several other bureaucrats had also noted Peters' request for a single hour of time-regression to January 1935 in the *Trans-Times*, but none knew the real reason for his proposed trip. The sun winked over the bunker behind the two men. They squinted as it reflected off the oversized yellow sign that proclaimed:

TIME PROBE CONTROL
Unit Four
Admittance with Official Clearance Only
—Esther Rubin, Admin.

"Classical music folks are weird, anyway. The old professor just retired, didn't he? Well, he's probably taking his life savings and spending it to see his mother."

A white-clad figure appeared on the horizon. It trudged slowly from the Time-Check Outpost toward the two time-techs and the probe control. Though almost a mile distant, Peters was clearly visible to the operatives. The centrix designers had selected the perfectly flat, barren terrain of the Oklahoma plains to enhance the security of the probe facilities.

---

This story by B. Lee Cooper and Larry S. Haverkos was originally printed as "Roll Over Beethoven" in the Spring 1987 issue of Olivet College's *Garfield Lake Review*. Reprint permission granted by the authors.

"He's probably going to hear a special concert by one of the greats."

"Yeah, Peters' mother was probably a kettle drum." Both men laughed. Neither knew a damn thing about either the ancients (Mozart, Bach, Tchaikovsky) or the moderns (Raimons, Kamahito, Nichewonge) of classical music. Both loved Voxpop.

Professor Arthur LeVan Peters marched toward the cone-shaped machine with determination if not vigor. At 78 he still swam daily and played tennis on weekends, but today his legs were not full of spring. It seemed absurd to hurry toward a mission from which he knew he would never return. From 100 yards away he could feel the eyes of the curious probe operators on him. They carefully examined the slightly stooped old man. His fringed bald head and searching blue eyes created a pathetic, if not comical appearance. A prickly face, too quickly shaved, complemented his overall careless appearance. He knew they were studying him, but he eased his nervousness by allowing his mind to roam, recalling the melody of his favorite aria.

"Good morning, Sir. May I see your clearance pass?" The plastic card switched hands. "Now, Dr. Peters, I'll need your TPC." The professor momentarily fumbled with the Travel Program Cartridge, and then presented it to the young man. "I know that you have passed all the security checks and that you have spent two weeks in the Time Probe Training Center, but I am required by Federal Code 432.90 to ask you to read this pledge aloud to me in the presence of a bonded witness." The guard gave Peters a plastic-coated paper bearing the flag and seal of the Federal Space/Time Administration. The words were simple. The meaning was clear. But Peters knew his next statement would be a lie.

"I promise to obey all of the rules of Time Travel as prescribed by law. I will remain in the probe during my entire allotment of past/time. If, for any reason, I am forced to open the time probe while in the past, I swear that while awaiting rescue I will not speak to another human being."

With the legal ritual completed, the smaller technician escorted Peters into the Probe Bunker, past the Nebulon Converter, and on to the capsule. "This is Chameleon IV." Peters experienced his first genuine fear as he confronted the capsule. He barely listened to the technical reassurances that his probe would be invisible to the world of 1935, a result of one-way plastifilm engineering. But he remained uneasy. "You'll begin your journey in exactly 37 minutes, at the 0800 hour. You'll return precisely one hour later. Please step into the capsule and fasten your seat clamp. I'll be placing your cartridge in the Neb-Co and then checking the probe environment until you depart. Is there anything else that I can tell you before I seal the hatch?"

Peters shook his head and the seven-foot diameter sphere was sealed. Its human cargo was secure. The technician went about his standard prep tasks. Everything seemed normal.

## PART II

Now Peters had time to contemplate his mission. Travel was a disagreeable business under any circumstances; this trip was no different. It was ironic to think that this was his first time away from the university in 25 years. Yet Peters knew that his sacrifice would change the course of musical history in America. Thus he was content to forfeit his personal savings, his time, and even his life for such a high cause. He owed the world no less. Failing in the music world as a serious composer, Peters had devoted his life to teaching about the compositions of others. But now he was on the eve of his first original contribution to the life of classical music. During the next hour he would singlehandedly rewrite the history of all contemporary music.

It was not pleasant to remember his recent quarrel with young Professor Witt Skinner. This seemingly minor incident had been the stimulus for his probe trip. Witt, who had joined the Conservatory Faculty three years earlier, was an advocate of diversionary nonsense. In fact, his dissertation had been a refutation of Waldo Wasserman's thesis that the final break between serious music and diversionary music (the infamous "Voxpop") had seriously retarded the cultural growth of the entire nation. Peters had drafted a lengthy rebuttal to Skinner's position. The prestigious *Journal of Classical Music* had placed the Skinner-Peters exchanges at the front of the October issue, and their debate had raged over the next two months—in print, over the phone, during departmental meetings, and finally, in a face-to-face tirade at the Faculty Club.

"You're completely off-beat," Skinner had snorted arrogantly. He labeled Peters an embarrassment to the music department and continued, "Surely you've noticed that practically no students ever sign up for your classes. The rest of us have been carrying you for two years." It was true that his enrollments had declined somewhat during the past few years, but Peters knew the difference between quality and quantity.

"You completely omit the folk humanities from your teaching. That kind of academic snobbery went out of style during the early 1960s." Skinner lectured him, waving his arms wildly and gesturing for effect as if he were addressing a freshman class. "And here you are four decades later, still spouting that ridiculous Wasserman shit."

Peters felt sick.

"You're living in a musical fantasy world that hasn't existed since before Jesse G inaugurated the rock revolution!" With these last words, Skinner jokingly leapt upon a lunch table and shook his right fist in a mock "victory" sign. This ungentlemanly display had been greeted with cheers by the other faculty members present. Even the ballerianic physicist had applauded. Peters had turned on his heel and gone directly to his office. The auto-type cranked out his resignation. In 20 minutes he had completely separated himself from the university which he had served for 37 years.

Now he had to vindicate himself. But how could one man prove that the rise of Voxpop had corrupted society? After weeks of brooding, Peters had the solution. Indeed, the solution had been provided during his last argument with Witt Skinner. "Not since Jesse G. . . ."

The application process for a probe trip was quite complicated. Of course, the high per-hour cost functioned as a terrific initial screening device. Still, security checks were made, personal interviews were conducted, and a seemingly endless series of classes in the rules of past/time travel were required. The only question mark that remained in the minds of the Probe Research/Security Office was whether Dr. Peters would actually be able to find what he claimed to be searching for in the past. Peters had rehearsed his fictitious story well.

"You're sure of that date, sir?" asked the young woman.

"That's right. Twelve noon, January 8, 1935. My parents were passing through Lee County in Mississippi when my brother was lost. I just want to see what happened to him. Just make sure that I land near Saltillo Street in East Tupelo."

"But we can't locate any records of your family ever residing in that area, . . . or of a police report about your brother being lost there. Didn't your bother die of cancer in 1940?"

"Yes, but he was lost to the family for three weeks in January 1935. When we found him, his mind was scrambled. Six years later he died, but he had never spoken a sane sentence since the eighth of January. I've got to know exactly what happened to him."

The lost brother story was a lie. But Sam Peters had died of cancer and the Peters family had been touring the southern states during the winter of 1934. Fortunately, there were no credit card records to mark gasoline, dining, or hotel locations. With no real evidence to the contrary, and Peters' harmless demeanor and unblemished scholarly credentials, the young lady had approved the probe trip.

Click! Click! Click! Click! Peters was startled as the time probe machinery began to flash into readiness. He was alerted by a blinking light to position his ear covers. Even through the flascolene muffs, the whine of the nebulon turbines was annoying. He felt strangely satisfied.

## *PART III*

He had approached his grisly task like an academic. Peters had carefully reread Winston Formaker's *The History of Modern American Music: From Rock to Voxpop*. The details of sound variations, of racial mixing in theme-lyric structures, of the cultural evolution of rhythm-and-blues, country, pop, rock, and folk, and the corresponding emergence of vocal superstars were interesting–though enraging–to Peters. The heart of the problem, he decided, was personality. Jesse G had emerged on the popular music scene in 1955 as a man who was able to synthesize all of the trends that had been blessedly disparate prior to his arrival. He had been a country boy reared to the turgid melodies of Bob Wills, Ernest Tubb, Roy Acuff, and Jimmie Rodgers; he had also imbibed the Negro blues from performers such as Bukka White, John Lee Hooker, Bill Broonzy, Howlin' Wolf, Muddy Waters, and Jimmy Reed; but what he had created by combining these styles with his own wild rock feeling had launched the revolution. The legend was too lurid to review. Hit after hit. The style of popular music solidified around his rock madness. The Beatles, the Rolling Stones, Grand Funk, Blind Treason, Eagle Mountain Pass, and then–Voxpop. The adoption of popular music as a universal medium of social communication. Even the news was delivered in lyrical form in 2002.

Peters was breathless. It was 7:57. Just three minutes to go. Chameleon IV was now the vortex of a thousand light beams. The power generators were near peak load. The probe operators were poised. Peters knew that he had planned his moves well. The great Jesse G and the Jordanaires would never be.

It was like being suddenly awakened from a sound sleep by falling out of bed. The whine had disappeared and in its place was the sound of a wind's gentle gust. The invisible sphere rested on a thin patch of grass alongside a rut-infested lane, facing a string of shabby one-story houses that were supported on concrete blocks. With no hesitation Peters drew back his spindly leg and kicked out at the hatch cover. It flipped open. Instantly, a calm mechanical voice filled the cabin of Chameleon IV. "Obviously, you've encountered some difficulty with the probe environment. Please step out and kneel beside the probe. A rescue ship will arrive in thirty minutes. Thank you."

The steadiness of the recorded voice which advised Peters to be calm was an impressive contrast to the violent spasm of activity at Probe Control. The alert horn sounded repeated intermittent blasts as the bunker lights undulated at an ominous heartbeat pace. The atmosphere within the bunker was laced with shouted instructions.

"Probe emergency! The integrity of the Chameleon IV has been compromised!" shouted the time-tech monitoring Peters' trip.

"Which one is it?"

"It's that music professor from the college–January, 1935."

"Quick! Beam the Wichita Centrix for clearance on an emergency TPC. Lock the marsupial capsule into transport position immediately."

"E.T.A. is thirty minutes. Let's pray that the old guy doesn't wander far from the capsule site."

Peters crawled out of the probe and began to walk across the dirt road. So singleminded was the elderly professor toward the fulfillment of his holy mission that he failed to notice the presence of another old man as he emerged from the probe.

"Ehhh–a magic man, uh?" snorted the dazed drunk. He was at least sixty years old, and he measured the professor through eyes that were not unaccustomed to beholding spectacular visions.

"Please don't be frightened." Peters' words of reassurance were unnecessary to his numbed observer. Undeniably, the image of an old man emerging "magically" from behind the Chameleon's plastic-film shield must have been shocking. Peters realized that he had been careless. He wouldn't let his mind wander again.

"Let's see another trick, buddy," implored Peters' unwanted audience of one.

"Please–!" Peters barely avoided the man's lunging grasp. The professor was becoming offended by his onlooker. The drunk wore the rags of depression-era Mississippi and, by the bacteria-conscious standards of Peters' time, he was totally unsanitary. The combined odors of alcohol and body filth were intolerably oppressive.

"I'll have to go now."

"C'mon mister, let's have some more tricks. Can you make me disappear, too?" The drunk was terribly loud and aggressive.

"You, sir, are disgustingly intoxicated and have obviously become a victim of some kind of narcotically induced delusion. You shall detain me no longer! I have some vitally important work to do. Is that quite clear?"

The professor's adversary, apparently impressed by Peters' firm demeanor, capped his bottle. "Are you from the hospital? You know that Vern's wife is having a baby, don't you?"

Which house, though, wondered Peters. The drunk responded to the unspoken question by pointing to the dilapidated frame structure located directly across the street. "Good day, sir. I have no time to prattle with you."

## *PART IV*

Vernon and Gladys were expecting their first child at any moment. The doctor was attending to the straining mother-to-be while the young father paced the living room floor. Uncle Vester and Aunt Delta Mae were also on hand to assist the physician and to calm their anxious relatives. The baby was born at 12:08 p.m. None of the people present in the house realized that Peters had slipped in unnoticed through the back door and was standing in the bedroom closet. Nor did they suspect that a second baby was on the way. Gladys lay on the bed in delirious exhaustion. Doc had carefully used a sterilized washcloth to clean the firstborn, wrapped him in a cotton bunting, and carried him into the living room to show the proud new father. All attention was focused on the babe. Doc accepted a glass of corn whiskey as an initial reward for his services.

Meanwhile the unanticipated second child, the would-be Jesse G continued to struggle toward existence. Gladys suddenly sensed the coming of another baby, and was relieved to feel the firm hands of assistance as she tightened her grip on the steel bed frame and breathed deeply. Peters' hands matter-of-factly covered the emerging baby's face. Jesse G was not to be born alive.

Moments later Doc returned to the bedroom to discover the stillborn child. His heart sank. He returned slowly to the living room with the lifeless body. "Vernon," he began slowly, "this is a day of joy and sorrow. There were to be two boys, but only one could hold on to life."

The father staggered. "I've already told Gladys," Doc comforted. "She needs you."

The next day three nonnewsworthy events occurred in Tupelo, Mississippi. An old man dressed in white silk-like coveralls and wearing strange rubber boots was found dead of an apparent heart attack beside the Old Saltillo Road. Since no kin could be located, he was buried in an unmarked grave. Close by, the Presley family was joined by Faye Harris, Orville Bean, Doc Williams, and several relatives as they laid their stillborn son, Jesse Garon, to rest in Priceville Cemetery. Later that same day, the grieving mother persuaded the elderly minister of the First Assembly of God Church to baptize her firstborn son. The preacher's hands dampened the crying infant's soft hair as he recited, "Elvis Aron Presley, I baptize you in the name of the Father, and of the Son, and of the Holy Ghost. Amen."

## REFERENCES

Albert, Richard N. (ed.). *From Blues to Pop: A Collection of Jazz Fiction*. Baton Rouge: Louisiana State University Press, 1990.

Baldwin, James. "Sonny's Blues," *Partisan Review*, XXIV (Summer 1957), pp. 327-358.

Burke, Martyn. *Ivory Joe*. New York: Ballantine Books, 1991.

Burnett, T-Bone. "Burning Love," *Musician*, No. 86 (December 1985), p. 114.

Carson, Tom. *Twisted Kicks*. Glen Ellen, California: Entwhistle Books, 1981.

Charters, Samuel Barclay. *Elvis Presley Calls His Mother After the Ed Sullivan Show: A Novel*. Minneapolis, Minnesota: Coffee House Press, 1992.

Charters, Samuel Barclay. *Jelly Roll Morton's Last Night at the Jungle Inn: An Imaginary Memoir*. London: Marion Boyars, 1984.

Childress, Mark. *Tender*. New York: Harmony Books, 1990.

Cooper, B. Lee. "Beyond *Flash Gordon* and *Star Wars*: Science Fiction and History Instruction," *Social Education*, XLII (May 1978), pp. 392-397.

Cooper, B. Lee. "Beyond Lois Lane and Wonder Woman: Exploring Images of Women Through Science Fiction, *Library-College Experimenter*, V (November 1979), pp. 7-15.

Cooper, B. Lee. "Bob Dylan, Isaac Asimov, and Social Problems: Non-Traditional Materials for Reflective Teaching," *International Journal of Instructional Media*, IV, No. 1 (1976-77), pp. 105-115.

Cooper, B. Lee. "Information Services, Popular Culture, and the Librarian: Promoting a Contemporary Learning Perspective," *Drexel Library Quarterly*, XVI (July 1980), pp. 24-42.

Cooper, B. Lee. "Popular Music, Science Fiction, and Controversial Issues: Sources for Reflective Thinking," *The History and Social Science Teacher*, XII (Fall 1976), pp. 31-45.

Cooper, B. Lee. *A Science Fiction Perspective on Contemporary Issues*. Dayton, Ohio: An Occasional Paper of the Ohio Council for the Social Studies, 1978.

Crow, Cameron. *Fast Times at Ridgemont High*. New York: Simon and Schuster, 1981.

Daniels, Charlie. *The Devil Went Down to Georgia*. Atlanta: Peachtree Publishers, Ltd., 1985.

Doyle, Roddy. *The Commitments*. Dublin: King Farouk Publishing, 1987.

Ellison, Harlan. *Spider Kiss*. New York: Ace Books, 1982.

Eskow, Jon. *Smokestack Lightning: A Novel of Rock and Roll*. New York: Delacorte Press, 1980.

Gelb, Jeff (ed.). *Shock Rock*. New York: Pocket Books, 1992.

Gelb, Jeff (ed.). *Shock Rock II*. New York: Pocket Books, 1994.

Goodman, Eric K. *The First Time I Saw Jenny Hall: A Novel*. New York: William Morrow, 1983.

Graham, Robert and Keith Baty. *Elvis–The Novel*. London: Granada Publications, 1984.

Grizzard, Lewis. *Elvis is Dead and I Don't Feel So Good Myself*. Atlanta: Peachtree Publishers, 1984.

Guralnick, Peter. *Nighthawk Blues*. New York: Shavirn Books, 1980.

Henderson, William McCranor. *Stark Raving Elvis*. New York: E.P. Dutton, 1984.

Hijuelos, Oscar. *The Mambo Kings Play Songs of Love*. London: Hamilton Books, 1989.

King, Stephen. *Christine*. New York: New American Library, 1983.

Kluge, Paul Frederick. *Eddie and the Cruisers*. New York: Viking Press, 1980.

Levy, Elizabeth. *All Shook Up*. New York: Scholastic Books, Inc., 1986.

Littlejohn, David. *The Man Who Killed Mick Jagger: A Novel*. New York: Pocket Books, 1977.

Lucas, George, Gloria Katz, and Willard Huyck. *American Graffiti*. New York: Ballantine Books, 1973.

Marcus, Greil. *Dead Elvis: A Chronicle of Cultural Obsession*. Garden City, New York: Doubleday and Company, Inc., 1991.

Martin, George R.R. *The Armageddon Rag*. New York: Poseidon Press, 1983.

Moody, Bill. "Jazz Fiction: It Don't Mean a Thing if It Ain't Got That Swing," *Journal of American Culture*, XIV (Winter, 1991), pp. 61-66.

Moorcock, Michael. *The Great Rock 'n' Roll Swindle* (second edition). London: Virgin Books, 1981.

Moorcock, Michael and Michael Butterworth. *The Time of the Hawklords*. London: Star (Wyndham) Books, 1976.

Newman, Charles. *White Jazz*. New York: Dial Press, 1984.

Norman, Philip. *Wild Thing*. London: J.M. Dent and Sons, Ltd., 1983.

O'Donnell, Jim. *Born to Rock–12 Rock Stories*. Jersey City, New Jersey: Peacock Books, 1981.

Parson, Tony. *Platinum Logic*. New York: Delilah Books, 1981.

Phillips, Jane J. *MoJo Hand: An Orphic Tale*. Berkeley, California: City Miner Press, 1986.

Price, Richard. *The Wanderers*. New York: Houghton Mifflin Company, 1974.

Robinson, Lisa. *Walk on Glass*. New York: New Market Press, 1982.

Smith, Joseph C. *The Day the Music Died*. New York: Grove Press, 1981.

Strete, Craig Kee. *Burn Down the Night*. New York: Warner Books, 1982.

Sublett, Jesse. *Rock Critic Murders*. New York: Dell Publishing Company, Inc., 1990.

Thomas, Bruce. *The Big Wheel*. London: Viking Books, 1990.

Wilson, F. Paul. "The Last 'One Mo' Once Golden Oldies Revival," in *Soft and Others: 16 Stories of Wonder and Dread* (New York: Tor Books, 1989), pp. 116-133.

Wilson, F. Paul. "The Years the Music Died," in *Soft and Others: 16 Stories of Wonder and Dread* (New York: Tor Books, 1989), pp. 136-149.

# Chapter 19

# Sex

## PERSONAL RELATIONSHIPS, LOVE, AND SEXUALITY

Throughout the twentieth century, courtship themes have dominated American lyrics. Love songs depict consistent behavioral patterns. Boy meets girl; a special relationship develops; love blooms; sexuality is explored; tensions are noted; rejection occurs; loneliness is felt; and (in a repetition of the pattern) boy meets another girl. Human interaction is never neat. Highly emotional personal involvements are not only less than neat, they are extremely volatile and likely to produce peaks of joy and valleys of depression. It would take not only a single chapter, but an entire book to illustrate accurately the variety of personal relationship themes that exist within the lyrics of popular songs during the past 35 years. The following pages examine selected hit recordings that depict the complex nature of male-female interaction.

Prior to the establishment of personal relationships, there is often an ideal mate who is initially conjured in the male or the female mind. Fantasy searches for reality. Actually, fantasy and reality duel in the hearts and minds of romantic dreamers as they seek the "right guy" or the "perfect girl" to make a successful relationship emerge. "This Magic Moment" (1968) is how Jay and the Americans describe such wish fulfillment. Meditation is sometimes a source of inspiration to would-be lovers.

The first essay by B. Lee Cooper was originally published as "Personal Relationships, Love, and Sexuality," in *A Resource Guide to Themes in Contemporary American Song Lyrics, 1950-1985* (Westport, Connecticut: Greenwood Press, 1986), pp. 131-181. Reprint permission granted by the author and Greenwood Press. The second essay by B. Lee Cooper is scheduled to be published as "Sultry Songs and Censorship: A Thematic Discography for College Teachers" in *International Journal of Instructional Media*. Reprint permission granted by the author, Editor Phillip J. Sleeman, and Baywood Publishing Company.

Andy Gibb and Victoria Principal declare "All I Have to Do Is Dream" (1981), but the notion simply echoes similar lyrical observations in "Dream Baby (How Long Must I Dream)" (1983), "Everybody's Dream Girl" (1983), "Dreamin'" (1982), and "Dream Lover" (1959). Other individuals appeal to mythical romantic authorities such as "Mister Sandman" (1981) or to voodoo specialists who can whip up "Love Potion No. 9" (1959). The goal remains the same in all cases: To secure "A Sunday Kind of Love" (1962).

Many young men utilize female traffic on downtown streets to stimulate their romantic imaginations. Recordings illustrating this voyeuristic behavior include "Standing on the Corner" (1956), "Kansas City" (1959), "Oh, Pretty Woman" (1964), and "Girl Watcher" (1968). Beyond ogling co-workers during lunch breaks or other female strangers at whatever time, there is the frustrating situation of being unable to initiate a loving relationship with a known friend. Such situations may arise from shyness, from social class and occupational distinctions, or from the recognition of prior relationships with someone else. Such themes appear in "Guess Who" (1959), "You Do Know Me" (1962), "Can't Take My Eyes off of You" (1967), "If I Were Your Woman" (1970), "My Eyes Adored You" (1974), "Jessie's Girl" (1981), "Somebody's Baby" (1982), "I've Made Love to You a Thousand Times" (1983), and "Scarlet Fever" (1983). Somehow the lonely hope of a beneficent "Cupid" (1961) to transform an "Imaginary Lover" (1978) into an "Angel Baby" (1960) or an "Earth Angel" (1954) is not satisfied very often. Regrettably, many folks must echo Stevie Wonder's lament that they "Never Had a Dream Come True" (1970). Christopher Cross declared that the best thing you can do is fall in love. This sentiment, expressed in "Arthur's Theme (Best That You Can Do)" (1981), is found in numerous Beatles' recordings including "All My Lovin'" (1964), "And I Love Her" (1964), "She Loves You" (1964), and "All You Need Is Love" (1967). Even though Paul McCartney acknowledges universal appeal of "Silly Love Songs" (1976), other singers have described the achievement of loving relationships as games, conquests, mutual agreements, evolutionary patterns, or even accidents. Songs depicting these situations are "It's All in the Game" (1958), "Game of Love" (1965), "Ten Commandments of Love" (1958), "Love Is Like an Itching in My Heart" (1966), "To the Aisle" (1957), "Love Is Strange" (1957), "Fooled Around and Fell in Love" (1976), "(Every Time I Turn Around) Back in Love Again" (1977), and "You Make My Dreams" (1981).

Teenage romance often begins with fantasies, but usually shifts from "Cowboys to Girls" (1968) and from dolls to "Boys" (1960). First kisses, first dates, and going steady are noted in numerous recordings that chronicle love among the young. It is interesting that such songs were particularly prevalent during the 1950s; however, they began to fade from hit charts in the late 1960s and practically disappeared by the late 1970s and early 1980s. Examples of these songs include "I Want You to Be My Girl" (1956), "A Rose and a Baby Ruth" (1956), "Too Young to Go Steady" (1956), "Young Love" (1956), "First Date, First Kiss, First Love" (1957), "Goin' Steady" (1957), "High School Romance" (1957), "Teenage Crush" (1957), "Wear My Ring Around Your Neck" (1958), "Sweet Nothin's" (1959), "A Teenager in Love" (1959), "Twixt Twelve and Twenty" (1959), "You're Sixteen" (1960), "Puppy Love" (1960), "Let's Go Steady Again" (1963), "I Saw Her Standing There" (1964), "Puppy Love" (1964), "Hold Me, Thrill Me, Kiss Me" (1965), "1-2-3" (1965), "I Second That Emotion" (1967), "When You're Young and in Love" (1967), "Put Your Head on My Shoulder" (1978), "Chuck E.'s in Love" (1979), and "P.Y.T. (Pretty Young Thing)" (1983). The immature, irrational, erratic behavior of lovers–particularly young and inexperienced romantics–is depicted in numerous songs such as "Fools Fall in Love" (1957), "A Fool in Love" (1960), "Foolish Little Girl" (1963), "Fools Rush In" (1963), and "Why Do Fools Fall in Love?" (1981).

The boundless euphoria of love is communicated in music throughout the past 35 years. General declarations include "Love Is a Many-Splendored Thing" (1955), "Dedicated to the One I Love" (1959), "I Only Have Eyes for You" (1959), "Every Beat of My Heart" (1961), "For Your Precious Love" (1963), "Goin' Out of My Head/Can't Take My Eyes off You" (1967), "Ain't No Mountain High Enough" (1970), "You're My Best Friend" (1976), "Crazy Little Thing Called Love" (1979), "Cupid I've Loved You for a Long Time" (1980), "The Closer You Get" (1983), and "Words and Music" (1983). Men in love are ecstatic about the virtues of their women. Examples of recordings illustrating this point include "Reet Petite (The Finest Girl You Ever Want to Meet)" (1957), "Portrait of My Love" (1961), "My Girl" (1965), "This Guy's in Love with You" (1968), "Baby I'm-a Want You" (1971), "Ain't No Woman (Like the One I've Got)" (1973), "How Sweet It Is (To Be Loved By You)" (1975), "Three Times a Lady" (1978), and "You're My Latest, My Greatest Inspiration" (1982). The same enthusiasm for male lovers is demonstrated by female singers in tunes such as "Baby It's You" (1961), "I've Told Every Little Star" (1961), "Baby, I'm Yours" (1965), "My Man" (1965), "Baby I Love You" (1967), "I Never Loved a Man (The Way I Love You)" (1967), "Love Eyes" (1967), "This Girl's in Love With You" (1969), "Best Thing That Ever Happened to Me" (1974), "I Honestly Love You" (1974), "Hopelessly Devoted to You" (1978), "I Only Want to Be with You" (1982), and "My

Guy" (1982). Both lyrically and in terms of harmonic declaration, some of the most memorable love songs have been recorded by male and female duos. Some of the most popular romantic tunes performed by singing partners are "True Love" (1956), "Baby (You've Got What It Takes)" (1960), "A Rockin' Good Way (To Mess Around and Fall in Love)" (1960), "I Need Your Loving" (1962), "Let It Be Me" (1964), "River Deep–Mountain High" (1966), "If I Could Build My Whole World Around You" (1967), "It Takes Two" (1967). "Ain't Nothing Like the Real Thing" (1968), "You're All I Need to Get By" (1968), "Never Ending Song of Love" (1971), "Only You Know and I Know" (1971). "Love Will Keep Us Together" (1975), "You Don't Have to Be a Star (To Be in My Show)" (1976), "Devoted to You" (1958), "You're the One That I Want" (1978), "Reunited" (1979), "My Guy/My Girl" (1980). "Endless Love" (1981), "Friends in Love" (1982), and "Islands in the Stream" (1983).

Although Wilson Pickett accurately observes "Everybody Needs Somebody to Love" (1967), there are numerous songs that illustrate the insecurity of romantic relationships. These tunes feature warnings to those seeking to break up an ongoing love affair, including "Bird Dog" (1958), "Don't Mess with Bill" (1966), and "Potential New Boyfriend" (1983) and complaints or fears about a partner's infidelity, such as "Butterfly" (1957) "Lipstick on Your Collar" (1959), "Mr. Blue" (1959), "Butterfly Baby" (1963), "Mama Didn't Lie" (1963), "Johnny One Time" (1969), "I've Got to Use My Imagination" (1973), "Don't Go Breaking My Heart" (1976), and "Let's Hang On" (1982). Feelings of helplessness in the wake of unfaithful behavior by a friend or lover are also communicated in "Cathy's Clown" (1960) and "Mama Said" (1961).

If the number of recordings describing "going steady/puppy love" relationships declined dramatically during the late 1960s and throughout the 1970s, it should be noted that songs describing sexual encounters increased dramatically during the same decades. The reasons are obvious. Prior taboos about overt references to intimate relations between the sexes were challenged during the 1960s and overthrown by the Woodstock generation. Similarly, the success of women's liberation contributed to greater social independence for females and generated more candid commentaries about working and playing interactions between men and women. Repeal of laws that prohibited contraception and the subsequent availability of birth control devices also liberalized sexual encounters by decreasing fears of unwanted pregnancies. It is particularly interesting to note that earthy lyrics from R&B music sources, once subject to sanitizing, sterilizing, and bowdlerizing in respect to sexual descriptions and innuendoes, are now translated directly as "crossover hits" into the pop, country, and rock realms. Finally, heavy metal bands, which often present bizarre sexual fantasies in their lyrics, were a staple of the 1980s youth culture.

The majority of sexual activity references in 1950s songs were oblique, metaphorical, and only mildly suggestive. This trend extended into the 1960s until the Rolling Stones, The Animals, and a variety of extremely popular black soul singers began to launch more overt sexual images. Typical commentaries on imagined or intended interactions in the more restrained pre-1965 period include "After the Lights Go Down Low" (1956), "Blueberry Hill" (1956), "Party Doll" (1957), "Chantilly Lace" (1958), "One Night" (1958), "Wiggle Wiggle" (1958), "You Got What It Takes" (1959), "Multiplication" (1961), "Lipstick Traces (on a Cigarette)" (1962), and "Let's Lock the Door (and Throw Away the Key)" (1964). The minority of overtly sexual recordings during the same period can be illustrated by tunes such as "Sixty-Minute Man" (1951), "Sexy Ways" (1954), "Shake, Rattle, and Roll" (1954), "Such a Night" (1954), "TV Mama" (1954), and "Work with Me Annie" (1954).

Post-British invasion lyrics demystified sex. Olivia Newton-John condemned small talk in favor of getting "Physical" (1981); Maria Muldaur described her wild exploits in "Midnight at the Oasis" (1974); AC/DC proclaimed, in mock sexual exhaustion, "You Shook Me All Night Long" (1980); Marvin Gaye pleaded "Let's Get It On" (1973) and requested "Sexual Healing" (1982); and while Tony Tennille proclaimed "You Never Done It Like That" (1978), the Rolling Stones challenged women to "Start Me Up" (1981) and Bob Seger extolled the unabashed joy of "The Horizontal Bop" (1980). Other highly suggestive recordings of the past 20 years include "In the Midnight Hour" (1965), "Something You Got" (1965), "Let's Spend the Night Together" (1967), "Light My Fire" (1967), "Love Me Two Times" (1967), "Sunshine of Your Love" (1968), "Touch Me" (1968), "Tonight I'll Be Staying Here With You" (1969), "Whole Lotta Love" (1969), "Make It with You" (1970), "Love Her Madly" (1971), "Reelin' and Rockin'" (1972), "Pillow Talk" (1973), "Can't Get Enough" (1974), "Love to Love You, Baby" (1975), "You Sexy Thing" (1975), "Tonight's the Night (Gonna Be Alright)" (1976), "Fire" (1978), "Sharing the Night Together" (1978), "Do That to Me One More Time" (1979), "Ring My Bell" (1979), "Urgent" (1981), "Jack and Diane" (1982), "Make a Move on Me" (1982), "Action" (1983), "Cold Blooded" (1983), "Get It Right" (1983), and "Love Don't Know a Lady (from a Honky Tonk Girl)" (1983).

If there were Olympic competition to determine champions of sexual prowess, physical attractiveness, and social self-confidence, contemporary songs could suggest a huge field of lyrical male and female champions.

The women who are depicted as sexual dynamos in modern recordings are "Long Tall Sally" (1956), "Good Golly, Miss Molly" (1958), "Big Leg Woman (with a Short, Short Mini Skirt)" (1970), "Maggie May" (1971), "Hot Legs" (1978), "My Sharona" (1979), "She's a Bad Mamajama (She's Built, She's Stacked)" (1981), "Super Freak" (1981), "Ms. Fine Brown Frame" (1982), "Gloria" (1983), "Ms. Got-The-Body" (1983), "(She's) Sexy + 17" (1983), and "Swing That Sexy Thang" (1983). The male counterparts of these sexy mamas are described in "Handy Man" (1959), "Lee Cross" (1967), "Steamroller Blues" (1973), "Da Ya Think I'm Sexy?" (1978), "Hot Blooded" (1978), "Hot Stuff" (1979), "Slow Hand" (1981), and "Candy Man" (1983).

Although the sexual Olympic competition idea may seem absurd, there is a strong strain of impersonalized sexual athletics depicted in modern lyrics. In several songs it appears that sex has very little to do with establishing or sustaining personal relationships. These casual sex scenarios are depicted in "Son-of-a-Preacher Man" (1968). "All Right Now"(1970), "One-Night Stand" (1971), "Spiders and Snakes" (1973), "Chevy Van" (1975), "Afternoon Delight" (1976), "Night Moves" (1976), "Paradise by the Dashboard Light" (1978), "We've Got Tonight" (1978). "Shakedown Cruise" (1979), "A Different Woman Every Night" (1983), and "Private Party" (1983). Of course, there must be mutual agreement to allow this kind of noncommittal sexual activity. That is, since it is neither rape nor prostitution, the persistence of random sexual encounters demands the kind of cooperation conveyed in "You Don't Have to Say You Love Me"(1966), "Angel of the Morning" (1968), "Until It's Time for You to Go" (1970), "Help Me Make It Through the Night" (1971), "Only the Good Die Young" (1978), "Do You Wanna Touch Me (Oh Yeah)" (1982), "Should I Do It" (1982), "The Woman in Me" (1982), and "Girls Just Want to Have Fun" (1983). There are a few songs that openly proclaim "It's Your Thing" (1969) so do what you want to do, but there are seldom recordings that respond "No" (1972) to proposals such as "Let's Spend the Night Together" (1967) or "Let's Pretend We're Married" (1983). Some authentically independent responses include "Will You Love Me Tomorrow" (1960), "Don't Touch Me" (1969), and the desire not to become just "Another Motel Memory" (1983).

Other recordings address more complex aspects of human sexual behavior. Extramarital relations are decried (or at least described) in "Ruby, Don't Take Your Love to Town" (1969), "Steppin' Out" (1976), "The Other Woman" (1982), "Don't Cheat in Your Hometown" (1983), "The Name of the Game Is Cheating" (1983), and "Stranger in My House" (1983); prostitution (examined later in this chapter) is illustrated recently in "Backstreet Ballet" (1983) and "I'm Alive" (1983); fear of contracting venereal disease is depicted in "You Ain't Seen Nothing Yet" (1974); birth control is the theme in "The Pill" (1975); and children born out of wedlock are mentioned in "Love-Child" (1968), "Gypsies, Tramps, and Thieves" (1971), "(You're) Having My Baby" (1974), and "Unwed Fathers" (1983). Clearly, the sexual revolution of the past quarter century is mirrored in popular lyrics.

Earlier in this section the pattern of fantasizing, establishing, enriching, and terminating male-female relationships was described as a recurring behavioral cycle. This is obviously an oversimplified approach to human interaction. In many cases, of course, dating leads to engagement, marriage, and a fulfilling family life. But for those who lose loved ones, there are often deeply emotional periods of loneliness and feelings of personal rejection. Just as popular songs celebrate the development of personal relations, they also document the sadness of breaking them.

The process of terminating a relationship is described from varying perspectives in popular recordings. Tommy Edwards noted that vacillating personal feelings are common; "It's All in the Game" (1958), he observes. Similar attitudes are voiced in "Build Me Up Buttercup" (1969) and "Break Up to Make Up" (1973). Sometimes one member of a couple senses unspoken tensions and elects to confront the problem directly. This approach appears in "Break-Up" (1958), "Breaking Up Is Hard to Do" (1962), "You Don't Bring Me Flowers" (1978), "Any Day Now" (1982), and "Break It to Me Gently" (1982). Rather than seeking to sustain a failing relationship though, some individuals feel trapped by an over-possessive lover and simply want their freedom. This attitude is expressed in "Let Me Go Lover" (1954), "Take These Chains from My Heart" (1963), and "Release Me (and Let Me Love Again)" (1967). Unfortunately, honesty does not always prevail when personal relationships begin to collapse. While one partner may bemoan the dishonesty of the other, lying, cheating, sneaking around, and emotional hardening often typify the behavior of a disenchanted partner. Recordings that provide examples of these activities are "Hearts of Stone" (1954), "It's Only Make Believe" (1958), "I Know (You Don't Love Me No More)" (1961), "It's My Party" (1963), "Lies" (1965) "(I Know) I'm Losing You" (1966), "Head Games" (1979), "Stop Draggin' My Heart Around" (1981), "Don't You Want Me" (1982), "Lies" (1983), and "Stop in the Name of Love" (1983). In spite of this type of behavior, some individuals continue to vow allegiance to even a wandering loved one. They beg their partner "Don't Be Cruel" (1956) to a heart that's true and declare that they "Ain't Too Proud to Beg" (1974) to retain a loving relationship. Other recordings that illustrate this situation are "The Great Pretender" (1955), "Love Me"

(1956), "I Can't Stop Loving You" (1958), "Forty Days" (1959), "He'll Have to Go" (1959), "Mr. Blue" (1959), "He Will Break Your Heart" (1960), "So Sad (to Watch Good Love Go Bad)" (1960), "I'm a Fool to Care" (1961), "Too Bad" (1962), "You've Lost That Lovin' Feelin'" (1964), "If You've Got a Heart" (1965), "The Thrill Is Gone" (1969), "Don't Pull Your Love/Then You Can Tell Me Goodbye" (1976), "Piece of My Heart" (1982), and "I Still Can't Get Over Loving You" (1983).

Heartbreak and loneliness over a lost lover is a universal theme in contemporary music. The recordings illustrating this situation are too numerous to mention here. Selected examples include "Heartbreak Hotel" (1956), "I Was the One" (1956), "Gone" (1957), "Since I Don't Have You" (1959), "Lonely Weekends" (1960), "Don't Get Around Much Anymore" (1961), "You Don't Know What You've Got (Until You Lose It)" (1961), "All Alone Am I" (1962), "Lover Please" (1962), "Hurt So Bad" (1965), "Yesterday" (1965), "Bang Bang (My Baby Shot Me Down)" (1966), "Cry Like a Baby" (1968), "I'll Never Fall in Love Again" (1969), "Yester-Me, Yester-You, Yester-day" (1969), "Can't Get Over Losing You" (1970), "Ain't No Sunshine" (1971), "I Can't Stand the Rain" (1978), "Ain't That a Shame" (1979), "Crying" (1981). "96 Tears" (1981), "Tryin' to Live My Life Without You" (1981), "I Fall to Pieces" (1982), "Always Something There to Remind Me" (1983), "Cuts Like a Knife" (1983), and "Singing the Blues" (1983).

Those who have suffered heartaches seem to be divided into two polarized categories. One group seems dejected and self-deprecating; the other remains self-confident and angry over the thoughtless behavior of a former friend and lover. Recordings that chronicle the feelings of depressed individuals include "Are You Lonesome Tonight?" (1960), "I Want to Be Wanted" (1960), "Born to Lose" (1962), "(I Was) Born to Cry" (1962), "I'm So Lonesome I Could Cry" (1962), "Another Saturday Night" (1963), "Whoever Finds This, I Love You" (1970), and "When Will I Be Loved?" (1975). But the dominant and occasionally cynical or vindictive position of a person who refuses to blame himself or herself for the collapse of a romance is much more intriguing. Songs depicting this position include "I Hear You Knocking" (1955), "Gonna Get Along Without You Now" (1956), "Goody Goody" (1957), "Who's Sorry Now?" (1958), "I Wanna Be Around" (1963), "Tired of Waiting for You" (1965), "You Can Have Her" (1965), "Cry Me a River" (1970), "Solitary Man" (1970), "Funny How Time Slips Away" (1982), and "What's New" (1983).

## SUGGESTIVE LYRICS AND CENSORSHIP

Lyricists have created commentaries on sexual situations throughout history. However the oral testimonies to adoration and lovemaking that echoed across Africa, Asia, and Europe for centuries have found new permanence and enlarged publicity since recording technology was perfected. After 1876 various forms of cylinders and discs have permitted the human voice to both produce and preserve love songs. Music, once solely a live experience, has become a mediated, repeatable, marketable item. Between 1950 and 1992 courtship themes have dominated popular music. When reviewing love songs as a general lyric category, one immediately notes that some compositions have harder edges than others. They are more direct, more suggestive, and more explicit in defining the nature and meaning of sexual relations. This study focuses on these tunes.

Recordings that openly address sex themes have been criticized for decades. Neither the reputations of classic pop lyricists (Cole Porter, Irving Berlin, or Richard Rogers) nor the literary quality of the specific imagery matter if a segment of listeners is seriously offended by a particular song. Censorship and popular music seem inalterably linked. Single words, short phrases, and entire songs have been alleged to be socially subversive. Naturally, profanity and overt vulgarity are the easiest targets for would-be censors. Suggestive phrasing and innuendoes are slightly more difficult to challenge. But many love songs hint at personal indiscretions or relate tales of infidelity, premarital sex, or promiscuous behavior without using either offensive words or double-entendre terminology. These are the most problematic foes of those who wish to "protect" society from prurient thoughts.

The spectrum of sex-related imagery featured in twentieth-century recordings cannot be understated. The intellectual freedom that a democratic society cherishes demands a responsible comprehension of commercially circulated popular culture materials that are consistently the objects of potential censorship. One need not be a "no-holds barred" libertarian to fear the mindless exclusion of popular materials. The legitimate issues of restricting the circulation of explicit recorded items are the breadth of sexual content in contemporary recorded music and the need to anticipate why certain topics may spawn cries for censorship. Clergy, politicians, women's groups, lawyers, parents, and people with fears about social disorder and individual depravation have sought to ban particular songs from both the airwaves and music stores. Libraries with sound recording collections are particularly susceptible to such censorship. Visual pornography and literary sex themes have ignited community outrage at various times in the past. The audio revolution presents yet another target for criticism, contempt, and censorship.

## Sex, Song Lyrics, and Censorship

Why are song lyrics, particularly recordings featuring sex-related themes, likely to come under increasing attack during the 1990s? Since the 1960s there has seemingly been a growing tolerance for the lyrical exploration of controversial topics. Church blacklisting of specific recordings has relented; Federal Communications Commission (FCC) pressures on radio playlists have declined; and principals and school boards, more cognizant of "free speech" issues, tend to ignore the lyrics of recorded music at school functions rather than challenging student-selected music and thus provoking unnecessary problems. The Parents Music Resource Center (PMRC), founded by Tipper Gore and other concerned Washington wives, has been partially satisfied by recording industry willingness to publicly label particularly provocative sexual material prior to sale. Finally, many performing artists have released edited or lyric-altered versions of sex-related songs in order to secure unhassled radio airplay. Such compromises, relaxations of control, and openness to muted sexual ideas would seem to toll the end of song lyricbanning.

This is clearly not the case. In fact, explicit sexual content and vulgar language are actually pawns in a much larger game of political censorship. The nature of popular music, at least since the mid-1950s, has been socially subversive. The demography of the recording industry's major audience practically dictates a thematic focus on issues of personal value exploration, identity definition, and challenges to existing traditions. Attacks on authority in contemporary lyrics are common. Sex is clearly the most emotional and potentially volatile issue confronting youth. The tendency of adults in American society is to cloak youthful vulnerability about sexual identity in myth. Songs such as "Love and Marriage," "That's the Way I Always Heard It Would Be," "To the Aisle," and "I'm Gonna Get Married" illustrate this idealistic perspective. Nevertheless, the lyrics of many, many popular recordings describe in graphic detail a very different process, expectation, and result. Yet the sex-only-after-marriage myth persists and is still championed by censors as the social covers are being pulled off by the lyrics of John Mellencamp, Marvin Gaye, Madonna, Color Me Badd, Tone-Loc, and others.

Sexual imagery in recordings offers an easy target for well-intentioned individuals or politically motivated interest groups to challenge. Morality and aesthetics are invariably debatable topics within a free society. Yet a more sinister threat lurks as the hand-maiden of sex lyric censors. The danger of restricting lyricists in one realm of human activity is that a chilling effect may expand to other crucial areas. Worse yet, new ideas or challenges to current practices might be still-born via rigorous control of lyrics by priests, politicians, police, or court officials who begin to abuse their power within the democratic framework. The antiauthoritarianism of popular lyrics, with historic challenges to government officials ("Won't Get Fooled Again"), to commercial hypocrisy ("Mr. Businessman"), to public education ("Kodachrome"), to police control ("For What It's Worth"), to environmental decay ("Pleasant Valley Sunday"), to world hunger ("Beds Are Burning"), or to international military adventures ("Undercover of the Night") is clearly at risk. Protecting and defending the rights of lyricists to explore sex-related issues is necessary in order to protect the freedom of composers to examine other controversial social and political topics.

### Classifying Themes

No single essay or book could list all sex-related recordings released during the past five decades. The remainder of this study consists of a table of 27 selected sex-related themes and popular recordings illustrating them. Each of these themes illustrates a specific topic that has been examined in several popular songs since 1950. Individual recordings are provided as illustrations of each theme. This material will allow teachers and other leaders to examine approaches taken by specific artists. Although this limited alphabetical table falls short of Linnaeus' systematic biological standard for taxonomy, it does help make the point that there is a broad spectrum of ideas, images, words, practices, and commentaries featured in sex-related recordings.

### Advocacy of Casual Sex

- "Angel of the Morning"
  (Bell 705)
  Merrilee Rush and the Turnabouts (1968)

- "Help Me Make It Through the Night"
  (Mega 0015)
  Sammi Smith (1971)

- "I Want Your Sex"
  (Columbia 07164)
  George Michael (1987)

- "Jack and Diane"
  (Riva 210)
  John Cougar (1982)

- "Let's Spend the Night Together"
  (London 904)
  The Rolling Stones (1967)
- "Love the One You're With"
  (Atlantic 2778)
  Stephen Stills (1970)

## Audio Insinuations of Sexual Activities

- "I Love Traci Lords"
  (Lonesome Town 112)
  Ronnie Mack (1986)
- "Love to Love You, Baby"
  (Oasis 401)
  Donna Summer (1975)
- "Pillow Talk"
  (Vibration 521)
  Sylvia (1973)
- "The Stripper"
  (MGM 13064)
  David Rose (1962)

## Dominant Females

- "Honky Tonk Women"
  (London 910)
  The Rolling Stones (1969)
- "Lady Marmalade"
  (Epic 50048)
  LaBelle (1975)
- "Maneater"
  (RCA 13354)
  Darryl Hall and John Oates (1982)
- "Mississippi Queen"
  (Windfall 532)
  Mountain (1970)
- "Wild Women Do"
  (EMI 50275)
  Natalie Cole (1990)

### Dominant Males

- "Hard to Handle"
  (Def America 19245)
  The Black Crowes (1991)

- "I'm a Man"
  (Checker 814)
  Bo Diddley (1955)

- "Medicine Man"
  (Event 3302)
  The Buchanan Brothers (1969)

- "Sixty-Minute Man"
  (Federal 12022)
  The Dominoes (1951)

- "Sledgehammer"
  (Geffen 28718)
  Peter Gabriel (1986)

- "Steamroller Blues"
  (RCA 0910)
  Elvis Presley (1973)

### Dreams and Sexual Fantasies

- "Girl Watcher"
  (ABC 11094)
  The O'Kaysions (1968)

- "Hot for Teacher"
  (Warner Brothers 29199)
  Van Halen (1984)

- "I Love Traci Lords"
  (Lonesome Town 112)
  Ronnie Mack (1986)

- "Oh, Pretty Woman"
  (Monument 851)
  Roy Orbison (1964)

- "Undercover Angel"
  (Pacific 001)
  Alan O'Day (1977)

### Female Control of a Sexual Situation

- "Baby, What You Want Me to Do?"
  (Vee-Jay 333)
  Jimmy Reed (1960)

- "Don't Touch Me"
  (Capitol 2382)
  Bettye Swann (1969)

- "Keep Your Hands to Yourself"
  (Elektra 69502)
  The Georgia Satellites (1986)

- "Lady Marmalade"
  (Epic 50048)
  LaBelle (1975)

- "Midnight at the Oasis"
  (Reprise 1183)
  Maria Muldaur (1974)

- "No"
  (Decca 32996)
  Bulldog (1972)

### Heavy Metal Macho Sexual Perspectives

- "Bang a Gong (Get It On)"
  (Reprise 1032)
  T. Rex (1972)

- "Black Dog"
  (Atlantic 2849)
  Led Zeppelin (1971)

- "Black and Blue"
  (Warner Brothers 27891)
  Van Halen (1988)

- "Finish What Ya Started"
  (Warner Brothers)
  Van Halen (1988)

- "You Shook Me All Night Long"
  (Atlantic 3761)
  AC/DC (1980)

## *Infidelity and Extramarital Sexual Involvements*

- "(If Loving You Is Wrong) I Don't Want To Be Right"
  (Koko 2111)
  Luther Ingram (1972)

- "Lyin' Eyes"
  (Asylum 45279)
  The Eagles (1975)

- "The Other Woman"
  (Arista 0669)
  Ray Parker, Jr. (1982)

- "Papa Was a Rollin' Stone"
  (Gordy 7121)
  The Temptations (1972)

- "Part-Time Lover"
  (Tamla 1808)
  Stevie Wonder (1985)

- "Ruby, Don't Take Your Love to Town"
  (Reprise 0829)
  Kenny Rogers (1969)

- "Run to You"
  (A&M 2686)
  Bryan Adams (1984)

## *Innuendoes and Sexual Suggestions*

- "Chantilly Lace"
  (Mercury 7133343)
  The Big Bopper (1958)

- "Love the One You're With"
  (T-Neck 930)
  The Isley Brothers (1971)

- "Me So Horny"
  (Skyywalker 130)
  The 2 Live Crew (1989)

- "Push It"
  (Next Plateau 315)
  Salt-N-Pepa (1987)

- "Push Push"
  (Laurie 3067)
  Austin Taylor (1960)

- "Spiders and Snakes"
  (MGM 14648)
  Jim Stafford (1973)

## *Interracial Dating and Sexual Relations*

- "Brown-Eyed Woman"
  (MGM 13959)
  Bill Medley (1968)

- "Brown Sugar"
  (Rolling Stone 19100)
  The Rolling Stones (1971)

- "Cinnamon Girl"
  (Reprise 0911)
  Neil Young (1970)

- "Lady Marmalade"
  (Epic 50048)
  LaBelle (1975)

- "Society's Child (Baby I've Been Thinking)"
  (Verve 5027)
  Janis Ian (1967)

## *Love Potions, Aphrodisiacs, and Spells*

- "Castin' My Spell"
  (Capitol 4168)
  Johnny Otis (1959)

- "Funky Cold Medina"
  (Delicious 104)
  Tone-Loc (1989)

- "I Put a Spell on You"
  (Okeh 7072)
  Screamin' Jay Hawkins (1956)

- "Love Potion No. 9"
  (United Artists 180)
  The Clovers (1959)

- "(You're My) Aphrodisiac"
  (Gordy 1737)
  Dennis Edwards (1984)

## *Outrageous Sexual Escapades*

- "Annie Had a Baby"
  (Federal 12195)
  The Midnighters (1954)

- "Dirty Diana"
  (Epic 07739)
  Michael Jackson (1988)

- "Sixty-Minute Man"
  (Fame 250)
  Clarence Carter (1973)

- "Wild Thing"
  (Delicious 102)
  Tone-Loc (1988)

- "Work with Me Annie"
  (Federal 12169)
  The Midnighters (1954)

- "You Ain't Seen Nothin' Yet"
  (Mercury 73622)
  Bachman-Turner Overdrive (1974)

## *Overt Sexuality*

- "Afternoon Delight"
  (Windsong 10588)
  The Starland Vocal Band (1976)

- "Chevy Van"
  (GRC 2046)
  Sammy Johns (1975)

- "Hurts So Good"
  (Riva 209)
  John Cougar (1982)

- "I Wanna Sex You Up"
  (Giant 19382)
  Color Me Badd (1991)

- "Sexual Healing"
  (Columbia 03302)
  Marvin Gaye (1982)

- "Sunshine of Your Love"
  (Atco 6544)
  Cream (1968)

- "Touch Me (I Want Your Body)"
  (Jive 1006)
  Samantha Fox (1986)

## *Playfully Suggestive Sexual Images*

- "After Midnight"
  (Atco 6784)
  Eric Clapton (1970)

- "After the Lights Go Down Low"
  (Decca 29982)
  Al Hibbler (1956)

- "Makin' Whoopee"
  (ABC-Paramount 10609)
  Ray Charles (1965)

- "Miss You"
  (Rolling Stone 19307)
  The Rolling Stones

- "(Night Time Is) The Right Time"
  (Atlantic 2010)
  Ray Charles (1959)

- "Wild Thing"
  (Fontana 1548)
  The Troggs (1966)

- "You Never Done It Like That"
  (A&M 2063)
  The Captain and Tennille (1978)

## *Pornography*

- "Blue Money"
  (Warner Brothers 7462)
  Van Morrison (1971)

- "I Love Traci Lords"
  (Lonesome Town 112)
  Ronnie Mack (1986)

- "Lady Godiva"
  (Capitol 5740)
  Peter and Gordon (1966)

## Pre-1950s Suggestive Songs

- "All Of Me"
  (Columbia 38163)
  Frank Sinatra (1948)

- "Baby, It's Cold Outside"
  (Capitol 567)
  Johnny Mercer and Margaret Whiting (1949)

- "Let It Snow! Let It Snow! Let It Snow!"
  (Victor 1759)
  Vaughn Monroe and His Orchestra (1945)

- "Let's Do It (Let's Fall In Love)"
  (Columbia 1701)
  Paul Whiteman and His Orchestra (1929)

- "Makin' Whoopee"
  (Victor 21831)
  Eddie Cantor (1929)

## Prostitution

- "Backstreet Ballet"
  (Mercury 814360)
  Savannah (1983)

- "Bad Girls"
  (Casablanca 988)
  Donna Summer (1979)

- "For the Love of Money"
  (Philadelphia International 3544)
  The O'Jays (1974)

- "Honky Tonk Women"
  (London 910)
  The Rolling Stones (1969)

- "The House of the Rising Son"
  (MGM 13264)
  The Animals (1964)
- "Sweet Cream Ladies, Forward March"
  (Mala 12035)
  The Box Tops (1968)

## *Sensual Physical Characteristics*

- "All Lips 'n' Hips"
  (Atco 98973)
  Electric Boys (1990)
- "Baby Got Back"
  (Def American 18947)
  SirMixaLot (1992)
- "Big Leg Woman (with a Short, Short Mini Skirt)"
  (Warren 106)
  Israel "Popper Stopper" Tolbert (1970)
- "Hot Legs"
  (Warner Brothers 8535)
  Rod Stewart (1978)
- "Legs"
  (Warner Brothers 29272)
  ZZ Top (1984)
- "39-21-46"
  (Minit 32007)
  The Showmen (1966)

## *Sex Objects–Female*

- "Addicted to Love"
  (Island 99570)
  Robert Palmer (1986)
- "Arlene"
  (Columbia 05724)
  Marty Stuart (1985)
- "California Girls"
  (Warner Brothers 29102)
  David Lee Roth (1985)

- "Cherry Hill Park"
(Columbia 44902)
Billy Joe Royal (1969)

- "Gloria"
(Dunwich 116)
The Shadows Of Knight (1966)

- "Party Doll"
(Roulette 4002)
Buddy Knox (1957)

- "Private Dancer"
(Capitol 5433)
Tina Turner (1985)

## Sex Objects–Male

- "Hot Stuff"
(Casablanca 978)
Donna Summer (1979)

- "Lee Cross"
(Columbia 44181)
Aretha Franklin (1967)

- "Love Is in Control (Finger on the Trigger)"
(Geffen 29982)
Donna Summer (1982)

- "Take It Easy"
(Asylum 11005)
The Eagles (1972)

## Sexual Imagery and Metaphors

- "Big Ten-Inch Record"
(King 4580)
Bull Moose Jackson (1953)

- "Crosscut Saw"
(Stax 201)
Albert King (1967)

- "Hanky Panky"
(Sire 19789)
Madonna (1990)

- "Ring My Bell"
  (Juana 3422)
  Anita Ward (1979)

- "Start Me Up"
  (Rolling Stone 21003)
  The Rolling Stones (1981)

- "Telephone Man"
  (GRT 127)
  Meri Wilson (1977)

### *Sexual Involvements with Underaged Partners*

- "Gypsies, Tramps, and Thieves"
  (Kapp 2146)
  Cher (1971)

- "I Recall a Gypsy Woman"
  (MCA 51151)
  B. J. Thomas (1981)

- "Jail Bait"
  (KMA 004)
  West Coast Crew (1986)

- "Jail Bait"
  (Fortune 837)
  Andre Williams (1957)

- "Son-of-a Preacher Man"
  (Atlantic 2580)
  Dusty Springfield (1968)

### *Sexually Stimulating Clothing*

- "Big Leg Woman (with a Short Short Mini Skirt)"
  (Warren 106)
  Isreal "Popper Stopper" Tolbert (1970)

- "Devil with a Blue Dress On" and "Good Golly Miss Molly"
  (New Voice 817)
  Mitch Ryder and the Detroit Wheels (1966)

- "Fishnet"
  (Warner Brothers 28201)
  Morris Day (1988)

- "One Piece Topless Bathing Suit"
  (Columbia 43093)
  The Rip Chords (1964)

- "Slip-In Mules (No High-Heel Sneakers)"
  (Checker 1073)
  Sugar Pie DeSanto (1964)

- "You Can Leave Your Hat On"
  (Capitol 5589)
  Joe Cocker (1986)

## Sexually Suggestive Comic Situations

- "Harper Valley P.T.A."
  (Plantation 3)
  Jeannie C. Riley (1968)

- "The Horizontal Bop"
  (Capitol 4951)
  Bob Seger and the Silver Bullet Band (1980)

- "Keep Your Hands to Yourself"
  (Elektra 69502)
  The Georgia Satellites (1986)

- "Lady Godiva"
  (Capitol 5740)
  Peter and Gordon (1966)

- "My Ding-a-Ling"
  (Chess 2131)
  Chuck Berry (1972)

- "My Toot-Toot"
  (Warner Brothers 28535)
  John Fogerty with Rockin' Sidney (1986)

- "Reelin' and Rockin'"
  (Chess 2136)
  Chuck Berry (1972)

- "Skinny Legs and All"
  (Dial 4063)
  Joe Tex (1967)

- "Something You Got"
  (Wand 181)
  Chuck Jackson and Maxine Brown (1965)

## *Uncontrollable Emotional Responses*

- "Breathless"
  (Sun 288)
  Jerry Lee Lewis (1958)

- "Fire"
  (Mercury 73643)
  The Ohio Players (1974)

- "Fire"
  (Planet 45901)
  The Pointer Sisters (1978)

- "Great Balls of Fire"
  (Sun 281)
  Jerry Lee Lewis (1957)

- "Hot Blooded"
  (Atlantic 3488)
  Foreigner (1978)

- "I'm So Excited"
  (Planet 13327)
  The Pointer Sisters (1982)

## *Unconventional Sexual Behaviors*

- "Dude (Looks Like a Lady)"
  (Geffen 28240)
  Aerosmith (1987)

- "Fat-Bottomed Girls"
  (Elektra 45541)
  Queen (1978)

- "Lola"
  (Reprise 0930)
  The Kinks (1970)

- "Obscene Phone Caller"
  (Motown 1731)
  Rockwell (1984)

- "Stoop Down, Baby"
  (La Val 871)
  Chick Willis (1972)

## Unexpected or Unwanted Pregnancies

- "Annie Had a Baby"
  (Federal 12195)
  The Midnighters (1954)

- "Gypsys, Tramps, and Thieves"
  (Kapp 2196)
  Cher (1971)

- "Half-Breed"
  (MCA 40102)
  Cher (1973)

- "Love Child"
  (Motown 1135)
  Diana Ross and the Supremes (1968)

- "Papa Don't Preach"
  (Sire 28660)
  Madonna (1986)

- "You're Having My Baby"
  (United Artists 454)
  Paul Anka and Odia Coates (1974)

## REFERENCES

Allen, Robert C. *Horrible Prettiness: Burlesque and American Culture*. Chapel Hill: University of North Carolina Press, 1991.

Ashmore, Harry. *Fear in the Air—Broadcasting and the First Amendment: The Anatomy of a Constitutional Crisis*. New York: W.W. Norton and Company, Inc., 1973.

Cooper, B. Lee. "Bear Cats, Chipmunks, and Slip-in Mules: The 'Answer Song' in Contemporary American Recordings 1950-1985," *Popular Music and Society*, XII (Fall 1988), pp. 57-77.

Cooper, B. Lee. "Personal Relationships, Love, and Sexuality," in *A Resource Guide to Themes in Contemporary American Song Lyrics 1950-1985* (Westport, Connecticut: Greenwood Press, 1986), pp. 131-181.

Cooper, B. Lee. "Response Recordings as Creative Repetition: Answer Songs and Pop Parodies in Contemporary American Music," *OneTwoThreeFour: A Rock 'n' Roll Quarterly*, No. 4 (Winter 1987), pp. 79-87.

Cray, Ed (comp.). *The Erotic Muse: American Bawdy Songs* (second edition). Urbana: University of Illinois Press, 1991.

Denisoff, R. Serge and William D. Romanowski. *Risky Business: Rock in Film.* New Brunswick, New Jersey: Transaction Books, 1991.

Denselow, Robin. *When the Music's Over: The Story of Political Pop.* London: Faber and Faber, 1989.

Edwards, Emily D. "Does Love Really Stink? The 'Mean World' of Love and Sex in Popular Music of the 1980s," in *Adolescents and Their Music: If It's Too Loud, You're Too Old*, edited by Jonathan S. Epstein (New York: Garland Publishing, Inc., 1994), pp. 225-249.

Evans, Simon. "Working with Annie . . ." *Blues and Rhythm*, No. 69 (May 1992), pp. 8-11.

Frith, Simon and Angela McRobbie. "Rock and Sexuality," in *On Record: Rock, Pop, and the Written Word*, edited by Simon Frith and Andrew Goodwin (New York: Pantheon Books, 1990), pp. 371-389.

Gore, Tipper. *Raising PG Kids in and X-Rated Society.* Nashville, Tennessee: Abington Press, 1987.

Grendysa, Peter. "You've Heard That Song Before: Record Censorship and Hysteria," *Goldmine*, No. 155 (July 4, 1986), p. 73.

Hoffmann, Frank. *Intellectual Freedom and Censorship.* Metuchen, New Jersey: Scarecrow Press, Inc., 1989.

Huffmann, James R. and Julie L. Huffmann. "Sexism and Cultural Lag: The Rise of the Jailbait Song, 1955-1985," *Journal of Popular Culture*, 21 (Fall 1987), pp. 65-83.

Isler, Scott. "Parent Terror–Insidious Rock Lyrics: The Inquisition Begins," *Musician*, No. 86 (December 1985), pp. 50-62.

Jarent, Charles and Jacqueline Boles. "Sounds of Seduction: Sex and Alcohol in Country Music Lyrics," in *America's Musical Pulse: Popular Music in Twentieth-Century Society*, edited by Kenneth J. Bindas (Westport, Connecticut: Praeger Books, 1992), pp. 257-267.

Keil, Charles. *Urban Blues.* Chicago: University of Chicago Press, 1966.

Lance, Larry M. and Christian Y. Berry. "Has There Been a Sexual Revolution? Human Sexuality in Popular Music, 1968-1977," *Journal of Popular Culture*, IX (Summer 1985), pp. 65-73.

Logsdon, Guy (comp.). *The Whorehouse Bells Were Ringing and Other Songs Cowboys Sing.* Urbana: University of Illinois Press, 1989.

Martin, Linda and Kerry Segrave. *Anti-Rock: The Opposition to Rock 'n' Roll.* Hamden, Connecticut: Archon Books, 1988.

McDonald, James R. "Censoring Rock Lyrics: A Historical Analysis of the Debate," *Youth and Society*, XIX (March 1988), pp. 294-313.

McDonald, James R. "Rock Censorship: Implications for Collectors and Libraries," *Popular Culture in Libraries*, I, No. 4 (1993), pp. 63-70.

Melton, Peter. "Censored! An Overview of the History of Banned and Censored Records in America," *Goldmine*, No. 276 (February 22, 1991), pp. 113-116.

Moonoogian, George. "Oh, That Annie!" *Record Exchanger*, No. 23 (1977), pp. 20-21.

Moonoogian, George and Chris Beachlery. "Lovin' Dan: A Look Thirty Years Later–Does He Have 59 to Go?" *It Will Stand*, No. 20 (1980), pp. 4-7.

Newman, Ralph M. "Whose Ding-a-Ling?" *Bim Bam Boom*, No. 9 (1973), pp. 16-17.

Oboler, Eli M. *Defending Intellectual Freedom: The Library and the Censor.* Westport, Connecticut: Greenwood Press, 1980.

Parents Music Resource Center. *Let's Talk About Rock: A Primer for Parents.* Arlington, Virginia: Parents Music Resource Center, Publishers, 1986.

Pratt, Ray. *Rhythm and Resistance: Explorations in the Political Uses of Popular Music.* New York: Praeger Publishers, 1990.

Robinson, Glen O. "The FCC and the First Amendment: Observations on 40 Years of Radio and Television Regulation," *Minnesota Law Review*, LII (November 1967), pp. 67-163.

Sandmel, Ben. "Whose Toot-Toot?" *Wavelength*, No, 56 (June 1985), pp. 24-28.

Savage, Jon. "The Enemy Within: Sex, Rock, and Identity," in *Facing the Music*, edited by Simon Frith (New York: Pantheon Books, 1988), pp. 131-172.

Schultze, Quentin J., Roy M. Anker, James D. Bratt, William D. Romanowski, John W. Worst, and Lambert Zuidervaart. *Dancing in the Dark: Youth, Popular Culture, and the Electronic Media.* Grand Rapids, Michigan: William B. Erdmans Publishing Company, 1991.

Simels, Steve. *Gender Chameleons: Androgeny in Rock 'n' Roll.* New York: Arbor House, 1985.

Snyder, Robert. "Cover Records: What? When? and Why?" *Record Digest*, I (July 1, 1978), pp. 3-18.

Stidom, Larry. "Dance with me, Henry," in *Izatso?! Larry Stidom's Rock 'n' Roll Trivia and Fact Book.* (Indianapolis, Indiana: L. Stidom, 1986), p. 57.

Tamarkin, Jeff. "The Censorship Debate: Four Opinions," *Goldmine*, No. 276 (February 22, 1991), pp. 52-54, 112-126.

Thompson, Stephen I. "Forbidden Fruit: Interracial Love Affairs in Country Music," *Popular Music and Society*, XIII (Summer 1989), pp. 23-37.

Tosches, Nick. *Hellfire: The Jerry Lee Lewis Story.* New York: Dell Publishing Company, Inc., 1982.

Weisman, Eric Robert. "Wine, Women, and Song: Frank Sinatra and the Rhetoric of Whoopee," *Pennsylvania Speech Communication Annual*, XXXII (1976), pp. 67-79.

Woodford, Chris. "Don't Mess with My Toot-Toot!" *Now Dig This*, No, 31 (October 1985), p. 25.

Young, Charles M. "My Talk with Tipper [Gore]," *Musician*, No. 106 (August 1987), pp. 21-26ff.

Zucker, Mark J. "The Saga of Lovin' Dan: A Study in the Iconography of Rhythm and Blues Music of the 1950s," *Journal of Popular Culture*, XVI (Fall 1982), pp. 43-51.

Chapter 20

# Soul Music

## CHICAGO SCENE

*Chicago Soul.* By Robert Pruter. Champaign-Urbana: University of Illinois Press, 1991. Illustrated. 408 pp.

From the founding of Vee Jay Records in 1953 to the demise of Chi-Sound Records in 1984, Chicago was a major producer of soul songs. This distinctive style of black music, amalgamating gospel emotion, rhythm 'n' blues raunchiness, and pop ballad sentiment, rose to national prominence during the late 1960s and early 1970s. Essayist and editor Robert Pruter pays loving homage to Chicago's soul artists—both large (Jerry Butler, Major Lance, Curtis Mayfield, Gene Chandler, Etta James, and The Dells) and small (Alvin Cash, The Dutones, Syl Johnson, McKinley Mitchell, and The Vibrations)—and to those recording companies that fostered Windy City soul. The author's boundless knowledge of performers, recordings, radio influences, local disc distribution techniques and record company personnel throughout Chicago is staggering. Similarly, his skillful use of black-and-white photographs and exceptionally broad print and interview research resources make this volume a treasure-trove of music information. *Chicago Soul* is the standard by which all future city-focused musical investigations will be judged.

Having produced such a magnificent though narrowly focused work, there are two new avenues of scholarly pursuit that should beckon Robert

The initial review by B. Lee Cooper was originally published as "Review of *Chicago Soul* by Robert Pruter," *Popular Culture in Libraries*, I, No. 1 (1993), pp. 146-148. Reprint permission granted by the author, Editor Frank Hoffmann, and The Haworth Press. The second review by B. Lee Cooper was published as "Review of *Soul Music A-Z* by Hugh Gregory," *Popular Music and Society*, XVI (Summer 1992), pp. 119-120. Reprint permission granted by the author, Editor R. Serge Denisoff, and Bowling Green State University Popular Press.

Pruter. The first challenge should also be of interest to Judith McCulloh, editor of the marvelous "Music in American Life" series for the University of Illinois Press. It is important to recognize Chicago as an urban mecca (not unlike New Orleans and Kansas City) for all types of music. Pruter's attention to Chicago's soul performers is undeniably laudable. Yet a genuinely comprehensive study of the interactions of Windy City jazz giants (e.g., Ahmad Jamal), bluesmen (e.g., Muddy Waters), rock 'n' rollers (e.g., Chuck Berry), pop nightclub performers (e.g., Lou Rawls), session players, and even bar bands would be a magnificent undertaking. From 1930 to 1990, the various musical styles of Chicago influenced not only every city in the United States, but a vast number of foreign metropolitan areas as well, including Liverpool (The Beatles) and London (the Rolling Stones).

The other topic for a historian/critic/fan of Robert Pruter's stature to pursue is the origins, impact, and demise of soul music throughout the United States and the world. Although pieces of this musical picture have already been painted by Cliff White, Peter Guralnick (*Sweet Soul Music*–1986), Jeff Hannusch (*I Hear You Knocking*–1985), Michael Haralambos, Gerri Hirshey (*Nowhere to Run*–1984), Nelson George, Tony Cummings, and others, no full-blown picture exists. Recent almanac-time-line publications by Lee Cotten and Galen Gart explore 1950s R&B music, but the emphasis of such investigations is on linking Wynonie Harris, Roy Brown, and The Dominoes more directly to the so-called "Golden Age of Rock and Roll," which ended–according to conventional wisdom–with the British Invasion of 1964. Pruter could provide a more comprehensive perspective by examining the rhythm 'n' blues, gospel, pop, and blues roots of not only his soulful Chicago idols, but also of Wilson Pickett, Solomon Burke, Aretha Franklin, James Brown, Otis Redding, and other American soul singing giants. It would also be helpful for him to speculate on the evolution of soul, identifying not only pre-1960s influences but also post-1980s spinoffs and current trends among contemporary black urban performers.

*Chicago Soul* bristles with facts, names, songs, and dates. It is scholarly, yet readable; it is opinionated, yet responsible. Nevertheless, a reviewer cannot avoid feeling the need for a more comparative overview, a vision that contrasts styles and achievements of The Impressions and The Temptations, Sugar Pie DeSanto and Irma Thomas, Curtis Mayfield and Otis Redding, and Dee Clark and Solomon Burke. No popular music fan, record collector, sound recording archivist, or music librarian should miss Robert Pruter's distinctive contribution to American music history.

# ENCYCLOPEDIA OF PERFORMERS

*Soul Music A-Z.* By Hugh Gregory. London: Blandford Press, 1991. Illustrated. 266 pp.

*Soul Music Who's Who.* By Ralph Tee. Rocklin, California: Prima Publishing, 1992. 309 pp.

Soul music emerged during the late 1960s as an amalgam of gospel, blues, and R&B stylings. Led by James Brown, Solomon Burke, Aretha Franklin, Wilson Pickett, and Otis Redding, soul sounds reasserted American musical dominance following two powerful waves of British invaders. Clearly, The Beatles and the Rolling Stones had drawn heavily on black precursors of the 1960s soul movement–singers as diverse as Arthur Alexander, Chuck Berry, Marvin Gaye, The Shirelles, Slim Harpo, and The Isley Brothers–and later found their own songs co-opted by new black musical giants from Atlantic, Stax, and Volt Records. London-born writer and film researcher Hugh Gregory has compiled an alphabetized encyclopedia listing nearly 600 vocalists, studio musicians, bands, song writers, record producers, disc jockeys, and other key music business personnel who sparked, spawned, supported, supplemented, and saw soul music conquer U.S. and U.K. record charts between 1965 and 1975. *Soul Music A-Z* is both a tribute and a celebration. It is also a marvelous roll call of talented artists and record industry maestros who saw beyond ragtime, jazz, blues, and rock 'n' roll to identify another indigenous audio vista in America's seemingly endless creative streams of original sound.

Gregory meticulously explains the profound difficulties of establishing inclusion/exclusion boundaries for his soul encyclopedia. The author elected to omit John Lee Hooker and Muddy Waters (too rural and stylistically narrow); Joe Turner and Sarah Vaughan (too jazz-oriented in vocal phrasing); most disco singers (too synthesized and repetitive); and nearly all rap or hip-hop groups. Those individuals included within the volume stretch from Gregory Abbott, Ewart Abner, Herb Abramson, and Johnny Ace to Stevie Wonder, Betty Wright, O.V. Wright, and The Zodiacs. Each entry features a short biographical sketch a selection of hit soul singles listed by both U.S. and U.K. chart numbers and years of release, and a brief album discography. The black-and-white photographs selected for the text are especially handsome.

It would seem difficult to find any fault with a study that so thoroughly highlights both giants (Ike and Tina Turner, Ray Charles, Curtis Mayfield, Diana Ross, and Sly and The Family Stone) and dwarfs (Big Al Downing, Alvin Cash, Ann Peebles, James Carr, Bobby Marchan, and Oscar Toney Jr.)

of soul. Yet there are serious omissions in biographical entries and biblio-graphic resources that flaw this work. Gregory should have cited most (if not all) of the following soul performers: Bobby King and Terry Evans, Marcia Ball, Lou Ann Barton, The Commitments, Freddy Fender, Narvel Felts, Taj Mahal, Michael Bolton, Billy Vera, Joe Cocker, Benny Spel-lman, Bettye Swann, The Soul Brothers Six, The Nylons, The Steve Miller Band, The Five Keys, The Five Satins, The Accents, Bonnie Raitt, and Eugene Church. In addition, the 30-book reference list at the end of Greg-ory's text should have been expanded to feature six to ten key biographical studies for each major soul artist cited.

Ralph Tee's *Soul Music Who's Who* is inferior to Gregory's volume in all aspects except the total number of biographical entries. Lacking any reasoned definition for "Soul Music," the study revels in minor black performers while either ignoring or downplaying major soul stylists. Why salute the Average White Band and omit The Righteous Brothers and Michael Bolton? Why include Etta James and exclude Johnny Ace, Jesse Belvin, and James Carr? Why list Chuck Berry and ignore Don and Dewey? The imbalance in length of descriptions allow Rose Royce, the Trammps, and Kim Weston to overshadow Solomon Burke, Wilson Pick-ett, and Otis Redding. This is nothing short of criminal.

Soul music fans will benefit by consulting Gregory's focused compen-dium of artists. However, until Britain's Cliff White and America's Peter Guralnick decide to pool their considerable black music knowledge in a co-authored music encyclopedia, there will be no definitive biographical resource guide available. Ben E. King defined this situation in two words–"Too Bad."

## *BLUE-EYED SOUL SINGERS*

*The Commitments* (MCAD 10286). Universal City, California: MCA Records, Inc. 1991. Fourteen Songs.

*The Commitments–Volume Two* (MCAD 10506). Universal City, California: MCA Records, Inc., 1992. Eleven Songs.

*Classic Recordings by the Original Artists of the Music Featured in the Motion Picture: The Commitments* (ATCO CD 7-91813-2). New York: ATCO/Atlantic Recording Corporation, 1991. Fourteen Songs.

John Belushi and Dan Aykroyd created Jake and Elwood as the televi-sion and motion picture soul-singing team The Blues Brothers. Between

1978 and 1981 they managed to chart four songs—"Soul Man," "Rubber Biscuit," "Gimme Some Lovin'," and "Who's Making Love." In 1986 Peter Guralnick issued his splendid study *Sweet Soul Music*. This examination of Memphis/Macon/Muscle Shoals music noted that the height of soul sound success was achieved through management and artistic cooperation among blacks and whites. In 1991 an Irish band, featuring lead vocals by Andrew Strong, Angeline Ball, Maria Doyle, Robert Arkins, and Niamh Kavanagh, revived a boatload of marvelous American soul songs. The Commitments were not lovable, laughable Blues Brothers, though. They were gritty, hungry, and only marginally successful. As a mythical Dublin-based band, they pounded out pure soul. Their reprise versions of "Mustang Sally," "In the Midnight Hour," "Try a Little Tenderness," "Show Me," and "Chain of Fools" prompted Atlantic Records to reissue the original soulful versions by Wilson Pickett, Otis Redding, Joe Tex, and Aretha Franklin. Soul music enthusiasts cheered!

One seldom encounters challenges to the performing genius of Ray Charles, James Brown, Percy Sledge, Solomon Burke, or hundreds of other black soul singers. Yet numerous white artists who have performed traditional soul tunes face dramatically mixed reviews. Is blue-eyed soul possible? Can white artists duplicate, emulate, or even create authentically soulful music? The Commitments' two CDs argue for the affirmative. So does the Simply Red triumph "If You Don't Know Me By Now" (1989). Michael Bolton has also achieved prominence over the past five years with classic tunes including "(Sittin' on) The Dock of the Bay" (1988), "Georgia on My Mind" (1990), and "When a Man Loves a Woman" (1991).

Many authors and rock journalists have sought to link 1940s and 1950s gospel, doo-wop, and rhythm 'n' blues to explain the emergence of 1960s and 1970s black soul music. What is really needed though, is a thorough, sensitive, longitudinal investigation of white soul singers. Where should such an examination begin? Clearly, the roots of blue-eyed soul reside in brown-eyed soul. But where does the magic manifestation of soulful translation occur? Not surprisingly, Elvis Presley is a key player. But just as the 1950s featured such diverse black talents as Jimmy Reed, Little Richard, Ray Charles, and Don and Dewey, they were also the tranquil days of black-influenced Elvis, Don and Phil Everly, Frankie Ford, and Bobby Darin. During the 1960s the blue-eyed soul movement jumped forward both domestically and internationally. Enter The Beatles and the Rolling Stones. But the most significant non-U.S. soul men were Tom Jones and Joe Cocker. Stateside it was Felix Cavaliere's Young Rascals, The Righteous Brothers, Johnny Rivers, Roy Head, and Dion DiMucci. The 1970s saw an expansion of white soul, headed by The Box Tops,

Michael McDonald and The Doobie Brothers, Dave Edmunds, Hall and Oates, and Tony Orlando. Finally, the 1980s and early 1990s featured the continuation of blue-eyed soul by Bill Medley and Delbert McClinton, the emergence of upbeat new players such as Robert Palmer and Michael Bolton, and the revelation of soulful diversity from UB40, Simply Red, and The Commitments.

During the 1950s black artists felt ravaged by white cover singers such as Pat Boone, The Crew Cuts, Georgia Gibbs, Gale Storm, The Hilltoppers, The Diamonds, and many others. The evolution of blue-eyed soul, however, is a labor of love and mutual respect rather than the money-grubbing machinations of music industry magnets. The two MCA *Commitments* discs and the accompanying ATCO *Classic Recordings* CD are invitations for scholarly research on blue-eyed soul music. The pursuit of this topic with sound-recordings archivists could be fascinating.

## REFERENCES

Bartlette, Reginald J. *Off the Record—Motown by Master Number, 1959-1989: Volume One–Singles*. Ann Arbor, Michigan: Popular Culture, Ink., 1991.

Belz, Carl. *The Story of Rock* (second edition). New York: Harper and Row, 1972.

Benjaminson, Peter. *The Story of Motown*. New York: Grove Press, 1979.

Bianco, David. *The Motown Fact Book*. Ann Arbor, Michigan: Pierian Press, 1988.

Blansky, Bob (comp.). *The Motown Era*. Detroit, Michigan: Jobete Music Company, Inc., 1971.

Brigerman, Chuck. *Record Collector's Fact Book–Volume One: 45 R.P.M., 1952-1965*. Westminster, Maryland: Disc Publishing, 1982.

Brown, Ashley. "The Alchemists," *The History of Rock*, No. 15 (1982), pp. 281-283.

Brown, Ashley. "The Roots of Soul," *The History of Rock*, No. 7 (1982), pp. 321-322.

Brown, Ashley and Michael Heatley (eds.). *The Motown Story*. London: Bedford Press, 1985.

Cooper, B. Lee. "Promoting Social Change Through Audio Repetition: Black Musicians as Creators and Revivalists, 1953-1978," *Tracking: Popular Music Studies*, II (Winter 1989), pp. 26-46.

Cooper, B. Lee. "Review of *Aretha Franklin–Queen of Soul: The Atlantic Recordings*," *Popular Music and Society*, XVI (Winter 1992), p. 109-111.

Cooper, B. Lee. "Review of *Atlantic Sisters of Soul*," *Popular Music and Society*, XVII (Summer 1993), p. 135.

Cooper, B. Lee. "Review of *Chicago Soul* by Robert Pruter," *Popular Culture in Libraries*, I, No. 1 (1993), pp. 146-148.

Cooper, B. Lee. "Review of *The Death of Rhythm and Blues* by Nelson George," *Popular Music and Society*, XIII (Summer 1989), pp. 117-119.

Cooper, B. Lee. "Review of *Heat Wave: The Motown Fact Book* by David Bianco," *Michigan Academician*, XXII (Summer 1990), pp. 304-306.

Cooper, B. Lee. "Review of *I Hear You Knockin': The Sound of Rhythm and Blues in New Orleans* by Jeff Hannusch," *Popular Music and Society*, Xi (Winter 1987), pp. 93-94.

Cooper, B. Lee. "Review of *Soul Music A-Z* by Hugh Gregory and *Soul Music Who's Who* by Ralph Tee," *Popular Culture in Libraries*, II, No. 1 (1994), pp. 103-104.

Cooper, B. Lee. "Review of *Sweet Soul Music: Rhythm and Blues and the Southern Dream of Freedom* by Peter Guralnick," *Popular Music and Society*, XI (Spring 1987), pp. 88-90.

Cummings, Tony. "Roots, Forerunners, and Originators," in *The Soul Book* by Ian Hoare, Tony Cummings, Clive Anderson, and Simon Frith (New York: Dell Publishing Company, Inc., 1976), pp. 1-38.

Cummings, Tony. *The Sound of Philadelphia.* London: Methuen Books, 1975.

Davis, Sharon. *Motown: The History.* New York: Sterling Books, 1989.

Downey, Pat. *The Golden Age of Top 40 Music (1955-1973) on Compact Disc.* Boulder, Colorado: Pat Downey Enterprises, 1992.

Edwards, Joseph (comp.). *Top 10's and Trivia of Rock and Roll and Rhythm and Blues 1950-1980.* St. Louis, Missouri: Blueberry Hill Publishing Company, 1981.

Garland, Phyl. "Basic Library of Rhythm-and-Blues," *Stereo Review*, XLII (May 1979), pp. 72-77.

Gart, Galen and Roy C. Ames, with Ray Funk, Rob Bowman, and David Booth. *Duke/Peacock Records: An Illustrated History with Discography.* Milford, New Hampshire: Big Nickel Publications, 1990.

George, Nelson. *The Death of Rhythm and Blues.* New York: Pantheon Books, 1988.

George, Nelson. *Where Did Our Love Go? The Rise and Fall of the Motown Sound.* New York: Omnibus Press, 1986.

Gillett, Charlie. *Making Tracks: Atlantic Records and the Growth of a Multi-Billion-Dollar Industry.* New York: E.P. Dutton and Company, 1974.

Gillett, Charlie. *The Sound of the City: The Rise of Rock and Roll* (revised and expanded edition). New York: Pantheon Books, 1983.

Given, Dave. *The Dave Given Rock 'n' Roll Stars Handbook: Rhythm and Blues Artists and Groups.* Smithtown, New York: Exposition Press, 1980.

Gray, Michael H. (comp.). *Bibliography of Discographies: Volume Three—Popular Music.* New York: Bowker Company, 1983.

Gregory, Hugh. *Soul Music A-Z.* London: Blandford Press, 1991.

Gribin, Anthony J. and Matthew M. Schiff. *Doo-Wop: The Forgotten Third of Rock 'n' Roll.* Iola, Wisconsin: Krause Publications, 1992.

Groia, Phil. *They All Sang on the Corner: New York City's Rhythm and Blues Vocal Groups of the 1950s.* Setauket, New York: Edmond Publishing Company, 1974.

Guralnick, Peter. "Soul," in *The Rolling Stone Illustrated History of Rock and Roll* (fully revised and updated), edited by Anthony DeCurtis and James Henke, with Holly George-Warren (New York: Random House, 1992), pp. 260-265.

Guralnick, Peter. *Sweet Soul Music: Rhythm and Blues and the Southern Dream of Freedom*. New York: Harper and Row, 1986.

Hansen, Barry. "Rhythm and Gospel," in *The Rolling Stone Illustrated History of Rock and Roll* (fully revised and updated), edited by Anthony DeCurtis and James Henke, with Holly George-Warren (New York: Random House, 1992), pp. 17-20.

Hirshey, Gerri. *Nowhere to Run: The Story of Soul Music*. New York: Da Capo Press, 1994 (c. 1984).

Landau, Jon. "Motown: The First Ten Years," in *It's Too Late to Stop Now: A Rock and Roll Journal* (San Francisco: Straight Arrow Books, 1972), pp. 143-150.

Lewis, George, Norm Cohen, Arnold Shaw et al. (comps.). "Black Music Bibliography," *Billboard*, XCI (June 9, 1979), pp. 32, 40-41 B.M.

Licks, Dr. *Standing in The Shadows of Motown: The Life and Music of Legendary Bassist James Jamerson*. Wynnewood, Pennsylvania: Dr. Licks Publishing, 1989.

Lipsitz, George. "'Ain't Nobody Here But Us Chickens': The Class Origins of Rock and Roll," in *Class Culture in Cold War America: A Rainbow at Midnight* (Brooklyn, New York: J.F. Bergin Publishers, Inc., 1981), pp. 195-225.

McEwen, Joe, and Jim Miller. "Motown," in *The Rolling Stone Illustrated History of Rock and Roll* (fully revised and updated), edited by Anthony DeCurtis and James Henke, with Holly George-Warren (New York: Random House, 1992), pp. 277-292.

McGowan, James A. *Here Today Here to Stay:A Personal History of Rhythm and Blues*. St. Petersburg, Florida: Sixth House Press, 1983.

Millar, Bill. "Rhythm and Blues," *The History of Rock*, No. 2 (1982); pp. 29-32.

Morse, David. *Motown and the Arrival of Black Music*. New York: Collier Books, 1971.

Osborne, Jerry, and Bruce Hamilton (comps.). *Blues/Rhythm and Blues/Soul: Original Record Collectors Price Guide*. Phoenix, Arizona: O'Sullivan, Woodside, and Company, 1980.

Partridge, Marianne (ed.). *The Motown Album: The Sound of Young America*. New York: St. Martin's Press, 1990.

Pavlow, Al (comp.). *Hot Charts 1940*. Providence, Rhode Island: Music House Publishing, 1994.

Pavlow, Al (comp.). *Hot Charts 1941*. Providence, Rhode Island: Music House Publishing, 1994.

Pavlow, Al (comp.). *Hot Charts 1942*. Providence, Rhode Island: Music House Publishing, 1994.

Pavlow, Al (comp.). *Hot Charts 1943*. Providence, Rhode Island: Music House Publishing, 1994.

Pavlow, Al (comp.). *Hot Charts 1944*. Providence, Rhode Island: Music House Publishing, 1994.

Pavlow, Al (comp.). *Hot Charts 1945*. Providence, Rhode Island: Music House Publishing, 1994.

Pavlow, Al (comp.). *Hot Charts 1946*. Providence, Rhode Island: Music House Publishing, 1994.

Pavlow, Al (comp.). *Hot Charts 1947*. Providence, Rhode Island: Music House Publishing, 1994.

Pavlow, Al (comp.). *Hot Charts 1948*. Providence, Rhode Island: Music House Publishing, 1994.

Pavlow, Al (comp.). *Hot Charts 1949*. Providence, Rhode Island: Music House Publishing, 1994.

Pavlow, Al (comp.). *Hot Charts 1950*. Providence, Rhode Island: Music House Publishing, 1990.

Pavlow, Al (comp.). *Hot Charts 1951*. Providence, Rhode Island: Music House Publishing, 1990.

Pavlow, Al (comp.). *Hot Charts 1952*. Providence, Rhode Island: Music House Publishing, 1990.

Pavlow, Al (comp.). *Hot Charts 1953*. Providence, Rhode Island: Music House Publishing, 1990.

Pavlow, Al (comp.). *Hot Charts 1954*. Providence, Rhode Island: Music House Publishing, 1990.

Pavlow, Al (comp.). *Hot Charts 1955*. Providence, Rhode Island: Music House Publishing, 1991.

Pavlow, Al (comp.). *Hot Charts 1956*. Providence, Rhode Island: Music House Publishing, 1991.

Pavlow, Al (comp.). *Hot Charts 1957*. Providence, Rhode Island: Music House Publishing, 1991.

Pavlow, Al (comp.). *Hot Charts 1958*. Providence, Rhode Island: Music House Publishing, 1992.

Pavlow, Al (comp.). *Hot Charts 1959*. Providence, Rhode Island: Music House Publishing, 1992.

Pruter, Robert. *Chicago Soul*. Champaign-Urbana: University of Illinois Press, 1991.

Redd, Lawrence N. "Rock! It's Still Rhythm and Blues," *Black Perspective in Popular Music*, XIII (Spring 1985), pp. 31-47.

Ruppli, Michel (comp.). *The Aladdin/Imperial Labels: A. Discography*. Westport, Connecticut: Greenwood Press, 1991.

Ruppli, Michel (comp.). *Atlantic Records: A Discography* (four volumes). Westport, Connecticut: Greenwood Press, 1979.

Ruppli, Michel, with Bill Daniels (comps.). *The King Labels: A Discography*. Westport, Connecticut: Greenwood Press, 1985.

Ruppli, Michel, with Bob Porter (comps.). *The Savoy Label: A Discography*. Westport, Connecticut: Greenwood Press, 1980.

Ryan, Jack. *Recollections–The Detroit Years: The Motown Sound by the People Who Made It*. Detroit, Michigan: J. Ryan, with Data Graphics and Whitlaker Marketing, 1982.

Ryan, Marc. *Trumpet Records: An Illustrated History with Discography*. Milford, New Hampshire: Big Nickel Publications, 1992.

Shapiro, Nat and Bruce Pollock (eds). *Popular Music, 1920-1979–A Revised Cumulation* (three volumes). Detroit, Michigan: Gale Research Company, 1985.

Shaw, Arnold. *Black Popular Music in America: From the Spirituals, Minstrels, and Ragtime to Soul, Disco, and Hip-Hop*. New York: Schirmer Books, 1986.

Shaw, Arnold. "Gospel Music and Soul," in *The World of Soul* (New York: Paperback Library, 1971), pp. 277-286.

Shaw, Arnold. *Honkers and Shouters: The Golden Years of Rhythm and Blues*. New York: Collier Books, 1978.

Shaw, Arnold. "Sh-Boom," in *The Rockin' 50s: The Decade That Transformed the Pop Music Scene* (New York: Hawthorn Books, Inc., 1974), pp. 73-79.

Shaw, Arnold. "Where It Started: Blues, Race, and Rhythm-and-Blues," in *The Rock Revolution* (New York: Paperback Library, 1971), pp. 26-54.

Stuessy, Joe. "The Emergence of Rock and Roll," in *Rock and Roll: Its History and Stylistic Development* (Englewood Cliffs, New Jersey: Prentice-Hall, Inc., 1990), pp. 31-45.

Tagg, Philip. "Open Letter–'Black Music,' 'Afro-American Music,' and 'European Music,'" *Popular Music*, VIII (October 1989), pp. 285-298.

Taraborrelli, Randy J. *Motown: Hot Wax, City Cool, and Solid Gold*. Garden City, New York: Doubleday and Company, Inc., 1986.

Tomashefsky, Steve. "The Apollo Theatre," *Living Blues*, No. 27 (May-June 1976), pp. 12-17.

Wade, Dorothy and Justine Picardie. *Music Man: Ahmet Ertegun, Atlantic Records, and the Triumph of Rock 'n' Roll*. New York: W.W. Norton and Company, Inc., 1990.

Waller, Don. *The Motown Story: The Inside Story of America's Most Popular Music*. New York: Charles Scribner's Sons, 1985.

Wexler, Jerry and David Ritz. *Rhythm and the Blues: A Life in American Music*. New York: Alfred A. Knopf, Inc., 1993.

# Chapter 21

# War

## INTERNATIONAL MILITARY ACTIVITY

*Fighting Songs and Warring Words: Popular Lyrics of Two World Wars*. By Brian Murdoch. London: Routledge, 1990. 288 pp.

*Rhythm and Resistance: Explorations in the Political Uses of Popular Music*. By Ray Pratt. New York: Praeger Publishers, 1990. 241 pp.

These two volumes assess the availability and influence of popular lyrics on twentieth Century listeners. Brian Murdoch focuses narrowly on war-related imagery, while Ray Pratt emphasizes much broader social and personal issues of conformity, individualism, and freedom. Both writers acknowledge that varying segments of a given society are attracted to or affected by lyrical observations in varying ways. Nevertheless Murdoch and Pratt are both convinced that recorded music is a key motivating factor in both private and political undertakings.

*Fighting Songs and Warring Words* is designed to ". . . extend the view of war poetry into areas sometimes dismissed as not worthy of consideration, such as the song, even though these have a far wider currency than some poetry; and to look at poetry that is not anti-war" (p. 21). Murdoch's success in this pursuit varies. On the positive side, he is brilliant in noting that the world wars produced lyrics of all persuasions–patriotism, mock-

---

The review by B. Lee Cooper was originally published as "Review of *Fighting Songs and Warring Words* by Brian Murdoch and *Rhythm and Resistance* by Ray Pratt," *Notes*, XLVIII (September 1991), pp. 140-141. Reprint permission granted by the author. The essay by B. Lee Cooper, titled "American Popular Music and the Myth of U.S. Military Morality," is scheduled to be published in *Journal of American Culture*. Reprint permission granted by the author, Managing Editor Pat Browne, and Bowling Green State University Popular Press.

*323*

ery, dissent, sentiment, reflection, and resignation. Beyond these diversities, the poems and songs sprang from lyricists of different national loyalties, different wartime involvements and different tongues. Murdoch skillfully translates hundreds of German and French compositions to accompany his numerous British and American illustrations. Being neither a militarist nor a pacificist, the academic author presents an objective overview of nearly 80 years of conflict-related lyrical commentary. On the negative side, Murdoch is too fastidious about his analytical neutrality, too repetitive in his translated lyrics, and far too traditional in his overemphasis on printed poetry instead of recorded popular songs. The study's central goal collapses under the verbose weight of a stodgy comparative literature review.

*Rhythm and Resistance* defines popular song as ". . . a collective dialog over popular identity and community purpose." (p. 213) Pratt moves from the nineteenth-century slavery era to the present in his argument that individual identity, freedom, and dignity are key factors in the lyrics of gospel, blues, jazz, country, folk, and rock music. The author rejects the proposition that popular refrains are functional tools of the elite class designed to instill correct behavior and proper respect for law and order. Instead Pratt views popular songs as emancipatory anthems that idealize, rationalize, and seek community support for increased freedom and well-being. Unlike Murdoch, Pratt is conversant with many of the foremost song-in-society theoreticians (R. Serge Denisoff, Simon Frith, Peter Guralnick, Paul Oliver, and Jerome Rodnitzky) and his thesis is reinforced by scholarship rather than burdened by it.

For the student seeking a model commentary linking song and social movement, *A Generation in Motion: Popular Music and Culture in the Sixties* by David Pichaske remains unparalleled. Pratt's study is superb, though he needs to move beyond Woody Guthrie and Bruce Springsteen to illustrate the diversity of freedom and individuality lauded by Otis Redding, Neil Young, Don Henley, Hank Williams Jr., and Paul Simon. Murdoch simply needs to listen to more Spike Jones ("Der Fuehrer's Face") and John Lennon ("Imagine") while reading knowledgeable essays on war songs by George W. Chilcoat, Hugo A. Keesing, Peter Hesbacher, and Les Waffen. Despite these injunctions, *Rhythm and Resistance* and *Fighting Songs and Warring Words* are still worthwhile reading for music historians, popular culture researchers, sociologists, and song nostalgia buffs. Both writers echo the haunting idea sung by Ray Charles: "That's why I'm so afraid of the progress that's being made . . . toward eternity."

# AMERICAN MILITARY EXPERIENCES
# IN THE TWENTIETH CENTURY

America's twentieth-century military adventures have been widely chronicled in print. However, wartime reveries are most frequently elicited through oral rather than literary resources. Popular songs, legacies of the commercial recording industry, Tin Pan Alley, ASCAP/BMI, and numerous singer/songwriters, are key items in understanding the public image of warfare in the United States. Since 1917 lyrics of war-related records have featured themes that have heartened troops, bolstered civilian morale, and defined a unique destiny for American society. The goal of national unity is unmistakable. Even so-called antiwar, pacifist, or protest songs allude to traditional ideals when challenging specific military involvement. The myth of military morality is conjured, circulated, and perpetuated in American popular music. Only by closely examining meanings of such image-driven militarism can the American public rationally decide whether the horrors of war are ever genuinely justified.

## Introductions

The United States is a military giant. American troops have seized naval bases in Mexico (1914), occupied Iceland and Greenland (1941), served as advisors in Greece (1947), led a United Nations police action in Korea (1950-1953), landed in the Dominican Republic (1965), halted an airfield expansion in Grenada (1983), participated in an international peace-keeping effort in Lebanon (1982-1984), bombed Libya (1986), and seized a dictator and drug czar in Panama (1989). The size, scope, and meaning of these military activities pale in comparison to the four major U.S. crusades of the twentieth century: World War I (1917-1918), World War II (1941-1945), the Vietnam War (1964-1973), and the Persian Gulf War (1991). Each of these four conflicts prompted a significant outpouring of popular songs. The lyrics of these war-related tunes contain key images and themes that capsule American values and beliefs about warfare. Even songs that dispute the need for immediate American involvement in overseas conflicts—those stressing isolationist sentiments, neutrality arguments, or pacificist contentions—are crafted around the same ideals that, ironically, are championed in promilitary tunes.

What are the most prominent, persistent themes in war-era songs? Ignoring contentious prewar debates and postwar frustrations over worldwide instability and personal dislocations, there are eleven central ideas that dominate the lyrics of war-related tunes. These themes are: (1) overt hostility toward international enemies, including ridiculing leaders, stereo-typing enemy nationalities, and belittling foreign soldiers as either sadists or cowards; (2) sympathy for conquered civilian populations and brave allied troops in occupied territories; (3) emphasis on long-term historical friendships between the United States, its military allies, and the invaded nations; (4) reinforcement of patriotic beliefs and emphasis on national symbols, previous military victories, and prior war heroes or national leaders; (5) support and admiration for U.S. soldiers, praise for their dedication and self-sacrifices, and grateful acknowledgment of their brav-ery and heroism; (6) empathy for loved ones—mothers, fathers, sweet-hearts, wives, and children—separated from U.S. soldiers; (7) confidence in U.S. leadership, with special praise for the wisdom of the President and for the courage of American generals; (8) support for the idealistic postwar goals of peace, prosperity, and the extension of democratic values abroad; (9) cynicism toward the articulated economic objectives and proposed post-war strategies of American politicians; (10) advocacy of resolving interna-tional disputes through nonmilitary strategies such as economic sanctions, political isolation, and the assertion of moral superiority; and (11) anger over the appearance of antiwar arguments expressed through allegations of cow-ardice, unpatriotic behavior, and giving aid and comfort to the enemy. These eleven themes are invariably intertwined in lyrics and cannot be viewed as singular or discrete commentaries.

Throughout the twentieth century, popular music has played a signifi-cant role in creating and reinforcing the myth of U.S. military morality. This highly subjective, ethnocentric perspective equates American involve-ment in international conflicts to religious crusades against infidels, to justifiable struggles against madmen, and to selfless sacrifices to advance the cause of worldwide human freedom. Very few song lyrics confront pragmatic issues such as balance of power politics, policies of economic strangulation, the threat of nuclear proliferation, key resource availability, geographical spheres of influence, and imperialistic expansion of political or economic control. By an unrelenting pursuit of theologically based patriotism, the music industry and its nationalistic troubadours undermine the debates that should characterize a democratic citizenry at war. Only during the lengthy Vietnam conflict did a significant number of antiwar sentiments emerge. Not surprisingly though, the artists' objections to Southeast Asian militarism were not grounded in rational assessments of real-world politics, but in the same kind of ethical and theological stances that fuel more common prowar lyrics.

The remainder of this study illustrates the wartime lyrical environments as generated through popular recordings between 1914 through 1991. The thematic structures outlined above are repeated time after time. The two world wars and the Persian Gulf War are amazingly consistent in promoting the U.S. military morality myth. Only the Vietnam War, and its mixed message aftermath, presented an opportunity for Americans to experience an audio forum of contrasting images and differing ideas. Rather than being a national embarrassment though, the music of the Vietnam era was actually the most open, democratic wartime debate of this century.

## Music as Public Memory

The American public has always envisioned international warfare through the hindsight of previous military conflicts. There are four distinct periods of wartime imagery in this century. The first spans 1914-1938 and is based upon experiences gained during the First World War; the second is 1939-1963 and includes events of the Second World War and the initial portion of the Cold War period; the third is 1964-1989 and involves the Vietnam War era; and the final frame is 1990-1991 and features the Persian Gulf War and its immediate aftermath.

This study examines the audio images of these four American war eras as featured on popular recordings. The lyrics reveal many of the assumptions that fuel public opinion about military policy. Commercially recorded commentaries both reflect and influence the perceptions of American society. Several persistent attitudes, topics, and themes are illustrated in war-related songs. Hindsight-driven international perspectives manifested in lyrics constitute a strange reversal of George Santayana's warning about remembering the past. Without a forward-thinking viewpoint, a reasoned and pragmatic sense of the present, and an open perspective on the future, a democratic society is threatened by citizen gridlock on foreign policy issues. More importantly, the President, U.S. Congress, and the State Department can also succumb to war imagery myths with even more drastic possibilities for mismanagement of America's vast military power.

Conventional wisdom asserts that while the American people may disagree about the specific reasons for becoming involved in a particular military conflict, bipartisan popular support will unite behind any U.S. war effort. This assumption is a subset of the notion that all foreign policy is conducted on a politically nonpartisan basis. Neither proposition is historically valid. Prior to the twentieth century, Americans quarreled, complained, and even killed each other during the Revolutionary War, the War of 1812, the Mexican War, the Civil War, and the Spanish-American War. Little changed after 1900. Woodrow Wilson hoped to make the world safe for democracy after 1917, but he encountered dramatic opposition from a hostile Senate when he brought his worldwide peace plan home. Franklin

Roosevelt benefited from Japan's 1941 sneak attack on Pearl Harbor and Germany's maniacal leader in amassing public support for involvement in World War II, but pacificists still campaigned throughout the conflict for an immediate end to hostilities. Lyndon Johnson and Richard Nixon both encountered fierce opposition to their ever-expanding southeast Asian military adventures. Even George Bush's quick, clinical annihilation of Iraq's huge conventional military machine during the Persian Gulf War was firmly opposed by many domestic peace groups.

Reality is seldom congruent with popular opinion. Short-term memory feeds public imagery. The function of contemporary songs as image sources about specific wars in the modern era has been explored in several studies. However, the idea that songs both reflect and influence postwar attitudes toward military conflict is rarely investigated or discussed. The following pages present a series of illustrations depicting the lengthy shadows of war-related recordings. This study was launched with three general assumptions in mind. First, with the significant exception of the Vietnam War, popular songs have functioned to support American military policies throughout the twentieth century. Second, postwar feelings about the validity of previous military involvements have been reinforced through the repetition of popular wartime tunes. Finally, American public opinion is much more susceptible to popular culture imagery about wars than to critical historical analysis, scholarly reinterpretations, or rapidly changing world conditions.

## FOUR WAR SONG ERAS

Music is a weapon in all wars, used to bolster morale or heap scorn on an enemy . . . .

–Robin Denselow,
*When the Music's Over: The Story of Political Pop* (1989)

The experience of war is staggering. The outbreak of hostilities invariably heightens the tensions that preceded the onset of military activities. Warfare itself psychologically batters solders, politicians, and civilian populations alike. The eventual cease-fire leaves victors and vanquished dissatisfied, while peace negotiations and postwar power realignments are invariably less than acceptable to the warring parties. Twentieth-century America has survived four war eras. These are World War I (1914-1938), World War II (1939-1963), the Vietnam War (1964-1989) and the Persian Gulf War (1990-1991). Generations that experience war eras also experience many, many war-related songs. The perspectives on these conflicts (outlined below) and the results interpreted in lyrics carry forward and influence future military images.

## Perspectives on Four War Eras in U.S. History
### 1914-1991

| Wars Eras | Prewar Perspectives | Wartime Perspectives | Postwar Perspectives |
|---|---|---|---|
| World War I (1914-1938) | isolationism<br>fear of European alliance<br>anger about economic blockades and submarine warfare<br>"Peace without Victory" sought | making the world safe for democracy<br>fight the war to end all wars<br>halt trade interference by European powers | patriotic nationalism<br>no foreign entanglements<br>"No" to League of Nations<br>return to normalcy sought |
| World War II (1939-1963) | neutrality<br>arsenal for democracy<br>fear of expansionism by Germany, Italy, and Japan | outrage at Japan's attack on Pearl Harbor<br>desire to conquer dictators in Germany, Italy, and Japan | "American Century" proclaimed<br>Marshall Plan<br>"Yes" to United Nations<br>Cold War and Iron Curtain<br>nuclear vulnerability<br>political cynicism<br>doubt about military superiority |
| Vietnam War (1964-1989) | fear of "domino effect" in Southeast Asia triggered by Hanoi's conquest of the Saigon regime | easy domination of Third World nation by naval support and air strikes<br>halt spread of Communism | political cynicism<br>doubt about military superiority |
| Persian Gulf War (1990-1991) | fear of Iraqi military domination of Arab states<br>concern about oil supply<br>invasion of Kuwait<br>fear of Iraqi nuclear ability | Crush Saddam Hussein's regime and restore Kuwaiti rulers<br>pinpoint bombing raids and blitzkrieg ground victory<br>heightened U.N. involvement/leadership<br>economic sanctions too slow | euphoria of quick victory<br>emerging New World Order<br>potential Arab/Israeli peace<br>praise for military |

World War I music heightened American nationalism, strengthened concern for civilians in Belgium, England, and France, increased the feeling of moral superiority toward European politicos, and created the belief that America had "saved" Europe. The music of the 1914-1938 period reinforced unity, patriotism, and confidence in the United States. World War II-era songs continued this trend. However, the postwar period became much more complicated. Expansion of atomic technology, reconstruction of Western Europe and Japan, the U.N. police action in Korea, McCarthyism, the Suez Crisis, the Cuban Missile Crisis, and numerous international incidents attributed to the machinations of a worldwide communist conspiracy created a domestic climate of unrest and insecurity. The Vietnam War era emerged in conflict, with music reflecting the disunity, uncertainty, complexity, and limited options of even a nuclear superpower. The music of the southeast Asian conflict was contentious and the postwar years featured a continuation of the dual perspectives of power and impotence, security and danger, and isolationistic patriotism and international humanitarianism. The Persian Gulf War, with its military brevity and patriotic zeal, found a new lyrical unity. The question that remains unanswered is whether the newest postwar period will continue the Vietnam disunity trend or mark a return to the heightened American nationalism and patriotic accord of earlier eras.

### World War I-Era Songs

> War songs as examples of propaganda have traditionally performed one dominant function: to create a sense (maybe an illusion) of unity and shared purpose. . . . Reviewing the songs of the Great War, one would hardly suspect that there was anything but the most whole-hearted acceptance of American involvement. And this is as it should be. The Tin Pan Alley songsmith's job was to communicate that sense of unity. The songs do not tell us that the country was divided on the issue of war. . . .
>
> –Timothy E. Scheurer,
> *Born in the U.S.A.* (1991)

The popular songs of the First World War were overwhelmingly patriotic, upbeat, and supportive of American soldiers. Sympathy for Great Britain and France, encouragement for President Woodrow Wilson, and commitment to defeating Germany and its allies was communicated in tunes such as "Lafayette (We Hear You Calling)," "Somewhere in France Is Daddy," and "I Think We've Got Another Washington (Wilson Is His Name)." The 1915 lament "I Didn't Raise My Boy to Be a Soldier" was overwhelmed by new patriotic lyrics. These tunes included "Let's All Be Good Americans Now," "Over There" (with five different hit versions during 1917 and 1918), and "Just Like Washington Crossed the Delaware, General Pershing Will Cross the Rhine." Emotion-rousing tributes to the flag and to national honor such as "The Battle Hymn of the Republic,"

"The Star-Spangled Banner," "The Stars and Stripes Forever March," and "You're a Grand Old Flag" also registered significant popular attention.

Positive perspectives of military service–duty, loyalty, and commitment–were echoed in songs aimed at soldiers, parents, and sweethearts. Service obligations were acknowledged in "America, Here's My Boy," "(Goodbye, and Luck Be with You) Laddie Boy," "Pack Up Your Troubles in Your Old Kit Bag and Smile, Smile, Smile," and "Send Me Away with a Smile." The sense of straightening out someone else's overseas problems was clearly communicated in "The Yanks Are At It Again." Homefront reactions to the dangers being faced by those loved ones who march off to Europe were contained in "Bring Back My Soldier Boy to Me," "God Be with Our Boys Tonight," and "Say a Prayer for the Boys Out There." Lyrical comments attributed to American troops were predictable: "I'm Gonna Pin My Medal on the Girl I Left Behind," "Life in a Trench in Belgium," and "Keep the Home Fires Burning." Humor was not overlooked, either. The GI viewpoint was delivered in "Oh, How I Hate to Get Up in the Morning" and "Would You Rather Be a Colonel with an Eagle on Your Shoulder or a Private with a Chicken on Your Knee."

The conclusion of the Great War provided lyrical reflection time. The European experience, particularly for young American servicemen in France, was heralded in several popular tunes: "Au Revoir But Not Goodbye, Soldier Boy," "Goodbye, France," "How Ya Gonna Keep 'Em Down on the Farm (After They've Seen Paree)," and "When Yankee Doodle Learns to Parlez Vous Francais." The humor of exchanging military ranks for civilian business roles was featured in the popular postwar tune "I've Got My Captain Working for Me Now."

The popular music of World War I was totally divorced from domestic political reality in the United States between 1914 and 1920. No references are made to the isolationist position or to fears of entangling alliances with any European powers. Neutrality was cherished. Woodrow Wilson's "He Kept Us Out of War" presidential campaign slogan swept him back into the White House in 1916. Songs do not reflect public reactions to the sinking of the British steamship Lusitania (1915), to the Zimmermann telegram (1917), or to any specific military events on the Continent. After the declaration of war by the U.S. Congress on April 6, 1917, American music was motivated by patriotic tradition, British propaganda about the heartless Huns, and the rules of political commentary dictated by George Creel's Committee on Public Information. The dream of a war to end all wars was given voice in U.S. popular recordings. When the Treaty of Versailles was defeated in the Senate in 1919, American music immediately switched from military themes to the romantic, dance-oriented sounds of the Jazz Age without missing a beat. With the exceptions of The Victor Symphony Orchestra's "Patriotic March Medley" (1929) and Jimmie Rodger's "The Soldier's Sweetheart" (1927), the interwar years were lyrically silent on the subject of warfare.

## World War II-Era Songs

The Second World War was a watershed period in British broadcasting, the requirements of the war effort prompting a fundamental re-evaluation of the purposes, functions, and applications of public radio service. It was a period in which the ideological uses of entertainment–its uses in binding people together in a common cause, its identification with and portrayal of national values, however contrived or self-regarding–were appreciated in very direct ways, and one that marked a distinct break with the principle of mixed programming and of catering for different interests and tastes within the context of one national network. As regards the broadcasting of popular music, the war years ushered in an era of greater reliance on gramophone records and considerably greater American domination of the music field as a whole.

–Stephen Barnard
*On the Radio: Music Radio in Britain* (1989)

The Good War. So we sum up the popular mythology centering around World War II. And so it seems it was–as wars go. There was a feeling of unity in the country. People's energies were focused again, business was humming, and the Depression was snapped. This is not to say there was not initial revulsion at the idea of another war.

–Timothy E. Scheurer
*Born in the U.S.A.* (1991)

As might be expected, both the singers and the songs of World War II differed from those of The Great War. Arthur Fields, John McCormack, Nora Bayes, Billy Murray, and Harry MacDonough yielded their wartime record chart positions to Glenn Miller, The Andrews Sisters, Spike Jones, Johnny Mercer, Kate Smith, Kay Kyser, Dinah Shore, and Harry James. Although most titles and lyrics were new, popular songs still served as domestic reinforcements for the overseas war effort. Both Germany and Japan were openly ridiculed in tunes such as "Der Fuehrer's Face," "Mussolini's Letter to Hitler," and "You're a Sap, Mr. Jap." Patriotism, military proficiency, and traditional American values were honored in songs such as "God Bless America," "Remember Pearl Harbor," "There's a Star-Spangled Banner Waving Somewhere," and "Yankee Doodle Boy." The Air Force was particularly lauded in "Comin' in on a Wing and a Prayer" and "He Wears a Pair of Silver Wings"; the U.S. Army was depicted in more realistic terms in "(Lights Out) 'Til Reveille," "Praise the Lord and Pass the Ammunition," and "This Is the Army, Mr. Jones."

Soldiers remained the central figures in American popular songs. The inconvenience and anxiety of the military draft system and the minimal pay received by U.S. troops were satirized in "Goodbye Dear, I'll Be Back in a Year" and "Twenty-One Dollars a Day–Once a Month." While fighting for the time when "(There'll Be Bluebirds Over) The White Cliffs of Dover," a few enlisted men found romance overseas. The most popular song illustrating this situation was "Johnny Doughboy Found a Rose in Ireland." Musical salutes to "The Boogie Woogie Bugle Boy" were far outnumbered by the sentimental feelings deploring lengthy separations from loved ones back home. Dispatched to military theaters in Africa, Italy, the South Pacific, and Western Europe, American soldiers were lyrically reminded "We Did It Before (and We Can Do It Again)" and that international peace and prosperity would be rekindled "When the Lights Go on Again (All Over the World)." However, the personal goals of fighting men and their sweethearts were more accurately captured in deeply sentimental songs such as "Cleanin' My Rifle (and Dreamin' of You)," "I'll Get By (As Long as I Have You)," and "It's Been a Long, Long Time."

Clearly, the Japanese attack on Pearl Harbor on December 7, 1941 was the galvanizing event for the American war effort. But popular music ignored the political debates prior to 1941 over isolationism, neutrality, and destroyers-for-bases deals with Great Britain, as well as the numerous peace campaigns launched by various groups. After the declaration of war, lyrics remained silent on the Nisei relocation issue, on government-enforced infringements on freedom of speech and civil rights, and even on the atomic blasts over Hiroshima and Nagasaki. Only after Hitler was defeated and Japan was occupied did singers begin to reckon with the irreversible change that victory had wrought in American life.

Between 1946 and 1964 an ever-so-slow evolution occurred in American popular song commentaries about warfare. References to worldwide annihilation appeared in a few country, blues, and R&B tunes. Bill Haley's "Thirteen Women" and Ray Charles' "The Danger Zone" illustrated this trend. But previous military involvements were heralded in "Ballad of the Alamo," "The Battle of New Orleans," "P.T. 109," and "Sink the Bismarck." Patriotic tunes continued to be charted–"Battle Hymn of the

Republic," "God Bless America," and "Stars and Stripes Forever"–along with a variety of military draft melodies–"The All-American Boy," "God, Country, and My Baby," and "Greetings (This Is Uncle Sam)." The recordings that most clearly signaled the dawning of a new age of popular music commentary were charted by a few popular folk artists. These tunes were: "Blowin' in the Wind," "If I Had a Hammer," and "Where Have All the Flowers Gone?". Nuclear proliferation, the McCarthy era, the Cold War and containment policies, and the civil rights struggle of the 1950s provided the historical and social background for America's impending southeast Asian involvement.

### Vietnam War-Era Songs

> In spite of the horrors of the atomic bomb and the Holocaust, Americans emerged from World War II much as they had from World War I–confident and eager to return to normal lives full of hope in the face of future anxiety.... [Many American people].... went into Vietnam with convictions that were shaped by the mythology of World War II.
>
> –Timothy E. Scheurer,
> *Born in the U.S.A.* (1991)

> It should perhaps be stressed that the Vietnam War was won by the Vietcong and the North Vietnamese, not by pop music, but music played an important role in helping to reflect and reinforce the anti-war mood in the U.S.A.
>
> –Robin Denselow,
> *When the Music's Over: The Story of Political Pop* (1989)

Songs related to the Vietnam War were more numerous, more complex, more divisive, and more politically oriented than those charted during either previous world war. This variety did not exclude tunes that championed traditional American ideals, lauded nationalism and patriotism, praised brave soldiers, and alluded joyfully to earlier military successes. These sentiments were spoken and sung in "The Americans (A Canadian's Opinion)," "The Ballad of the Green Berets," "Battle Hymn of the Republic," "Gallant Men," "Okie from Muskogee," "Pledge of Allegiance," and "Stout-Hearted Men." Yet even in the reinterpretations of traditional songs such as "Seven O'Clock News/Silent Night" and "The Star-Spangled Banner," it was clear that the times were a-changing. Confusion and argumentation thrived in popular lyrics; unrest and agitation swept the radio airwaves; unanswered questions spawned greater and greater lyrical hostility toward military activities. Songs of uncertainty included "America, Communicate with Me," "Ball of Confusion (That's What the World Is Today)," "Eve of Destruction," "Fortunate Son," "For What It's Worth (Stop, Hey What's That Sound)," "2 + 2 = ?," "What's Going On," and "Who Will Answer?"

Images of soldiers also became much more complex. As always, the military draft led to unwanted separations from domestic life. However, the risk of life and limb in the jungles of Southeast Asia lacked the glamour or the sense of patriotic sacrifice for European homelands that was necessary to sustain domestic popular support. Songs frequently reflected this fact. Lyrics both fearful and satirical were presented in "Billy, Don't Be a Hero, "Dear Uncle Sam," "The Draft Dodger Rag," "I Feel-Like-I'm-Fixin'-To-Die Rag" and "Where Have All the Flowers Gone." Battlefield deaths, the horrors of war, and unwarranted profiteering of munitions dealers gained lyrical attention in "Battle Hymn of Lt. Calley," "Billy and Sue," "I Ain't Marching Anymore," "Masters of War," "Military Madness," "The Universal Soldier," and "The Unknown Soldier." Youthful cynicism and anger echoed in "War" and "Won't Get Fooled Again." In this context, it is understandable why so many songs of peace emerged. Lyrics of pacifist tunes tended to ignore the complexities of negotiated settlements, national goals, disputed boundaries, and political objectives in favor of the immediate cessation of hostilities and the need for worldwide humanitarian healing. Songs of this genre included "Give Peace a Chance," "Imagine," "Lay Down (Candles in the Rain)," "Stop the War Now," and "We Got to Have Peace."

From the French military defeat at Dien Bien Phu in 1954 until the Gulf of Tonkin Incident ten years later, the American government had encountered no popular music criticism related to its Southeast Asian policies. Yet the dimensions of lyrical commentary throughout the long and bloody Vietnam conflict were dramatic and detailed. From selective service practices to the My Lai massacre, no topic seemed to escape the composer's pen or the troubadour's tongue. The gentle early 1960s folk criticism by The Kingston Trio and Peter, Paul, and Mary escalated into full-throated screams for the warring to end from Barry McGuire, Bob Dylan, John Fogerty, Phil Ochs, Edwin Starr, and Neil Young.

The period from the end of the Vietnam War until the Iraqi invasion of Kuwait was unlike any other postwar period in the twentieth century. The war of words continued. Song lyrics perpetuated the debate about the validity of war as a means of achieving political, economic, or any idealistic ends. America was not being torn apart by unpatriotic malcontents who happened to be musicians. The public simply continued to resonate to the issues being discussed in vinyl grooves, on cassette tapes and on compact discs. The Vietnam debate continued to rage after the Vietnam War. A few examples of songs from the interwar period are: "Born in the U.S.A.," "Goodnight Saigon," "In America," "Still in Saigon," "Used to Be," "War," and "War Games."

## Persian Gulf War-Era Songs

> No nation can survive without a myth; no nation profits from holding onto a myth that cannot plausibly include recent historical experience. The respective result can only be a cynical realism or a self-deluding fantasy.
>
> —John Hellman
> *American Myth and the Legacy of Vietnam* (1986)

> The war had greater power as a cultural event than a political one. Waiters automatically offer tabasco sauce, which all soldiers seem to relish, at favored military hangouts. Many Saudis are indulging their newfound taste for country-and-western music, developed after listening to Armed Forces Radio, and those illegal satellite dishes now tune in to Israeli TV–despite public warnings that the Israeli Secret Service is trying to corrupt Saudi society over the airwaves.
>
> —Ray Wilkinson
> *"One Year Later," Newsweek* (1991)

Although military and diplomatic preparations for the attacks on Kuwait and Iraq extended over several months, the Persian Gulf War itself was measured in days of saturation bombing and hours of successful land-force operations. Thus, the popular songs related to this conflict were derivative rather than original. That is, images or ideas contained in earlier hit songs were adapted to the Saudi Arabian launching site of Operation Desert Storm. Patriotic fervor was fanned through songs such as "The Star-Spangled Banner" and "God Bless the U.S.A."; support for American soldiers was echoed in "Somewhere Out There" and "Wind Beneath My Wings"; personal dedications from wives and sweethearts were delivered as voice-overs on "From a Distance"; and the homefront support for returning servicemen was articulated in the 1973 chestnut "Tie a Yellow Ribbon 'Round the Ole Oak Tree." Disc jockeys reinforced the use of oldies either to depict or to interpret Gulf area military activities. "Rock the Casbah" was played as a warning to those dwelling in Baghdad about imminent U.S. bombing raids; "Welcome to the Jungle" was dedicated from Uncle Sam's troops to the Iraqi Army; "Another One Bites the Dust" was played to honor the U.S. soldiers operating Patriot Anti-Missile Batteries (so-called "Scudbusters"); and, in the war's frenzied aftermath, "Catch Us if You Can" was the song used to describe the frantic flight of Iraqi Republican Guard units.

For the brief premilitary period when international economic sanctions were being utilized in an attempt to force Saddam Hussein to relinquish his military control of Kuwait, a musicians' collaboration performance version of "Give Peace a Chance" was somewhat popular. However, as American policy shifted from the Desert Shield of defense to the Desert Storm of offense, such pacifist tunes virtually disappeared from the charts. The massive air strikes that defined the initial phase of Operation Desert Storm and the blitzkrieg land invasion and speedy victory produced public euphoria in the United States. General Norman Schwarzkopf was an instant hero. So were his troops. Celebrity Choir Messages were delivered in "Voices That Care." A variety of patriotic songs, very few that attained *Billboard* chart listing, praised the valor of troops, condemned the stupidity of Saddam Hussein, and promised heroic welcomes for returning U.S. soldiers. These songs included: "American Kid in Arabian Sand," "The Ballad of Saddam Hussein," "The Beast in the Middle East," "Desert Storm," "The Flags Fly High," "Iraq Is Robbin'," "K-K-Kuwaitis," "Letter to Saddam Hussein (You Must Be Insane)," "Proud to Be an American for Freedom," "A Symbol in the Storm," "These Colors Never Run," "Welcome Home Soldier," "When Johnny Comes Marchin' Home Again," and "Who'll Put a Bomb on Saddam Saddam Saddam."

President George Bush was quick to proclaim that the shadow of the Vietnam War had finally been lifted and that a New World Order of international solidarity had commenced. Clearly, the Republican President heard little from popular music realms to contradict his preliminary conclusions. Middle East concerns voiced in earlier American song lyrics were related to oil and hostages—"The Crude Oil Blues," "Get That Gasoline Blues," "A Message to Khomeini," and "Bomb Iran." All tunes that were played concerning the Persian Gulf, though, lauded Bush's diplomacy, praised U.S. military planning and execution, and promised love, honor, and domestic tranquility to returning U.S. troops. Even such potentially embarrassing actions as playing such old pop tunes as "Ahab the Arab," "The Sheik of Araby," or "Midnight at the Oasis" over military radio stations in Saudi Arabia had apparently been avoided.

The future of post-Gulf War music remains a question mark. If President Bush's fondest wish is fulfilled, popular music will continue its uniformly patriotic stance. Lyricists and performers will forget Saigon, will ignore Baghdad, and will adopt only heroic themes when they comment on all aspects of U.S. military activity. However, another track of behavior may emerge. The failure to establish a fully acceptable peace in the Middle East might spark a new era of lyrical debate. Will Kuwait become a more democratic state? Will Saddam Hussein remain the dictator in Iraq? Will the Kurds be safe? Can Israel be successfully integrated into the body politic of the Middle East to signal a genuinely New World Order? Can the United States expect an uninterrupted flow of crude oil from its former Persian Gulf wartime partners?

## Themes in War-Related Popular U.S. Songs 1917-1991

| Theme | World War I | World War II | Vietnam War | Persian Gulf War |
|---|---|---|---|---|
| 1. Overt hostility toward international enemies | yes | yes | yes | yes |
| 2. Sympathy toward conquered civilian populations | yes | yes | no | yes |
| 3. Emphasis on long-term historical associations or friendships | yes | yes | no | no |
| 4. Reinforcement of patriotic beliefs and traditional national symbols | yes | yes | yes | yes |
| 5. Support and admiration for U.S. troops | yes | yes | yes | yes |
| 6. Empathy for loved ones separated from American soldiers | yes | yes | yes | yes |
| 7. Confidence in U.S. political and military leadership | yes | yes | yes | yes |
| 8. Support for the idealistic postwar goals of world peace and prosperity | yes | yes | yes | yes |

| Theme | World War I | World War II | Vietnam War | Persian Gulf War |
|-------|-------------|--------------|-------------|------------------|
| 9. Cynicism toward and criticism of stated political objectives and publicized military strategies | no | no | yes | no |
| 10. Advocacy of resolving international disputes through nonmilitary strategies | no | no | yes | no |
| 11. Anger over antiwar arguments | no | no | yes | yes |

## *Preliminary Conclusions*

> Some would say that myth does nothing but feed fantasies and distort reality, but the crucial point about myth is that it provides a greater reality.

—Timothy E. Scheurer
*Born in the U.S.A.* (1991)

> Some generation of mankind was eventually bound to face the task of abolishing war, because civilization was bound to endow us sooner or later with the power to destroy ourselves. We happen to be that generation, though we did not ask for the honor and do not feel ready for it. There is nobody wiser who will take the responsibility and solve this problem for us. We have to do it ourselves.

—Gwynne Dyer
*War* (1985)

During four major military conflicts of the twentieth century, popular music played a role designed to reinforce patriotism at home and among U.S. troops abroad. In three of these conflicts—World War I, World War II, and the Persian Gulf War—there was little if any lyrical debate about the validity of general military goals, about the propriety of wartime strategy, or about the honor and dignity of all Americans involved in battle field activities. The Vietnam War is an anomaly in this situation. From the inception of the conflict, antiwar lyrics burst forth with the same prominence as prowar tunes. During the postwar periods following the two World Wars, popular music tended to downplay military themes. However, the 1946-1963 period featured a greater trend toward examining war-related phenomena than the 1919-1938 period had. Once again, the period following the Southeast Asian conflict was a hotbed of debate and conflict about military life, American foreign policy, the results of warfare, and the domestic implications of pursuing military conquests in foreign lands. The postwar lyrical climate of the Persian Gulf conflict has yet to emerge. It would seem unlikely that a civilian population that had become accustomed to lyrical debate concerning military activity would define the coming years as free if single-minded super patriotism dominated the airwaves. The final lyrical interpretations of Operation Desert Storm have yet to be delivered by Bruce Springsteen, Midnight Oil, U2, Stevie Wonder, Don Henley, John Fogerty, Merle Haggard, Bruce Hornsby, and others who sing with the courage of their convictions.

## *Coda*

Establishing the morality of military activity in a democratic society is contingent upon public acceptance of numerous "just cause" arguments. Lyrics of American popular songs furnish such arguments in very broad strokes. The propaganda value of oft-repeated tunes understandably exceeds the influence of singular political speeches, newspaper editorials, and magazine articles. Of course, the complexity of international relations is unrealistically simplified—if not ignored—in favor of perpetuating traditional themes that cast U.S. military action as a moral necessity, an ethical obligation, or an historical inevitability. Honor demands human sacrifice. Freedom requires military defense. Lyrics make warfare morally palatable. The flag, historical allies, national honor, democratic values, traditions of loyal service, and images of future peace and prosperity demand continuing American involvement in the bloodiest of human enterprises.

The role of antiwar songs in America's myth-making system for justifying warfare is unique. From the end of the Second World War in 1945 to the outbreak of the precision bombing raids over Iraq and Kuwait in 1991, a few singers have "worried" aloud about nuclear annihilation ("The Danger Zone"), potential superpower confrontations, deaths of countless soldiers without positive resolution of either conflicts or tensions, international racism and imperialism ("Undercover of the Night"), and political leaders ("Won't Get Fooled Again") or weapons dealers ("Masters of War"). Yet the most concerned musicians—John Lennon, Ray Charles, Peter, Paul, and Mary, Barry McGuire, Bob Dylan, John Fogerty, and others—invariably communicate their lyrical messages ("Give Peace a Chance," "Blowin' in the Wind," and "Eve of Destruction") in myth-shrouded imagery. They tout ideals of peace, brotherhood, democracy, justice, equality, freedom, and other fundamental American virtues. Not surprisingly, prowar and antiwar songs preach the same national mythology. The fact that complicated, messy reality rarely coincides with these simple images—just as urban life in the Bronx contrasts sharply with the images proclaimed in "America the Beautiful"—tend to reinforce the theoretical morality of war. Fighting to sustain or secure universal ideals is invigorating to a democratic populace; arguing in favor of neutrality, economic sanctions, isolationism, humanitarianism, or other heavy philosophical imperatives promotes only minimal enthusiasm. Medals, parades, and the roar of canons overwhelm carefully phrased antiwar anthems. Few democratic politicians choose to openly attack those singers and songwriters who challenge the U.S. military morality myth. Instead, they wisely praise the freedom of speech principle that permits vinyl voicing of "unpopular," "illogical," or even "unwise" positions. Popular music is thus easily defused as a source of genuinely radical thought. Tradition is much more readily served by song lyrics. Military myths are especially precious to generations of veterans. The influence of popular songs on public perceptions of war is an issue worthy of further investigation.

## REFERENCES

Adams, Michael C. C. *The Best War Ever: America and World War II*. Baltimore, Maryland: Johns Hopkins University Press, 1994.

Auslander, Ben H. "If Ya Wanna End War and Stuff, You Gotta Sing Loud: A Survey of Vietnam-Related Protest Music," *Journal of American Culture*, IV (Summer 1981), pp. 108-113.

Bindas, Kenneth J. and Craig Houston. "Takin' Care of Business: Rock Music, Vietnam, and the Protest Myth," *The Historian*, LII (November, 1989), pp. 1-23.

Bolger, Daniel P. *Americans At War, 1975-1986: An Era of Violent Peace*. Novato, California: Presidio Press, 1988.

Bowman, Kent. "Echoes of Shot and Shell: Songs of the Great War," *Studies in Popular Culture*, X (Winter 1987), pp. 27-41.

Boyer, Paul. *By the Bomb's Early Light: American Thought and Culture at the Dawn of the Atomic Age*. New York: Pantheon Books, 1985.

Brown, Sheldon. "The Depression and World War II as Seen Through Country Music," *Social Education*, XLIX (October 1985), pp. 588-594.

Cawelti, John. *Adventure, Mystery, Romance: Formula Stories as Art and Popular Culture*. Chicago: University of Chicago Press, 1976.

Chilcoat, George W. "The Images of Vietnam: A Popular Musical Approach," *Social Education*, XLIX (October 1985), pp. 601-603.

Chinn, Jennie A. "There's a Star-Spangled Banner Waving Somewhere: Country-Western Songs of World War II," *JEMF Quarterly*, XVI (Summer 1980), pp. 74-80.

Cleveland, Les. *Dark Laughter: War in Song and Popular Culture*. Westport, Connecticut: Praeger Books, 1994.

Cooper, B. Lee. "Examining the Audio Images of War: Lyrical Perspectives on America's Major Military Crusades, 1914-1991," *International Journal of Instructional Media*, XIX, No. 3 (1992), pp. 277-287.

Cooper, B. Lee. "I'll Fight for God, Country, and My Baby: Persistent Themes in American Wartime Songs," *Popular Music and Society*, XVI (Summer 1992), pp. 95-111.

Cooper, B. Lee. *Images of American Society in Popular Music: A Guide to Reflective Teaching*. Chicago: Nelson-Hall, Inc., 1982.

Cooper, B. Lee. "Military Conflicts," in *A Resource Guide to Themes in Contemporary American Song Lyrics, 1950-1985* (Westport, Connecticut: Greenwood Press, 1986), pp. 101-109.

Cooper, B. Lee. *Popular Music Perspectives: Ideas, Themes, and Patterns in Contemporary Lyrics*. Bowling Green, Ohio: Bowling Green State University Popular Press, 1991.

Cooper, B. Lee. "Popular Song, Military Conflicts, and Public Perceptions of the United States at War," *Social Education*, LVI (March 1992), p. 160-168.

Cooper, B. Lee. "The Record(s) of America at War, 1941-1991: An Audio Perspective" (Mimeographed paper presented at the Annual Conference of the Midwest Popular Culture Association in Cleveland, Ohio on October 1, 1991), pp. 1-13.

Cooper, B. Lee. "Review of *Fighting Songs and Warring Words: Popular Lyrics of Two World Wars* by Brian Murdoch and *Rhythm and Resistance: Exploration in the Political Uses of Popular Music* by Ray Pratt," *Notes*, XLVIII (September 1991), pp. 140-141.

Cooper, B. Lee. "Rumors of War: Lyrical Continuities, 1914-1991," in *Continuities of Popular Culture*, edited by Ray B. Browne and Ronald J. Ambrosetti (Bowling Green, Ohio: Bowling Green State University Popular Press, 1993), pp. 121-142.

Cooper, B. Lee. "Tapping a Sound Recording Archive for War Song Resources to Investigate America's Major Military Involvements, 1914-1991," *Popular Culture in Libraries*, I, No. 4 (1993), pp. 71-93.

Denisoff, R. Serge. "Fighting Prophecy with Naplam: 'The Ballad of the Green Berets,'" *Journal of American Culture*, XIII (Spring 1990), pp. 81-93.

Denisoff, R. Serge. *Sing a Song of Social Significance* (second edition). Bowling Green, Ohio: Bowling Green State University Popular Press, 1983.

Denisoff, R. Serge. *Songs of Protest, War, and Peace: A Bibliography and Discography*. Santa Barbara, California: American Bibliographical Center and Clio Press, Inc., 1973.

Denisoff, R. Serge and William D. Romanowski. "Gooooood Morning, Vietnam!" in *Risky Business: Rock in Film* (New Brunswick, New Jersey: Transaction Books, 1991), pp. 605-651.

Denselow, Robin. *When the Music's Over:The Story of Political Pop*. London: Faber and Faber, 1990.

Dittmar, Linda and Gene Michaud. *From Hanoi to Hollywood: The Vietnam War in American Film*. New Brunswick, New Jersey: Rutgers University Press, 1990.

Doherty, Thomas. *Projections of War: Hollywood, American Culture, and World War II*. New York: Columbia University Press, Gwynne Dyer, *War*. New York: Crown Publishers, 1985.

Ellison, Mary. "War–It's Nothing But a Heartbreak: Attitudes to War in Black Lyrics," *Popular Music and Society*, X (Fall 1986), pp. 29-42.

Elshtain, Jean B. *Women and War*. New York: Basic Books, 1987.

Geltman, Max. "The Hot Hundred: A Surprise," *National Review*, XVIII (September 6, 1966), pp. 894-896.

Girgus, Sam. *The American Self: Myth, Popular Culture, and the American Ideology*. Albuquerque, New Mexico: University of New Mexico Press, 1980.

Graff, Gary. "War Likely to Make Music, But Not Like That of the '60s," *The Detroit Free Press* (February 3, 1991), pp. 1G, 4G.

Hellmann, John. *American Myth and the Legacy of Vietnam*. New York: Columbia University Press, 1986.

Hesbacher, Peter. "War Recordings: Incidence and Change, 1940-1980," *Popular Music and Society*, VIII (Summer/Fall 1982), pp. 177-101.

Hibbard, Don J. and Carol Kaleialoha. "Anti-War Songs," in *The R & B Rock: A Guide to the Social and Political Consequences of Rock Music* (Englewood Cliffs, New Jersey: Prentice-Hall, Inc., 1983), pp. 55-60.

Holsinger, M. Paul and Mary Anne Schofield (eds.). *Visions of War: World War II in Popular Literature and Culture*. Bowling Green, Ohio: Bowling Green State University Popular Press, 1992.

"It's Time for the Americans!" *Rhythm and News*, I (March), p. 3.

Jasen, David A. "The Alley Goes to War (1940-1949)," in *Tin Pan Alley–The Composers, the Songs, the Performers, and Their Times: The Golden Age of American Popular Music from 1886 to 1956* (New York: Donald I. Fine, 1988), pp. 246-278.

Keesing, Hugo A. "Pop Goes to War: The Music of World II and Vietnam" (Mimeographed paper presented in April 1979 at the 9th Annual Convention of the Popular Culture Association), pp. 1-8.

Keesing, Hugo A. "Recorded Music and the Vietnam War: The First 25 Years" (Mimeographed paper presented in March 1987 at the 17th Annual Convention of the Popular Culture Association), pp. 1-10.

Landon, Philip J. "From Cowboy to Organization Man: The Hollywood War Hero, 1940-1955," *Studies in Popular Culture*, XII (Winter 1989), pp. 28-41.

Lees, Gene. "1918-1986: From Over There to Kill for Peace," *High Fidelity*, XVIII (November 1968), pp. 56-60.

Lees, Gene. "War Songs: Bathos and Acquiescence," *High Fidelity*, XXVIII (December 1978), pp. 41-44.

Lees, Gene. "War Songs II: Music Goes AWOL," *High Fidelity*, XXIX (January 1979), pp. 20-22.

Lello, John. "Using Popular Songs of the Two World Wars in High School History," *The History Teacher*, XIV (November 1980), pp. 37-41.

Limeberry, John. "Did America View 'From a Distance' from a Distance?: An Overview of Culture and Popular Music from Vietnam to the Persian Gulf," *Popular Music and Society*, XVI (Fall 1992), pp. 75-87.

Lipsitz, George. *Time Passages: Collectives Memory and American Popular Culture*. Minneapolis, Minnesota: University of Minnesota Press, 1990.

Lund, Jens. "Country Music Goes to War: Songs for the Red-Blooded American," *Popular Music and Society*, I (Summer 1972), pp. 210-230.

Marsh, Dave. "Life During Wartime," *Rock and Roll Confidential*, No. 86 (March 1991), pp. 1-4.

McLaurin, Melton A. "Proud to be an American: Patriotism in Country Music," in *America's Musical Pulse: Popular Music in Twentieth-Century Society*, edited by Kenneth J. Bindas (Westport, Connecticut: Praeger Publishers, 1992), pp. 23-32.

McNeil, William K. " 'We'll Make the Spanish Grunt': Popular Songs About the Sinking of the *Maine*," *Journal of Popular Culture*, II (Spring 1969), pp. 537-551.

Mohrmann, G.P. and F. Eugene Scott. "Popular Music and World War II: The Rhetoric of Continuation," *Quarterly Journal of Speech*, LXII (February 1976), pp. 145-156.

Mondak, Jeffrey J. "Protest Music as Political Persuasion," *Popular Music and Society*, XII (Fall 1988), pp. 25-38.

Murdoch, Brain. *Fighting Songs and Warring Words: Popular Lyrics of Two World Wars*. London: Routledge Publishing, Ltd., 1990.

Palmer, Roy. "War and Peace," in *The Sound of History: Songs and Social Comment* (New York: Oxford University Press, 1988), pp. 271-302.

Philbin, Marianne (ed.). *Give Peace a Chance: Music and the Struggle for Peace*. Chicago: Chicago Review Press, 1983.

Pratt, Ray. *Rhythm and Resistance: Explorations in the Politic Uses of Popular Music*. New York: Praeger Publishers, 1990.

Reynolds, Clay. "Vietnam's Artistic Legacy: The Need to Understand," *Journal of American Culture*, XIV (Summer 1991), pp. 9-11.

Rodnitzky, Jerome L. *Minstrels of the Dawn: The Folk-Protest Singer as a Cultural Hero*. Chicago: Nelson-Hall, Inc., 1976.

Scheurer, Timothy E. *Born in the U.S.A.: The Myth of America in Popular Music From Colonial Times to the Present*. Jackson: University Press of Mississippi, 1991.

Scheurer, Timothy E. "Myth to Madness: America, Vietnam, and Popular Culture," *Journal of American Culture*, IV (Summer 1981), pp. 149-165.

Scodar, Christine. "Operation Desert Storm as 'Wargames': Sport, War, and Media Intertextuality," *Journal of American Culture*, XVI (Spring 1993), pp. 1-5.

Sealey, Don. "Saudi Update," *Goldmine*, No. 277 (March 8, 1991), p. 7.

Student, Menachem. *In the Shadow of War: Memories of a Soldier and Therapist*. Philadelphia: Temple University Press, 1991.

Suid, Lawrence. *Guts and Glory: Great American War Movies*. Reading, Massachusetts: Addison-Wesley Publishing Company, 1978.

Tischler, Barbara. "One Hundred Percent Americanism and Music in Boston During World War I," *American Music*, IV (Summer 1986), pp. 164-176.

Turner, Donald W. "I Ain't Marchin' Anymore: The Rhetorical Potential in Anti-War Song Lyrics During the Vietnam Conflict for the Left" (PhD Dissertation: Pennsylvania State University, 1982).

Van Creveld, Martin. *The Transformation of War*. New York: Free Press, 1991.

Van Devanter, Lynda and Joan Furey (eds.). *Visions of War, Dreams of Peace: Writings of Women in the Vietnam War*. New York: Warner Books, 1991.

Waffen, Les and Peter Hesbacher. "War Songs: Hit Recordings During the Vietnam Period," *ARSC Journal*, (Spring 1981), pp. 4-18.

Whitburn, Joel. *Pop Memories, 1890-1954: The History of American Popular Music*. Menomonee Falls, Wisconsin: Record Research, Inc. 1986.

Whitburn, Joel. *Top Pop Singles, 1955-1990*. Menomonee Falls, Wisconsin: Record Research Inc., 1991.

Whitfield, Stephen J. *The Culture of the Cold War*. Baltimore, Maryland: Johns Hopkins University Press, 1991.

Wiener, Jonn. "Give Peace a Chance: An Anthem For the Anti-War Movement," in *Give Peace a Chance: Music and the Struggle for Peace*, edited by Marianne Philbin (Chicago: Chicago Review Press, 1983).

Wilkinson, Ray. "One Year Later," *Newsweek*, CXVIII (July 29, 1991), pp. 28-32.

Wolfe, Charles. "Nuclear Country: The Atomic Bomb in Country Music," *Journal of Country Music*, VI (January 1978), pp. 4-22.

Woll, Allen L. "From Blues in the Night to Ac-cent-tchu-ate the Positive: Film Music Goes to War, 1939-1945," *Popular Music and Society*, IV (Spring 1975), pp. 77-85.

Women's Division of Soka Gakkai (eds.). *Women Against War*. New York: Kodansha International, Ltd., 1986.

Woodward, William. "America as a Culture (I): Some Emerging Lines of Analysis," *Journal of American Culture*, XI (Spring 1988), pp. 1-16.

Woodward, William. "America as a Culture (II): A Fourfold Heritage," *Journal of American Culture*, XI (Spring 1988), pp. 17-32.

# Chapter 22

# Women

## GENDER STUDIES
## WITH POPULAR CULTURE RESOURCES

A new wind is blowing through American classrooms. This stiff breeze is dislodging the blinding cobwebs of male chauvinism, scattering the dusty female stereotypes of past days, and blowing closed forever the pages of sexist textbooks. This is fine. But what kinds of new teaching resources should be used to stimulate the minds and hearts of young students to investigate the historical and contemporary achievements of women?

All effective teaching activities must be directed by clearly defined goals. Although no single set of general objectives has been generated to cover the entire women's studies movement, the following list embodies a broad range of ideas that undergird the ideology of the liberationist instructional goals.

1. To examine the numerous stereotypes and social myths that surround the images of women in contemporary American society.
2. To illustrate the variety of professional activities and avocational pursuits that women have historically pursued and in which they currently participate.
3. To provide a series of models that can be used as focal points for student sex-role investigations.
4. To study contemporary social issues through the intellectual context of women's studies.

---

The essay by B. Lee Cooper was originally published as "The Traditional and Beyond: Resources for Teaching Women's Studies," *Audiovision Instruction*, XXII (December 1977), pp. 14-18, 45. Reprint permission granted by the author. The review of *She's a Rebel* by Gillian G. Gaar is scheduled to be published in *Journal of American Culture*. Reprint permission granted by the author, Managing Editor Pat Browne, and Bowling Green State University Popular Press.

5. To review the writings of historical commentators and contemporary thinkers on the issues of civil liberty, social equality, and women's liberation.
6. To note the variety of methods and resources that have been used to publicize the women's movement.
7. To examine the literature of the women's movement in its written and oral contexts.
8. To improve the self-image of female students and to enhance the understanding of all students concerning the historical circumstances of women in America.
9. To establish a logical basis for securing constructive social and political reforms to benefit women in contemporary American society.

These goals address several elements that are essential for stimulating student interest. They aim at defining female identity/self-image; they emphasize the functional reality of politics along with the reality of promoting change in both thought and action; and they involve the pursuit of historical truth about human relations. Though some scholars might argue that these objectives are too contemporary for historical study, there is ample reason to argue that these instructional goals are historically and pedagogically sound.

The following are a variety of suggestions about valuable, factual, and innovative resources currently available in the field of women's studies. The recommended books, articles, and songs are divided into three categories: traditional textbook and periodical resources, popular music resources, and science fiction resources. These categories subdivide into socially relevant themes. The final section of each category offers teachers a series of professional commentaries about teaching and studying with these resources.

## Traditional Textbook and Periodical Resources

The real challenge of altering the sexist slant of contemporary society rests in reforming informal socialization processes that have dulled the sensitivities of students to the contributions of females to American life. Polemics aside, students must be encouraged to examine reflectively the full range of historical roles that women have occupied. Historian Anne Firor Scott has capsuled this goal:

In some ideal world there would be no such thing as women's history since social historians would recognize that males and females make up society, create mores, pattern the culture; economic historians would be aware that women have always been part of the labor force and have contributed to economic choices; legal historians would know that case law and to some degree statute law had been shaped by the needs and demands of women; political historians would be aware of the people who organized the precincts as well as the people who met at the summit.

The following books and articles offer resources for both students and teachers to overcome the sexist attitudes and perspectives described by Scott.

## History, Culture, and Politics

- Banner, Lois W. *Women in Modern America: A Brief History.* New York: Harcourt, Brace, Jovanovich, 1974.

- Chafe, William H. *The American Woman: Her Changing Social, Economic, and Political Roles, 1920-1970.* New York: Oxford University Press, 1972.

- Cooper, James L. and Sheila McIsaac Cooper (eds.). *The Roots of American Feminist Thought.* Boston: Allyn & Bacon, 1973.

- Cott, Nancy F. (ed.). *Roots of Bitterness: Documents of the Social History of American Women.* New York: E. P. Dutton and Company, 1972.

- Flexner, Eleanor. *Century of Struggle: The Women's Rights Movement in the United States.* New York: Atheneum Press, 1974.

- Friedan, Betty. *It Changed My Life: Writings on the Women's Movement.* New York: Random House, 1976.

- Friedman, Jean E. and William G. Shade (eds.). *Our American Sisters.* Boston: Allyn & Bacon, 1973.

- Gluck, Sherna (ed.). *From Parlor to Prison: Five American Suffragists Talk About Their Lives: An Oral History.* New York: Vintage Books, 1976.

- Janeway, Elizabeth. *Man's World, Woman's Place: A Study in Social Mythology.* New York: Dell Publishing Company, 1971.

- Kraditor, Aileen S. *The Ideas of the Woman Suffrage Movement, 1890-1920.* New York: Columbia University Press, 1965.

- Kraditor, Aileen S. (ed.). *Up from the Pedestal: Selected Writings in the History of American Feminism.* Chicago: Quadrangle Books, 1968.

- Lerner, Gerda. *The Woman in American History.* Reading, MA: Addison Wesley Publishing Company, 1971.

- Morgan, Robin (ed.). *Sisterhood Is Powerful: An Anthology of Writings from the Women's Liberation Movement.* New York: Random House, 1970.

- Morgan, Robin (ed.). *Black Woman in White America: A Documentary History.* New York: Vintage Books, 1972.

- O'Neill, William L. *Everyone Was Brave: The Rise and Fall of Feminism in America.* Chicago: Quadrangle Books, 1969.

- Parker, Gail (ed.). *The Oven Birds: American Women on Womanhood, 1820-1920.* Garden City, NY: Doubleday and Company, 1972.

- Riegel, Robert E. *American Women: A Story of Social Change.* Rutherford, NJ: Fairleigh Dickinson University Press, 1970.

- Scott, Anne Firor. *The Southern Lady: From Pedestal to Politics.* Chicago: University of Chicago Press, 1970.

- Scott, Anne Firor. *Women in American Life.* Boston: Houghton Mifflin Company, 1970.

- Sinclair, Andrew. *The Better Half: The Emancipation of the American Women.* New York: Harper and Row, 1965.

- Smith, Page. *Daughters of the Promised Land: Women in American History.* Boston: Little, Brown and Company, 1970.

## Teaching Approaches, Resources, and Criticism

- Domann, Cathy and Mary Lee Wright. "Teaching the Big Ideas: What Is Liberation? A Closer Look at the Women's Equal Rights Amendment," in Allan O'Kownslar (ed.), *Teaching American History: The Quest for Relevancy* (Washington: National Council for the Social Studies, 1974) pp. 57-79.

- Grambs, Jean D. "Sex Stereotypes in Instructional Materials, Literature, and Language: A Survey of Research," *Women's Studies Abstracts*, Vol. I (December 1972), pp. 1-4, 91-94.

- Grambs, Jean D. (ed.). *Teaching About Women in the Social Studies: Concepts, Methods and Materials.* Washington: National Council for the Social Studies, 1976.

- Hartmand, Mary and Lois W. Bannder (eds.). *Clio's Consciousness Raised: New Perspectives in Women's History.* New York: Harper and Row, 1974.

- Lerner, Gerda. "New Approaches to the Study of Women in American History," *Journal of Social History*, Vol. 3 (1970), pp. 53-62.

- O'Faolain, Julia and Laura Martines (eds.). *Not in God's Image: Women in History from the Greeks to the Victorians*. New York: Harper and Row, 1973.

- Rosen, Ruth. "Sexism in History or Women's History is a Tricky Business," *Journal of Marriage and the Family*, Vol. 33 (August 1971), pp. 541-544.

- Scott, Anne Firor. "Women in American Life," in William H. Cartwright and Richard L. Watson (eds.), *The Reinterpretation of American History and Culture* (Washington, DC: National Council for the Social Studies, 1973), pp. 151-163.

- Sochen, June. "The Role of Women in History," *The Chronicle of Higher Education*, Vol. 10 (April 21, 1975), p. 11.

- Trecker, Janice Law. "Teaching the Role of Women in American History," in James A. Banks (ed.), *Teaching Ethnic Studies* (Washington, DC: National Council for the Social Studies, 1973), pp. 279-292.

- "Women in U.S. History High School Textbooks." *Social Education*, Vol. 35 (March 1971), pp. 249-261ff.

## *POPULAR MUSIC RESOURCES*

The classroom must become an active arena for exploding the pervasive stereotype of the submissive female. The following section suggests that teachers can profit by adopting audio resources to examine the pluralistic American society of the past two decades. Since the field of popular music has produced rich resources of social commentary by and about women, it offers ample instructional resources for critical study. An additional benefit of using the audio medium is found in the large number of female performers who have attained celebrity status as both singers and songwriters since 1960.

Unfortunately, the lyrics of contemporary singers are rarely discussed in the classroom. E.G. Campbell, a student of present history-teaching techniques, has criticized the shortsightedness of the omission of both the arts and women's studies from traditional history classes by noting:

> The simple fact of women's virtual exclusion from the "seamless web" of United States history is well substantiated. . . . Historians

have tended to treat women in much the same way with the arts, music, and literature; they have set them apart in separate chapters as vignettes which tend to render them trivial. Have women and artistic expression been deemed inappropriate for inclusion in the seamy male world of politics, wars, and industrialization? Since they have been relegated more often to the wings of historical consideration, it has devolved to the contemporary historian to redress the balance. This belated process is currently moving ahead.

Although the scholarly books and articles of Simone de Beauvoir, Betty Friedan, Elizabeth Janeway, Aileen S. Kraditor, Gerda Lerner, and Margaret Mead continue to stimulate thoughtful, creative investigations in the area of women's studies, their works have failed to spark similar innovative thinking in the realm of instructional resources. Why is this true? One reason might be that the process of assembling evidence on the female past has followed the traditional scholarly tendency of relying solely upon written sources—newspaper articles and editorials; official records from city governments, state legislatures, and both houses of Congress; books and essays by poets, journalists, politicians, and clergy; as well as other standard literary resources. This approach has rendered women's history speechless. In several instances the rich oral testimony of contemporary women has been considered and investigated, but more classes should study women's oral history. If teachers neglect the use of oral resources in history courses, they perpetuate student disinterest and even foster youthful distrust about the credibility of the analytical writings of Friedan, Mead, and others.

The most productive approach for adding a voice to the mute texts of women's studies in American history is to use popular recordings to reconstruct the pluralistic image of women in contemporary society. This can be accomplished by selecting a series of significant social themes for classroom study. Once identified, these themes will provide a framework for students to arrange recorded commentaries in a fashion that will reveal the multiplicity of female images in contemporary American culture. Hopefully, the interplay of ideas within each thematic structure will encourage each member of the class to develop a personal position on each issue.

### Stereotypes, Paternalism, and Discrimination

- "Born a Woman"
  (MGM 13501)
  Sandy Posey

- "Dreams of the Everyday Housewife"
  (Capitol 2224)
  Glenn Campbell

- "Down on Me"
  (Mainstream 662)
  Big Brother and the Holding Company (Janis Joplin)

- "Half-Breed"
  (MCA 40102)
  Cher

- "I'm Livin' in Shame"
  (Motown 1139)
  Diana Ross and the Supremes

- "Society's Child (Baby, I've Been Thinking)"
  (Verve Forecast 5027)
  Janis Ian

- "Trouble in Mind"
  (Colpix 175)
  Nina Simone

- "When Will I Be Loved?"
  (Capitol 4050)
  Linda Ronstadt

### *Individualism, Pride, and Confidence*

- "Brand New Key"
  (Neighborhood 4201)
  Melanie

- "Don't Make Me Over"
  (Scepter 1239)
  Dionne Warwick

- "Don't Rain on My Parade"
  (Columbia 33161)
  Barbra Streisand

- "Different Drum"
  (Capitol 2004)
  Stone Poneys (Linda Ronstadt)

- "Fancy"
  (Capitol 2675)
  Bobbie Gentry

- "I Am Woman"
  (Capitol 3350)
  Helen Reddy

- "I'm a Woman"
  (Reprise 1319)
  Maria Muldaur

- "Mr. Big Stuff"
  (Stax 0088)
  Jean Knight

- "Respect"
  (Atlantic 2403)
  Aretha Franklin

- "These Boots Are Made for Walkin' "
  (Reprise 0432)
  Nancy Sinatra

- "Think"
  (Atlantic 2528)
  Aretha Franklin

### *Dependence, Selflessness, and Submission*

- "Angel of the Morning"
  (Bell 705)
  Merilee Rush

- "Chain of Fools"
  (Atlantic 2464)
  Aretha Franklin

- "Help Me Make It Through the Night"
  (Mega 615-0015)
  Sammi Smith

- "Midnight Train to Georgia"
  (Buddah 383)
  Gladys Knight and the Pips

- "Mixed-Up, Shook-Up Girl"
  (Herald 590)
  Patty and the Emblems

- "Oh Me, Oh My (I'm a Fool for You Baby)"
  (Atlantic 2838)
  Aretha Franklin

- "Piece of My Heart"
  (Shout 221)
  Erma Franklin

- "Where You Lead"
  (Columbia 45414)
  Barbra Streisand

- "You Keep Me Hangin' On"
  (Motown 1101)
  The Supremes

## Domination, Courage, and Power

- "Don't Mess with Bill"
  (Tamla 54126)
  The Marvelettes

- "Harper Valley P.T.A."
  (Plantation 3)
  Jeannie C. Riley

- "How Does That Grab You, Darlin'?"
  (Reprise 0461)
  Nancy Sinatra

- "Lady Marmalade"
  (Epic 50048)
  LaBelle

- "Lucretia MacEvil"
  (Columbia 45235)
  Blood, Sweat, and Tears

- "Mother-in-Law"
  (Minit 623)
  Ernie K-Dee

- "Polk Salad Annie"
  (Monument 1104)
  Tony Joe White

- "Swamp Witch"
  (MGM 14496)
  Jim Stafford

## *Aggression, Rebellion, and Deviance*

- "Devil with a Blue Dress On' and 'Good Golly Miss Molly"
(New Voice 817)
Mitch Ryder and the Detroit Wheels

- "Evil Ways"
(Columbia 45069)
Santana

- "Honky Tonk Woman"
(London 910)
The Rolling Stones

- "Mary Lou"
(Roulette 4177)
Ronnie Hawkins

- "Mean Woman Blues"
(Monument 824)
Roy Orbison

- "Mississippi Queen"
(Windfall 532)
Mountain

- "Mrs. Robinson"
(Columbia 44511)
Simon and Garfunkel

- "Night Owl"
(Altantic 2648)
Wilson Pickett

- "Suzanne"
(Reprise 0615)
Noel Harrison

- "Sweet Cream Ladies, Forward March"
(Mala 12035)
The Box Tops

- "Witchy Woman"
(Asylum 11008)
The Eagles

## *Teaching Approaches, Resources, and Criticism*

- Brown, Roger L. and Michael O'Leary. "Pop Music in an English Secondary School System," *American Behavioral Scientist*, Vol. 14 (January/February 1971), pp. 401-413.

- Browne, Ray B. and Ronald J. Ambrosetti (eds.). *Popular Culture and Curricula*, revised edition. Bowling Green, OH: Bowling Green University Popular Press, 1972.

- Collins, Judy. *The Judy Collins Songbook.* New York: Grosset and Dunlap, 1969.

- Cooper, B. Lee. "Chuck Berry's Golden Decade (2 vols.) and The London Chuck Berry Sessions," *The History Teacher*, Vol. 8 (February 1975), pp. 300-301.

- Cooper, B. Lee. "Examining Social Change Through Contemporary History: An Audio Media Proposal," *The History Teacher*, Vol. 6 (August 1973), pp. 523-534.

- Cooper, B. Lee. "Images of the Future in Popular Music: Lyrical Comments on Tomorrow," *Social Education*, Vol. 39 (May 1975), pp. 276-285.

- Cooper, B. Lee. "Popular Music and Academic Enrichment in the Residence Hall," *HASPA Journal*, Vol. 11 (Winter 1974), pp. 50-57.

- Cooper, B. Lee. "Rock Music and Religious Education: A Synthesis," *Religious Education*, Vol. 70 (May-June 1975), pp. 289-299.

- Cooper, B. Lee and Larry S. Haverkos. "Using Popular Music in Social Studies Instruction," *Audiovisual Instruction*, Vol. 17 (November 1972), pp. 86-88.

- Denisoff, R. Serge and Richard A. Peterson (eds.). *The Sounds of Social Change: Studies in Popular Culture.* Chicago: Rand McNally and Company, 1972.

- DeTurk, David A. and A. Poulin, Jr. (eds.). *The American Folk Scene: Dimensions of the Folksong Revival.* New York: Dell Publishing Company, 1967.

- Dufty, David and John Anthony Scott. *How to Use Folk Songs.* Washington, DC: National Council for the Social Studies, 1969.

- Graves, Barbara Farris and Donald J. McBain (eds.). *Lyric Voices: Approaches to the Poetry of Contemporary Song.* New York: John Wiley and Sons, 1972.

- Heyman, Scott. "And Music," in Thomas F. Powell, *Humanities and the Social Studies.* Washington, DC: National Council for the Social Studies, 1969, pp. 80-87.

- Hosher, Harold F. Jr. "The Lyrics of American Pop Music: A New Poetry," *Popular Music and Society,* Vol. 1 (Spring 1972), pp. 167-176.

- Lyons, Anne W. "Creative Teaching in Interdisciplinary Humanities: The Human Values in Pop Music," *Minnesota English Journal,* Vol. 10 (Winter 1974), pp. 23-31.

- Morse, David E. "Avant-Rock in the Classroom," *English Journal,* Vol. 58 (February 1969), pp. 196-200ff.

- Sander, Ellen. "Pop in Perspective: A Profile," *Saturday Review,* Vol. 51 (October 26, 1968), pp. 80-93.

- Spinner, Stephanie (ed.). *Rock Is Beautiful: An Anthology of American Lyrics, 1953-1968.* New York: Dell Publishing Company, 1970.

- "Why Won't Teachers Teach Rock? Some Answers," in Jonathan Eisen (ed.). *The Age of Rock/2: Sights and Sounds of the American Cultural Revolution.* New York: Vintage Books, 1970, pp. 28-33.

- "Youth and Music," in Robert D. Barr (ed.). *Values in Youth: Teaching Social Studies in an Age of Crisis–No. 2.* Washington, DC: National Council for the Social Studies, 1971, pp. 99-103.

- "Youth Music–A Special Report." *Music Educators Journal,* Vol. 56 (November 1969), pp. 43-73.

## *SCIENCE FICTION RESOURCES*

The recent introduction of nontraditional materials–simulation games, role-playing activities, and historical fiction–as educational resources marks only a feeble beginning in expanding the spectrum of alternative teaching tools that should be employed in the classroom. Science fiction stories can be valuable additions to the growing arsenal of instructional materials being used by imaginative teachers of women's studies. The science fiction literary heritage is long-standing and diversified. Speculative fiction tales invariably involve imaginative situations where the author uses intellect as well as emotion in the story line. The genre has attracted such distinguished writers as Jack London, Rudyard Kipling, Herman Melville, and Mark Twain. Speculative essays are consciously written with regard to significant social and political dilemmas of present and future concern, and the authors generally commit themselves to presenting proposed solutions to the problems they have identified. Just as the future-oriented books by Jules Verne and H.G. Wells revolutionized and stimulated the minds of past generations, so too the stories of Poul Anderson, Frederik Pohl, Robert Heinlein, Philip Jose Farmer, Ursula K. LeGuin, Kurt Vonnegut Jr., and Harlan Ellison have created intellectual passages and dangerous visions that enable individuals to glimpse beyond the future shock of the 1970s.

Strangely, the use of popular culture materials in women's studies has only recently gained academic respectability. Science fiction advocates have been only marginally successful in justifying their materials as classroom resources. It should be acknowledged that science fiction stories can provide rich, varied, and stimulating resources for examining social issues. Commentaries on the most relevant cultural themes—including race relations, sex practices, death, ecology, and patriotism—are elements prevalent in popular culture media.

### Love, Marriage, and Motherhood

- Anderson, Poul. "Journeys End," in Robert Silverberg (ed.), *Mind to Mind: Nine Stories of Science Fiction* (New York: Dell Publishing Company, 1971), pp. 223-235.

- Asimov, Isaac. "The Ugly Little Boy," in Damon Knight (ed.), *Dimension X: Five Science Fiction Novellas* (New York: Simon and Schuster, 1970), pp. 303-350.

- Carr, Carol. "Look, You Think You've Got Troubles," in Damon Knight (ed.), *The Best of Orbit* (New York: Medallion Books, 1976), pp. 193-203.

- Del Rey, Lester. "Helen O'Loy," in Sam Moskowitz (ed.), *The Coming of the Robots* (New York: Collier Books, 1963), pp. 47-65.

- Kuttner, Henry and C. L. Moore. "The Children's Hour," in Anthony Boucher (ed.), *A Treasury of Great Science Fiction: Volume One* (Garden City, NY: Doubleday and Company, 1959), pp. 255-287.

- Rankine, John. "Two's Company," in John W. Milstead, Martin Harry Greenberg, Joseph D. Orlander, and Patricia Warrick (eds.), *Sociology Through Science Fiction* (New York: St. Martin's Press, 1974), pp. 281-292.

- Zelazny, Roger. "A Rose for Ecclesiastes," in Judith Merril (ed.), *The Year's Best SF 10th Annual Edition* (New York: Delacorte Press, 1965), pp. 211-248.

### Feminine Roles and the Social Order

- Anderson, Poul. *Virgin Planet*. New York: Warner Paperback Library, 1959.
- Elliott, George P. "Sandra," in Anthony Boucher (ed.), *A Treasury of Great Science Fiction: Volume One* (Garden City, NY: Doubleday and Company, 1959), pp. 370-379.
- Heinlein, Robert A. "Delilah and the Space-Rigger," in *The Past Through Tomorrow: Future History Stories* (New York: Berkley Publishing Corp., 1975), pp. 213-225.
- Heinlein, Robert A. "The Menace from Earth," in Isaac Asimov (ed.), *Tomorrow's Children: 18 Tales of Fantasy and Science Fiction* (Garden City, NY: Doubleday and Company, 1966), p. 259.
- LeGuin, Ursula K. *The Left Hand of Darkness*. New York: Walker Books, 1969.
- Levin, Ira. *The Stepford Wives*. Greenwich, CT: Fawcett Publications, 1972.
- Merril, Judith. "Survival Ship," in Robert A. Heinlein (ed.), *Tomorrow, the Stars* (New York: Berkley Publishing Corp., 1967), pp. 138-146.
- Panshin, Alexei. *Rite of Passage* (New York: Ace Books, 1973).
- Russ, Joanna. *The Female Man* (New York: Bantam Books, 1975).
- Wilhelm, Kate. "The Funeral," in Pamela Sargent (ed.), *More Women of Wonder: Science Fiction Novelettes by Women About Women* (New York: Vintage Books, 1976), pp. 175-213.

### Deviant Behavior

- Bloch, Robert. "Lizzie Borden Took an Axe . . . ," in Peter Heining (ed.), *Beyond the Curtain of Dark* (New York: Pinnacle Books, 1972), pp. 17-31.
- Bloch, Robert. "A Toy for Juliette," in Harlan Ellison (ed.), *Dangerous Visions* (New York: New American Library, 1967), pp. 115-121.
- Farmer, Philip Jose. "Mother," in Robert Silverberg (ed.), *Alpha 4* (New York: Ballantine Books, 1973) pp. 215-244.
- Merril, Judith. "That Only a Mother," in Daniel Roselle (ed.), *Transformations: Understanding World History Through Science Fiction* (Greenwich, CT: Fawcett Publications, 1973), pp. 115-126.

- Russ, Joanna. "When It Changed," in Isaac Asimov (ed.), *Nebula Award Stories 8* (New York: Berkley Medallion Books, 1973), pp. 90-99.

- Tushnet, Leonard. "Aunt Jennie's Tonic," in Donald A. Wollheim, *The 1972 Annual World's Best SF* (New York: DAW Books, 1972), pp. 207-225.

- Weinbaum, Stanley G. "Adaptive Ultimate," in *The Best of Stanley G. Weinbaum* (New York: Ballantine Books, 1974), pp. 51-74.

- Wilhelm, Kate. "Baby You Were Great," in Pamela Sargent (ed.), *Women of Wonder: Science Fiction Stories by Women About Women* (New York: Vintage Books, 1974), pp. 139-158.

### Adventure Stories

- Heinlein, Robert A. "Searchlight," in *The Past Through Tomorrow: Future History Through Stories* (New York: Berkley Publishing Corp., 1975), pp. 343-346.

- Mitchison, Naomi. *Memoirs of a Spacewoman.*

- Moore, C.L. "Jirel Meets Magic," in Pamela Sarlient (ed.), *More Women of Wonder: Science Fiction Novelettes by Women About Women* (New York: Vintage Books, 1976), pp. 3-52.

### Teaching Approaches, Resources, and Criticism

- Allen, L. David. *The Ballantine Teacher's Guide to Science Fiction: A Practical Creative Approach to Science Fiction in the Classroom.* New York: Ballantine Books, 1975.

- Bradbury, Ray. "If I Were a Teacher," *Learning: The Magazine for Creative Teachers*, Vol. I (May 1973), pp. 14-17.

- Calkins, Elizabeth and Barry McGhan. *Teaching Tomorrow: A Handbook of Science Fiction* (Dayton, OH: Pflaum/Standard, 1972).

- Cooper, B. Lee. "Bob Dylan, Isaac Asimov, and Social Problems: Non-traditional Materials for Reflective Teaching," *International Journal of Instructional Media*, Vol. 9 (1976-1977), pp. 105-115.

- Cooper, B. Lee. "Futurescope," *Audiovisual Instruction*, Vol. 21 (January 1976), pp. 42-48.

- Friend, Beverly. "Reaching the Future Through Paperback Fiction," *Media and Methods*, Vol. 2 (November 1974), pp. 35-36ff.

- Hollister, Bernard C. "Teaching American History with Science Fiction," *Social Education*, Vol. 39 (February 1975), pp. 81-85.

- Hollister, Bernard C. and Dean C. Thompson. *Grokking the Future: Science Fiction in the Classroom*. Dayton, OH: Pflaum/Standard, 1975.

- Millies, Suzanne. *Science Fiction Primer for Teachers*. Dayton, OH: Pflaum Publishers, 1975.

- Paine, Doris M. and Dianna Martinez. *Guide to Science Fiction: Exploring the Possibilities and Alternatives*. New York: Bantam Books, 1974.

- Rogers, Chester B. "Science Fiction and Social Studies," *Social Studies*, Vol. 66 (November/December 1975), pp. 261-264.

- Sargent, Pamela. "Introduction," in *More Women of Wonder: Science Fiction Novelettes by Women About Women* (New York: Vintage Books, 1976), pp. xi-xiii.

- Sargent, Pamela. "Women in Science Fiction," in *Women of Wonder: Science Fiction Stories by Women About Women* (New York: Vintage Books, 1974), pp. xiii-xiv.

- Williamson, Jack. "Science Fiction: Teaching and Criticism," in Reginald Bretnor (ed.), *Science Fiction: Today and Tomorrow* (Baltimore, Maryland: Penguin Books, 1974), pp. 309-328.

## *Conclusion*

E.G. Campbell, not only a teacher and learner but also an eloquent critic of current social studies teaching, has declared: "The 'bucolic' canard that the 'place' for women is at home, pregnant, barefoot, and mute typically characterizes the historians' treatment of them." This observation is painfully relevant; and until formal scholarship and classroom approaches related to women's studies are synthesized, the true value of examining female images will never be realized. This article suggests only three innovative instructional approaches as models for classroom study. The ability of teachers to adopt nontraditional resources in any context remains both a question mark and a challenge. Without the introduction of such innovative instructional techniques, the majority of female (and male) students may continue to question the validity of American history in their lives. That would be tragic.

# ROCK 'N' ROLL WOMEN

*She's a Rebel: The History of Women in Rock and Roll.* By Gillian G. Gaar. Seattle, Washington: Seal Press, 1992. Illustrated. 467 pp.

Adapting the title from The Crystals' 1962 hit song to a female model, Seattle journalist and rock newspaper editor Gillian G. Gaar presents a revisionist history of women's influence in American popular music since 1950. Perhaps the author should have titled her study *The Rebel Girl* in honor of WWI heroine Elizabeth Gurley Flynn and in recognition of Joe Hill's song of that title. The second verse of Hill's tune is especially appropriate with regard to Gaar's perspective about the male-dominated commercial recording industry:

> And the grafters in terror are trembling,
> When her spite and defiance she'll hurl.
> For the only and thoroughbred lady,
> Is the rebel girl.

Examinations of women rock performers are not uncommon. Two of the most interesting studies are *Girl Groups: The Story of a Sound* by Alan Betrock (Delilah, 1982) and *Will You Still Love Me Tomorrow? Girl Groups From the '50s On . . .* by Charlotte Greig (Virago, 1989.) Rather than focusing on groups though, Gaar expands her perspective to include individual artists (Dusty Springfield, Janis Joplin, and Sinead O'Connor), singer/songwriters (Carole King, Joni Mitchell, and Joan Armatrading), women's magazine founders (Lori Twerskyi), and recent record company initiators (Lisa Fancher and Judy Dlugacz.) Gaar contends that rock journalists and popular culture historians have either totally ignored or inadequately chronicled the contributions of women in rock. The breadth of Gaar's perspective–from "Big Mama" Thornton, Ruth Brown, and LaVern Baker in the 1950s to Madonna, Janet Jackson, and Queen Latifah in the 1990s–and the detail of her interviews, commentaries, research, and insights make *She's a Rebel* a distinctive sociological contribution.

Does this competently conceived study miss any bases or overlook any key persons? Yes. The shortcomings are found in historical imbalance and biographical omissions. In her effort to emphasize aesthetics and morality over materialism and commercial success, Gaar tends to underestimate the impact of nonpolitical singing stars (Gogi Grant, Anne Murray, Brenda Lee, Crystal Gayle, Irma Thomas, and Carla Thomas); cover artists (Georgia Gibbs, Kay Starr, and Gale Storm); novelty performers (Millie Jackson, Toni Basil, Damita Jo, and Dodie Stevens); traditional pop singers

(Patti Page, Doris Day, Teresa Brewer, and Rosemary Clooney); wives in husband-and-wife duos (Mary Ford, Toni Tennille, Keely Smith, and Valerie Simpson); women in mixed male-and-female groups (Marilyn McCoo, Chaka Khan, and Mavis Staples); and honky tonk performers (Lou Ann Barton, Marcia Ball, and Angela Strehli). Beyond performers though, Gaar needs to investigate the female business roots of the rock music industry. This valuable study would include Lillian McMurry of Trumpet Records, Estelle Axton of Stax Records, and Vivian Carter Bracken of Vee-Jay Records.

The power of *She's a Rebel* resides in the author's commitment to unearthing the often hidden but influential role of women in American music. The rich bibliography illustrates Gaar's scholarly pursuits; the expansive "Song Title Index" and "Album Title Index" demonstrates her understanding that lyrics are audio resources too often ignored by well-meaning but traditionally trained cultural historians. This volume blends strident revisionism with thorough knowledge and critical perspective. Gaps exist. Imbalances can be identified. But Gaar has significantly outdistanced Betrock, Greig, and other women-in-rock observers with a fascinating, fact-filled study. The most powerful portion of this investigation is the post-1970 period. If Gaar revisits this topic, she should strive to tackle American recorded music from 1940 through the 1960s with much more zeal. Meanwhile scholars, music fans, librarians, and women's movement enthusiasts should secure this superb study.

## REFERENCES

Balfour, Victoria. *Rock Wives: The Hard Lives and Good Times of the Wives, Girlfriends, and Groupies of Rock and Roll.* New York: Beech Tree Books/ Williams Morrow and Company, 1986.

Bayton, Mavis. "Feminist Musical Practice: Problems and Contradictions," in *Rock and Popular Music: Politics/Policies/Institutions*, edited by Tony Bennett, Simon Frith, Lawrence Grossberg, John Shepherd, and Graeme Turner (London: Routledge, 1993), pp. 177-192.

Bufwack, Mary A. and Robert K. Oermann. *Finding Her Voice: The Saga of Women in Country Music.* New York: Crown Publishers, Inc., 1993.

Burks, John and Jerry Hopkins. *Groupies and Other Girls: A Rolling Stone Special Report.* New York: Bantam Books, 1970.

Cooper, B. Lee. "Challenging Sexism Through Popular Music," in *Images of American Society in Popular Music: A Guide to Reflective Teaching* (Chicago: Nelson-Hall, Inc., 1982), pp. 28-37.

Cooper, B. Lee. "A Popular Music Perspective: Challenging Sexism in the Social Studies Classroom," *Social Studies*, LXXI (March-April 1980), pp. 71-76.

Cooper, B. Lee. "Review of *She's a Rebel: The History of Women in Rock and Roll* by Gillian G. Gaar," *Journal of American Culture*, XVII (Spring 1994), pp. 99-100.

Cooper, B. Lee. "Searching for Personal Identity in the Social Studies: Male and Female Perspectives in Contemporary Lyrics," *International Journal of Instructional Media*, VI (1978-1979), pp. 351-360.

Cooper, B. Lee. "Sultry Songs and Censorship: A Thematic Discography for College Teacher," *Instructional Journal of Instructional Media*, XX, No. 2 (1993), pp. 181-194.

Cooper, B. Lee. "Sultry Songs as High Humor," *Popular Music and Society*, XXVII (Spring 1993), pp. 71-85.

Cooper, B. Lee. "The Traditional and Beyond: Resources for Teaching Women's Studies," *Audiovisual Instruction*, XXII (December 1977), pp. 14-18ff.

Cooper, B. Lee. "Women's Studies and Popular Music: Using Audio Resources in Social Studies Instruction," *The History and Social Science Teacher*, XIV (Fall 1978), pp. 29-40.

Des Barres, Pamela. *I'm with the Band: Confessions of a Groupie*. New York: Beech Tree Books, 1987.

Gaar, Gillian G. *She's a Rebel: The History of Women in Rock and Roll*. Washington, DC: Seal Press, 1992.

Gammon, Larriane and Margaret Marshment (eds.). *The Female Gaze: Women as Viewers of Popular Culture*. Seattle, Washington: Real Comet Books, 1989.

Garon, Paul and Beth Garon. *Woman with Guitar: Memphis Minnie's Blues*. New York: Da Capo Books, 1992.

Gottlieb, Joanne and Gayle Wald. "Smells Like Teen Spirit: Riot Grrrls, Revolution, and Women in Independent Rock," in *Microphone Fiends: Youth Music and Youth Culture*, edited by Andrew Ross and Tricia Rose (New York: Routledge, 1994), pp. 250-274.

Jordan, Sass. "When Will Women Rockers Get Respect?" *Musician*, No. 188 (June 1994), pp. 16, 44.

Koskoff, Ellen (ed.). *Women and Music in Cross-Cultural Perspective*. Champaign-Urbana: University of Illinois Press, 1989.

Lewis, Lisa A. *Gender Politics and MTU: Voicing the Difference*. Philadelphia: Temple University Press, 1990.

McClary, Susan. *Feminine Endings: Music, Gender, and Sexuality*. Minneapolis: University of Minnesota Press, 1991.

Mellers, Wilfrid. *Angels of the Night: Popular Female Singers of Our Time*. New York: Basil Blackwell, Inc., 1986.

Pavletich, Aida. *Sirens of Song: The Popular Female Vocalist in America*. New York: Da Capo Books, 1980.

Potter, John. "The Singer, Not the Song: Women Singers as Composer-Poets," *Popular Music*, XIII, No. 2 (May 1994), pp. 191-199.

Shapiro, Nat and Bruce Pollock (eds.). *Popular Music 1920-1979—A Revised Cumulation* (three volumes). Detroit, Michigan: Gale Research Company, 1985.

Steward, Sue and Sheryl Garratt. *Signed, Sealed, and Delivered: True Life Stories of Women in Pop*. Boston: South End Press, 1984.

Tobler, John (ed.). *Who's Who in Rock and Roll*. New York: Crescent Books, 1991.

Vaughan, Ronald. "Review of *She's a Rebel* by Gillian A. Gaar," *DISCoveries*, No. 71 (April 1994), pp. 116-119.

Wenner, Hilda E. and Elizabeth Freilicher (comps.). *Here's to the Women: 100 Songs for and about American Women*. Syracuse, New York: Syracuse University Press, 1987.

# Bibliography

## *Books*

Allen, Bob (ed.). 1994. *The Blackwell Guide to Recorded Country Music.* Cambridge, Massachusetts: Blackwell Publishers, Inc.

Baker Jr., Houston A. 1993. *Black Studies, Rap, and the Academy.* Chicago: University of Chicago Press.

Bane, Michael. 1992 (c. 1982). *White Boy Singin' the Blues: The Black Roots of White Rock.* New York: Da Capo Press.

Barlow, William and Cheryl Finley. 1994. *From Swing to Soul: An Illustrated History of African American Popular Music from 1930 to 1960.* Washington, DC: Elliott and Clark Publishing.

Barnard, Stephen. 1989. *On the Radio: Music Radio in Britain.* Milton Keynes, England: Open University.

Bayles, Martha. 1994. *Hole in Our Soul: The Loss of Beauty and Meaning in American Popular Music.* New York: The Free Press.

Beaton, Virginia and Stephen Pedersen. 1992. *Maritime Music Greats: Fifty Years of Hits and Heartbreak.* Halifax, Nova Scotia: Numbus Publishing, Ltd.

Bennett, Tony, Simon Frith, Lawrence Grossberg, John Shepherd, and Graeme Turner (eds.). 1993. *Rock and Popular Music: Politics/Policies/Institutions.* London: Routledge.

Bernard, Stephen. 1993. *Rock Companion.* New York: HarperCollins.

Best, Kenneth. 1992. *Eight Days a Week: An Illustrated Record of Rock 'n' Roll.* Thornhill, Ontario, Canada: Pomegranate Pacific Press.

Binds, Kenneth J. (ed.). 1992. *America's Musical Pulse: Popular Music in Twentieth-Century Society.* Westport, Connecticut: Praeger Books.

Biracree, Tom. 1993. *The Country Music Almanac.* New York: Prentice Hall General Reference.

Booth, Stanley. 1991. *Rhythm Oil: A Journey Through the Music of the American South.* New York: Pantheon Books.

Bradley, Dick. 1992. *Understanding Rock 'n' Roll: Popular Music in Britain, 1955-1964.* Buckingham, England: Open University Press.

Bronson, Fred. 1992. *The Billboard Book of Number One Hits* (third edition, revised and enlarged). New York: Billboard Books.

Brooks, Elston. 1981. *I've Heard Those Songs Before: The Weekly Top Ten Tunes for the Past Fifty Years.* New York: Morrow/Quill Paperbacks.

Buchanan, Scott (ed.). 1994. *Rock 'n' Roll: The Famous Lyrics.* New York: Harper Perennial Books.

Bufwack, Mary A. and Robert K. Oermann. 1993. *Finding Her Voice: The Saga of Women in Country Music*. New York: Crown Publishers, Inc.

Bunch, William. 1994. *Jukebox America: Down Back Streets and Blue Highways in Search of the Country's Greatest Jukebox*. New York: St. Martin's Press.

Cackett, Alan. 1994. *The Harmony Illustrated Encyclopedia of Country Music*. New York: Crown Paperbacks.

Cagle, Van M. 1995. *Reconstructing Pop/Subculture: Art, Rock, and Andy Warhol*. Thousand Oaks, California: Sage Publications, Inc.

Carlin, Richard. 1995. *The Big Book of Country Music: A Biographical Encyclopedia*. New York: Penguin Books.

Carney, George O. (ed.) 1994. *The Sounds of People and Places: A Geography of American Folk and Popular Music* (third edition). Lanham, Maryland: Rowman and Littlefield Publishers, Inc.

Charlton, Katherine. 1990. *Rock Music Styles: A History*. Dubuque, Iowa: William C. Brown Publishers.

Chilton, John. 1994. *Let the Good Times Roll: The Story of Louis Jordan and His Music*. Ann Arbor, Michigan: University of Michigan Press.

Christgau, Robert. 1990. *Christgau's Record Guide: The '80s*. New York: Pantheon Books.

Christgau, Robert. 1990. *Rock Albums of the '70s: A Critical Guide*. New York: Da Capo Press.

Cianci, Bob. 1989. *Great Rock Drummers of the Sixties*. Milwaukee, Wisconsin: Third Earth Productions, Inc./Hal Leonard Publishing Corp.

Cimino, Al. 1992. *Great Record Labels: An Illustrated History of the Labels Behind the Stars*. Secaucus, New Jersey: Chartwell Books, Inc.

Clark, Alan. 1993. *Legends of Sun Records–Number Three*. West Covina, California: National Rock and Roll Archives.

Cohen, Barry and Jim Quirin (comps.). 1992. *Rock One Hundred: An Authoritative Ranking of the Most Popular Songs for Each Year, 1954 Through 1991* (fifth edition). Los Angeles: Chartmasters.

Cohn, Lawrence. 1993. *Nothing But the Blues: The Music and the Musicians*. New York: Abbeville Press.

Cooper, B. Lee. 1986. *A Resource Guide to Themes in Contemporary American Song Lyrics, 1950-1985*. Westport, Connecticut: Greenwood Press.

Cooper, B. Lee and Wayne S. Haney. 1995. *Rock Music in American Popular Culture: Rock 'n' Roll Resources*. Binghamton, New York: Harrington Park Press.

Crafts, Susan D., Daniel Cavicchi, and Charles Keil. 1993. *My Music*. Hanover, New Hampshire: University Press of New England.

Davis, Francis. 1995. *The History of the Blues: The Roots, the Music, and the People from Charley Patton to Robert Cray*. New York: Hyperion Books.

Dawson, Jim. 1994. *Nervous Man Nervous: Big Jay McNeely and the Rise of the Honking Tenor Sax!* Milford, New Hampshire: Big Nickel Publications.

DeCurtis, Anthony and James Henke, with Holly George-Warren (eds.). 1992. *The Rolling Stone Album Guide*. New York: Random House.

Denisoff, R. Serge. 1975. *Solid Gold: The Popular Record Industry.* New Brunswick, New Jersey: Transaction Books.

DeWitt, Howard A. 1985. *The Beatles: Untold Tales.* Fremont, California: Horizon Books.

DeWitt, Howard A. 1993. *Elvis: The Sun Years–The Story of Elvis Presley in the Fifties.* Ann Arbor, Michigan: Popular Culture, Ink.

DiMartino, Dave. 1994. *Singer-Songwriters: Pop Music's Performer-Composers, From A to Zevon.* New York: Billboard Books.

Dister, Alain (translated by Tovla Ballas). 1993. *The Age of Rock: Smash Hits and Superstars.* New York: Harry N. Abrams, Inc.

Dolgins, Adam. 1993. *Rock Names: From Abba to ZZ Top–How Rock Groups Got Their Names.* New York: Citadel Press.

Downey, Pat, George Albert, and Frank Hoffmann. 1994. *Cash Box Pop Singles Charts, 1950-1993.* Englewood, Colorado: Libraries Unlimited, Inc.

Downey, Pat. 1994. *Top 40 Music on Compact Disc, 1955-1981.* Boulder, Colorado: Pat Downey Enterprises.

Dunne, Michael. 1992. *Metapop: Self-Referentiality in Contemporary American Popular Culture.* Jackson: University Press of Mississippi.

Duxbury, Janell R. 1985. *Rockin' the Classics and Classicizin' the Rock: A Selectively Annotated Discography.* Westport, Connecticut: Greenwood Press.

Duxbury, Janell R. 1991. *Rockin' the Classics and Classicizin' the Rock: A Selectively Annotated Discography–First Supplement.* Westport, Connecticut: Greenwood Press.

Eberly, Philip K. 1982. *Music in the Air: America's Changing Tastes in Popular Music, 1920-1980.* New York: Hastings House.

Editors of *Country Music Magazine.* 1994. *The Comprehensive Country Music Encyclopedia.* New York: Times Books/Random House.

Ellis, Allen (ed.). 1992. *Popular Culture and Acquisitions.* Binghamton, New York: The Haworth Press.

Ellison, Curtis W. 1995. *Country Music Culture: From Hard Times to Heaven.* Jackson: University Press of Mississippi.

Elson, Howard. 1982. *Early Rockers.* New York: Proteus Books.

Ennis, Philip H. 1992. *The Seventh Stream: The Emergence of Rock 'n' Roll in American Popular Music.* Hanover, New Hampshire: Wesleyan University Press.

Epstein, Jonathan S. (Ed.). 1994. *Adolescents and Their Music: If It's Too Loud, You're Too Old.* New York: Garland Publishing, Inc.

Erlewine, Michael, with Chris Woodstra and Vladimir Bogdanov (eds.). 1994. *All Music Guide: The Best CDs, Albums, and Tapes* (second edition). San Francisco: Miller Freeman Books.

Escott, Colin, with Martin Hawkins. 1991. *Good Rockin' Tonight: Sun Records and the Birth of Rock 'n' Roll.* New York: St. Martin's Press.

Evans, Liz. 1994. *Women, Sex, and Rock 'n' Roll: In Their Own Words.* San Francisco: Pandora/HarperCollins.

Fancourt, Les (comp.) 1991. *Chess R&B: A Discography of the R&B Artists on the Chess Labels, 1947-1975* (second edition). Faversham, Kent, England: Les Fancourt.

Ferlingere, Robert D. (comp.) 1976. *A Discography of Rhythm & Blues and Rock 'n' Roll Vocal Groups, 1945 to 1965.* Hayward, California: California Trade School.

Fidler, Linda M. and Richard S. James (eds.). 1990. *International Music Journals.* Westport, Connecticut: Greenwood Press.

Finn, Julio. 1992. *The Bluesman: The Musical Heritage of Black Men and Women in the Americas.* Brooklyn, New York: Interlink.

Finson, Jon W. 1994. *The Voices That Are Gone: Themes in 19th-Century American Popular Song.* New York: Oxford University Press.

Fogo, Fred. 1994. *I Read the News Today: The Social Drama of John Lennon's Death.* Lanham, Maryland: Littlefield Adams.

Fornatale, Pete. 1987. *The Story of Rock 'n' Roll.* New York: William Morrow.

Frame, Pete. 1983. *The Complete Rock Family Trees–Books I and II.* London: Omnibus Press.

Frame, Pete, John Tobler, Ed Hanel, Roger St. Pierre, Chris Trengove, John Beecher, Clive Richardson, Gary Cooper, Marsha Hanlon, and Linda Sandahl. 1989. *The Harmony Illustrated Encyclopedia of Rock* (sixth edition). New York: Harmony Books.

Freeman, Scott. 1995. *Midnight Riders: The Story of the Allman Brothers Band.* Boston: Little, Brown, and Company.

Frith, Simon, Andrew Goodwin, and Lawrence Grossberg (eds.). 1993. *Sound and Vision: The Music Video Reader.* London: Routledge.

Frith, Simon (ed.). 1989. *World Music, Politics, and Social Change: Papers from the International Association for the Study of Popular Music.* Manchester, England: Manchester University Press.

Gaar, Gillian G. 1992. *She's a Rebel: The History of Women in Rock and Roll.* Seattle, Washington: Seal Press.

Gambaccini, Paul, Tim Rice, and Jonathan Rice (comps.). 1992. *British Hit Albums* (fifth edition). Enfield, Middlesex, England: Guinness Publishing, Ltd.

Gambaccini, Paul, Tim Rice, and Jonathan Rice (comps.). 1991. *British Hit Singles* (eighth edition). Enfield, Middlesex, England: Guinness Publishing, Ltd.

Gans, Herbert J. 1974. *Popular Culture and High Culture: An Analysis and Evaluation of Taste.* New York: Basic Books.

Garofalo, Reebee (ed.). 1992. *Rockin' the Boat: Mass Music and Mass Movements.* Boston: South End Press.

Gart, Galen and Roy C. Ames, with contributions from Ray Funk, Rob Bowman, and David Booth. 1990. *Duke/Peacock Records: An Illustrated History with Discography.* Milford, New Hampshire: Big Nickel Publications.

Gart, Galen (comp.). 1993. *First Pressings: The History of Rhythm and Blues– Special 1950 Volume.* Milford, New Hampshire: Big Nickel Publications.

Gart, Galen (comp.). 1991. *First Pressings: The History of Rhythm and Blues: Volume One–1951.* Milford, New Hampshire: Big Nickel Publications.

Gart, Galen (comp.). 1989. *First Pressings: The History of Rhythm and Blues: Volume Three–1953*. Milford, New Hampshire: Big Nickel Publications.

Gart, Galen (comp.). 1989. *First Pressings: The History of Rhythm and Blues: Volume Four–1954*. Milford, New Hampshire: Big Nickel Publications.

Gart, Galen (comp.). 1990. *First Pressings: The History of Rhythm and Blues: Volume Five–1955*. Milford, New Hampshire: Big Nickel Publications.

Gart, Galen (comp.). 1991. *First Pressings: The History of Rhythm and Blues: Volume Six–1956*. Milford, New Hampshire: Big Nickel Publications.

Gart, Galen (comp.). 1993. *First Pressings: The History of Rhythm and Blues: Volume Seven–1957*. Milford, New Hampshire: Big Nickel Publications.

Gart, Galen (comp.). 1986. *First Pressings–Volume One, 1948-1950: Rock History as Chronicled in Billboard Magazine*. Milford, New Hampshire: Big Nickel Publications.

Gart, Galen (comp.). 1986. *First Pressings–Volume Two, 1951-1952: Rock History as Chronicled in Billboard Magazine*. Milford, New Hampshire: Big Nickel Publications.

Gart, Galen. 1987. *R & B Stars of 1953: Thirty-six Authentic-Looking Postcards in Glorious Full Color*. Milford, New Hampshire: Big Nickel Publications.

Gatten, Jeffrey N. (comp.). 1993. *The Rolling Stone Index: Twenty-five Years of Popular Culture, 1967-1991*. Ann Arbor, Michigan: Popular Culture, Ink.

Gelfand, Steve. 1994. *Television Theme Recordings: An Illustrated Discography, 1951-1994*. Ann Arbor, Michigan: Popular Culture, Ink.

Goddard, Peter and Philip Kamin (comps.). 1989. *Shakin' All Over: The Rock 'n' Roll Years in Canada*. Toronto: McGraw Hill Ryerson, Ltd.

Goodall Jr., H. L. 1991. *Living in the Rock 'n' Roll Mystery: Reading Context, Self, and Others as Clues*. Carbondale: Southern Illinois University Press.

Goodfellow, William D. 1990. *Where's That Tune? An Index to Songs in Fakebooks*. Metuchen, New Jersey: Scarecrow Press, Inc.

Goodwin, Andrew. 1992. *Dancing in the Distraction Factory: Music Television and Popular Culture*. Minneapolis: University of Minnesota Press.

Gordon, Robert. 1995. *It Came from Memphis*. Boston: Faber and Faber.

Green, Archie (ed.). 1993. *Songs About Work: Essays in Occupational Culture for Richard A. Reuss*. Bloomington: Indiana University Press.

Gregory, Hugh. 1991. *Soul Music A-Z*. London: Blandford Press.

Griggs, Bill. 1994. *A "Who's Who" of West Texas Rock 'n' Roll Music*. Lubbock, Texas: William F. Griggs/*Rockin' 50s* Magazine.

Guiheen, Anna Marie and Marie-Reine A. Pafik. 1992. *The Sheet Music Reference and Price Guide*. Paducah, Kentucky: Collector Books.

Guralnick, Peter. 1989. *Feel Like Going Home: Portraits in Blues and Rock 'n' Roll*. New York: Harper and Row.

Guralnick, Peter. 1994. *Last Train to Memphis: The Rise of Elvis Presley*. Boston: Little, Brown, and Company.

Guralnick, Peter. 1982. *Listener's Guide to the Blues*. New York: Facts on File.

Guralnick, Peter. 1989. *Lost Highway: Journeys and Arrivals of American Musicians*. New York: Harper and Row.

Halberstam, David. 1993. *The Fifties.* New York: Villard Books.

Hamm, Charles. 1979. *Yesterdays: Popular Song in America.* New York: W. W. Norton.

Harris, James F. 1993. *Philosophy at 33 1/3 R.P.M.: Themes of Classic Rock Music.* La Salle, Illinois: Open Court Publishing.

Haskins, Jim. 1994 (c. 1977). *The Cotton Club.* New York: Hippocrene Books.

Havlice, Patricia Pate (comp.). 1975. *Popular Song Index.* Metuchen, New Jersey: Scarecrow Press.

Havlice, Patricia Pate (comp.). 1978. *Popular Song Index–First Supplement.* Metuchen, New Jersey: Scarecrow Press.

Havlice, Patricia Pate (comp.). 1984. *Popular Song Index–Second Supplement.* Metuchen, New Jersey: Scarecrow Press.

Havlice, Patricia Pate (comp.). 1989. *Popular Song Index–Third Supplement.* Metuchen, New Jersey: Scarecrow Press.

Hayes, Cedric J. and Robert Laughton (comps.). 1993. *Gospel Records, 1943-1969: A Black Music Discography* (Two Volumes). Milford, New Hampshire: Big Nickel Publications.

Heatley, Michael (ed.). 1993. *The Ultimate Encyclopedia of Rock: The World's Most Comprehensive Illustrated Rock Reference.* New York: HarperCollins.

Heatley, Michael (ed.). 1993. *The Virgin Encyclopedia of Rock.* London: Virgin Publishing.

Hemming, Roy and David Hajdu. 1991. *Discovering Great Singers of Classic Pop: A New Listener's Guide to the Sounds and Lives of Top Performers and Their Recordings, Movies, and Videos.* New York: Newmarket Press.

Herzhaft, Gerard (translated by Brigette Debord). 1992. *Encyclopedia of the Blues.* Fayetteville: University of Arkansas Press.

Hildebrand, Lee. 1994. *Stars of Soul and Rhythm and Blues.* New York: Billboard Books.

Hirshey, Gerri. 1994 (c. 1984). *Nowhere to Run: The Story of Soul Music.* New York: Da Capo Press.

Hischak, Thomas S. 1995. *The American Musical Theatre Song Encyclopedia.* Westport, Connecticut: Greenwood Press.

Hoffmann, Frank W. (comp.). 1989. *Intellectual Freedom and Censorship: An Annotated Bibliography.* Metuchen, New Jersey: Scarecrow Press, Inc.

Hoffmann, Frank W. 1995. *American Popular Culture: A Guide to the Reference Literature.* Englewood, Colorado: Libraries Unlimited, Inc.

Hoffmann, Frank and B. Lee Cooper. 1995. *The Literature of Rock III, 1984-1990.* Metuchen, New Jersey: Scarecrow Press, Inc.

Holt, Sid (ed.) 1989. *The Rolling Stone Interviews: The 1980s.* New York: St. Martin's Press/Rolling Stone Press.

Hyland, William G. 1995. *The Song is Ended: Songwriters and American Music, 1900-1950.* New York: Oxford University Press.

Jacobs, Dick and Harriet Jacobs. 1994. *Who Wrote That Song?* (second edition, updated and expanded). Cincinnati, Ohio: Writer's Digest.

Jahn, Mike. 1973. *Rock: From Elvis Presley to The Rolling Stones*. New York: Quadrangle Books.

Jeffries, Neil (ed.) 1993. *Kerrang! Directory of Heavy Metal: The Indispensable Guide to Rock Warriors and Headbangin' Heroes*. London: Virgin Publishing.

Jones, Steve. 1992. *Rock Formation: Music, Technology, and Mass Communication*. Newbury Park, California: Sage Publications.

Kallmann, Helmut and Gilles Potvin (eds.). 1992. *Encyclopedia of Music in Canada* (second edition). Toronto, Ontario, Canada: University of Toronto Press.

Kantor, Kenneth Aaron. 1982. *The Jews on Tin Pan Alley: The Jewish Contribution to American Popular Music, 1830-1940*. New York: Ktav Publishing.

Kelly, Michael Bryan. 1991. *The Beatle Myth: The British Invasion of American Popular Music, 1956-1969*. Jefferson, North Carolina: McFarland and Company.

Kernfeld, Barry (ed.). 1991. *The Blackwell Guide to Recorded Jazz*. Cambridge, Massachusetts: Blackwell Publishers.

Kingsbury, Paul (ed.). 1993. *Country on Compact Disc: The Essential Guide to the Music by The Country Music Foundation*. New York: Grove Press.

Kingsbury, Paul and The Country Music Foundation (eds.). 1994. *Country: The Music and the Musicians—From the Beginnings to the '90s (revised and updated edition)*. New York: Abbeville Publishing Group.

Kreiter, Jeff. 1993. *45 R.P.M. Group Collector's Record Guide: A Guide to Valuable Recordings of Rhythm & Blues/Doo-Wops/Vocal Group Sound From 1950-1992*. Wheeling, West Virginia: Boyd Press.

LaBlanc, Michael L. (ed.). 1989. *Contemporary Musicians—Volume One: Profiles of the People in Music*. Detroit, Michigan: Gale Research, Inc.

LaBlanc, Michael L. (ed.). 1990. *Contemporary Musicians—Volume Two: Profiles of the People in Music*. Detroit, Michigan: Gale Research, Inc.

LaBlanc, Michael L. (ed.). 1990. *Contemporary Musicians—Volume Three: Profiles of the People in Music*. Detroit, Michigan: Gale Research, Inc.

LaBlanc, Michael L. (ed.). 1991. *Contemporary Musicians—Volume Four: Profiles of the People in Music*. Detroit, Michigan: Gale Research, Inc.

LaBlanc, Michael L. (ed.). 1991. *Contemporary Musicians—Volume Five: Profiles of the People in Music*. Detroit, Michigan: Gale Research, Inc.

LaBlanc, Michael L. (ed.). 1992. *Contemporary Musicians—Volume Six: Profiles of the People in Music*. Detroit, Michigan: Gale Research, Inc.

LaBlanc, Michael L. (ed.). 1992. *Contemporary Musicians—Volume Seven: Profiles of the People in Music*. Detroit, Michigan: Gale Research, Inc.

Lanza, Joseph. 1994. *Elevator Music: A Surreal History of Muzak, Easy-Listening, and Other Moodsong*. New York: St. Martin's Press.

Larkin, Colin (ed.). 1993. *The Guinness Encyclopedia of Popular Music (Four Volumes)*. Enfield, Middlesex, England: Guinness Superlatives, Ltd.

Larkin, Colin (ed.). 1993. *The Guinness Who's Who of Blues Music*. Enfield, Middlesex, England: Guinness Books.

Larkin, Colin (ed.). 1993. *The Guinness Who's Who of Country Music*. Enfield, Middlesex, England: Guinness Books.

Larkin, Colin (ed.). 1993. *The Guinness Who's Who of Fifties Music*. Enfield, Middlesex, England: Guinness Books.

Larkin, Colin (ed.). 1993. *The Guinness Who's Who of Folk Music*. Enfield, Middlesex, England: Guinness Books.

Larkin, Colin (ed.). 1993. *The Guinness Who's Who of Seventies Music*. Enfield, Middlesex, England: Guinness Books.

Larkin, Colin (ed.). 1993. *The Guinness Who's Who of Soul*. Enfield, Middlesex, England: Guinness Books.

Laufenberg, Frank (edited by Hugh Gregory). 1992. *Rock and Pop Day by Day: Birthdays, Deaths, Hits, and Facts*. London: Blandford Books.

Leichter, Albert. 1975. *Discography of Rhythm & Blues and Rock & Roll, Circa 1946-1964: A Reference Manual*. Staunton, Virginia: A. Leichter.

Levine, Lawrence. 1988. *Highbrow/Lowbrow: The Emergence of Cultural Hierarchy in America*. Cambridge, Massachusetts: Harvard University Press.

Lewis, George H. (ed.). 1993. *All That Glitters: Country Music in America*. Bowling Green, Ohio: Bowling Green State University Popular Press.

Lewis, Jerry Lee and Charles White. 1993. *Killer!* London: Century Books, Ltd.

Lewis, Lisa A. 1990. *Gender, Politics, and MTV: Voicing the Difference*. Philadelphia: Temple University Press.

Leyser, Brady J., with additional research by Pol Gosset. 1994. *Rock Stars/Pop Stars: A Comprehensive Bibliography, 1955-1994*. Westport, Connecticut: Greenwood Press.

Lipsitz, George. 1994. *Rainbow at Midnight: Labor and Culture in the 1940s*. Urbana: University of Illinois Press.

Lipsitz, George. 1990. *Time Passages: Collective Memory and American Popular Culture*. Minneapolis: University of Minnesota Press.

Loder, Kurt. 1990. *Bat Chain Puller: Rock and Roll in the Age of Celebrity*. New York: St. Martin's Press.

Lofman, Ron. 1994. *Goldmine's Celebrity Vocals: Surprising, Unexpected, and Obscure Recordings by Actors, Sports Heroes, and Celebrities*. Iola, Wisconsin: Krause Publications.

Lomax, Alan. 1993. *The Land Where the Blues Began*. New York: Pantheon Books.

Love, Robert (ed). 1993. *The Best of Rolling Stone: Twenty-Five Years of Journalism on the Edge*. New York: Doubleday.

Loza, Steven. 1993. *Barrio Rhythm: Mexican American Music in Los Angeles*. Urbana: University of Illinois Press.

Lull, James. 1992. *Popular Music and Communication* (second edition). Newbury Park, California: Sage Publications Inc.

MacDonald, Ian. 1994. *Revolution in the Head: The Beatles' Records and the Sixties*. New York: Henry Holt and Company.

MacLeod, Bruce A. 1993. *Club Date Musicians: Playing the New York Party Circuit*. Urbana: University of Illinois Press.

Marcus, Greil. 1991. *Dead Elvis: A Chronicle of Cultural Obsession*. Garden City, New York: Doubleday.

Marcus, Greil. 1989. *Lipstick Traces: A Secret History of the Twentieth Century.* Cambridge, Massachusetts: Harvard University Press.

Marcus, Greil. 1993. *Ranters and Crowd Pleasers: Punk in Pop Music, 1977-1992.* New York: Doubleday.

Marsh, Dave. 1985. *Fortunate Son.* New York: Random House.

Marsh, Dave. 1989. *The Heart of Rock and Soul: The 1001 Greatest Singles Ever Made.* New York: New American Library.

Marsh, Dave. 1993. *Louie Louie: The History and Mythology of The World's Most Famous Rock 'n' Roll Song.* New York: Hyperion Books.

Marsh, Dave and James Bernard. 1994. *The New Book of Rock Lists.* New York: Fireside Books/Simon and Schuster.

Martin, George, with William Pearson. 1994. *With a Little Help from My Friends: The Making of Sgt. Pepper.* Boston: Little, Brown, and Company.

Martin, Linda and Kerry Segrave. 1993. *Anti-Rock: The Opposition to Rock 'n' Roll.* New York: Da Capo Press.

Mawhinney, Paul C. (ed.). 1993. *Music Master: The CD-5 Singles Directory—From the Beginning to 1994.* Pittsburgh: Record-Rama Sound Archives.

Mawhinney, Paul C. (ed.). 1992. *Music Master: The 45 RPM Singles Directory/ Supplement—44 Years of Recorded Music from 1948 to 1992 Listed Alphabetically By Artist.* Pittsburgh: Record-Rama Sound Archives.

Mawhinney, Paul C. (comp.). 1983. *Music Master: The 45 RPM Record Directory, 1947-1982 (Volume I-Artist).* Pittsburgh: Record-Rama.

Mawhinney, Paul C. (comp.). 1983. *Music Master: The 45 RPM Record Directory, 1947-1982 (Volume II-Title).* Pittsburgh: Record-Rama.

McAleer, Dave (comp.). 1994. *The All-Music Book of Hit Singles: Top Twenty Charts from 1954 to the Present Day.* San Francisco: Miller Freeman Books.

McAleer, Dave. 1994. *The Fab British Rock 'n' Roll Invasion of 1964.* New York: St. Martin's Press.

McAleer, Dave. 1993. *Hit Parade Heroes: British Beat Before the Beatles.* London: Hamlyn Books.

McAleer, Dave. 1990. *The Omnibus Book of British and American Hit Singles, 1960-1990.* London: Omnibus Press.

McDonough, Jack. 1985. *San Francisco Rock: The Illustrated History of San Francisco Rock Music.* San Francisco: Chronicle Books.

McLaurin, Melton and Richard Peterson (eds.). 1992. *You Wrote My Life: Lyrical Themes in Country Music.* New York: Gordon and Breach.

Middleton, Richard. 1989. *Studying Popular Music.* Milton Keynes, England: Open University Press.

Miller, Terry E. 1986. *Folk Music in America: A Reference Guide.* New York: Garland Publishers.

Moore, Allan F. 1993. *Rock, the Primary Text: Developing a Musicology of Rock.* Philadelphia: Open University Press.

Murray, Charles Shaar. 1993. *Blues on CD: The Essential Guide.* London: Kyle Cathie, Ltd.

Nash, Bruce and Allan Zullo. 1993. *The Wacky Top 40*. Holbrook, Massachusetts: Bob Adams.

Negus, Keith. 1992. *Producing Pop: Culture and Conflict in the Popular Music Industry*. New York: Edward Arnold.

Nickerson, Marina, with photographs by Cynthia Farah. 1982. *Country Music: A Look at the Men Who've Made It*. El Paso, Texas: C. M. Publishing Co.

Norman, Philip. 1982. *The Road Goes on Forever: Portraits from a Journey Through Contemporary Music*. New York: Fireside Books.

Obrecht, Jas (ed.). 1990. *Blues Guitar: The Men Who Made the Music*. San Francisco: Guitar Player.

Obrecht, Jas (ed.). 1987. *Texas Guitar*. Cupertino, California: Guitar Player.

Oermann, Robert K., with Douglas Green. 1983. *The Listener's Guide to Country Music*. New York: Facts On File.

Oliver, Paul. 1990. *Blues Fell This Morning: Meaning in the Blues*. Cambridge, England: Cambridge University Press.

Oliver, Vaughan, Storm Thorgerson, and Roger Dean (eds.). 1993. *Album Cover Album 6*. London: Dragon's World Books.

O'Neil, Thomas. 1993. *The Grammys: For the Record*. New York: Penguin Books.

Otis, Johnny. 1993. *Upside Your Head! Rhythm and Blues on Central Avenue*. Hanover, New Hampshire: Wesleyan University Press/University Press of New England.

Paikos, Mike (comp.). 1993. *R&B Covers and Re-Recordings*. Moraga, California: M. Paikos.

Patterson, Daniel W. (ed.). 1991. *Sounds of the South*. Chapel Hill: Southern Folklore Collection at the University of North Carolina.

Pattillo, Craig W. 1990. *TV Theme Soundtrack Directory and Discography with Cover Versions*. Portland, Oregon: Braemar Books.

Pavlow, Al (comp.). 1983. *Big Al Pavlow's the R&B Book: A Disc-History of Rhythm and Blues*. Providence, Rhode Island: Music House Publishing.

Pavlow, Al (comp.). *Hot Charts 1940*. Providence, Rhode Island: Music House Publishing.

Pavlow, Al (comp.). 1994. *Hot Charts 1941*. Providence, Rhode Island: Music House Publishing.

Pavlow, Al (comp.). 1994. *Hot Charts 1942*. Providence, Rhode Island: Music House Publishing.

Pavlow, Al (comp.). 1994. *Hot Charts 1943*. Providence, Rhode Island: Music House Publishing.

Pavlow, Al (comp.). 1994. *Hot Charts 1944*. Providence, Rhode Island: Music House Publishing.

Pavlow, Al (comp.). 1994. *Hot Charts 1945*. Providence, Rhode Island: Music House Publishing.

Pavlow, Al (comp.). 1994. *Hot Charts 1946*. Providence, Rhode Island: Music House Publishing.

Pavlow, Al (comp.). 1994. *Hot Charts 1947*. Providence, Rhode Island: Music House Publishing.

Pavlow, Al (comp.). 1994. *Hot Charts 1948*. Providence, Rhode Island: Music House Publishing.

Pavlow, Al (comp.). 1994. *Hot Charts 1949*. Providence, Rhode Island: Music House Publishing.

Pavlow, Big Al (comp.). 1990. *Hot Charts 1952*. Providence, Rhode Island: Music House Publishing.

Pavlow, Big Al (comp.). 1990. *Hot Charts 1953*. Providence, Rhode Island: Music House Publishing.

Pavlow, Big Al (comp.). 1990. *Hot Charts 1954*. Providence, Rhode Island: Music House Publishing.

Pavlow, Big Al (comp.). 1991. *Hot Charts 1955*. Providence, Rhode Island: Music House Publishing.

Pavlow, Big Al (comp.). 1991. *Hot Charts 1956*. Providence, Rhode Island: Music House Publishing.

Pearce, Chris. 1991. *Jukebox Art*. London: H.C. Blossom.

Peters, Richard. 1992. *Elvis: The Music Lives On—The Recording Sessions, 1954-1976*. London: Pop Universal/Souvenir Press.

Pike, Jeff. 1993. *The Death of Rock 'n' Roll: Untimely Demises, Morbid Pre-occupations, and Premature Forecasts of Doom in Pop Music*. Boston: Farber and Farber.

Pollock, Bruce (ed.). 1989. *Popular Music 1988—Volume 13: An Annotated Guide To American Popular Songs*. Detroit, Michigan: Gale Research, Inc.

Pollock, Bruce (ed.). 1990. *Popular Music: Volume 14, 1989*. Detroit, Michigan: Gale Research, Inc.

Pollock, Bruce (ed.). 1991. *Popular Music: Volume 15, 1990*. Detroit, Michigan: Gale Research, Inc.

Pollock, Bruce (ed.). 1993. *Popular Music: Volume 17, 1992*. Detroit, Michigan: Gale Research, Inc.

Pruter, Robert (ed.). 1993. *The Blackwell Guide to Soul Recordings*. Oxford, England: Basil Blackwell.

Raymond, Jack. 1992. *Show Music on Record: The First 100 Years*. Washington, DC: Smithsonian Institution Press.

Reuss, Jerry (comp.). 1995. *Joel Whitburn's Top Pop Singles CD Guide, 1955-1979*. Menomonee Falls, Wisconsin: Record Research, Inc.

Richards, Tad and Melvin B. Shestack (comps.) 1993. *The New Country Music Encyclopedia*. New York: Fireside Books/Simon and Schuster.

Roberty, Marc. 1994. *Eric Clapton: The Eric Clapton Album—Thirty Years of Music and Memorabilia*. New York: Viking Studio Books/Penguin Books U.S.A.

*Rockabilly!* 1993. Milwaukee, Wisconsin: Hal Leonard Publishing Corp.

Roland, Tom. 1991. *The Billboard Book of Number One Country Hits*. New York: Watson-Guptill Publications/Billboard Books.

Romanowski, Patricia (ed.). 1983. *The Rolling Stone Rock Almanac: The Chronicles of Rock and Roll*. New York: Rolling Stone Press/Collier Books.

Rose, Tricia. 1994. *Black Noise: Rap Music and Black Culture in Contemporary America*. Hanover, New Hampshire: University Press of New England.

Ross, Andrew and Tricia Rose (eds.). 1994. *Microphone Fiends: Youth Music and Youth Culture*. New York: Routledge.

Rubiner, Julia M. (ed.). 1993. *Contemporary Musicians—Volume Eight: Profiles of the People in Music*. Detroit, Michigan: Gale Research, Inc.

Rubiner, Julia M. (ed.). 1993. *Contemporary Musicians—Volume Nine: Profiles of the People in Music*. Detroit, Michigan: Gale Research, Inc.

Ruppli, Michel and Ed Novitsky (comps.). 1993. *The Mercury Labels: A Discography* (Five Volumes). Westport, Connecticut: Greenwood Press.

Rust, Brian and Allen G. Debus. 1989. *The Complete Entertainment Discography from 1897 To 1942* (revised second edition). New York: Da Capo Press.

Ryan, Marc. 1992. *Trumpet Records: An Illustrated History with Discography*. Milford, New Hampshire: Big Nickle Publications.

Rypens, Arnold. 1987. *The Originals: "You Can't Judge a Song by the Cover."* Brussels, Belgium: BRT Vitgrave.

Sammon, Paul M. (ed.). 1994. *The King Is Dead: Tales of Elvis Postmortem*. New York: Delta Books.

Sanjek, Russell and David Sanjek. 1991. *The American Popular Music Business in the 20th Century*. New York: Oxford University Press.

Santell, Robert. 1993. *The Big Book of the Blues: A Biographical Encyclopedia*. New York: Penguin Books.

Santoro, Gene. 1994. *Dancing in Your Head: Jazz, Blues, Rock, and Beyond*. New York: Oxford University.

Savary, Louis M. 1967. *The Kingdom of Downtown: Finding Teenagers in Their Music*. New York: Paulist Press.

Savore, Chris (comp.). 1993. *U.K. Black Music 45s, 1950-1980*. New Castle Under Lyme, Staffordshire, England: Soul Care Publications.

Scherman, Tony (ed.). 1994. *The Rock Musicians—15 Years of Interviews: The Best of Musicians Magazine*. New York: St. Martin's Press.

Scheurer, Timothy E. 1991. *Born in the U.S.A.: The Myth of America in Popular Music from Colonial Times to the Present*. Jackson, MS: University Press of Mississippi.

Schipper, Henry. 1992. *Broken Record: The Inside Story of the Grammy Awards*. Secaucus, New Jersey: Birch Lane Press.

Schwichtenberg, Cathy (ed.). 1992. *The Madonna Connection: Representational Politics, Subculture Identities, and Cultural Theory*. Boulder, Colorado: Westview Press.

Scott, Barry. 1994. *We Had Joy, We Had Fun: The "Lost" Recording Artists of the Seventies*. Boston: Faber and Faber.

Seeger, Pete and Bob Reiser. 1991. *Carry It On! The Story of America's Working People in Song and Picture*. Bethlehem, Pennsylvania: Sing Out Publications.

Sexton, Adam (ed.). 1995. *Rap on Rap: Straight-Up Talk on Hip-Hop Culture*. New York: Dell Publishing.

Shank, Barry. 1994. *Dissonant Identities: The Rock 'n' Roll Scene in Austin, Texas*. Hanover, New Hampshire: University Press of New England.

Shapiro, Bill. 1988. *The CD Rock and Roll Library: Thirty Years of Rock and Roll on Compact Disc*. Kansas City, Missouri: Andrews and McMeel.

Simpson, Jeff (ed.). 1992. *Radio One's Classic Interviews: 25 Rock Greats in Their Own Words*. London: BBC Books.

Sonnier Jr., Austin. 1994. *A Guide to the Blues: History, Who's Who, Research Sources*. Westport, Connecticut: Greenwood Press.

Spencer, Jon Michael. 1993. *Blues and Evil*. Knoxville: University of Tennessee Press.

Stanley, Lawrence A. (ed.). 1992. *Rap: The Lyrics*. New York: Penguin Books.

Stone, Al. 1990. *Jingles: How to Write, Produce, and Sell Commercial Music*. Cincinnati, Ohio: Writer's Digest.

Studwell, William. 1994. *The Popular Song Reader: A Sampler of Well-Known Twentieth-Century Songs*. Binghamton, New York: The Haworth Press.

Sultanof, Jeff (editorial director). 1992. *The Most Fantastic Fakebook in the World*. Secaucus, New Jersey: Warner Brothers Publications.

Sumrall, Harry. 1994. *Pioneers of Rock and Roll: 100 Artists Who Changed the Face of Rock*. New York: Billboard Books.

Sutton, Allan (comp.). 1993. *A Guide to Pseudonyms on American Recordings, 1892-1942*. Westport, Connecticut: Greenwood Press.

Swern, Phil and Shaun Greenfield. 1990. *30 Years of Number Ones: The U.K. and U.S. Chart-Toppers, 1960-1989*. London: British Broadcasting Corporation.

Tee, Ralph. 1991. *Who's Who in Soul Music*. London: Weidenfield and Nicolson.

Tharin, Jr., Frank C. (comp.). 1980. *Chart Champions: 40 Years of Rankings and Ratings*. San Francisco: Chart Champions.

Tichi, Cecelia. 1994. *High Lonesome: The American Culture of Country Music*. Chapel Hill: University of North Carolina Press.

Tichi, Cecelia. (ed.). 1995. *Readin' Country Music: Steel Guitars, Opry Stars, and Honky Tonk Bars*. Durham, North Carolina: Duke University Press.

Titon, Jeff Todd (ed.). 1990. *Downhome Blues Lyrics: An Anthology from the Post-World War II Era* (second edition). Urbana: University of Illinois Press.

Titon, Jeff (general editor). 1992. *Worlds of Music: An Introduction to the Music of the World's Peoples* (Second Edition). New York: Schirmer Books.

Tobler, John (ed.). 1992. *The NME Rock and Roll Years*. London: Hamlyn Books.

Torme, Mel. 1994. *My Singing Teachers: Reflections on Singing Popular Music*. New York: Oxford University Press.

Tosches, Nick. 1982. *Hellfire: The Jerry Lee Lewis Story*. New York: Dell Publishing.

Tosches, Nick. 1991. *Unsung Heroes of Rock 'n' Roll: The Birth of Rock in the Wild Years Before Elvis* (revised edition). New York: Harmony Books.

Umphred, Neal (comp.). 1994. *Goldmine's Price Guide to Collectible Jazz Albums, 1949-1969* (second edition). Iola, Wisconsin: Krause Publications.

Umphred, Neal, with special contributions by Norman Feinberg and Gary Johnson (comps.). 1994. *Goldmine's Price Guide to Collectible Record Albums* (fourth edition). Iola, Wisconsin: Krause Publications.

Walker, Clinton (ed.). 1985. *The Next Thing: Contemporary Australia Rock.* Beaverton, Oregon: Kangaroo Press.

Walker, Donald E. and B. Lee Cooper. 1995. *Baseball and American Culture.* Jefferson, North Carolina: McFarland and Company.

Walser, Robert. 1993. *Running with the Devil: Power, Gender, and Madness in Heavy Metal Music.* Hanover, New Hampshire: University Press of New England.

Warner, Jay. 1992. *The Billboard Book of American Singing Groups: A History, 1940-1990.* New York: Billboard Books.

Weinstein, Deena. 1991. *Heavy Metal: A Cultural Sociology.* New York: Lexington Books.

West, John Foster. 1993. *Lift Up Your Head, Tom Dooley: The True Story of the Appalachian Murder That Inspired One of America's Popular Ballads.* Asheboro, North Carolina: Down Home Press.

Wexler, Jerry and David Ritz. 1993. *Rhythm and the Blues: A Life in American Music.* New York: Alfred A. Knopf.

Whitburn, Joel (comp.). 1995. *Billboard Music Yearbook 1994.* Menomonee Falls, Wisconsin: Record Research, Inc.

Whitburn, Joel (comp.). 1994. *Billboard Pop Album Charts, 1965-1969.* Menomonee Falls, Wisconsin: Record Research, Inc.

Whitburn, Joel (comp.). 1994. *Billboard Singles Reviews–1958.* Menomonee Falls, Wisconsin: Record Research, Inc.

Whitburn, Joel (comp.). 1992. *Bubbling Under the Hot 100, 1959-1985.* Menomonee Falls, Wisconsin: Record Research, Inc.

Whitburn, Joel (comp.). 1993. *Daily #1 Hits, 1940-1992.* Menomonee Falls, Wisconsin: Record Research, Inc.

Whitburn, Joel (comp.). 1991. *1990 Music and Video Yearbook.* Menomonee Falls, Wisconsin: Record Research, Inc.

Whitburn, Joel (comp.). 1992. *1991 Music and Video Yearbook.* Menomonee Falls, Wisconsin: Record Research, Inc.

Whitburn, Joel (comp.). 1993. *1992 Music and Video Yearbook.* Menomonee Falls, Wisconsin: Record Research, Inc.

Whitburn, Joel (comp.). 1994. *1993 Music Yearbook.* Menomonee Falls, Wisconsin: Record Research, Inc.

Whitburn, Joel (comp.). 1995. *Pop Annual, 1955-1994.* Menomonee Falls, Wisconsin: Record Research, Inc.

Whitburn, Joel (comp.). 1994. *Pop Hits 1940-1954.* Menomonee Falls, Wisconsin: Record Research, Inc.

Whitburn, Joel (comp.). 1991. *Pop Singles Annual, 1955-1990.* Menomonee Falls, Wisconsin: Record Research, Inc.

Whitburn, Joel (comp.). 1993. *Top Adult Contemporary, 1961-1993.* Menomonee Falls, Wisconsin: Record Research, Inc.

Whitburn, Joel (comp.). 1994. *Top Country Singles, 1944-1993.* Menomonee Falls, Wisconsin: Record Research, Inc.

Whitburn, Joel (comp.). 1993. *Top Pop Album Tracks, 1955-1992.* Menomonee Falls, Wisconsin: Record Research, Inc.

Whitburn, Joel (comp.). 1995. *Top Pop Singles CD Guide, 1955-1979.* Menomonee Falls, Wisconsin: Record Research, Inc.

Whitburn, Joel (comp.). 1994. *Top Pop Singles, 1955-1993.* Menomonee Falls, Wisconsin: Record Research, Inc.

Whitburn, Joel (comp.). 1993. *Top 1000 × 5.* Menomonee Falls, Wisconsin: Record Research, Inc.

Whitcomb, Ian. 1982. *Whole Lotta Shakin': A Rock 'n' Roll Scrapbook.* London: Arrow Books.

White, Adam. 1990. *The Billboard Book of Gold and Platinum Records.* New York: Billboard Books.

White, Adam and Fred Bronson. 1993. *The Billboard Book of Number One Rhythm and Blues Hits.* New York: Billboard Books/Watson-Guptill Publications.

White, Charles. 1984. *The Life and Times of Little Richard: The Quasar of Rock.* New York: Da Capo Press.

Wilcock, Donald E., with Buddy Guy. 1993. *Damn Right I've Got The Blues: Buddy Guy and the Blues Roots of Rock-and-Roll.* San Francisco: Woodford Press.

Williams, Paul. 1993. *Rock and Roll: The 100 Best Singles.* New York: Carroll and Graf Publishers, Inc.

Wolff, Daniel, with S. R. Crain, Clifton White, and G. David Tenenbaum. 1995. *You Send Me: The Life and Times of Sam Cooke.* New York: William Morrow.

Woods, Bernie. 1994. *When the Music Stopped: The Big Band Era Remembered.* New York: Barricade Books.

Wynn, Ron, with Michael Erlewine and Vladimir Bogdanov (eds.). 1994. *All Music Guide to Jazz: The Best CDs, Albums, and Tapes.* San Francisco: Miller Freeman Books.

Young, Jordan R. 1994. *Spike Jones off the Record: The Man Who Murdered Music.* Beverly Hills, California: Past Times Publishing.

## *Articles*

Blair, M. Elizabeth and Eva M. Hyatt. 1992. "Home Is Where The Heart Is: An Analysis of Meanings of the Home in Country Music." *Popular Music and Society*, XVI, Winter, pp. 69-82.

Bradby, Barbara. 1993. "Sampling Sexuality: Gender, Technology, and the Body in Dance Music." *Popular Music*, XII, May, pp. 155-176.

Caputi, Jane. 1993. "Nuclear Power and the Sacred; or, Why a Beautiful Woman Is Like a Nuclear Power Plant." *Ecofeminism and the Sacred*, edited by Carol J. Adams. New York: Continuum Press, pp. 229-250.

Christianen, Michael. 1995. "Cycles in Symbol Production? A New Model to Explain Concentration, Diversity, and Innovation in the Music Industry." *Popular Music*, XIV, January, pp. 55-93.

Colman, Stuart. 1993. "Lest We Forget." *Now Dig This*, No. 128, November, pp. 5-6.

Cooper, B. Lee. 1973. "Social Change, Popular Music, and the Teacher." *Social Education*, XXXVII, December, pp. 776-781.

Cooper, B. Lee. 1975. "Images of the Future in Popular Music: Lyrical Comments on Tomorrow." *Social Education*, XXXIX, May, pp. 276-285.

Cooper, B. Lee. 1976a. "Oral History, Popular Music, and Les McCann." *Social Studies*, LXVII, May/June, pp. 115-118.

Cooper, B. Lee. 1976b. "Resources for Teaching Popular Music: A Checklist." *Popular Culture Methods*, III, Spring, pp. 37-38.

Cooper, B. Lee. 1977. "The Traditional and Beyond: Resources for Teaching Women's Studies." *Audiovisual Instruction*, XXII, December, pp. 14-18ff.

Cooper, B. Lee. 1977-1978. "Popular Songs as Oral History: Teaching Black History Through Contemporary Audio Resources." *International Journal of Instructional Media*, V, pp. 185-195.

Cooper, B. Lee. 1978a. "The Image of the Black Man: Contemporary Lyrics as Oral History." *The Journal of the Interdenominational Theological Center*, V, spring, pp. 105-122.

Cooper, B. Lee. 1978b. "Women's Studies and Popular Music: Using Audio Resources in Social Studies Instruction." *The History and Social Science Teacher*, XIV, Fall, pp. 29-40.

Cooper, B. Lee. 1979a. "Jerry Lee Lewis and Little Richard: Career Parallels in the Lives of the Court Jesters of Rock 'n' Roll." *Music World and Record Digest*, No. 46, May, p. 6.

Cooper, B. Lee. 1979b. "Popular Music: A Creative Teaching Resource." *Audiovisual Instruction*, XXIV, March, pp. 37-43.

Cooper, B. Lee. 1979c. "Popular Music: An Untapped Resource for Teaching Contemporary Black History." *Journal of Negro Education*, XLVIII, Winter, pp. 20-36.

Cooper, B. Lee. 1979-1980. "'Cruisin' and Playin' the Radio': Exploring Images of the American Automobile Through Popular Music." *International Journal of Instructional Media*, VII, pp. 327-334.

Cooper, B. Lee. 1980a. "Information Services, Popular Culture, and the Librarian: Promoting a Contemporary Learning Perspective." *Drexel Library Quarterly*, XVI, July, pp. 24-42.

Cooper, B. Lee. 1980b. "Nothin' Outrun My V-8 Ford: Chuck Berry and the American Motorcar, 1955-1979." *JEMF Quarterly*, XVI, Spring, pp. 18-23.

Cooper, B. Lee. 1980c. "A Popular Music Perspective: Challenging Sexism in the Social Studies Classroom." *Social Studies*, LXXI, March/April, pp. 71-76.

Cooper, B. Lee. 1980-1981. "Contemporary Music Discographies: Guides to Recorded Teaching Resources." *International Journal of Instructional Media*, VIII, pp. 81-93.

Cooper, B. Lee. 1981a. "Jerry Lee Lewis: Rock 'n' Roll's Living Legend." *Music World*, No. 90, October, pp. 28-36.

Cooper, B. Lee. 1981b. "Music and the Metropolis: Lyrical Images of Life in American Cities, 1950-1980." *Teaching History: A Journal of Methods*, VI, Fall, pp. 72-84.

Cooper, B. Lee. 1981c. "Popular Music in the Social Studies Classroom: Audio Resources for Teacher." (How To Do It–Series 2, No. 13) Washington, DC: N.C.S.S., pp. 1-8.

Cooper, B. Lee. 1981-1982. "Popular Music Bibliographies: Literary Resource Guides to Contemporary Songs, Singers, Styles, and Sounds from 1950-1980." *International Journal of Instructional Media*, IX, pp. 173-184.

Cooper, B. Lee. 1982/1983. "Johnny Rivers and Linda Ronstadt: Rock 'n' Roll Revivalists." *JEMF Quarterly*, XVIII, Nos. 67/68, Fall/Winter, pp. 166-177.

Cooper, B. Lee. 1983. "Oral History, Popular Music, and American Railroads, 1920-1980." *Social Studies*, LXXIV, November/December, pp. 223-231.

Cooper, B. Lee. 1984. "The Fats Domino Decades, 1950-1969." *R.P.M.*, No. 5, May, pp. 56-58.

Cooper, B. Lee. 1985. "Mick Jagger as Herodotus and Billy Joel as Thucydides? A Rock Music Perspective, 1950-1985." *Social Education*, XLIX, October, pp. 596-600.

Cooper, B. Lee. 1986a. "Controversial Issues in Popular Lyrics, 1960-1985: Teaching Resources from the English Classroom." *Arizona English Bulletin*, XXIX, Fall, pp. 174-187.

Cooper, B. Lee. 1986b. "Human Relations, Communication Technology, and Popular Music: Audio Images of Telephone Use in the United States, 1950-1985." *International Journal of Instructional Media*, XIII, No. 1, pp. 75-82.

Cooper, B. Lee. 1988a. "Christmas Songs: Audio Barometers of Tradition and Social Change in America, 1950-1987." *Social Studies*, LXXIX, November/December, pp. 278-280.

Cooper, B. Lee. 1988b. "Images from Fairy Tales and Nursery Rhymes in the Lyrics of Contemporary Recordings." *International Journal of Instructional Media*, XV, No. 2, pp. 183-193.

Cooper, B. Lee. 1988c. "Social Concerns, Political Protest, and Popular Music." *Social Studies*, LXXIX, March/April, pp. 53-60.

Cooper, B. Lee. 1989a. "Creating an Audio Chronology: Utilizing Popular Recordings to Illustrate Ideas and Events in American History, 1965-1987." *International Journal of Instructional Media*, XVI, No. 2, pp. 167-179.

Cooper, B. Lee. 1989b. " 'Do You Hear What I Hear?' Christmas Recordings as Audio Symbols of Religious Tradition and Social Change in Contemporary America." *International Journal of Instructional Media*, XVI, No. 3, pp. 265-270.

Cooper, B. Lee. 1989c. "Repeating Hit Tunes, A Cappella Style: The Persuasions as Song Revivalists, 1967-1982." *Popular Music and Society*, XIII, Fall, pp. 17-27.

Cooper, B. Lee. 1989d. "Rhythm 'n' Rhymes: Character and Theme Images from Children's Literature in Contemporary Recordings, 1950-1985." *Popular Music and Society*, XIII, Spring, pp. 53-71.

Cooper, B. Lee. 1989e. "Rick Nelson: A Review Essay." *Popular Music and Society*, XIII, Winter, pp. 77-82.

Cooper, B. Lee. 1990. "From Anonymous Announcer to Radio Personality; From Pied Piper to Payola: The American Disc Jockey, 1950-1970." *Popular Music and Society*, XIV, Winter, pp. 89-95.

Cooper, B. Lee (comp.). 1991a. "Baseball on Record: A Selected Discography of 45 R.P.M. Recordings." *Popular Music and Society*; XV, Summer, pp. 58-62.

Cooper, B. Lee. 1991b. "Dancing: The Perfect Educational Metaphor." *Garfield Lake Review*, Spring, pp. 14-15.

Cooper, B. Lee. 1991c. "Having a Screaming Ball in Dracula's Hall." *Popular Music and Society*, XV, Spring, pp. 103-105.

Cooper, B. Lee. 1991d. "Lyrical Commentaries: Learning from Popular Music." *Music Educators Journal*, LXXVII, April, pp. 56-59.

Cooper, B. Lee. 1992a. "*Dracula* and *Frankenstein* in the Classroom: Examining Theme and Character Exchanges in Film and in Music." *International Journal of Instructional Media*, XIX, No. 4, pp. 339-347.

Cooper, B. Lee. 1992b. "Examining the Audio Images of War: Lyrical perspectives on America's Major Military Crusades, 1914-1991." *International Journal of Instructional Media*, XIX, No. 3, pp. 277-287.

Cooper, B. Lee. 1992c. "I'll Fight for God, Country, and My Baby: Persistent Themes in American Wartime Songs." *Popular Music and Society*, XVI, Summar, pp. 95-111.

Cooper, B. Lee (comp.). 1992d. "Popular Culture Research and Library Services: A Selected Bibliography." *Popular Culture Association Newsletter*, XIX, May, pp. 5-7.

Cooper, B. Lee. 1992e. "A Resource Guide to Studies in the Theory and Practice of Popular Culture Librarianship." *Popular Culture and Acquisitions*, edited by Allen Ellis. Binghamton, New York: The Haworth Press, pp. 131-146.

Cooper, B. Lee. 1993a. "Awarding an 'A' Grade to Heavy Metal: A Review Essay." *Popular Music and Society*, XVII, Fall, pp. 99-102.

Cooper B. Lee. 1993b. "Can Music Students Learn Anything of Value by Investigating Popular Recordings?" *International Journal of Instructional Media*, XX, No. 3, pp. 273-284.

Cooper, B. Lee. 1993c. "The Coasters–What Was the Secret of Their Succes? A Review Essay." *Popular Music and Society*, XVII, Summar, pp. 115-119.

Cooper, B. Lee. 1993d. "The Drifters: From Gospel Glory to Rock Royalty." *Popular Music and Society*, XVII, Winter, pp. 125-128.

Cooper, B. Lee. 1993e. "From the Outside Looking In: A Popular Culture Researcher Speaks to Librarians." *Popular Culture in Libraries*, I, No. 1, pp. 37-46.

Cooper, B. Lee. 1993f. "Jackie Wilson–Mr. Excitement? Mr. Musical Diversity? Mr. Song Stylist? or Mr. Stage Show? A Review Essay." *Popular Music and Society*, XVII, No. 2, Summer, pp. 119-122.

Cooper, B. Lee. 1993g. "Processing Health Care Images from Popular Culture Resources: Physicians, Cigarettes, and Medical Metaphors in Contemporary Recordings." *Popular Music and Society*, XVII, Winter, pp. 105-124.

Cooper, B. Lee. 1993h. "Rumers of War: Lyrical Continuities, 1914-1991." *Continuities of Popular Culture*, edited by Ray B. Browne and Ronald J. Ambrosetti. Bowling Green, Ohio: Bowling Green State University Popular Press, pp. 121-142.

Cooper, B. Lee. 1993i. "Searching for the Most Popular Songs of the Year . . . with Menomonee Joe, Big Al, Louisiana Jim, and Bayou Barry." *Popular Culture in Libraries*, I, No. 2, pp. 125-130.

Cooper, B. Lee. 1993j. "Sultry Songs and Censorship: A Thematic Discography for College Teachers." *International Journal of Instructional Media*, XX, No. 2, pp. 181-194.

Cooper, B. Lee. 1993k. "Sultry Songs as High Humor." *Popular Music and Society*, XXVII, Spring, pp. 71-85.

Cooper, B. Lee. 1993l. "Tapping a Sound Recording Archive for War Song Resources to Investigate America's Major Military Involvement, 1914-1991." *Popular Culture in Libraries*, I, No. 4, pp. 71-93.

Cooper, B. Lee. 1994. "Sex, Songs, and Censorship: A Thematic Taxonomy of Popular Recordings for Music Librarians and Sound Recording Archivists." *Popular Culture in Libraries*, II, No. 4, pp. 11-47.

Cooper, B. Lee and Laura E. Cooper. 1992. "Commercial Recordings and Cultural Interchanges: Studying Great Britain and the United States, 1943-1967." *International Journal of Instructional Media*, XIX, No. 2, pp. 183-189.

Cooper, B. Lee and James A. Creeth. 1983. "Present at the Creation: The Legend of Jerry Lee Lewis on Record, 1956-1963." *JEMF Quarterly*, XIX, Summer, 122-129.

Cooper, B. Lee and Larry S. Haverkos. 1973. "The Image of American Society in Popular Music: A Search for Identity and Values." *Social Studies*, LXIV, December, pp. 319-322.

Cooper, B. Lee and William L. Schurk. 1981. "William L. Schurk—Audio Center Director: A Close Encounter with a Librarian of a Different Kind." *Twentieth-Century Popular Culture in Museums and Libraries*, edited by Fred E. H. Schroeder. Bowling Green, Ohio: Bowling Green State University Popular Press, pp. 210-225.

Cooper B. Lee and William L. Schurk. 1987. "Food for Thought: Investigating Culinary Images in Contemporary American Recordings." *Internatinal Journal of Instructional Media*, XIV, No. 3, pp. 251-262.

Cooper, B. Lee and William L. Schurk. 1989. "From 'I Saw Mommy Kissing Santa Claus' to 'Another Brick in the Wall': Popular Recordings Featuring Pre-teen Performers, Traditional Childhood Stories, and Contemporary Pre-adolescent Perspectives, 1945-1985." *International Journal of Instructional Media*, XVI, No. 1, pp. 83-90.

Cooper, B. Lee and William L. Schurk. 1993. "A Haunting Question: Should Sound Recording Archives Promote the Circulation of Horror Material?" *Popular Culture in Libraries*, I, No. 3, pp. 45-58.

Cooper B. Lee and William L. Schurk. 1994. "Smokin' Songs: Examining Tobacco Use as an American Cultural Phenomenon Through Contemporary

Lyrics." *International Journal of Instructional Media*, XXI, No. 3, pp. 261-268.

Cooper, B. Lee and Verdan D. Traylor. 1979-1980. "Liberal Education and Technology in Small Colleges: Popular Music and The Computer." *International Journal of Instructional Media*, VII, pp. 25-35.

Cooper, B. Lee and Donald E. Walker, 1990. "Baseball, Popular Music, and Twentieth-Century American History." *Society Studies*, LXXXI, May-June, pp. 120-124.

Cooper, B. Lee and Donald E. Walker, with assistance from William L. Schurk. 1991. "The Decline of Contemporary Baseball Heroes in American Popular Recordings." *Popular Music and Society*, XV, Summar, pp. 49-58.

Cooper, B. Lee, Simon Frith, Bernhard Hefele, Frank Hoffmann, David Horn, Toru Mitsui, and Robert Springer (comps.). 1990. "Booklist." *Popular Music*, IX, October, pp. 389-405.

Cooper, B. Lee, Simon Frith, Bernhard Hefele, Frank Hoffmann, Toru Mitsui, Lynne Sharma, and Robert Springer (comps.). 1991. "Booklist." *Popular Music*, X, October, pp. 361-378.

Cooper, B. Lee, Frank Hoffman, Simon Frith, Bernhard Hefele, David Horn, Jaap Gerritse, Antoine Hennion, and Toru Mitsui (comps.). 1992. "Booklist." *Popular Music*, XI, October, pp. 385-404.

Cooper, B. Lee, David Buckley, Simon Frith, Jaap Gerritse, Bernhard Hefele, Frank W. Hoffmann, and Toru Mitsui (comps.). 1993. "Booklist." *Popular Music*, XII, October, pp. 331-352.

Cooper, B. Lee, Michael Marsden, Barbara Moran, and Allen Ellis. 1993. "Popular Culture Materials in Libraries and Archives." *Popular Culture in Libraries*, I, No. 1, pp. 5-35.

Cooper, B. Lee, Jaap Gerriste, Bernhard Hefele, Frank Hoffmann, Toru Mitsui, and Motti Regev (comps.). 1994. "Booklist." *Popular Music*, XIII, No. 3, October, pp. 375-399.

Cooper, Laura E. and B. Lee Cooper. 1990. "Exploring Cultural Imperialism: Bibliographical Resources for Teaching About American Domination, British Adaptation, and the Rock Music Interchange, 1950-1967." *International Journal of Instructional Media*, XVII, No. 2, pp. 167-177.

Cooper, Laura E. and B. Lee Cooper. 1993a. "From American Forces Network to Chuck Berry, from Larry Parnes to George Martin: The Rise of Rock Music Culture in Great Britain, 1943 to 1967 and Beyond—A Biblio-Historical Study." *Popular Cultures in Libraries*, I, No. 2, pp. 33-64.

Cooper, Laura E. and B. Lee Cooper. 1993b. "The Pendulum of Cultural Imperialism: Popular Music Interchanges between the United States and Britain, 1943-1967." *Journal of Popular Culture*, XXVII, Winter, pp. 61-78.

Cusic, Don. 1993. "Comedy and Humor in Country Music." *Journal of American Culture*, XVI, Summer, pp. 45-50.

Cutietta, Robert A. 1991. "Popular Music: An Ongoing Challenge." *Music Educators Journal*, LXXXVII, April, pp. 26-29.

Dawson, Jim. 1995. "And the Twist Goes Round and Round." *Goldmine*, No. 389, June 23, pp. 42-58, 154.

Duxbury, Janell R. 1988. "Shakespeare Meet the Backbeat: Literary Allusion in Rock Music." *Popular Music and Society*, XII, Fall, pp. 19-23.

Endres, Thomas G. 1993. "A Dramatic Analysis of Family Themes in the Top 100 Country Songs of 1992." *Popular Music and Society*, XVII, Winter, pp. 29-46.

Epstein, Jonathon S. and David J. Pratto. 1990. "Heavy Metal Rock Music, Juvenile Delinquency, and Satanic Identification." *Popular Music and Society*, XIV, Winter, pp. 67-76.

Fitzgerald, Jon. 1995. "Motown Crossover Hits 1963-1966 and the Creative Process." *Popular Music*, XIV, January, pp. 1-11.

Geiger, Pat. 1993. "I Wrote a Letter to the Postman: How Elvis Received a Stamp of Approval." *Goldmine*, No. 326, January 26, pp. 44-46, 92, 94.

Goebel, Bruce. 1993. "Diversity, Conformity, and Democracy: A Critique of Arthur M. Schlesinger's *The Disuniting of America: Reflections on a Multicultural Society.*" *Journal of American Culture*, XVI, Winter, pp. 73-77.

Hicks, Jeffrey Alan. 1992. "Television Theme Songs: A Content Analysis." *Popular Music and Society*, XVI, Spring, pp. 13-20.

Johnson-Grau, Brenda. 1989. "Prodigal Sons on a Lost Highway: Records in Rock and Roll." *One, Two, Three, Four: A Rock 'n' Roll Quarterly*, No. 7, Winter, pp. 21-36.

Knickerbockers, I. M. 1994. "Does Howard A. DeWitt Really Exist?" *DISCoveries*, No. 72, May, pp. 10-12.

Lemlich, Jeffrey M. 1994. "Twistin' with Tricky: A Richard Nixon Dickography." *Goldmine*, No. 36, May, p. 15.

Lewis, George H. 1991. "Duellin' Values: Tension, Conflict, and Contradiction in Country Music." *Journal of Popular Culture*, XXIV, Spring, pp. 103-107.

Lewis, George L. 1983. "The Meaning's in the Music and the Music's in Me: Popular Music as Symbolic Communication." *Theory, Culture, and Society*, I, No. 3, pp. 133-141.

Martin, Christopher. 1993. "Traditional Criticism of Popular Music and the Making of a Lip-Synching Scandal." *Popular Music and Society*, XVII, Winter, pp. 63-81.

McDonald, James R. 1988. "Censoring Rock Lyrics: A Historical Analysis of the Debate." *Youth and Society*, XIX, March, pp. 294-313.

McDonald, James R. 1988. "Politics Revisited: Metatextual Implications of Rock and Roll Criticism." *Youth and Society*, XIX, June, pp. 485-504.

McDonald, James R. 1993. "Rock and Memory: A Search for Meaning." *Popular Music and Society*, XVII, Fall, pp. 1-17.

McDonald, James R. 1993. "Rock Censorship: Implications for Collectors and Libraries." *Popular Culture in Libraries*, I, No. 4, pp. 63-70.

Milberg, David A. 1993. "Saluting Summer: Pop Music's Second Most Favorite Time of the Year." *DISCoveries*, No. 62, July, pp. 31-35.

Miller, Doug. 1995. "The Man Within the Tone: African Retentions in Rhythm and Blues Saxophone Style in Afro-American Popular Music." *Popular Music*, XIV, May, pp. 155-174.

Neustadter, Roger. 1994. "The Obvious Child: The Symbolic Use of Childhood in Contemporary Popular Music." *Popular Music and Society*, XVIII, Spring, pp. 51-67.

Pruter, Robert. 1990. "A Historical Overview of Soul Music in Chicago." *Black Music Research Bulletin*, XII, Fall, pp. 1-4.

Riccio, Barry D. 1993. "Popular Culture and High Culture: Dwight MacDonald, His Critics, and the Ideal of Cultural Hierarchy in Modern America." *Journal of American Culture*, XVI, Winter, pp. 7-8.

Schurk, William L. 1992. "Uncovering the Mysteries of Popular Recordings Collection Development." *The Acquisitions Librarian*, No. 8, pp. 91-98.

Scott, Linda M. 1990. "Understanding Jingles and Needle-Drop: A Rhetorical Approach to Music in Advertising." *Journal of Consumer Research*, XVII, September, pp. 223-237.

Shumway, David R. 1991. "Rock and Roll as a Cultural Practice." *South Atlantic Quarterly*, XC, Fall, pp. 753-769.

Tunnell, Kenneth D. 1992. "99 Years is Almost for Life: Punishment for Violent Crime in Bluegrass Music." *Journal of Popular Culture*, XXV, Winter, pp. 165-181.

Von Nordheim, Deloris. 1993. "Vision of Death in Rock Music and Musicians." *Popular Music and Society*, XVII, No. 2, Summer, pp. 21-31.

Walker, Donald E. and B. Lee Cooper. 1993. "Baseball Cards, Hispanic Players, and Public School Instruction." *Popular Culture in Libraries*, I, No. 3, pp. 85-104.

Walker, Donald E. and B. Lee Cooper. 1991. "Black Players and Baseball Cards: Exploring Racial Integration with Popular Culture Resources." *Social Education*, LV, March, pp. 169-173, 204.

Woodford, Chris. 1993. "British Beat Before the Beatles." *Now Dig This*, No. 126, September, pp. 9-10.

Woodford, Chris. 1993. "British Beat Before the Beatles." *Now Dig This*, No. 127, October, pp. 24-26.

Woodford, Chris. 1993. "British Beat Before the Beatles." *Now Dig This*, No. 129, December, pp. 24-25.

Woodward, William. 1989. "History and Popular Culture . . . and Vice Versa." *Popular Culture Association Newsletter*, XVI, February, pp. 1-3.

Young, Jordan R. 1994. "Spike Jones: Off the Record." *Discoveries*, No. 77, October, pp. 20-29.

Young, Jordan R. 1994. "Spike Jones—Off the Record: Part Two." *Goldmine*, No. 373, November 11, pp. 34-39.

## *Unpublished Materials*

Lam, R. Errol and William L. Schurk. 1988. "My Yellow Jacket Girl: The Image of the Asian-American in 20th Century Popular Music." Mimeographed paper presented at the 15th Annual Convention of the Midwest Popular Culture Association.

Schurk, William L. 1994. " 'Blue Moon': The Story of An American Classic." Mimeographed paper presented at the 21st Annual Convention of the Midwest Popular Culture Association.

Schurk, William L. 1995. "From 'Daisy Bell' to Queen: A Century of Bicycling in Popular Song." Mimeographed paper presented at the 17th Annual Convention of the American Cultural Association.

# Index

Brown, Charles, 263
Brown, Clarence "Gatemouth," 264
Brown, James, 314,315,317
Brown, Roy, 145,257,314
Brown, Ruth, 16,363
Browne, Ray B., xii,98,99,118
Bryant, Felice and Boudleaux, 168
Buchanan and Goodman, 228
Burke, Solomon, 314,315,316,317
Bultman, Scott, 227,228
Burns, Gary, 99
Burns, George, 146
Bush, George, 328,337
Butler, Jerry, 313
Byrne, Jane, 59

Cain, Robert, 176
Campbell, E.G., 351,362
Cantor, Eddie, 153
Cantor, Louis, 69
*Cape Fear*, 136
Capitol Steps, 148-149
Carmichael, Hoagy, 174
Carney, George O., 249,250
"Carol," 35
Carr, James, 315,316
Cars, 29-37
Carter, Jimmy, 70
*Cash Box*, xi
Casper the Friendly Ghost, 117
Casting Spells, 104,130
Cats and the Fiddle, 84
Cawelti, John, 99
Celebrity choir messages, 337
Censorship, 293-309
Chan, Charlie, 146
Chandler, Gene, 313
Chaney, Jr., Lon, 119,122,137
Changing Image of Metropolis, 62
Chantels, 86
Charles, Ray, 154,174,315,317,324,
    333,340
*Cheyenne*, 56
Chicago, Illinois, 58-59

*Chicago Soul*, 313-314
Chilcoat, George W., 324
Chi-Sound Records, 313
Christian, Charlie, 264
Chronology of horror-related
    recordings, 132-134
Chronology of tobacco-related
    recordings (1947-1993),
    44-52
Church, Eugene, 316
Cigarettes, 43-53
City Life, 55-68
City life and Black Americans,
    63-64
"Clap for the Wolfman," 127
Clapton, Eric, 254
Clark, Dee, 314
Clark, Dick, 169,171
Classical Music, 221
Clooney, Rosemary, 364
Clovers, 84
Coasters, 145-148
Cocker, Joe, 206,252,316,317
Cohen, Norm, 99,236
*Collecting Phil Spector; The Man,
    The Legend, The Music,*
    171-172
*Collecting Rare Records*, 85-87
Collins, Albert, 262,264
Collins, Phil, 170
Color Me Badd, 294
"Come On," 32
Commitments, 316,317
*Commitments*, 74,316-317
Connor, Joanna, 259
Cooke, Sam, 16
Cooper, B. Lee, xiii,97
Cooper, Jack L., 70
Cooper, Michael, 233
Copland, Aaron, 260
Costello, Elvis, 270
Cotten, Lee, 96,314
Count Dracula, 127
    and other vampires, 106
Cray, Robert, 225